THE 5 POWERS OF
GØD

THE 5 POWERS OF
GØD

PAUL M. GOULET

THOMAS NELSON
Since 1798

NASHVILLE DALLAS MEXICO CITY RIO DE JANEIRO BEIJING

Published in Nashville, TN, by Thomas Nelson. Thomas Nelson is a trademark of Thomas Nelson, Inc.

Thomas Nelson, Inc. titles may be purchased in bulk for educational, business, fund-raising, or sales promotional use. For information, please e-mail SpecialMarkets@ThomasNelson.com.

All Scripture quotations, unless otherwise indicated, are taken from The New King James Version (NKJV®), copyright 1979, 1980, 1982, Thomas Nelson, Inc., Publishers.

Other Scripture references are from The Holy Bible, New International Version® (NIV). Copyright © 1973, 1978, 1984, International Bible Society. Used by permission of Zondervan Bible Publishers.

Library of Congress Cataloging-in-Publication Data

Goulet, Paul M.
    The 5 powers of God / by Paul M. Goulet.
        p. cm.
    ISBN 13: 978-0-529-12229-2
    ISBN 10: 0-5291-2229-4
    1. Christian life. 2. Power (Christian theology) I. Title. II.
Title: Five powers of God.
BV4501.3.G68 2007
248.4—dc22
2006034925

Printed in the United States of America
07 08 09 10 11 QW 9 8 7 6 5 4 3 2 1

CONTENTS

CONTENTS

ACKNOWLEDGMENTS

I am deeply indebted to all those who have imparted into my life such as my parents, brothers, sisters, coaches, teachers, professors, and Campus Crusade for Christ staff members, who imparted John 10:10 in my life and discipled me. To my pastors, teachers, and leaders, who poured into me for several years and introduced me to the power of the Holy Spirit. To Claudio Freidzon, whom God used to give me a second chance. To Denise, my bride, who constantly inspires me. To my children, who are reflecting so well the grace of God and the impartations of their parents. To my colleagues, who have encouraged me to do the research and write books. To my mentors Dr. Dobbins, Dr. David Lim, and Dr. James Marocco. I would have been lost without your love and influence. Finally, to the staff, board, and congregation of ICLV. The list could be much longer since it is only the tip of the iceberg in terms of those who have imparted into my life. I am thankful God used all of you to mold, make, and heal me. May this book be God's tool to fill you to overflowing.

INTRODUCTION

THE POWER OF GOD

The power of God became a reality for me in 1997. A well-known Argentinean pastor, Claudio Freidzon, waved his hand at me and said, "Take it." Expectations became exasperation when his hand knocked me in the nose. I do have a pronounced nasal fixture (according to my two daughters), but the shock of being hit in the nose at an emotionally vulnerable moment was overwhelming. I didn't know if I should laugh or cry.

Please allow me to digress for a moment to help you understand the importance at that moment in my life. Two years prior, I had told the Holy Spirit to pull back His power in my life. I had become embarrassed by His touch and the move of the Spirit in our services. The outpouring of the Holy Spirit that touched me in October 1994 caused great controversy in our church. At that time, I did not know how to pastor the people through a revival. Instead of navigating them through the storms, I bailed out. For more than two years, I felt the sting of my betrayal of the Holy Spirit. I knew that I had grieved Him.

The revival quickly ended, but the church started to grow again. During the two-year lull of the visible manifestation of His power, I began asking God for a second chance. To my surprise the church began growing. This led us to an invitation to a conference in Branson, Missouri, with Steve Hill, Claudio Freidzon, and Jack Deere. We were involved with a movement that invited its one hundred largest churches to attend. Although our church had grown so much, deep in my heart I yearned for the move of God again. I yearned for His power to flow through me. My expectation at the altar was huge: God, give me another chance.

Have you ever noticed that church altars can be one of the most exciting and unsafe places in the world? I have been spat on, pushed down, shouted at, stepped on, shoved aside, and ignored. Why do we keep going back for more? It must be that deep down we want more of God, and we are desperate enough to do almost anything to get Him. Aren't you hungry for more of God? Didn't a hungry seeker refer to herself as a dog eating the crumbs from under the table?

"Yes, Lord," she said, "but even the dogs eat the crumbs that fall from their masters' table." (Matthew 15:27 NIV)

She wasn't afraid to admit the revolting truth that we are desperate for a touch from God. If we are willing to humble ourselves, then we will see God and eat at His table. For each of us to experience God, we must put our pride aside. We can no longer call the shots. My experience with Claudio sealed this truth in my heart.

After Claudio smacked me in the nose, strange thoughts rushed through my mind. Should I be mad, embarrassed, disappointed, or amused? Before I could decide, something knocked me on my back. It felt like a linebacker had stopped me on the five-yard line. My eyes and mouth were now wide open. Waves of power rushed through my body. "Take it, take it, and take it!" he cried out. Each time a flood of power washed through me.

Although I have a master's degree in psychology, I find it difficult to explain the events of that overwhelming evening. As I lay on the ground for over an hour, the Holy Spirit filled me to overflowing. It wasn't just a flow of power; it was Him—the Holy Spirit. He then started to deal with my personal issues. He spoke so clearly to my mind. Was I willing to die to myself so that He could truly use me? Would I allow Him to crucify areas of my life? I could literally see my pride, fear, people-pleasing, and ego nailed to the cross. God had knocked me to the floor that night to do surgery. Falling to the ground is not the big issue. It is what happens after you get up that reveals the legitimacy of the experience.

I wept bitterly at my sin that night. I realized I had grieved Him so many times. When Claudio said, "Take it," I learned that "it" is everything the Holy Spirit wanted to pour into me at that moment. When Claudio prayed, God imparted through him.

Impartation is being filled with the Holy Spirit and allowing Him to deal with us from the inside out. It is not about falling, shaking, crying, laughing, or healing, although these often occur. The media, critics, and misguided individuals have placed the emphasis on the outward reaction to an inward event. While the debate rages about manifestations, the Holy Spirit is grieved. The critics are in danger of calling a Holy Spirit movement "satanic."

> *"I tell you the truth, all the sins and blasphemies of men will be forgiven them. But whoever blasphemes against the Holy Spirit will never be forgiven; he is guilty of an eternal sin."* He said this because they were saying, *"He has an evil spirit."* (Mark 3:28–30 NIV)

Have we forgotten the stern warning against cursing the Holy Spirit? Have the critics bothered to verify the fruit of the meetings? Before we place judgment on a church or a movement, shouldn't we thoroughly investigate the testimonies? Would we find reconciled marriages, invigorated ministries, saved souls, recovering drug addicts, revitalized Christians, and the fruits of the Spirit? Perhaps not in every case, but in many cases there have been legitimate changes.

There is another danger that is almost as insidious: men, women, and young people who have an experience but fail to let the Holy Spirit transform their character. In many cases we are unwilling to embrace the fellowship of His sufferings, to pick up our crosses and walk, to sell everything we have, to give to the poor. Following Him is difficult.

Then he said to them all: "If anyone would come after me, he must deny himself and take up his cross daily and follow me. For whoever wants to save his life will lose it, but whoever loses his life for me will save it." (Luke 9:23–24 NIV)

FILLED, NOT SPILLED

We desire the experience of being filled but not the expense of being spilled for Him. If you really want to be filled, get ready to be spilled. Paul the apostle testified this was his experience: "*But even if I am being poured out like a drink offering on the sacrifice and service coming from your faith, I am glad and rejoice with all of you*" (Philippians 2:17 NIV).

There is no impartation without a pouring out. In other words, you can only keep it if you give it away. Jesus exhorted His disciples to "*Heal the sick, raise the dead, cleanse those who have leprosy, drive out demons. Freely you have received, freely give*" (Matthew 10:8 NIV).

The most important purpose of a filling is a future spilling. The condition I am referring to may be compared to the problems in the first-century Corinthian church. There was tremendous movement of the Holy Spirit in Corinth, but the people were unwilling to harness their character problems. There was also a lack of love, self-sacrifice, and selflessness. We must not fall into these traps.

After my experience with the Holy Spirit, I faced four major challenges. I needed wisdom to travel this new road.

1. **What happened to me?** I knew it was real and it was God, but how did it fit biblically? The Bible had always helped me understand my experiences and the truth. I had been through Bible studies, Bible college, and seminary, but no one had prepared me for that type of impartation. It took awhile for me to adjust and to absorb the tremendous move of God.

2. **Could God impart through me, as He had through Claudio Freidzon?** Was this experience something that could be repeated? If so, when, where, and how? Could I bring it back to our church in Las Vegas? What would happen when I prayed for people? Would there be transference of power or spirit? Do you remember Elijah's response to Elisha's request to have a double portion of his spirit?

   When they had crossed, Elijah said to Elisha, "Tell me, what can I do for you before I am taken from you?" "Let me inherit a double portion of your spirit," Elisha replied. "You have asked a difficult thing," Elijah said, "yet if you see me when I am taken from you, it will be yours—otherwise not." (2 Kings 2:9–10 NIV)

3. **How could I protect this new impartation in my life?** I knew it wasn't just an emotional reaction to a heartfelt need. It was the power of God that filled my body. It was more than just a power; it was "the power," the *dunamos* from heaven, the Holy Spirit Himself. To protect and feed the power, I had to protect and further my relationship with the Holy Spirit. The power

we feel when we are filled with the Holy Spirit should not be our focus; He wants to be our focus. Many believers are enamored with the flame while neglecting the fire, but He desires intimacy with us.

4. **What is the concept of biblical impartation?** Why had I never heard about this before? Nobody that I knew had ever boldly said, "I have something I want to impart into you, something I want to pour into you!" In the professional realm we often hear about coaching and mentoring. They claim to want to pour into students through teaching, seminars, or tapes. Fortune 500 companies pay heavy fees to motivational speakers to inspire their employees. Isn't this impartation? As I spent time reviewing my childhood, I realized that people had been imparting into me my entire life. Some poured life, some poured death, and some poured fluff.

God can impart into us through many different vehicles. He can use His Word, a song, articles, a person, a set of circumstances, or His presence. People also impart in a similar way through their words, actions, letters, books, articles, and presence. The purpose of this book is to help you understand how God imparts in you and through you. Knowing that impartation is always a reality, your eyes will be open to the impact that you are making on others and other are making on you.

This book will help you define who and how people have poured into you. It will enable you to throw out impartations that brought insecurity, fear, guilt, shame, and death. It will also inspire you to choose who will pour into you and whom you will pour into. You can be empowered to be a vessel of impartation with tremendous impact. Is this what you want? How badly do you want it? Is there a spiritual hunger deep within you?

I would like to challenge you to read this book with a desire to answer these four questions. It is my prayer that through my experiences and those of our congregation, you will embrace the Holy Spirit. He is a very real person who wants to fill you, transform you, and pour Himself into others through you. Our experiences are not meant to be normative. We are simply living epistles.

Clearly you are an epistle of Christ, ministered by us, written not with ink but by the Spirit of the living God, not on tablets of stone but on tablets of flesh, that is, of the heart. (2 Corinthians 3:3)

Your relationship with the Holy Spirit will be unique and personal. He is God, and we are not. He wants to impart through you. When you pray for people, He wants to flow through you with great intensity. He will transform you into a vessel of impartation if you will let Him.

IMPARTATION IS FOR TODAY

Webster's dictionary defines *impartation*, "to give a share or portion of." It seems that we have heard the term used more often in the past few years. There is renewed interest in the relationship between coaches and athletes, business experts and students, pastors and leaders. The revival that is spreading around the world has certainly reawakened the question, "What is the impact of teaching, preaching, coaching, laying of hands, and prayer?"

My own experience has caused me to study this principle. I want to understand

- how impartation takes place,
- where it happens,
- when it occurs,
- why it happens, and
- what impact it has on people.

I have spent many hours studying, praying, and experiencing this principle. I have come to a few clear conclusions that will help you become an imparter. There are seven primary methods of imparting:

1. **Teaching**—Hopefully, you received something through your education. I am sure your teachers were trying to give you knowledge, wisdom, and character.

   For though you might have ten thousand instructors in Christ, yet you do not have many fathers; for in Christ Jesus I have begotten you through the gospel. (1 Corinthians 4:15)

2. **Preaching**—The Bible offers more explanations of this great impartation than any other. I have preached for almost twenty

years, and I can assure you my intention has always been to give the listeners a life-changing truth.

Did I commit sin in humbling myself that you might be exalted, because I preached the gospel of God to you free of charge? (2 Corinthians 11:7)

3. **Modeling**—Our actions speak louder than our words. Paul understood this principle and encouraged the Corinthians to live it.

You are our epistle written in our hearts, known and read by all men; clearly you are an epistle of Christ, ministered by us, written not with ink but by the Spirit of the living God, not on tablets of stone but on tablets of flesh, that is, of the heart. (2 Corinthians 3:2–3)

4. **Anointing with oil and the laying of hands with prayer**— What kind of supernatural transference occurs when we exercise these biblical practices? These connections are for a holy reason. Does God use us as vessels to pour into others? Are we useful conduits of the power and graces of God?

As each one has received a gift, minister it to one another, as good stewards of the manifold grace of God. If anyone speaks, let him speak as the oracles of God. If anyone ministers, let him do it as with the ability which God supplies, that in all things God may be glorified through Jesus Christ, to whom

belong the glory and the dominion forever and ever. Amen.
(1 Peter 4:10–11)

5. **Gifts of the Spirit**—What happens when we allow the gifts of the Holy Spirit to be loosed through us? Great things are released into peoples' lives!

   Do not neglect the gift that is in you, which was given to you by prophecy with the laying on of the hands of the eldership. (1 Timothy 4:14)

6. **Our words and actions**—Every word is a seed that will either bear fruit or die. Our actions will feed the seeds that have been planted in people's hearts and minds.

   But we were gentle among you, just as a nursing mother cherishes her own children. So, affectionately longing for you, we were well pleased to impart to you not only the gospel of God, but also our own lives, because you had become dear to us. For you remember, brethren, our labor and toil; for laboring night and day, that we might not be a burden to any of you, we preached to you the gospel of God. (1 Thessalonians 2:7–9)

7. **Worship and prayer**—Do you believe that every time you worship and pray something is happening in heaven? I do. When we worship or pray, God does something in the seen or unseen world. I have discovered the incredible power of worship and prayer, and I know you will too.

But the hour is coming, and now is, when the true worshipers will worship the Father in spirit and truth; for the Father is seeking such to worship Him. God is Spirit, and those who worship Him must worship in spirit and truth. (John 4:23–24)

WHAT THE BIBLE SAYS ABOUT IMPARTATION

The Old Testament does not use the word *impartation*. Instead it uses other words such as *give, confer, bestow, hand over, put, place*, and *inherit*. The New Testament also uses several words to communicate the principles of giving.

In Matthew 10:8, Jesus taught His disciples to give what they had received from Him: *"Heal the sick, cleanse the lepers, raise the dead, cast out demons. Freely you have received, freely give."* He uses the Greek term *didomi*, meaning "to give." Clearly Jesus is referring to the anointing power and authority He had given to them. With these gifts they could give to others. Isn't this the model that was given to the apostles and disciples?

In Acts 3:6–7, Peter seems to believe he had something to give to a crippled man at the beautiful gate. Peter *"lifted him up."* Can you imagine the risk he took? He used the same term Jesus used in Matthew 10:8, *didomi*.

Although the Old Testament doesn't use the term *impart*, we need to spend some time reviewing the use of this principle in the Old Testament to discover how God lays a firm foundation for a dynamic New Testament reality.

OLD TESTAMENT IMPARTATION

God has always wanted to pour His Spirit into open vessels. In the Old Testament, leaders were recognized by their anointing or Spirit. God desired to spread this same Spirit on the multitudes. God is no respecter of individuals. He has always wanted to raise up an extreme army of anointed people. In Numbers 11:16–17, God instructs Moses to collect the seventy elders of Israel so He could take the Spirit that was on him and place it on them.

The LORD said to Moses: "Bring me seventy of Israel's elders who are known to you as leaders and officials among the people. Have them come to the Tent of Meeting, that they may stand there with you. I will come down and speak with you there, and I will take of the Spirit that is on you and put the Spirit on them. They will help you carry the burden of the people so that you will not have to carry it alone." (NIV)

The purpose of this impartation was to divide the burdens of the people; Moses couldn't do it alone. Their needs weren't being met. God didn't send these leaders to a weekend seminar (although those can be helpful). He didn't create more institutions of higher learning. He knew the elders needed Moses' spirit.

I have been privileged to attend many wonderful conferences for leaders and pastors. I graduated from a university, attended a Bible college, and completed a graduate degree in psychology and pastoral counseling. My life and ministry have been improved by the information given to me. However, I have been changed dramatically by the impartations of spiritual gifts in the past five years. I am talking about a supernatural infusion of the Holy Spirit and His gifts. We need impartation of knowledge. We need solid role models to emulate. We need to develop the disciplines of study and prayer. Most of all, we need Jesus Christ and His power.

My purpose in attending seminars has changed. Yes, I want information, but I really want to catch the person's spirit. I am very selective. In some settings, I like the material, but I am uncomfortable with the spirit. In my opinion, professionalism, marketing, pride, and ego have ruined many great leaders. I have purposely sought out men like Tommy Barnett, Dr. Richard Dobbins, Reinhard Bonnke, Claudio Freidzon, and Carlos Annacondia. Like Elisha, I have cried out to God, "Please give me a double portion of the Spirit you placed on them." I have never heard any leader encourage this type of behavior. It seems almost too spiritual, unnatural, or even too mystical. In our culture we are taught that we do not need anyone; we can go directly to God.

Perhaps this philosophy is a reflection of Protestant theology, a reaction to a hierarchical form of church leadership. Perhaps it's a reaction to the abuses of the past. Power-hungry, manipulative charlatans have plagued the church for centuries. I do not know why the subject of impartation is mentioned but never explained or discussed. It may be fear and ignorance. Maybe we are afraid to admit someone has something we don't, or we are afraid that admitting it would give them too much power over our lives. One purpose of this book is to open the subject for investigation, prayer, and consideration.

Many conditions can stop us from biblical impartation. Fear, sin, pride, and ignorance are probably the most significant. Regardless of how we feel about it, we need to answer the big question. Is it biblical? If it is, then we need to answer the whys, wheres, whats, and hows of this dynamic subject.

As you read this book, you will become convinced that impartation is not only biblical but is also part of the rich history of the church through the ages. God has always wanted to increase the leadership base in the body of believers. John Maxwell teaches leaders to develop more leadership. One of his powerful mottos has inspired me: "There is no success without a successor." Our church has adopted this as a ministry must. He imparted this truth into our church through his seminar tapes and books.

In the book of Numbers, the day of impartation finally came for the multitudes of Israel.

> So Moses went out and told the people what the LORD had said. He brought together seventy of their elders and had them stand around the Tent. Then the LORD came down in the cloud and spoke with him, and he took of the Spirit that was on him and put the Spirit on the seventy elders. When the Spirit rested on them, they prophesied, but they did not do so again. (Numbers 11:24–25 NIV)

God is demonstrating a powerful truth to Moses: impartation leads to multiplication. Multiplication leads to shared leadership and lighter burdens. The immediate impact of this event was that sixty-eight prophesied around the tabernacle and two prophesied in the camp. The significance of the two in the camp cannot be overlooked. First, it demonstrated how impartation could work whether the leaders were with Moses or not. These two who could not see Moses received the same blessing. They couldn't touch him or experience the atmosphere of the tabernacle, but God still filled them with the Spirit. Second, it revealed God's desire to spread the anointing to the general populace. The impartation of the gifts and the anointing are not meant only for the church and the priests but also for all the people. The Spirit is given for daily living. God wants the anointing and anointed ones to exit church buildings and spread the glory. Revival must occur outside the four walls of buildings where anointed ones can spread this fire at work, on the streets, and in their homes.

PART I

THE 5 POWERS
OF GOD

ONE

DO YOU KNOW JACK?

The English translations of the Bible do not perfectly reflect the original languages. The most common examples of this are the words translated "love." In the Greek text four words are translated as love. They are:

1. *agape*—unconditional love
2. *phileo*—brotherly love
3. *storgé*—family love
4. *éros*—erotic love

The same principle holds true for the power of God. In the New Testament at least five root words can be translated "power." They are:

1. *exousia*—delegated authority
2. *dunamis*—miraculous dynamite power
3. *energeia*—energy
4. *kratos*—dominion
5. *ischus*—strength

The evangelical world and Pentecostal world are divided by a misunderstanding of the power of God. Many Christians believe the power of God is evidenced by falling down, crying, shaking, laughing, dancing, or shouting. Others see the power of God in a strong sermon, a dynamic altar call, or a moving song. Others see the power as a miraculous healing or deliverance. Still others see the power of God in His Word, a tract, a film, or a Christ-centered novel. Others see the power in the gifts of the Spirit described in Acts, Romans, and Corinthians. The question most people ask is, "Who's right and wrong?"

Could it be they are all right? Could it be that God shows His powers in all of these ways because He has different types of power for different purposes? Could it be that He gives these powers to different people at different times for different purposes? The purpose of this book is to dispel the myths, confusions, and misunderstandings of the power of God.

I will explain the five different words used in the New Testament for the concept of power. Each word is distinct. Unfortunately, their subtleties are hidden by English translation. Let's take time to study each word in context to discover the five powers of God.

THE WORD OF GOD

Have you ever heard someone say, "They don't know jack"? This phrase means someone does not understand.

My people are destroyed for lack of knowledge. (Hosea 4:6a)

Jesus answered and said to them, "You are mistaken, not knowing the Scriptures nor the power [dunamis] *of God."* (Matthew 22:29)

In other words, these religious people didn't know jack. They were religious leaders who fasted, prayed, went to the synagogue, and worshiped. They seemed to do everything right, but Jesus told them that they didn't know jack. He told them they did not know the Word of God, and they did not know the power of God. I see a lot of Christians who live just like that. They really don't know the Word of God, and they really don't know the power of God.

THE IMPORTANCE OF
KNOWING THE WORD

How can you fight the devil if you don't know the Word of God? The only offensive tool in a Christian's weaponry (according to Ephesians) is the sword of the Spirit, which is the Word of God.

Stand therefore, having girded your waist with truth, having put on the breastplate of righteousness, and having shod your feet with the preparation of the gospel of peace; above all, taking the shield of faith with which you will be able to quench all the fiery darts of the wicked one. And take the helmet of salvation, and the sword of the Spirit, which is the word of God. (Ephesians 6:14–17)

What happens if you don't know the Word of God? You are constantly playing defense against Satan. I want you to know the Word of God is important, and it is your sword.

Knowing the Word helps you overcome Satan's lies. Isn't he called the father of all lies?

You are of your father the devil, and the desires of your father you want to do. He was a murderer from the beginning, and does not stand in the truth, because there is no truth in him. When he speaks a lie, he speaks from his own resources, for he is a liar and the father of it. (John 8:44)

Timothy was a great example of someone who was raised in the Word. This knowledge raised him above his peers.

But evil men and impostors will grow worse and worse, deceiving and being deceived. But you must continue in the things which you have learned and been assured of, knowing from whom you have learned them, and that from childhood you have known the Holy Scriptures, which are able to make you wise for salvation through faith which is in Christ Jesus. All Scripture is given by inspiration of God, and is profitable for doctrine, for reproof, for correction, for instruction in righteousness, that the man of God may be complete, thoroughly equipped for every good work. (2 Timothy 3:13–17).

Timothy was complete and equipped because he was intimate with the Word of God. All of us must be proficient in the use of the sword. It is our only offensive weapon. The Word of God is "God breathed." It means that a breath of God came into the authors who wrote the Bible. The authors did not write it; God breathed through them into these Scriptures. Peter, in his second epistle, makes this completely clear, as does the writer of Hebrews. There is no room for debate. You must have confidence in the sword of the Spirit.

Knowing this first, that no prophecy of Scripture is of any private interpretation, for prophecy never came by the will of man, but holy men of God spoke as they were moved by the Holy Spirit. (2 Peter 1:20–21)

For the word of God is living and powerful, and sharper than any two-edged sword, piercing even to the division of soul and spirit, and of joints and marrow, and is a discerner of the thoughts and intents of the heart. (Hebrews 4:12)

When you read the Bible it is active in your life, even if you don't feel it. Our military has ammunition that can hit a target and then explode. It's active: it doesn't just hit and penetrate; it penetrates, then explodes. It has explosive power when it hits its mark. That's what the Word of God is like; it's living and active. We are promised that not one of His words will return void.

So shall My word be that goes forth from My mouth;
It shall not return to Me void,
But it shall accomplish what I please,
And it shall prosper in the thing for which I sent it.

(Isaiah 55:11)

Often we make decisions based on our emotions; we don't always *feel* like reading our Bibles. We don't feel like going to church. We may not feel like being holy. The Word will help you overcome feelings and circumstances. When the Word is read, quoted, memorized, or meditated, it activates change in your will, mind, emotions, and choices. As a result, your character changes. People start noticing the change in you. In other words, you have a testimony that glorifies Jesus.

That He might sanctify and cleanse her with the washing of water by the word. (Ephesians 5:26)

Make a choice today to dive into His Word, study it, and teach it. Some of my greatest changes came as a result of teaching Sunday school. It freed me to become disciplined. It freed me to study and stretch myself, to use His Word to change me from the inside out.

If you want to know jack, you've got to know the Word. If you're going to lead people to Jesus, you've got to know the Word. If you're going to defend yourself against enemies' lies, you need to know the truth of the Word. If the enemy lies to me and I believe him, my feelings will change. If it changes the way I feel, then it can change how I plan my life and react to others. It changes my attention, options, and choices, which change the way I live and what I experience. So if our major weapon in warfare is the Word, which is living and active, then this sword penetrates the enemies' lies. Let's become experts in the Word of God and become successful warriors for God.

THE WORD IS NEEDED
FOR OPPORTUNE TIMES

Now when the devil had ended every temptation, he departed from Him until an opportune time. (Luke 4:13)

The devil always looks for opportunities. If you defeat him today, he will look for another time next week. He doesn't have a lot of resources, so he picks his fights where he can. So why did the devil leave Jesus in Luke 4? Because he had been defeated. Think of how Jesus fought the devil. Jesus kept quoting the Word. He used it because it was an offensive weapon. If Jesus had to use the Word, do you think that we as mere mortals should use the Word too? Three times Satan tempted Jesus; three times Jesus fought back with the Word.

1. **Satan's lie:** *"And the devil said to Him, 'If You are the Son of God, command this stone to become bread'"* (Luke 4:3).

   God's truth: *"But Jesus answered him, saying, 'It is written, "Man shall not live by bread alone, but by every word of God"'"* (Luke 4:4).

2. **Satan's lie:** *"Then the devil, taking Him up on a high mountain, showed Him all the kingdoms of the world in a moment of time. And the devil said to Him, 'All this authority I will give You, and their glory; for this has been delivered to me, and I give it to whomever I wish. Therefore, if You will worship before me, all will be Yours'"* (Luke 4:5–7).

   God's truth: *"And Jesus answered and said to him, 'Get behind Me, Satan! For it is written, "You shall worship the LORD your God, and Him only you shall serve"'"* (Luke 4:8).

3. **Satan's lie:** *"Then he brought Him to Jerusalem, set Him on the pinnacle of the temple, and said to Him, 'If You are the Son of God, throw Yourself down from here. For it is written: "'He shall give His angels charge over you, To keep you," and, "In their hands they shall bear you up, lest you dash your foot against a stone"'"* (Luke 4:9–11).

   God's truth: *"And Jesus answered and said to him, 'It has been said, "You shall not tempt the LORD your God"'"* (Luke 4:12).

Then Jesus returned in the power [dunamis] *of the Spirit to Galilee, and news of Him went out through all the surrounding region.* (Luke 4:14)

Jesus' knowledge and use of the Word caused Him to return to Galilee in power. The power used here is *dunamis*, which is the dynamite, miracle-working power of God. To be guilty of knowing jack means that we must become more acquainted with His Word. This will give us more power. Let us get to know His power.

EXOUSIA POWER

The Holy Spirit touches you with power in five different ways. There are five powers available to us as Christians, and I want to look at each of these so you can begin to walk in them.

The word *power* is used one hundred twenty-four times in the New Testament. The revelation of power was developed in the teaching of Jesus and His disciples. When Christ came to the earth, He brought full revelation. Before Christ came there was not full revelation, so when He came He introduced the concept of spiritual warfare and opened the Word of God for us. He also taught about power.

When Jesus told the religious leaders they did not know the Word of God or the power of God, the word translated *know* means "to see, perceive, and understand." So Jesus was telling these leaders they really could not understand the Scriptures. Second, He was telling them they could not perceive or understand the power of God. I don't want you to be like these religious leaders; I don't want you to be ignorant about the power of God.

EXOUSIA DEFINED

Exousia—the authority, the power, or right to act. The ability, privilege, force, capacity, competency, freedom, mastery, or delegated influence.

Exousia is used 103 times in the New Testament, so it must be important!

EXAMPLES OF THE USE OF *EXOUSIA*

1. **Jesus had authority to lay down His life and pick it up again.**
   "No one takes it from Me, but I lay it down of Myself. I have power [exousia] to lay it down, and I have power to take it again. This command I have received from My Father" (John 10:18).

The debate has raged for years whether the Jews or Romans killed Jesus. Mel Gibson's movie, *The Passion of the Christ*, stirred up accusations of anti-Semitism due to its graphic depiction of the sufferings of Christ at the hands of the leaders of His time. This scripture puts to rest any such discussion—no one had the authority to kill Jesus. He alone had the authority to give up His life. He could have called legions of angels, but refused to do so because by His authority He laid His life down.

2. **Jesus has authority to forgive and heal.** *"'But that you may know that the Son of Man has power* [exousia] *on earth to for-give sins'—then He said to the paralytic, 'Arise, take up your bed, and go to your house'"* (Matthew 9:6).

Have you ever said that you just can't forgive? Although you may feel like you cannot forgive, you actually have divine authority to forgive sins. This means when you commit a sin or someone commits a sin against you, you can choose to forgive others and exercise the authority that has been given to you.

And when He had called His twelve disciples to Him, He gave them power [exousia] *over unclean spirits, to cast them out, and to heal all kinds of sickness and all kinds of disease.* (Matthew 10:1)

No demon can stand against you because you have authority over them. God has made you the boss over demons. He has given you that authority, but you have a choice not to take it. You have authority over unclean spirits; you can cast them out in Jesus's name. You have authority to heal all kinds of sicknesses. You have this authority because He gave it to you, and it is yours to take. Jesus gave the five powers to the twelve disciples, then the seventy, then to all believers (Acts 2:4). In the New Testament we see the genius of His strategy to impart to all followers: men, women, young, old, Gentile, and Jew.

3. **Jesus has all authority in heaven and on earth.** *"And Jesus came and spoke to them, saying, 'All authority [exousia] has been given to Me in heaven and on earth. Go therefore and make disciples of all the nations, baptizing them in the name of the Father and of the Son and of the Holy Spirit'"* (Matthew 28:18–19).

Due to the fact that Jesus had all authority, He gave His followers the Great Commission (Matthew 16:15–18). As Christians, we have authority in our campuses, workplaces, and families. Jesus was given authority by the Father, He gave it to us, and now He instructs us to use that authority to make disciples of all nations.

4. **Jesus has authority to give more authority.** *"And he said to him, 'Well done, good servant; because you were faithful in a very little, have authority [exousia] over ten cities'"* (Luke 19:17).

Now when He came into the temple, the chief priests and the elders of the people confronted Him as He was teaching, and said, "By what authority [exousia] are You doing these things? And who gave You this authority [exousia]?" (Matthew 21:23)

Do you have authority to heal? Do you have authority to cast out demons? Do you have authority to lead people to Christ?

The answer is yes, but by whose authority? By the authority of Jesus Christ, which He has given to you.

5. **We have authority to become children of God.** *"But as many as received Him, to them He gave the right* [exousia] *to become children of God, to those who believe in His name"* (John 1:12).

Believing is not good enough, you have to receive it. You have to receive the authority that comes with adoption. The Bible says when you received Christ you were given authority to become a child of God. He gave you authority to be a child of God and to live like a child of God. When you are a child of God, you live differently than when you were not.

6. **Simon wanted to buy the authority.** *"Saying, 'Give me this power* [exousia] *also, that anyone on whom I lay hands may receive the Holy Spirit'"* (Acts 8:19).

The authority that the disciples had was so attractive that Simon thought he could buy it. His intentions seemed good, but his method revealed his heart. The power that he saw was evident and dynamic. He was willing to do whatever it took to acquire this same power.

7. **We have been called to set people free from the authority of Satan.** *"Open their eyes, in order to turn them from darkness to light, and from the power* [exousia] *of Satan to God, that they*

may receive forgiveness of sins and an inheritance among those who are sanctified by faith in Me" (Acts 26:18).

The devil also has *exousia*, but Jesus is greater than the devil because all authority was given to Him. Jesus received all authority from the Father, and now He gives it to us as believers. So we are called to dispossess Satan from his authority because we have greater authority; He who is in us is greater than he who is in the world (1 John 4:4).

And you He made alive, who were dead in trespasses and sins, in which you once walked according to the course of this world, according to the prince of the power [exousia] *of the air, the spirit who now works in the sons of disobedience.* (Ephesians 2:1–2)

Once again the word for power is *exousia*. Satan is the prince of the authority of the air. Satan takes authority over different cities, homes, and families, but God has given us even greater authority than what the devil has. This authority is not just over spiritual aspects of our lives, but over our finances, children, families, and crises. Some have taken authority over one area but not other areas of life. We have to exercise the authority God has given us, otherwise the enemy will take authority because we forfeited the authority God has given us.

8. We will one day be rewarded with authority over nations.
"And he who overcomes, and keeps My works until the end, to

him I will give power [exousia] *over the nations*" (Revelation 2:26).

Can you believe this promise? God is planning your next graduation—wow! After we overcome all the trials, He will give us authority over nations. In other words, we become nation changers, and that's exciting!

APPLICATION

Jesus has all authority, and He chooses to delegate all of it to us.

> *"He who hears you hears Me, he who rejects you rejects Me, and he who rejects Me rejects Him who sent Me." Then the seventy returned with joy, saying, "Lord, even the demons are subject to us in Your name." And He said to them, "I saw Satan fall like lightning from heaven. Behold, I give you the authority* [exousia] *to trample on serpents and scorpions, and over all the power of the enemy, and nothing shall by any means hurt you." (Luke 10:16–19)*

The pattern displayed by Jesus with His followers:

- He delegated authority to the twelve disciples.
- Then He gave it to the seventy.
- We too are given this authority over all sicknesses.

We have authority to heal, deliver, war, become sons and daughters, save nations, and forgive.

How to increase authority:

- Know the Word.
- Be faithful.
- Ask Him to fill you with *exousia*.
- Begin to exercise authority in every realm of your life.

QUESTIONS

Q. How familiar are you with the Word of God?

Q. Have you experienced more power because of it?

Q. How well do you know His power?

Q. Are you walking in your divinely delegated authority?

TWO

MIRACLE-WORKING POWER

The *Dunamis* of God

Dunamis—might, force, energy, dynamite, miraculous power.

Dunamis is mentioned 116 times in the New Testament.

When I was born again I was involved in Campus Crusade for Christ. I liked a girl, so I started going to her church. As I started reading the Bible I realized it was not consistent with what they were teaching at her church. They said the power of God no longer exists for us; they did not believe in the baptism of the Holy Spirit, miracles, healing, or the gifts of the Spirit. They said everything stopped after the first century.

This was a church that genuinely loved God and won souls, but they didn't believe in the power of God. They cut out most of the Bible. I finally concluded the Bible was true, so I no longer wanted to attend this church. That's how I began my Christian walk, believing simply what the Bible said about the power of God.

Many of you have experienced this power, but we must be able to explain it biblically, otherwise we are walking away from God's truth regarding His power.

MY FIRST ENCOUNTER
WITH THE POWER OF GOD

My family and I were in a very traditional religion, and we attended church only twice a year. I didn't get along with my father, so I moved away from home when I was sixteen; I moved back when I was seventeen.

I played junior hockey and was very violent at the time, but I achieved much success. I needed God, so one night as I was lying in bed I stretched my hands to heaven and said, "Lord, come into my life."

I had never heard about being born again, about the baptism of the Holy Spirit, or about receiving Jesus—I was just desperate for God. In my own faith I asked the Lord to come into my life. Right then something filled me, and I started praying in another language. I didn't know what was happening. I stopped after about two to three minutes, and I thought to myself, *I am going crazy.* But I also remember thinking, *If I'm going crazy, this is awesome! I feel great!* I kept speaking in this weird language; it sounded like baby talk to me, but it made me feel good.

The next night, I remembered how good I had felt after that experience, so I lifted up my hands and asked the Lord to come into my life again. I started speaking in tongues again. I felt incredibly filled with something from heaven.

That was the beginning of what completely changed my life. No one had ever explained the baptism of the Holy Spirit to me; no one had ever talked with me about the gifts of the Spirit. I didn't know anything! But in my own childlike faith I asked the Lord to come into my life. So no one can tell me the baptism of the Holy Spirit isn't real or the power of God isn't real—because I have experienced it for myself.

THE POWER OF DISCOVERY

That I may know Him and the power [dunamis] *of His resurrection, and the fellowship of His sufferings, being conformed to His death.* (Philippians 3:10)

The word *know* in this Scripture connotes intimacy. It is one thing to just know something as intellectual knowledge; it's another thing to want to know something or someone intimately. Paul wanted to know God's power intimately. He wanted to become intimate with the *dunamis* power of God. Jesus promised this *dunamis* to us as believers. Shouldn't we also desire to be intimate with this *dunamis* God has given us?

And He said to them, "It is not for you to know times or seasons which the Father has put in His own authority [exousia]. *But you shall receive power* [dunamis] *when the Holy*

21

Spirit has come upon you; and you shall be witnesses to Me in Jerusalem, and in all Judea and Samaria, and to the end of the earth." (Acts 1:7–8)

Jesus prophesied that as people were baptized in the Holy Spirit they would receive *dunamis*. The purpose of this *dunamis* is to empower us to be witnesses in our cities, states, nations, and world.

THE SECOND COMING OF JESUS

Immediately after the tribulation of those days the sun will be darkened, and the moon will not give its light; the stars will fall from heaven, and the powers [dunamis] *of the heavens will be shaken. Then the sign of the Son of Man will appear in heaven, and then all the tribes of the earth will mourn, and they will see the Son of Man coming on the clouds of heaven with power* [dunamis] *and great glory.* (Matthew 24:29–30)

Whenever you read about the second coming of Christ, He is always coming in *dunamis* power. Jesus will arrive on a white horse to conquer, and He will come with dynamite. His return will be explosive! *"Jesus said to him, 'It is as you said. Nevertheless, I say to you, hereafter you will see the Son of Man sitting at the right hand of the Power* [dunamis], *and coming on the clouds of heaven'"* (Matthew 26:64). We will see Jesus sitting on the right hand of dynamite.

FEEL THE POWER

You can receive the *exousia* without feeling anything, but you can feel the *dunamis* of God. When you are baptized in the Holy Spirit, you receive force, and you can always feel force.

> *And Jesus, immediately knowing in Himself that power* [dunamis] *had gone out of Him, turned around in the crowd and said, "Who touched My clothes?"* (Mark 5:30)

Jesus felt when the *dunamis* left His body, and the woman felt when that *dunamis* took away her disease.

> *And the whole multitude sought to touch Him, for power* [dunamis] *went out from Him and healed them all.* (Luke 6:19)

These two Scriptures reveal how Jesus literally felt the power leave His body. And each of those times the power was specified as *dunamis*. I received the *dunamis* of God in 1994 for the first time. I was a born-again Christian, I had been filled with the Holy Spirit, but I didn't really have the *dunamis* until this experience. I didn't know how to walk or function with the dynamite of God until then. Since then, I can feel the power of God flow through me. I believe that a sign of a true believer is the *dunamis* that flows through them on a daily basis. I often ask people if they felt the power when we prayed, and the answer is usually a resounding yes.

PAUL'S TESTIMONY

I was with you in weakness, in fear, and in much trembling. And my speech and my preaching were not with persuasive words of human wisdom, but in demonstration of the Spirit and of power [dunamis], *that your faith should not be in the wisdom of men but in the power* [dunamis] *of God.* (1 Corinthians 2:3–5)

Your faith is not supposed to be dependent on the wisdom of men. I've seen people fall away after leaders in the church fell because their faith was dependent on a person instead of on God Himself. Your faith must be based on the power of God and the Word of God. Paul encouraged the believers in Corinth to build their faith on the *dunamis* of God.

EXAMPLES OF *DUNAMIS*

And Stephen, full of faith and power [dunamis], *did great wonders and signs among the people.* (Acts 6:8)

Stephen was full of faith and full of dynamite. Dynamite power produces signs and wonders. One person cannot be filled with dynamite and change the world; it has to be all of us. When you have dynamite power, signs and wonders will follow. It's not limited to any of us; it's given to all of us. Stephen was a simple table server who had *dunamis* flowing in his life.

And to one he gave five talents, to another two, and to another one, to each according to his own ability [dunamis]; and immediately he went on a journey. (Matthew 25:15)

He gave them each talents according to their own dynamite. The talents that God deposits in us are drawn by the *dunamis* power in our lives. That's why it looks like some people have all the gifts; it is because they have had a larger dose of *dunamis*. Now this dynamite is given to everybody according to his or her own faith. If you want more dynamite, God will give it to you. When you get more dynamite, He will give you more talents. It's not that God is playing favorites; He is simply showing us that gifts are attracted by the anointing in your life. The more anointing in your life, the more He will pour gifts and blessings toward you. I have had such favor in my life, but it's not because of something that I've done, it's become of something that I have received by faith.

QUESTIONS

Q. Have you received the *dunamis* to change your circumstances, environment, and family?

Q. Are you using the *dunamis* power from God to have a life of miracles?

Q. Are you baptized in the Holy Spirit?

Q. Has this baptism given you the *dunamis* to become a great witness for the church?

THREE

THE ENERGIZER BUNNY IN YOU

The *Energeia* of God

Energeia—effective, energetic, efficient, working different operations.

This word is used eight times in the New Testament.

In 1994 I felt the power of God flow through me for the first time. Not only did God give me *dunamis*, but His *energeia* went through me too. I was in a conference in Canada, and I asked someone to come and pray for Las Vegas. He wanted to pray for me instead. God hit me with His power, and I fell on the floor. I told God, "While I'm down here, why don't You do whatever You want to do to me?"

Little did I know that He put dynamite into me. It felt like someone had hooked up my head and my toes to electric wires and then turned the switch on. I was lying on the ground, shaking like crazy and contracting my muscles.

I had felt this kind of electricity before. After an accident, I went through physical therapy. They would take some pads and place them on different parts of my body that were hurting, and then they would turn on the electricity. They would send an electric current through my muscles, and my muscles would contract and then release. That is how it felt when the power of God hit me at the conference in Canada. Every time the *energeia* would flow through my body I would contract and release. I didn't understand what was happening to me then, but now I know what God was doing—He was imparting His *energeia* into me.

When you feel heat, it is typically the *energeia* going through you. Have you ever felt pumped up after a service? This too is the *energeia* of God. Sometimes you may even feel invigorated when the *energeia* of God flows through you.

THE RELATIONSHIP BETWEEN
DUNAMIS AND *EXOUSIA*

To this end I also labor, striving according to His working [energeia] *which works* [energeo] *in me mightily* [dunamis]. (Colossians 1:29)

Paul works with the energy God gave him to be charged by His dynamite power. We can move in *dunamis* power because of the *exousia* that He has given us.

And Jesus came and spoke to them, saying, "All authority
[exousia] has been given to Me in heaven and on earth. Go
therefore and make disciples of all the nations, baptizing
them in the name of the Father and of the Son and of the
Holy Spirit, teaching them to observe all things that I have
commanded you; and lo, I am with you always, even to the
end of the age." Amen. (Matthew 28:18–20)

Then He called His twelve disciples together and gave them
power [dunamis] and authority [exousia] over all demons,
and to cure diseases. (Luke 9:1)

The extension of the kingdom of God is based on this fact:
all evangelism should be empowered by the Word of God by
the demonstration of *dunamis* and *exousia*. We're supposed to
be functioning in both authority and dynamite. It's not one or
the other; He wants us all to function in both in order to be the
most effective.

That the Gentiles should be fellow heirs, of the same body,
and partakers of His promise in Christ through the gospel, of
which I became a minister according to the gift of the grace
of God given to me by the effective working [energeia] of His
power [dunamis]. (Ephesians 3:6–7)

The *energeia* of His *dunamis* enabled Paul to minister. It is the
energy flowing from His dynamite. We walk with supernatural
ability and potential because of the *energeia* that is in us. When

the dynamite of God fills your life, there is a release of energy in your body, soul, and mind. Have you ever felt goose bumps when the Holy Spirit shows up? It is a physical reaction to a spiritual manifestation.

Now to Him who is able to do exceedingly abundantly above all that we ask or think, according to the power [dunamis] *that works* [energeo] *in us.* (Ephesians 3:20)

Have you ever seen the Energizer Bunny and desired that kind of energy? Haven't we all struggled and become tired at times? We need God's energy. You may not need His *dunamis* for the tasks ahead of you today, but you may need His supernatural *energeia*. God will give you whatever kind of power you need.

WHAT THE ENERGY OF GOD CAN DO

1. **There are different types of energy.** "*And there are diversities of activities* [energema], *but it is the same God who works* [energeo] *all in all*" (1 Corinthians 12:6).

This Scripture tells us there are varieties of energy. In other words, just because God touches someone with dynamite and someone else with *energeia*, it is still the same God.

Many people come to the altar desiring power and leave the altar disappointed because they didn't get blown away. But maybe God didn't want to blow them away with *dunamis*; maybe He wanted to give them *energeia* for the road ahead. Maybe all He wants to do is give you authority. You don't feel a thing, but there is a deposit of authority and you now have victory over your struggles. You may walk away disappointed, but God knows what you need. God has a variety of powers for different times, different people, and different places, but we make the mistake of expecting only one thing, one way.

> *But the manifestation of the Spirit is given to each one for the profit of all.* (1 Corinthians 12:7)

The word *manifestation* means "a shining forth from within." A manifestation is not when someone falls or cries; that is a physical reaction to the deposit of the Spirit of God in your life. Manifestation is what is being deposited in you and what is going to come out. It may be the gift of prophecy, maybe the gift of miracles. Manifestations are from the Father, through the Son, to the body of Christ.

Wednesdays tend to be long for our pastoral staff. We work all day and then serve at night. During the past thirteen years at ICLV, I often have not come home for dinner. Recently, I decided to get some Grandma's molasses cookies from the candy dispenser, to energize me for the service. I put my money in the machine and pushed E14 for the cookies. To my shock and dismay there was a malfunction in the system. E14 did not give up its reservoir of cookies; instead, F10 gave me the hot cinnamon candy I really dislike. I was disgusted because I didn't get what I paid for.

In many services, Christians leave the altar disappointed or disillusioned because they wanted *dunamis*, but got energy. They wanted *ischus* (strength), but they got *dunamis*. They were so embarrassed by the falling or crying that they never wanted to return again. God doesn't always give us what we want; He gives us what the world needs through us. We seek God for E14, but He gives us F10 because He is the one who decides what to give us. Many have made huge mistakes by demanding what we want how we want it, instead of seeking God with an open mind and heart. If He wants to pour dynamite in you, are you willing? If He wants to pour more authority instead, are you open? If He wants to give you gifts, will you let Him?

2. **The energy to subdue all things.** *"For our citizenship is in heaven, from which we also eagerly wait for the Savior, the Lord Jesus Christ, who will transform our lowly body that it may be conformed to His glorious body, according to the working* [energeia] *by which He is able even to subdue all things to Himself"* (Philippians 3:20–21).

There is an energy working in me at all times because I am a born-again Christian and I'm full of the Spirit. The energy is working in me in such a way that one day this lowly body is going to conform to His glorious body.

3. **The energy fills us so we can win souls.** *"Him we preach, warning every man and teaching every man in all wisdom, that we may present every man perfect in Christ Jesus. To this end I also*

labor, striving according to His working [energeia] *which works* [energeo] *in me mightily* [dunamis]" (Colossians 1:28–29).

Do you know ministry and discipleship are not easy? Our church's goal is to lead people to Christ and present them perfect to Jesus. This is the energy of God that helps us win souls and see them transformed. If you preach for twenty minutes, it's worth eight hours of work, physically and emotionally. But there is an energy that energizes us. Working for God is difficult, but He has energy to deposit inside of you.

4. **The energy helps us do His will.** "*For it is God who works* [energeo] *in you both to will and to do for His good pleasure*" (Philippians 2:13).

The Lord energizes us to do His will. As God releases His *energeia* in me, it's working on my will so I am willing and capable to do His will.

5. **The energy that flows from the prayer of a righteous man or woman.** "*Confess your trespasses to one another, and pray for one another, that you may be healed. The effective* [energeo]*, fervent prayer of a righteous man avails* [ischuo] *much*" (James 5:16).

When a righteous man or woman prays, there is a righteous force released through their lives. When you pray, something is happening. You don't see it, but it enters the throne room of

God like a beam of electricity. When you pray, energy and strength are released.

6. **Faith and love energize us as believers.** "*For in Christ Jesus neither circumcision nor uncircumcision avails* [ischuo] *anything, but faith working* [energeo] *through love*" (Galatians 5:6).

Faith energized by love makes you strong. When your motivation is love, it increases your faith and you're energized. When you feel loved, you are motivated, energized, and compelled to give.

7. **Authority releases energy to work on peoples' hearts and minds.** "*And you He made alive, who were dead in trespasses and sins, in which you once walked according to the course of this world, according to the prince of the power* [exousia] *of the air, the spirit who now works* [energeo] *in the sons of disobedience*" (Ephesians 2:1–2).

Satan has certain authority over the earth and the sons of disobedience. Because he has this authority, he energizes the sons of disobedience. Have you ever wondered what motivates a terrorist to murder innocent men and women? Do you ever wonder what motivates people to abuse children, murder families, or rape women?

The enemy is able and has authority to energize the sons of disobedience. How does he energize them? He stimulates them to think thoughts and make choices that will destroy their lives.

All of us have three potentials: demonic potential, natural potential (developed by natural means), and divine potential. Divine potential is what we can do if we are filled with the *dunamis* of God, the *exousia* of God, and the *energeia* of God. This is what we can be as the power of God fills our lives, transforms us, and uses us to transform others.

The enemy does not have authority over the children of God, but he does have authority over the sons and daughters of disobedience. Satan has no authority to stimulate your mind to think thoughts that will lead to destruction. He can try to speak and lie to you, but he does not have authority over you.

The enemy tries to speak to our minds to help us reach our demonic potential. Why does he do this? How can we reach our demonic potential? By life choices. There are four choices: demonic, destructive, creative, and divine. The enemy is trying to energize you to make decisions that will lead to your destruction or your demonic potential. Your choices will lead you to reach your potential either demonically or divinely. But if you are a child of God, then you can take authority over the enemy and choose to deflect his energy.

The minute you give your life to Christ, Satan has no right to speak to your mind. When you have a thought and take it captive, you must discern where it is coming from. If it is not coming from the Father, then it is coming from Satan who has no authority over you. The reason the Bible says we can have the mind of Christ is because Satan has no authority, no right, to speak to your mind anymore. When you begin to take thoughts captive, your mind can become the mind of Christ.

BENEFITS OF THE *ENERGEIA* OF GOD

When you are filled with the *energeia* of God, you will

- be more effective,
- have the energy to tackle challenges,
- be energized for soul winning,
- be able to work things out, and
- be able to do His will.

When I pray, the energy of God is released. When I read the Word, the energy of God is released. When the energy of God is released, I become more effective because creativity and problem solving are released.

QUESTIONS

Q. Are you being filled with His energy?

Q. When was the last time Jesus got excited about your involvement in His mission?

FOUR

GOD, GIVE ME STRENGTH, PLEASE!

The *Ischus* of God

Ischus—force, ability, strength.

> *Jesus answered him, "The first of all the commandments is: 'Hear, O Israel, the LORD our God, the LORD is one. And you shall love the LORD your God with all your heart, with all your soul, with all your mind, and with all your strength [ischus].' This is the first commandment."* (Mark 12:29–30)

> *Confess your trespasses to one another, and pray for one another, that you may be healed. The effective, fervent prayer of a righteous man avails much.* (James 5:16)

The energy that comes from the prayer of a righteous man

avails (*ischus*) much. The active, effective prayer is powerful. The
prayer of a man is effective and energetic; it is also *ischus*.

> *If anyone speaks, let him speak as the oracles of God. If any-*
> *one ministers, let him do it as with the ability* [ischus] *which*
> *God supplies, that in all things God may be glorified through*
> *Jesus Christ, to whom belong the glory and the dominion for-*
> *ever and ever. Amen.* (1 Peter 4:11)

> *For in Christ Jesus neither circumcision nor uncircumcision*
> *avails* [ischuo] *anything, but faith working* [energeo] *through*
> *love.* (Galatians 5:6)

> *And what is the exceeding greatness of His power* [dunamis]
> *toward us who believe, according to the working* [energeia]
> *of His mighty* [ischus] *power* [kratos]. (Ephesians 1:19)

> *Finally, my brethren, be strong in the Lord and in the power*
> [kratos] *of His might* [ischus]. (Ephesians 6:10)

QUESTIONS

Q. Are you using the power of God to extend His rule and
dominion in your home and workplace?

Q. Are you praying God's dominion will be expanded on
this earth?

Q. How can we use the five keys to expand His kingdom?

FIVE

WHO'S THE BOSS?

The *Kratos* of God

And what is the exceeding greatness of His power [dunamis]
toward us who believe, according to the working [energeia]
of His mighty [ischus] *power* [kratos]. (Ephesians 1:19)

Kratos—dominion or reigning authority.

DUNAMIS ENERGEIA
ISCHUS EXOUSIA

God's ability to impart *exousia, dunamis, energeia,* and *ischus* is
based on His total dominion. God's dominion, *kratos,* is the basis

of all of the powers. The reason you can walk in power, dynamite, energy, and authority is because Christ has dominion. From *kratos* come the other four words *exousia, dunamis, energeia,* and *ischus*. The purpose of the power is to cause the expansion of God's kingdom.

> *He worked* [energeia] *in Christ when He raised Him from the dead and seated Him at His right hand in the heavenly places, far above all principality and power* [exousia] *and might* [dunamis] *and dominion* [kuriotes] *and every name that is named, not only in this age but also in that which is to come.* (Ephesians 1:20–21)

Jesus has dominion over every power, authority, dominion, and character, *"and He put all things under His feet, and gave Him to be head over all things to the church, which is His body, the fullness of Him who fills all in all"* (Ephesians 1:22–23).

Christ has dominion over everything; whether we yield to that dominion or not is up to us.

EXPANDING GOD'S FRANCHISE

> *Finally, my brethren, be strong* [dunamis] *in the Lord and in the power* [kratos] *of His might* [ischus]. *Put on the whole armor of God, that you may be able to stand against the wiles of the devil.* (Ephesians 6:10–11)

Since you have the strength, you've been endowed with dynamite; you are now part of the dominion of Jesus Christ. God releases dynamite, authority, energy, and strength to expand His kingdom. Because you have received these things now, put on the full armor of God. God gives you power to go to war. We are called to be the most radical army in the world, and our objective should be to expand the kingdom of God on this earth. He has now empowered us to go forth as warriors and expand His kingdom. The question is—are we going to spread His kingdom or our own kingdoms?

America is not a kingdom, but it is a democracy. We are not trying to spread our kingdom, but we are trying to spread democracy. England is a kingdom that expanded its borders and realm. As it expanded, it freed nations and conquered nations, expanding the borders, rulership, dominion, and wealth.

Scripturally, Jesus Christ gives us power based on His dominion, and He wants to fill you with His power, His energy, and His strength so that you expand His dominion. We were not saved just to get to heaven; we were saved to expand His kingdom. Now that you are saved from hell, you are supposed to be part of the greatest expansion of all time.

When Americans travel overseas, we always look for restaurants or coffee shops that we have in the United States. We do this because these franchises are familiar to us. This is like Jesus; He gives us His power so wherever we go, we all bring the same quality. We are into franchising the anointing so that we can all carry it wherever we go.

KINGDOM DEFINED

Kingdom—basilica, royalty, rule, realm. Kingdom is used three hundred thirty-nine times in the Bible.

> *Strengthened with all might* [dunamis], *according to His glorious power* [kratos], *for all patience and longsuffering with joy.* (Colossians 1:11)

If Jesus is not reigning in your life, you will not experience the power of God. You cannot have Him just as your Savior; you must have Him as your Lord. The more God reigns in your life, the more power He releases. The amount of power is based on the amount of surrender. The minute we come under the dominion of Christ and submit to Him, all the power of heaven is released into our lives. God extends His kingdom through empowered followers who use their delegated authority.

You have authority over addictions and fears. He is the head, and He will not let those control you anymore. When Jesus is your head, He becomes your covering; when He is your covering, you receive all the blessings from heaven.

The disciples of Jesus were taught the kingdom could come down to earth. I'm glad that you're going to heaven, but that is not the only purpose of you getting saved, filled with the Holy Spirit, and filled with His power and love. The purpose is for you to expand His kingdom on earth, expand the influence of the power of God, and expand the dominion of God in every realm. This makes us the heads and not the tails! Once you submit to His dominion, He helps you overcome all other dominions. What dominion will God use you to overcome?

PRAYERS FOR EXPANSION

Who alone has immortality, dwelling in unapproachable light, whom no man has seen or can see, to whom be honor and everlasting power [kratos]. *Amen.* (1 Timothy 6:16)

Paul is praying for Christ to have everlasting dominion.

If anyone speaks, let him speak as the oracles of God. If anyone ministers, let him do it as with the ability [ischus] *which God supplies, that in all things God may be glorified through Jesus Christ, to whom belong the glory and the dominion* [kratos] *forever and ever. Amen.* (1 Peter 4:11)

In this passage, Peter acknowledges Christ's dominion. When you speak you can have courage because He is empowering you to expand His kingdom.

To Him be the glory and the dominion [kratos] *forever and ever. Amen.* (1 Peter 5:11)

To God our Savior,
Who alone is wise,
Be glory and majesty,

Dominion [kratos] *and power* [exousia],
Both now and forever. Amen. (Jude 25)

These disciples continued to pray for the expansion of the kingdom of God. It was a constant prayer of the saints of God.

And every creature which is in heaven and on the earth and
under the earth and such as are in the sea, and all that are
in them, I heard saying:
"Blessing and honor and glory and power [kratos]
Be to Him who sits on the throne,
And to the Lamb, forever and ever!" (Revelation 5:13)

Twenty-four hours a day a heavenly host is proclaiming this in the throne room of God. They are interceding for you so you can expand His kingdom. Your life has purpose as you live out this expansion. When you are working at your job, know that you have the ability to prophesy, pray for the sick, lead a lost person to Christ, and deliver people from demons and addictions.

THE LORD'S PRAYER

Your kingdom come. Your will be done on earth as it is in
heaven. And do not lead us into temptation, but deliver us
from the evil one. For Yours is the kingdom and the power
and the glory forever. Amen. (Matthew 6:10, 13)

The disciples had asked Jesus to teach them how to pray, so He gave them a model prayer. At the conclusion of the Lord's Prayer, He ends with a request that His kingdom and His dominion be established forever. Why did the disciples give their lives? Why do missionaries still suffer and die? Because they know they are part of the greatest expansion of all time. They know that Jesus Christ is greater than any persecution, He is greater than any terrorist, and He is greater than anyone out there. He wants to have dominion worldwide, and He is going to do it through you and me. The advancement of His reign on the earth should be our number one priority as believers.

Jesus has dominion over everything; however, He will not force His dominion upon you. You can only surrender your will to Christ. It must be voluntary as He takes dominion over your life. Jesus will never take dominion over someone's free will. His dominion and authority can only be exercised when you are surrendered to Him totally and allow Him dominion over your life.

The Lordship of Christ is a daily thing because we all have wills and we all want to have control. It is as if we believe we know better than God. Coming under His *kratos* is a daily thing as we surrender to Him.

But seek first the kingdom of God and His righteousness, and all these things shall be added to you. (Matthew 6:33)
And Jesus went about all the cities and villages, teaching in their synagogues, preaching the gospel of the kingdom, and healing every sickness and every disease among the people. (Matthew 9:35)

If we are Christians, should we not act like Christ? A Christian is a little Christ, and Christ taught the gospel of the kingdom. Wherever He went He brought the kingdom—healing every sickness and disease among the people.

But if I cast out demons by the Spirit of God, surely the kingdom of God has come upon you. (Matthew 12:28).

How do we expand the kingdom of God?

- Teach
- Preach
- Heal
- Cast out devils

RECEIVING HIS *KRATOS*

And I will give you the keys of the kingdom of heaven, and whatever you bind on earth will be bound in heaven, and whatever you loose on earth will be loosed in heaven. (Matthew 16:19)

He gave the disciples the keys of the kingdom. Not long ago my son, Samuel, turned sixteen, and I wanted to buy him a car. I found a PT Cruiser, which reminded me of my youth. I asked Samuel what he thought of this car, and he really liked it. I then gave him the keys. When I gave him the car I gave him authority to drive the car, and I have authority to take it away. As long as he submits to my *kratos* and obeys my rules, he has authority to drive the car. In the same way God gives us the keys to reign and rule with Him.

And heal the sick there, and say to them, "The kingdom of God has come near to you." (Luke 10:9)

When we submit to the dominion of Christ, He releases the powers into our lives. As I walk into a place, the kingdom of God is approaching people because it is living in me. As Jesus reigns and rules in my life, the kingdom of God comes with me wherever I go. The five powers are available so that we can help expand His influence and His dominion over the lives we encounter and touch; we are bringing the kingdom to them. It is one thing to invite someone to your church, but it is another thing to bring the kingdom to them. The goal is for you to take everything God has placed in you to a hurting community.

QUESTIONS

Q. Have you allowed Christ to take dominion in your life? Is He truly your Lord?

Q. Have you humbled yourself to God so that He can lift you up?

PART II

PREPARE FOR
HIS POWER

SIX

PUSH THE EJECT BUTTON

And heal the sick there, and say to them, "The kingdom of God has come near to you." (Luke 10:9)

Miracles are not reserved for superstar Christians; they are for those willing to do menial tasks. While we are out doing our menial tasks, we strengthen the strength-less. We don't have to stand up and preach in front of thousands of people; we just have to be willing to help those who are weak.

After you are fed, filled with the power, you should be ejected into your world, workplace, and family to make a difference for the expansion of the kingdom of God.

1. **Send forth—eject.** "*After these things the Lord appointed seventy others also, and sent them two by two before his face*

into every city and place where He Himself was about to go" (Luke 10:1).

Jesus sent them out two by two, for accountability and strength. Do not be lone rangers; you were designed to go out two by two—to be accountable and have support. You have to develop a strong support system around your life.

2. **The harvest is great, but the laborers are few.** *"Then He said to them, 'The harvest truly is great, but the laborers are few; therefore pray the Lord of the harvest to send out laborers into His harvest'"* (Luke 10:2).

The harvest needs laborers. Your city is ripe for harvest; consider the opportunity you have right now to become harvesters for Jesus Christ. Get a vision for the harvest. Jesus is not looking for superstars; He is looking for laborers. He is looking for those who will love others by making a phone call to someone who is lonely, visiting someone in the hospital, mowing the lawn for a neighbor, or baking cookies for someone. He is looking for those who are laborers and will do menial tasks.

3. **You are His lambs.** *"Go your way; behold, I send you out as lambs among wolves"* (Luke 10:3).

You may be lambs, but you are heavily armed lambs! We have the powers of God flowing through our lives, making us heavily armed.

4. Don't depend on your own strength, and don't get distracted. "*And remain in the same house, eating and drinking such things as they give, for the laborer is worthy of his wages. Do not go from house to house. Whatever city you enter, and they receive you, eat such things as are set before you. And heal the sick there, and say to them, 'The kingdom of God has come near to you'*" (Luke 10:7–9).

What a great strategy! Go to one house and use it as a foothold to impact that city. If you change one family, then you start changing that city. That one family knows another family, who knows another family, and each family knows at least five or six other families. This is a strategy to help you win your city.

Jesus didn't want to give them a task that was too big for them, so He instructed them to start with one house. So go to your house, begin changing your family, your kids, your grandkids, and your relatives. You are bringing God's kingdom on earth. Set up your home as a lighthouse for your community. From your home you can reach your community, and your community can then reach your city.

The very dust of your city which clings to us we wipe off against you. Nevertheless know this, that the kingdom of God has come near you. But I say to you that it will be more tolerable in that Day for Sodom than for that city. He who hears you hears Me, he who rejects you rejects Me, and he who rejects Me rejects Him who sent Me. (Luke 10:11–12, 16)

How they treat you is how they treat Christ and the Father; it is delegated authority. When you are overseas and enter an American embassy, it is no longer the territory of the country you are visiting; you are on American soil. The ambassador is the delegated authority from our president, Congress, and Senate, and whatever the ambassador says is what the president says. Whatever that country does to the American ambassador, they do to our president and to America. In the same way, Jesus is saying whatever they do to us they are really doing it to Him because we are ambassadors of Christ; this is delegated authority!

Then the seventy returned with joy, saying, "Lord, even the demons are subject to us in Your name." And He said to them, "I saw Satan fall like lightning from heaven. Behold, I give you the authority to trample on serpents and scorpions, and over all the power of the enemy, and nothing shall by any means hurt you. Nevertheless do not rejoice in this, that the spirits are subject to you, but rather rejoice because your names are written in heaven." (Luke 10:17–20)

I paraphrase this passage: To overcome physical challenges you will encounter when I send you out again, I will give you all power (*dunamis*) over the enemy and the demonic forces that come from the one who hates you. Nothing shall by any means hurt you. And nothing, nothing, nothing shall be unjust toward you. It is great that demons submit to you, but I have a book in heaven, and I have already written your name in it. This book represents all those who get to go to the next level.

What is the next level for us? God wants to promote you with new authority.

And he who overcomes, and keeps My works until the end, to him I will give power (exousia) *over the nations.* (Revelation 2:26)

Those who subdue and guard will receive *exousia* over the nations. God expects you to subdue, and He expects me to have dominion over spirits and demons. Jesus does not expect something we cannot do, so we must be able to do this through Jesus Christ.

We are not weak Christians; we are powerful in Jesus Christ. God wants to elevate you to be someone who oversees nations. Why are we letting the enemy run over our children, our workplaces, our campuses, our homes, and our families? This is a wake-up call for all of us; we are called to rule nations, to overcome the problems in our families, and to subject spirits in the name of Jesus Christ!

The seventy discovered the anointing was not only for the twelve; the anointing was for every one of them who followed Christ. These seventy realized the spirits were subjected to them in Jesus' name.

These seventy were told to say that the kingdom of God was near because it was near. It was in them. Jesus is in us, and we are the temple of the Holy Spirit. We are bringing the presence of God with us wherever we go. When we walk into a room, the kingdom of God is near to these people. Wherever you are, you should carry a presence with you because you are over every evil spirit.

> *In that hour Jesus rejoiced in the Spirit and said, "I praise You, Father, Lord of heaven and earth, that You have hidden these things from the wise and prudent and revealed them to babes. Even so, Father, for so it seemed good in Your sight."* (Luke 10:21)

Jesus rejoiced, which means He started shouting and leaping with joy. This reality made Jesus leap for joy. Imagine Jesus not stoic but full of joy and happiness. In this context Jesus was laughing, joyful, dancing, and thrilled with what God was doing through these followers. Jesus rejoices when you walk in His delegated authority.

> *Then Jesus cried out and said, "He who believes in Me, believes not in Me but in Him who sent Me. And he who sees Me sees Him who sent Me."* (John 12:44–45)

> *Most assuredly, I say to you, he who receives whomever I send receives Me; and he who receives Me receives Him who sent Me.* (John 13:20)

Just like the Father sent the Son, the Son is now sending us. If they mistreat you, then they are mistreating the Son and the Father. The same power, the same authority, the same unction, the same gifts that were given to Jesus Christ, He gives them to us. Because Jesus had all authority, He gave authority to us and told us to go into the world. Jesus gave us the authority that the Father gave Him.

AUTHORITY MULTIPLIED

If I give my son the keys to my car, then he will have authority over my car. If my son then gives my keys to his friend, his friend has authority over my car. So whatever my son's friend does to my car is going to impact him, my son, and me. This is the same concept. The Father gave the Son authority; the Son in turn gives all authority to us. Just as the Father walks in this authority, now you can walk in this authority.

First the Father had authority; He gave it to the Son, who then gave it to the twelve and the seventy. On the day of Pentecost this power and authority was given to one hundred twenty. Now it is not only eighty-one people who are full of the power of God, it is more than one hundred twenty people who are now saved and filled with the Holy Spirit. A few years later there was a great persecution of the thousands the one hundred twenty had touched. These Jewish believers scattered across the world, and they took this same authority to others. These people then went out and did the same thing. Many were persecuted because they were trying to stop the most dynamic force ever witnessed—people walking in the authority that Jesus gave them.

DELEGATED AUTHORITY

Most assuredly, I say to you, he who believes in Me, the works that I do he will do also; and greater works than these he will do, because I go to My Father. And whatever you ask in My name, that I will do, that the Father may be glorified in the Son. If you ask anything in My name, I will do it. (John 14:12–14)

You have delegated authority. Because of your association with Jesus Christ and the Holy Spirit, you have the power and authority to change people's lives. You have authority and power to see people healed and delivered. You have power and authority to hear words of knowledge, wisdom, and prophecy. Jesus looks forward to ejecting you into your city. He looks forward to seeing you change cities and make history.

QUESTIONS

Q. Have you activated the power of God in your life?

Q. Are you using His power to heal the sick and change lives?

SEVEN

THE INDESTRUCTIBLE LIFE

And I will give you the keys of the kingdom of heaven, and whatever you bind on earth will be bound in heaven, and whatever you loose on earth will be loosed in heaven. (Matthew 16:19)

Who has come, not according to the law of a fleshly commandment, but according to the power [dunamis] *of an endless life.* (Hebrews 7:16)

An endless life means an indestructible life—you cannot dilute it, and you can not dissolve it. Jesus Christ lived a life that was indestructible. Satan tried to destroy His life, but he could not. You have the same ability to live an indestructible life. There is something in you, as a believer, that is greater than anything in the world, and it is Jesus Christ and the power of the Holy Spirit.

THE PROGRESSION OF THE KEYS

Jesus' statement to Peter introduces the concept of the keys to the kingdom. This is an important analogy because everyone understands that keys unlock doors and help us enter through them into a new environment. The keys that Jesus promised Peter referred to the powers, gifts, and abilities that would unlock the prison doors to so many people caught in the lies of the enemy. These keys were not just for Peter but for every person who would believe and receive Jesus Christ. Peter probably did not know what keys Jesus was referring to, but he did know that it would help him bind and loose.

1. **The seventy were given an assignment.** *"After these things the Lord appointed seventy others also, and sent them two by two before His face into every city and place where He Himself was about to go"* (Luke 10:1).

2. **Jesus gave the seventy two keys: heal the sick and proclaim the message.** *"And heal the sick there, and say to them, 'The kingdom of God has come near to you'"* (Luke 10:9).

They were given a limited agenda, but discovered that they had more power than needed.

3. **Jesus gave the twelve four keys: power, authority, healing, and preaching.** *"Then He called His twelve disciples together and gave them power* [dunamis] *and authority* [exousia] *over all demons, and to cure diseases. He sent them to preach the kingdom of God and to heal the sick"* (Luke 9:1–2).

4. **The seventy came back with a progress report.** *"Then the seventy returned with joy, saying, 'Lord, even the demons are subject to us in Your name'"* (Luke 10:17).

The seventy were very excited because most of what they did was not part of their assignment. The four keys were not given to them, but they were able to perform these things anyway. They had dominion over demons. They were not expecting demons to be subject to them. These seventy had more power than they even knew.

5. **Jesus responded to their success.** Jesus recognized the impact of their ministry, and in Luke 10:18 said, *"I saw Satan fall like lightning from heaven."*

What is interesting here is that these seventy were the ones defeating the enemy, not Jesus Himself. He gave them power to damage the kingdom of darkness in His name; He authorized it. Jesus wants you to have the gratification of tearing down the kingdom of your accuser, the one who lies and steals from you. Jesus has given you the keys to defeat your enemy and the enemy of your family, church, and city.

6. **The seventy got a promotion when Jesus gave them more authority.** *"Behold, I give you the authority* [exousia] *to trample on serpents and scorpions, and over all the power* [dunamis] *of the enemy, and nothing shall by any means hurt you. Nevertheless do not rejoice in this, that the spirits are subject to you, but rather rejoice because your names are written in heaven"* (Luke 10:19–20).

The seventy were given the power to heal and a message from Jesus to deliver. After they received these two keys and exercised their authority, Jesus decided to give them more keys. It is interesting to note the following in this Scripture:

- Jesus told them to rejoice that their names were written in heaven, not because the spirits were subject to them.
- Jesus agreed the spirits were subject to them.
- Jesus then extended their authority to include natural dangers.

Mark 16:18 seems to expand upon this authority a little more.

They will take up serpents; and if they drink anything deadly, it will by no means hurt them; they will lay hands on the sick, and they will recover.

Paul's experience with a serpent is a real example of how the first-century church benefited from this promise (Acts 28:1–5).

The venom of the snake did not kill Paul. This proved to be a huge testimony to the people of Malta. When believers demonstrate authority, it creates a huge platform for ministry.

> But when Paul had gathered a bundle of sticks and laid them on the fire, a viper came out because of the heat, and fastened on his hand. So when the natives saw the creature hanging from his hand, they said to one another, "No doubt this man is a murderer, whom, though he has escaped the sea, yet justice does not allow to live." But he shook off the creature into the fire and suffered no harm. (Acts 28:3–5)

God will protect you from Satan's attacks in the natural realm. Do you know how many car accidents He has saved you from? Do you know how many times He has cured physical diseases that could have impacted you? By His grace and mercy He protects us so we can continue to spread His dominion on this earth.

> And over all the power [dunamis] of the enemy, and nothing shall by any means hurt you. (Luke 10:19b)

They were given power over all demons. You have authority over the *dunamis* of the enemy. God gives you power and authority over all of Satan's power, which includes his power to steal, kill, and destroy in the natural and supernatural.

MATTHEW'S PERSPECTIVE OF THE MISSION

Luke heard the report of the twelve from Peter, but Matthew was an eyewitness; he was actually there. This is how Matthew tells it:

And when He had called His twelve disciples to Him, He gave them power over unclean spirits, to cast them out, and to heal all kinds of sickness and all kinds of disease. (Matthew 10:1)

We now have a new key: authority over unclean spirits.

And as you go, preach, saying, "The kingdom of heaven is at hand." Heal the sick, cleanse the lepers, raise the dead, cast out demons. Freely you have received, freely give. (Matthew 10:7–8)

They were instructed to do the following:

- Spread the message
- Heal the sick
- Cleanse the lepers
- Raise the dead
- Cast out demons
- Freely give what they had received

God gave you the keys free. Now that you have received them, give them to someone else. We are called to pass them along!

For I long to see you, that I may impart to you some spiritual gift, so that you may be established. (Romans 1:11)

Paul wanted to give something he had in excess. It is the picture of someone who has two coats and gives one away to someone else. Paul has all kinds of gifts—plenty to hand out to others in Jesus' name.

Then Peter said, "Silver and gold I do not have, but what I do have I give you: In the name of Jesus Christ of Nazareth, rise up and walk." And he took him by the right hand and lifted him up, and immediately his feet and ankle bones received strength. So he, leaping up, stood and walked and entered the temple with them—walking, leaping, and praising God. (Acts 3:6–8)

Peter did not have any silver or gold because Jesus' original assignment instructed them not to bring any silver or gold (Matthew 10:9). Peter followed the original instructions and what he freely received, he gave. Peter did not have silver and gold, but what he did have he received in Matthew 16:19—the keys to the kingdom! Peter had the power given by Jesus to heal all sicknesses and cure every disease. Christ gave the provisions for us to implement the power. The provision has been paid for by Jesus Christ, but we are involved in the implementation. Someone can give you orders, but your must implement those orders. We have been given the ability to bind and to loose. If someone is bound by sin, we can loose them; if someone is filled with a demon, we can bind the devil. We have authority to bind and loose.

Jesus gave five ways to expand His kingdom:

- Message—The gospel and the kingdom of God are in you.
- Mission—We should bring heaven down to earth.
- Power—The five different powers are:

  1. *exousia*—delegated authority
  2. *dunamis*—miraculous dynamite power
  3. *energeia*—energy
  4. *kratos*—dominion
  5. *ischus*—strength

- Authority—We are to heal the sick.
- Gifts—We must use our gifts to expand His kingdom.

THE GIFTS

Now concerning spiritual gifts, brethren, I do not want you to be ignorant. (1 Corinthians 12:1)

But the manifestation of the Spirit is given to each one for the profit of all: for to one is given the word of wisdom through the Spirit, to another the word of knowledge through the same Spirit, to another faith by the same Spirit, to another gifts of healings by the same Spirit, to another the working of mira-

cles, to another prophecy, to another discerning of spirits, to another different kinds of tongues, to another the interpretation of tongues. But one and the same Spirit works all these things, distributing to each one individually as He wills. (1 Corinthians 12:7–11)

These gifts are supposed to be used in your life to bring the kingdom of heaven down to earth. Every one of you has at least ten to fifteen people in your sphere of influence. You should be so full of power, so full of authority, so full of gifts that you can give it to other people, knowing there is plenty more where that came from.

My friend and mentor Dr. David Lim has done an amazing work titled *Spiritual Gifts—A Fresh Look.* The exegesis of this passage and full description of the gifts will help you understand the nature of the gifts. The Greek word for gift is *charisma,* which means a (divine) gratuity, i.e. deliverance (from danger or passion); (specifically) a (spiritual) endowment, i.e. (subjectively) religious qualification, or (objectively) miraculous faculty—(free gift).[1] God's gifts are the favors that He deposits in our lives. We don't deserve any of them; they are favors given to us by God to reach a broken world.

AFTER THE RESURRECTION

Jesus gave authority and power to heal and to have dominion over every demon and evil spirit. The twelve disciples used this authority and power and had incredible results. The seventy received this same authority and power and had even greater results. After the resurrection of Christ, the power, gifts, and authority increased. The same authority, power, and gifts were passed on to the second and third generations of believers. These second-generation Christians had the same power and authority as the first-generation believers. In fact, after the resurrection of Christ they became more powerful.

For God has not given us a spirit of fear, but of power and of love and of a sound mind. (2 Timothy 1:7)

God did not give you a spirit that makes you timid or cowardly; He gave you a spirit of *dunamis*, a feeling of *agape*, and a sound mind. A sound mind means discipline and self-control.

Do not neglect the gift that is in you, which was given to you by prophecy with the laying on of the hands of the eldership. (1 Timothy 4:14)

Timothy was instructed to not neglect the gifts. The word translated as *neglect* means "to be careless of, make light of, neglect, be negligent, not regard."[2]

And He said to them, "Go into all the world and preach the gospel to every creature. He who believes and is baptized will be saved; but he who does not believe will be condemned. And these signs will follow those who believe: In My name they will cast out demons; they will speak with new tongues; they will take up serpents; and if they drink anything deadly, it will by no means hurt them; they will lay hands on the sick, and they will recover." (Mark 16:15–18)

All believers are given this assignment:

- Cast out demons in Jesus' name
- Speak in new tongues
- Have dominion over natural threats
- Heal the sick

Everywhere we go these signs should follow us.

QUESTIONS

Q. How much power and authority has God given you?

Q. Have you used these powers and this authority well?

Q. Have you freely given what was given to you? If so, how? If not, why?

Q. What have you received from Jesus?

Q. Have you neglected these gifts?

Q. Do you need to rekindle them?

Q. What have you done with the power, authority, and message Christ has given you?

EIGHT

Seven Steps to Prepare Yourself for His Power

Are you ready for a holy impartation of God's power and presence? I hope that you are. These seven steps will help you *seize* a divine opportunity so you can use the keys to the kingdom. God wants to prepare you for a holy visitation. Holy visitations can become holy habitations, if we walk in obedience.

STEP 1: GET RIGHT WITH GOD

In order to get right with God, we must start with total submission to Him. A yielded life is one God can mold and shape into a vessel of honor.

Submit yourselves, then, to God. Resist the devil, and he will flee from you. (James 4:7 NIV)

Submission will enable us to be transformed by Him. Every experience of life can be surrendered to his care. He can use every situation, even those from sin or the devil.

God sees the big picture of our trials, and tribulations. He sees the context of our calling, purpose, and destiny, and the context of the world's needs and people's needs. He sees us from an eternal perspective. Everything is evaluated with eternal values.

Circumstances overwhelm us because we can't see the final product. We become anxious because we can't see God's hand in our trials. We must recognize we are in the furnace for a purpose. Whether the author of our trial is the enemy, ourselves, or God, we must surrender our problems to God so He can use them. The fiery trials are purifying. Their pressure and heat and perfect us. Pure vessels become vessels worthy of containing His glory.

In 2 Timothy, the apostle Paul realized the process that God was bringing Timothy through.

In a large house there are articles not only of gold and silver, but also of wood and clay; some are for noble purposes and some for ignoble. If a man cleanses himself from the latter, he will be an instrument for noble purposes, made holy, useful to the Master and prepared to do any good work. Flee the evil desires of youth, and pursue righteousness, faith, love and peace, along with those who call on the Lord out of a pure heart. (2 Timothy 2:20–22 NIV)

Could it be that God would spend years refining us to use us for a habitation of His glory? Yes, of course. How many years did it take for the Messiah to come? How long will it take for Him to return? How long has it taken Him to prepare a place for us? God's timing and values are different than ours: "*With the Lord a day is like a thousand years, and a thousand years are like a day*" (2 Peter 3:8 NIV).

I heard a preacher once say that it took a few days for the Hebrews to get out of Egypt, but it took over forty years for God to get Egypt out of the Hebrews. Would it help us to deal with the trials of daily life with this view in mind? God rarely sends tragedies and trials to us, but when they occur we can yield them to Him. We can surrender the pain and confusion to Him. Doesn't John 10:10 (NIV) clearly tell us, "*The thief comes only to steal and kill and destroy; I have come that they may have life, and have it to the full*"?

God wants to give us an abundant life, but we must submit ourselves to Him. We have to surrender our hearts and minds to Him. Are you right with God? Are you so right that you can receive everything He has to offer?

Do you clean your home before important guests arrive? Do you add decorations or furniture when you receive houseguests? My mom recently spent a month and a half with my wife and me. My father had passed away, so we opened our home to her. My wife, Denise, spent time and money preparing a room and bathroom for her. We wanted her to feel comfortable, loved, and cherished. The room was rearranged, and a new comforter, sheets, and towels were added. The room looked great! My mom felt welcomed, wanted, and appreciated. Is this how the Holy Spirit feels with us?

Jesus refers to this principle in the parable of the new wine and old wineskins: "*And no one pours new wine into old wineskins. If he does, the new wine will burst the skins, the wine will run out and the wineskins will be ruined. No, new wine must be poured into new wineskins*" (Luke 5:37–38 NIV). The new wineskins are our hearts and minds.

Our minds, emotions, and spirits must be ready to receive the God of glory. When Solomon built the temple, he used the finest materials. Purity was a crucial specification. God gave the details of every article of the temple. If God would spend this much time describing the details of a building and its ornaments, would He not be as concerned about our hearts and minds? Are we not the temple of the Holy Spirit?

Do you not know that your body is a temple of the Holy Spirit, who is in you, whom you have received from God? You are not your own. (1 Corinthians 6:19 NIV)

On many occasions I have confronted men, women, and young people who wanted impartation but were not right with God. Our altars have been filled with people who confessed to being backsliders and lukewarm. Doesn't God say if we are lukewarm He will vomit us out of His mouth?

So, because you are lukewarm—neither hot nor cold—I am about to spit you out of my mouth. (Revelation 3:16 NIV)

I take this warning seriously. We fool ourselves if we are expecting an impartation of spiritual gifts with a lukewarm, compromised life. We should expect judgment and discipline. It is crucial that we repent of compromise, apathy, sins, reproach, and so many other conditions that will rob us of God's gifts. Many Christians have lost a holy, healthy fear of God. We must pray for a spirit of repentance. If we ask God to forgive us, then He will. John clearly explains, *"If we confess our sins, he is faithful and just and will forgive us our sins and purify us from all unrighteousness"* (1 John 1:9 NIV).

The Greek word for sin is *hamartia*, which means "to miss the mark." This Greek word is a word picture of an archer who shoots an arrow but misses the target; it is when we miss or disobey God's commands. That is why, *"for God so loved the world that he gave his one and only Son, that whoever believes in him shall not perish but have eternal life"* (John 3:16–17 NIV).

Repentance means to turn 180 degrees from the behavior or attitude. If you honestly repent for a sin, you will experience a real character change.

Take a moment now and ask the Holy Spirit to reveal to you any behavior that grieves Him. David asked the same question of God in Psalm 51:10 (NIV): *"Create in me a pure heart, O God, and renew a steadfast spirit within me."* It is so easy to rationalize our sin. We deceive ourselves so frequently. Solomon had such deep insight when he wrote,

There is a way that seems right to a man, but in the end it leads to death. (Proverbs 14:12 NIV)

STEP 2: GET RIGHT WITH OTHERS

Do not let any unwholesome talk come out of your mouths, but only what is helpful for building others up according to their needs, that it may benefit those who listen. And do not grieve the Holy Spirit of God, with whom you were sealed for the day of redemption. Get rid of all bitterness, rage and anger, brawling and slander, along with every form of malice. Be kind and compassionate to one another, forgiving each other, just as in Christ God forgave you. (Ephesians 4:29–32 NIV)

Has your heart and life become cluttered with hurts and angers from the past? Do you struggle with moments of jealousy and envy? If your answer is yes to these pressing questions, then Ephesians 4:29–32 is for you.

Paul is emphatic about the correlation between our relationships and the Holy Spirit: *"Do not grieve the Holy Spirit."* Every time we allow hurtful words, bitterness, resentment, rage, anger, and reproach to dwell in our lives, we grieve the Holy Spirit. There is no impartation when the Holy Spirit is grieved, only a deafening silence from heaven. It is of primary importance to get rid of all these hindrances. Easier said then done, isn't it? What can you do with all the excess relational garbage? Here are a few steps to clean up the mess.

THE PATH OF RECONCILIATION

Matthew 18:15–17 is our detailed biblical map to reconciliation. Let us follow these directions to the path of peace.

If your brother sins against you, go and show him his fault, just between the two of you. If he listens to you, you have won your brother over. But if he will not listen, take one or two others along, so that "every matter may be established by the testimony of two or three witnesses." If he refuses to listen to them, tell it to the church; and if he refuses to listen even to the church, treat him as you would a pagan or a tax collector. (NIV)

Step 1: If a friend, relative, mentor, or colleague offends you, then work it out honestly between the two of you. Don't minimize it or allow fear to stop you. Just do it.

Step 2: If you can't resolve it one-on-one, then ask for an objective third party to mediate and serve as a witness. The mediator will have to be spiritually mature.

Step 3: Ask your church leadership to help if steps 1 and 2 fail. This stage ensures the elders of the church will use their anointing, experience, and knowledge to help resolve the conflict.

Step 4: If every step fails, realize that someone is acting ungodly. Remember that it takes two to reconcile. Follow biblical council, and make sure that you aren't the problem. If you are pointing the finger at them, beware of the three that are directed at you.

Step 5: Forgive him, forgive him forgive him, and forgive him. Then ask God to heal your hurts and deal with your anger. In most cases I encourage people to start the process with forgiveness. It tends to take the tension and anger out of our conversations.

Matthew also deals with situations when *we* have offended someone.

> *Therefore, if you are offering your gift at the altar and there remember that your brother has something against you, leave your gift there in front of the altar. First go and be reconciled to your brother; then come and offer your gift.* (Matthew 5:23–24 NIV)

The Holy Spirit will remind us of unresolved conflicts so that we can get them right. We may not be aware that we have hurt someone until God wakes us up.

Our goal in any relational wedge must be *reconciliation*. This term means "to bring to peace two parties that are at war." We have to take up the courage to take the first step with a desire to reconcile; we must want peace. If you are willing to follow these biblical guidelines, you will begin to live in relational peace. Most conflicts can be resolved with very little intervention. It is worth the effort.

STEP 3: GET RIGHT WITH OURSELVES

This step may sound redundant, but it is not. I have noticed at altars all around the world that God does care about our emotions. My wife is an excellent illustration of this truth. While we were at a conference in Canada, we discovered God wanted to heal her before He would pour His power into her. During the first night's services, Denise responded to the altar call. She wanted to experience God's power like the others. Unexpectedly, the woman who prayed for her discerned an unresolved hurt. The altar worker wanted to pray for healing rather than the impartation of power or gifts. Denise was not happy with this situation.

At the conference, Denise experienced this three separate times. Each worker discerned the need for healing. On the third attempt, Denise finally received the healing prayer. The next evening, my wife was ready for other impartations, and she received them for the first time.

There have been times in my life when it took me twenty to thirty minutes to deal with all my emotional baggage before I could receive anything from God. Now is the time to deal with issues that need to be resolved. Do not hope that He will wipe them all away in some glorious rapture experience. With God's help, the altar experience can free you of fears, guilt, shame, insecurities, and rejection. Jesus Christ is still the Great Physician. Why would He fill you with His power when your heart is broken? It would be like filling a gas tank with cracks in it. God is more concerned about you than He is about a goose-bump experience. He wants to give you good gifts, but will you be able to contain them? Have you spent the time forgiving and receiving forgiveness?

If you, then, though you are evil, know how to give good gifts to your children, how much more will your Father in heaven give good gifts to those who ask him! (Matthew 7:11 NIV)

STEP 4: BREAK ALL TIES WITH THE DEMONIC

Submit yourselves, then, to God. Resist the devil, and he will flee from you. Come near to God and he will come near to you. Wash your hands, you sinners, and purify your hearts, you double-minded. (James 4:7–8 NIV)

James admonishes us to defeat the devil's schemes by submitting to God, resisting the devil, drawing near to God, washing our hands, and purifying our hearts. These will bring spiritual victory and renewal. In Ephesians, Paul explains how some satanic strongholds are born in unresolved anger. God always has an antidote for satanic strongholds. Satan will do everything in his power to defile us and keep us from receiving God's blessings. The spirit world is an invisible battleground. In order for us to receive these blessings, we must take active measures to free ourselves from the grasp of satanic forces.

During our impartation services, we encourage the people to break these ties by verbally working through the five R's:

1. **Repent:** "*Repent, then, and turn to God, so that your sins may be wiped out, that times of refreshing may come from the Lord*" (Acts 3:19 NIV).

2. **Resist:** "*Submit yourselves, then, to God. Resist the devil, and he will flee from you*" (James 4:7 NIV).

3. **Renounce:** "*Renounce your sins by doing what is right, and your wickedness by being kind to the oppressed. It may be that then your prosperity will continue*" (Daniel 4:27 NIV).

4. **Rebuke:** "*The LORD said to Satan, 'The LORD rebuke you, Satan! The LORD, who has chosen Jerusalem, rebuke you! Is not this man a burning stick snatched from the fire?'*" (Zechariah 3:2 NIV).

5. **Reclaim:** "*In that day the Lord will reach out his hand a second time to reclaim the remnant that is left of his people from Assyria, from Lower Egypt, from Upper Egypt, from Cush, from Elam, from Babylonia, from Hamath and from the islands of the sea*" (Isaiah 11:11 NIV).

God wants to reclaim souls, families, and friends. You must break the demonic ties by verbally taking your stand for Christ. You must clean out your house of any items that open the door to the demonic. There is a popular song that talks about going to the enemy's camp to take back what Satan has stolen from us. Jesus wants to work through us to reclaim lost ground and blessings. A Scripture I have claimed for my life is: "*And the God of all grace, who called you to his eternal glory in Christ, after you have suffered a little while, will himself restore you and make you strong, firm and steadfast"* (1 Peter 5:10 NIV). Don't be afraid, saint. Take back the territory that God has already seized for you.

FACING THE DEMONIC

Our ministry with the demonic has been greatly aided by Dr. James Marocco's book, *Closing the Forbidden Doors,* and Carlos Annacondia's book, *Listen to Me, Satan.* I will never forget a personal experience that illustrates the need for each person to break his or her ties with the demonic.

I was helping Claudio Freidzon lead a crusade and pastors' school in Lima, Peru. Claudio had become my friend after he ministered to me in 1997. He invited me to be part of this great outreach to the people of Peru. Although I was honored to be invited, I was intimidated by the oppression in the location of the stadium. Taxi drivers would not drive me to the stadium because of the gang violence that surrounded it. The first night was overwhelming.

I was asked to testify for twenty minutes to the twenty-five thousand people in attendance. What a rush! The heaviness of spiritual warfare was extreme. Praise, worship, the Word, and anointing broke it. The Holy Spirit began to touch the great crowd on the second night of the crusade. A spirit of joy filled the place. I was supposed to share a testimony that night, but God took over. The leaders started dancing, and the people shouted and danced as God broke through the darkness of poverty and pain from their past.

All of a sudden my safe little existence was rattled by Claudio's invitation for "all the drug addicts, gang members, and demon-possessed people to come to the platform." To my surprise respondents started shaking the locked gates to get on the field. The security guards hesitated, but Claudio insisted. Can you imagine what fifty to sixty drug addicts, gang members, and demon-possessed people looked like as they ran toward me? I couldn't believe my eyes.

Claudio was safely positioned ten feet high, while I was on the grass ten feet from the gang. Things got worse as some of the respondents were screaming and throwing up. They were truly demon-possessed. Living in Las Vegas I have encountered a few possessed people, but nothing like this! Not even in Asia had I seen what the Bible calls demoniacs. These poor souls were Grade A, 100 percent demoniacs.

I tried to show that I was not afraid. I took a few steps toward them to demonstrate my confidence. Actually, I was scared out of my wits. Just when I thought things couldn't get worse, Claudio told me to take care of the two who were the most disruptive.

These two demoniacs were vomiting, screaming, and foaming at the mouth. I was dressed in my best suit, so I decided to stand about eight feet away (a safe distance, I thought). Instantly the fear left me and the Holy Spirit took over. I started to shout at the demons in English. I told them they would have to let go when I counted to three. Now remember that these people were Peruvian. They did not understand English, but the demons did.

I counted to three, then . . . POW. The power knocked about eight of them down. For a moment I felt pretty impressed with my new authority. *Wow, Lord, even the demons obey me in Your name*, I thought. But then in front of twenty-five thousand people I learned a valuable lesson. Claudio looked down and said, "No Paul, not yet." I thought that I had done what Claudio asked me to do: take care of the worst demon-possessed people who were disrupting what he was trying to do, but Claudio was going to lead the multitudes who responded in a prayer of repentance and renouncing of all spirits. In saying these words, demon-possessed people become involved in their own deliverance. If they are actually involved in their own deliverance, they will have the tools to stay free. Remember that the Bible warns us how to stay delivered (Luke 11:24–26).

Well, being corrected in front of the stadium was not fun, but I learned a valuable lesson. The eight who had fallen down and been delivered were picked up and led in prayer. They gained a great victory and received a great tool. I pushed the dust off my pride, took a deep breath, and went back to work for God. It was awesome! As the conference continued, altar workers and desperate parents would bring their demon-possessed children for deliverance. It was glorious. God used a scared pastor from Las Vegas to deliver the worst in Peru.

You too can experience the power of deliverance. Take a moment to make sure that every bondage is broken. The five powers will help you in this process. You must Repent, Renounce, Resist, Rebuke, and Reclaim. Ask the Holy Spirit to reveal any open doors to demonic spirits and ask Him to set you free forever.

STEP 5: TOTALLY SURRENDER
YOUR LIFE TO CHRIST

A surrendered life is one that can be filled and led by the presence of the Holy Spirit. This is more, much more that just accepting Jesus in your heart. In my opinion, a true conversion experience requires total surrender. This surrender decision will occur throughout your life. We will all face our Calvary at crucial points in our lives. Paul admonished the church in Rome: "*Therefore, I urge you, brothers, in view of God's mercy, to offer your bodies as living sacrifices, holy and pleasing to God—this is your spiritual act of worship*" (Romans 12:1 NIV).

God is looking for men and women who will say, "*Father, if you are willing, take this cup from me; yet not my will, but yours be done*" (Luke 22:42 NIV). Have you made this type of radical commitment to Christ? Are you totally surrendered to the leading of the Holy Spirit, or do you argue and fight with God? In countless hours of impartation services I have discovered that God pours into surrendered vessels. Others struggle to receive a drop from heaven, but the surrendered are spoiled by God's generosity. Get ready to be spoiled.

REALITY CHECK

Have you ever experienced a reality check? It is a pivotal moment when reality crashes through our defense mechanisms and denial. I was widely awakened by such an event. It all began in

1995 when the Holy Spirit first fell on our church in an unfamiliar way. I had been fasting and praying on Fridays for over a year. I was desperate for God's help. I remember praying for revival without really knowing what it meant. Can you relate to this? Although our church had experienced sizeable growth (from 270 to 400 attending Sunday services) in just one year, I was struggling with my role as senior pastor, the church's growth, and the role of the Holy Spirit.

Our services focused on providing emotional healing and hope. I was reviewing the seeker-sensitive approach when the Holy Spirit touched me in a service. I was filled with an unexplainable joy. My wife noticed I was laughing quietly and asked me what was so funny. I had no answer. I couldn't stop the fountain of joy that filled me.

After the service we were invited to a conference on the Holy Spirit and revival. We accepted the opportunity with curious skepticism. The chain of events that followed changed our lives, family, and ministry forever. The next two years were both glorious and difficult.

Heaven and hell seem so close at critical crossroads of our lives. The details of my first experience with the Holy Spirit impartation are in my book *The Power of Impartation*. For now, I need to emphasize that I had to make a choice to either follow the Holy Spirit totally or yield to public opinion and grieve the Holy Spirit. During the past four years I have experienced the words of Paul: *"I have been crucified with Christ and I no longer live, but Christ lives in me. The life I live in the body, I live by faith in the Son of God, who loved me and gave himself for me"* (Galatians 2:20 NIV).

I had to decide whether I wanted to please God or man. Would I put to death my pride and ego, or would I allow Him to make me successful? These choices became so real to me. Are they for you? I hope so. It boils down to a daily choice to die to self and embrace the Holy Spirit. Perhaps it is the most difficult step.

It is also crucial that you seek God on His terms and not yours. Don't tell God what He needs to do. Spend time at His altar seeking His face. Linger in His presence. It seems that those who wait for prayer are the ones who are touched. I have often said the last wine is always the best. We need to reinstitute the tarrying services of early Pentecost in our churches. In light of this idea, our church regularly opens the altars and allows time for the Surgeon to do His work in us. We anoint with oil, lay hands on the sick, and pray for God to touch and transform. We "tarry"—waiting at length for the work of the Holy Spirit. True spiritual hunger cannot be measured in a one-hour service and a five-minute altar call. God is looking for signs of spiritual hunger and desperation.

STEP 6: FAITH IS A PORTAL

Faith is a portal of impartation as large as a garage door. Do you want the windows of heaven to open? Do you cry out to God, "Pour out a blessing on us that we cannot contain it"? If so, we must *"walk by faith"* (2 Corinthians 5:7).

A minister mentioned recently that faith is an action. Isn't this true? If you desire impartation, then you must demonstrate faith. Are you going to the altar expecting a transforming touch from God? Are you going to the altar to be altered? Will you leave without your blessing, or will you wrestle your way into a blessing like Jacob did?

> *So Jacob was left alone, and a man wrestled with him till daybreak. When the man saw that he could not overpower him, he touched the socket of Jacob's hip so that his hip was wrenched as he wrestled with the man. Then the man said, "Let me go, for it is daybreak." But Jacob replied, "I will not let you go unless you bless me." The man asked him, "What is your name?" "Jacob," he answered. Then the man said, "Your name will no longer be Jacob, but Israel, because you have struggled with God and with men and have overcome."* (Genesis 32:24–28 NIV)

What are you hoping for? How badly do you want it? Are you like the deer panting for water? Do you seek God with confidence that He will meet with you eventually? Jacob had this confidence; he had tried to maneuver his way into his destiny before. This time he knew only God could do it. King David had this same confidence: *"Surely goodness and love will follow me all the days of my life, and I will dwell in the house of the LORD forever"* (Psalm 23:6 NIV).

Remember the definition of faith: *"Now faith is being sure of what we hope for and certain of what we do not see"* (Hebrews 11:1 NIV).

Feed your faith with the Word and stories of glorious revivals. Take steps of faith. I challenge you to be a giver, a goer, a forgiver, a carrier, and a lover. You and your world will never be the same.

- **Giver:** *"Give, and it will be given to you. A good measure, pressed down, shaken together and running over, will be poured into your lap. For with the measure you use, it will be measured to you"* (Luke 6:38 NIV).
- **Goer:** *"He said to them, 'Go into all the world and preach the good news to all creation'"* (Mark 16:15 NIV).
- **Forgiver:** *"For if you forgive men when they sin against you, your heavenly Father will also forgive you. But if you do not forgive men their sins, your Father will not forgive your sins"* (Matthew 6:14–15 NIV).
- **Carrier:** *"Carry each other's burdens, and in this way you will fulfill the law of Christ"* (Galatians 6:2 NIV).
- **Lover:** *"Dear friends, let us love one another, for love comes from God. Everyone who loves has been born of God and knows God"* (1 John 4:7 NIV).

When you take these risky faith steps, God enters the scene. He becomes part of a miracle equation. Not only are you demonstrating faith, but you also are activating the involvement of God. I want God to be involved in my life. What about you?

STEP 7: HAVE PURPOSE FOR THE IMPARTATION OF GOD'S POWER

Why would God pour a spiritual gift into you? Jesus taught His disciples to do something with His investment in their lives.

Heal the sick, raise the dead, cleanse those who have leprosy, drive out demons. Freely you have received, freely give. (Matthew 10:8 NIV)

What are your plans for the gift from heaven? Have you been faithful with past impartations? Although we live in a selfish society, God is looking for *selfless* people—people who will pour it out as faithfully as He pours it in. Isaiah 6:8 demonstrates this divine yearning: "*Then I heard the voice of the Lord saying, 'Whom shall I send? And who will go for us?' And I said, 'Here am I. Send me'*" (NIV). What was God looking for? A mouthpiece, a candidate, a life to use to touch His people. Who responded? Isaiah did. God is still looking for Isaiahs, Gideons, Jeremiahs, Jonahs, Esthers, and Marys. The illustration of the woman with a flask of oil is a classic example of this principle.

She left him and afterward shut the door behind her and her sons. They brought the jars to her and she kept pouring. When all the jars were full, she said to her son, "Bring me another one." But he replied, "There is not a jar left." Then the oil stopped flowing. (2 Kings 4:5–6 NIV)

The oil continued to pour as long as there were empty jars. What happened when all the jars were full? The oil stopped. Has the oil stopped flowing in your life or ministry? Could it be that you have stopped pouring? I know there are still plenty of empty people left in your world. I can assure you that there are countless empty jars in my world. If there is a shortage of oil, the problem is not with God's oil dispenser—it is with us. Why would God pour into you when you haven't even used the last blessing? Pour yourself into God's purposes, and get ready for the gifts and anointing to flow through you. Paul's words echo true at this point: "*But even if I am being poured out like a drink offering on the sacrifice and service coming from your faith, I am glad and rejoice with all of you*" (Philippians 2:17 NIV).

There is a divine objective, target, reasoning, or need for a visitation or impartation. God is looking for available people who will not hoard it but pour it. Are you willing to be a pourer? Or are you the next member of the "bless me club"? Second Timothy 2:20–21 (NIV) summarizes this principle so well: "*In a large house there are articles not only of gold and silver, but also of wood and clay; some are for noble purposes and some for ignoble. If a man cleanses himself from the latter, he will be an instrument for noble purposes, made holy, useful to the Master and prepared to do any good work.*"

"Prepare for any good work." God wants us to be equipped and prepared for *any* good work.

WHY DO WE CHOOSE OTHER WAYS?

You and I are in a great house. We are part of a glorious family, the family of God. We are brothers and sisters in Christ. In the church body there are different types of people. All those who are born again are forgiven. If we remain in Christ we will inherit eternal life because of Jesus Christ. However, not everyone will be used as a vessel of gold or silver. This is the choice of every believer. Isn't this an incredible opportunity? We get to choose honor or dishonor, value or disgrace, dignity or indignity. The options seem so obvious. It would be insane for a believer to choose the latter. Unfortunately many Christians still do not choose what's behind door number one. Why, you ask? Ignorance, apathy, deception, or sin. Only God knows the heart of every person. Do you want to be useful or useless in the Master's hands? What can you do to make sure that you will be useful? Timothy gives a clear and simple one-step program.

If a man cleanses himself . . . he will be an instrument for noble purposes, made holy, useful to the Master and prepared to do any good work. (2 Timothy 2:21 NIV)

We can cleanse ourselves by willfully, specifically following Timothy's advice. The secret to becoming a vessel of honor is to make it my sole purpose. I have to decide that the purpose of my life is to be an instrument of gold and silver, an instrument of honor. You cannot be "*a double-minded man, unstable in all he does*" (James 1:8 NIV).

You cannot leave the purpose of your life to chance. Once you set this target, all other decisions and actions must fall in line. Your road becomes narrow and your choices clearer because you have a set purpose. Everything else in life will help you achieve this goal.

It is important that we totally purge ourselves of sin. The word Paul uses for purge, *ekkathairo*, means "to cleanse thoroughly." In this computer age we can identify with purging old files, deleting ancient commands, and thoroughly cleansing the hard drive. Without this process our computer programs will freeze and overload the hardware. There may not be enough room for more updated programs. I am convinced that most people do not consciously choose to hold on to their sins. Paul referred to his ability to fall into the same destructive habits over and over again: "*What a wretched man I am! Who will rescue me from this body of death?*" (Romans 7:24 NIV). Can you relate to this destructive tendency?" Praise God that Paul realized victory could only come through Christ.

> *Therefore, there is now no condemnation for those who are in Christ Jesus, because through Christ Jesus the law of the Spirit of life set me free from the law of sin and death.* (Romans 8:1–2 NIV)

It is simple to slip into compromise and failure. If you don't shoot for a specific target, then you will hit something else. As a child, I had a dartboard in our garage. Initially I aimed for the dartboard, but eventually I became more proficient. I could aim for a number and hit it. After a little more practice I could hit the double or triple of most numbers. My life has progressed like this since I received Jesus Christ in 1978. I no longer want God's permissive will; I want His perfect will.

> *Therefore, I urge you, brothers, in view of God's mercy, to offer your bodies as living sacrifices, holy and pleasing to*

God—this is your spiritual act of worship. Do not conform any longer to the pattern of this world, but be transformed by the renewing of your mind. Then you will be able to test and approve what God's will is—his good, pleasing and perfect will. For by the grace given me I say to every one of you: Do not think of yourself more highly than you ought, but rather think of yourself with sober judgment, in accordance with the measure of faith God has given you. (Romans 12:1–3 NIV)

I want to be on target, making choices that will help me achieve the targets and visions that God has given me.

Brothers, I do not consider myself yet to have taken hold of it. But one thing I do: Forgetting what is behind and straining toward what is ahead. (Philippians 3:13 NIV)

Go ahead and make your choice. Seek His face, and then set a target that is clear and bright. It is the best position for a visitation and impartation from God.

PART III

THE SEVEN KEYS TO UNLOCK THE POWER OF GOD IN YOUR LIFE

NINE

How Can You Become a
Releaser of God's Power?

The term *intimacy* is generally used in relationships. It refers to a close relationship between two people—a relationship that necessitates communication, tenderness, and understanding. Until we became senior pastors, Denise and I conducted marriage seminars. During these couples' weekends, we would illustrate the true meaning of this term by playing with it a little. Intimacy became "into-me-you-see." I'm pretty sure we didn't come up with this illustration, but it makes so much sense. Into-me-you-see is the essence of every healthy relationship and of this book.

Denise and I have been married for over twenty-five years. Some aspects of my wife are very familiar and unforgettable.

There are days that I can predict her exact response to a given situation. I know how she drives, sleeps, sings, cooks, cleans, prays, preaches, cries, and laughs. I love how she plays with our puppy, how she imitates Mr. Bean, and how she laughs at my jokes. Sometimes she is so predictable, but other times we get so close that I see a different side of her. Something I have never seen in twenty-five years will come out, something that makes the fire of our relationship burn even brighter. It is this journey of discovery that makes a relationship intimate. Only time, perseverance, and love can chart a course of intimacy. Can you handle more intimacy in your relationships?

Intimacy with God will take time, perseverance, vulnerability, and trust. In Ephesians, Paul tells the Christians in Ephesus they will embark upon a journey of discovery. He underlined the role of the power of God in this journey.

For this reason I kneel before the Father, from whom his whole family in heaven and on earth derives its name. I pray that out of his glorious riches he may strengthen you with power through his Spirit in your inner being, so that Christ may dwell in your hearts through faith. And I pray that you, being rooted and established in love, may have power, together with all the saints, to grasp how wide and long and high and deep is the love of Christ, and to know this love that surpasses knowledge—that you may be filled to the measure of all the fullness of God. Now to him who is able to do immeasurably more than all we ask or imagine, according to his power that is at work within us, to him be glory in the church and in Christ Jesus throughout all generations, for ever and ever! Amen. (Ephesians 3:14–21 NIV)

Let's look more closely at these verses.

1. *"He may strengthen you with power."* When was the last time you were strengthened with His power?
2. *"Through His Spirit in your inner being . . ."* Paul ties the power to the relationship. The power comes through the Holy Spirit. The Holy Spirit is the Spirit of Christ. He reflects perfectly who Christ is. Intimacy with the Spirit of Christ will bring us into a realm of discovery. In this context, the discovery will be of His power. It is as real as when we discovered His grace in weaknesses, His mercy in repentance, and His love in salvation.

In many Christian churches the journey of discovery stops at the head. We all want to know the Word, understand the will of God, and grow in wisdom. There are great achievements worthy of our time and energy. However, our pilgrimage cannot stop there. There are other characteristics of God still left to experience and receive.

Take a moment and think about the names of God that are found in the Old Testament: *Jehovah Jireh*—"YHWH the provider"; *Jehovah Raphe*—"YHWH the healer"; *Jehovah Tsidekenu*—"YHWH is righteousness"; *Jehovah Shalom*—"YHWH of peace." So you can proclaim, "God is my provider, God is my healer, God is my righteousness, and God is my peace."

Whether God was identifying Himself, or a patriarch was

trying to describe Him, each name reflects a very personal side of God's nature. Not only is He Yahweh of peace, Isaiah also prophesied that the Messiah would be the Prince of Peace (Isaiah 9:6). God's nature was being described in relation to our reality, our needs, and our desperation. How can finite humans describe the God who created a hundred billion galaxies in the universe with one word? Human words or thought cannot embrace the true nature of God. He is the God in relationship with us humans. Wow! Doesn't that sound deep? If the truth be told, it is deep.

Each name was a reflection of our patriarchs' experiences with God Almighty. They didn't think up these names through weeks of deep thought. The Hebrews experienced their God. The names simply reflected one more incredible aspect of God they were introduced to. To some He was their deliverer, to others their healer, and to others their peace. But He is not only one way with each person. He is everything to all of us.

And what agreement has the temple of God with idols? For you are the temple of the living God. As God has said: "I will dwell in them and walk among them. I will be their God, and they shall be My people." (2 Corinthians 6:16)

We see through the Scriptures the relational God penetrating our logic and worldly wisdom to dwell in our hearts. He is truly the God of experience, discovery, and intimacy. He doesn't only want understanding; He wants my heart. The power of God helps experience a level of into-me-you-see. Christ will dwell, not just visit, in my heart. He won't dwell in my thoughts alone;

He wants to go deeply into me. His power is the part of Him that helps me experience Him on such an intimate level.

Didn't He command us to *"love the LORD your God with all your heart . . ."* (Luke 10:27, quoting Deuteronomy 6:5)? He wants not only our minds; He wants all of our hearts—every one of our thoughts, feelings, desires, and energies. This whole-hearted devotion creates an environment where God dictates the atmosphere. In other words, the atmosphere that we function in is different than the world's atmosphere. The Bible teaches us that Satan is the prince of the power of the air; however, those of us who are 100 percent sold out for God are aliens in this world. Our bodies are the temple of the Holy Spirit (1 Corinthians 6:19). We breathe oxygen from heaven—the Holy Spirit.

If you become intimate with God, you will become intimate with His power. You will become a holy lightning rod for God. You will attract His presence and power wherever you go. You will also attract the support of others who are like-minded. God will bring pastors, coaches, mentors, and teachers into your life who will help you grow. He will also bring to you people who need you to pour into them. Lightning rods attract lightning. Lightning rods for God attract God's attention. The Bible teaches us that *"we are surrounded by so great a cloud of witnesses"* (Hebrews 12:1). These witnesses are in heaven.

Debate has raged for years whether people in heaven can see what happens on the earth. I certainly believe these great men and women of God can see what's going on in some contexts. Are there bleachers in heaven? Do you think we have heaven's attention? When we become intimate with God there is a supernatural crowd surrounding our daily choices. Doesn't Paul say that all creation is waiting for the revelation of the sons of God (Romans 8:19)? Doesn't Luke remember, *"He shall give His angels charge over you"* (Luke 4:10)?

Not just one angel, but *angels.* Intimacy with God is so rare that God is looking for examples to show His love, power, mercy, and grace. Consider for a moment those notable leaders in the past two hundred years who seemed to have divine insight and connection. The Wigglesworths, Wesleys, Moodys, Whitefields, Brights, Grahams, Kulhmans, and so many others are bright lights pointing to something deeper, greater, and more intimate. Heaven is surely waiting to draw more of us into this inner circle. Will you get heaven's attention?

I have also discovered during the first twenty years of my ministry experience that intimacy with God also attracts Satan's attention. It has shocked me how our lives have been threatened several times. My family has received death threats. Why would anyone want to kill my family and me? In some cases, we have encountered other forms of resistance and opposition. I am sure this is why Paul taught the Ephesians to put on the full armor of God. But please don't dwell on the battles and opposition that come from being a sold-out believer.

Finally, brethren, whatever things are true, whatever things are noble, whatever things are just, whatever things are pure, whatever things are lovely, whatever things are of good report, if there is any virtue and if there is anything praiseworthy—meditate on these things. (Philippians 4:8)

Our battles only come for a season. If we resist the devil, he will flee from us. He has to flee from us because God's infallible Word says so. When you know someone really well, you learn to trust them; you learn that you can count on them in many situations. Intimacy with God provides a trusted relationship that becomes a firm foundation to weather the storms of life.

> And the rain descended, the floods came, and the winds blew and beat on that house; and it did not fall, for it was founded on the rock. But everyone who hears these sayings of Mine, and does not do them, will be like a foolish man who built his house on the sand: and the rain descended, the floods came, and the winds blew and beat on that house; and it fell. And great was its fall. (Matthew 7:25–27)

Your relationship with the Holy Spirit must become so deep and close that when circumstances come to contradict your assurance, you can proclaim with certainty, "I know that I have these circumstances, but I also know God will take these trials and turn them into trophies. I don't know how, but I do know Him."

Job must have had this level of connection with God. His words of commitment should echo firmly in our spirits, affirming in our hearts that there is more to our relationship with God. "*Though He slay me, yet will I trust Him. Even so, I will defend my own ways before Him*" (Job 13:15).

I believe this book is all about "deep calling out to deep." It is about living our lives with all the resources of God flowing through us. We cannot be successful in this world with a half-hearted faith and a lukewarm experience with God. Nothing in this present world is halfway. Jesus said you are either with Him or against Him (Luke 9:50).

PRAYER

Oh, Father, thank you that you call us sons and daughters. I need this relationship to go even deeper. Help me have the courage and the strength needed to develop it. I want to live like a real son or daughter.

TEN

KNOW HIM INTIMATELY

I want to know Christ and the power of his resurrection and the fellowship of sharing in his sufferings, becoming like him in his death. (Philippians 3:10 NIV)

Though I myself have reasons for such confidence. If anyone else thinks he has reasons to put confidence in the flesh, I have more: circumcised on the eighth day, of the people of Israel, of the tribe of Benjamin, a Hebrew of Hebrews; in regard to the law, a Pharisee. (Philippians 3:4–5 NIV)

Paul had experienced tremendous success as a Jewish leader and scholar. He was a Pharisee. You might say that he had a lot to be proud of. When he wrote to the church in Philippi he had also achieved much as the "least of the apostles." He was a church planter who backed his preaching with signs and wonders.

> But I will come to you very soon, if the Lord is willing, and then I will find out not only how these arrogant people are talking, but what power they have. For the kingdom of God is not a matter of talk but of power. (1 Corinthians 4:19–20 NIV)

Paul had the gift to bring a revival or a riot to any city he visited. Although he already had a personal relationship with Christ, his first goal was "to know Him." He wanted to develop an intimate relationship with Jesus; titles, positions, degrees, experience, and reputation meant very little to him. Paul wanted to know Him more. He admits that every other morsel of knowledge was worth nothing compared to truly knowing Jesus Christ.

> What is more, I consider everything a loss compared to the surpassing greatness of knowing Christ Jesus my Lord, for whose sake I have lost all things. I consider them rubbish, that I may gain Christ. (Philippians 3:8 NIV)

Is this your deepest desire? Is this your number one goal? Do you have enough humility to recognize that you don't know Him enough?

The Lord recently revealed to me the deep meaning of this Scripture. As I preached in David Mohan's church in Madras, India, the Lord spoke to me very clearly. Dr. Mohan's church is world famous: sixteen thousand souls attend the services, and they have started over 120 churches. Some of the world's greatest preachers have graced this pulpit. I was quite intimidated. What did I have to offer this great church? What could I say to make a difference? I was desperate to receive a word from God for these people. Stale sermons from a file would not do. A preacher should seek God for a fresh word every time he or she stands at the pulpit. As I was worshiping God with the congregation, God spoke this word: "Paul, tell them there is more." My first reaction to this word was shock. God, won't they be offended? They have already accomplished so much. Won't I sound arrogant? Who am I to say something like this? The Lord quietly confirmed His word to me when I saw a banner on one of the walls. It was in English, "The year of increase."

Thank God this pastor was not sitting back on his laurels. Thank God he was not living in pride and conceit. Thank God he was still willing to risk, to stretch, and to reach for more. I believe this is a problem with many churches and Christians. It is the sin of complacency, pride, comfort, and success. At what point will you grow satisfied with the size of your church, its outreaches, and its impact around the world? Have you lost a desperate hunger for God, souls, and disciples? Did you ever have this thirst for more of Him?

Blessed are those who hunger and thirst for righteousness, for they will be filled. (Matthew 5:6 NIV)

At what point did you grow satisfied with your soul winning, prayer life, holiness, biblical knowledge, or love for others? The closer I get to Him, the worse I look. His light gets brighter and exposes my weaknesses, attitudes, thoughts, and motives. Don't you want to know Him more?

I have been married to Denise for more than twenty-six years. I love her more today then ever before. I know her more today then ever before. I know her strengths, weaknesses, likes, and dislikes, but I still love her more than ever before. We have both counted the cost of having each other and decided that it is more than worth it. We love each other more because we know each other more.

The more we know Christ, the more we love Him; the more we give Him, the more we will want to know Him. Jesus wanted Peter to feel this way. Do you remember what He said to Peter? *"When they had finished eating, Jesus said to Simon Peter, 'Simon son of John, do you truly love me more than these?'"* (John 21:15 NIV). Jesus wanted to be *agaped*.

I had a desperate need to know the heart of God for this church. There have been many seasons in my life without that desperate desire. This hunger only surfaces when I am faced with insurmountable odds or challenges. Can you relate to what I am sharing from my heart? Are you desperate to know Him on a consistent basis or only when the roof is caving in? When your church reaches sixteen thousand people, will it be enough or will you want more?

Paul tells them there is more. Can you imagine how I felt that day in front of sixteen thousand? Do I confront the temptation to reach an invisible plateau? What is your plateau? Have you grown impressed with your success? Have you believed the accolades of your friends or denomination? These past few years have taught me an incredible lesson: I must please God even when it risks the rejection of man. I took a risk that day, but God moved in a great way. The pastor seemed very pleased with our visit, souls were saved, the sick were healed, and the church was encouraged. I was so nervous that day. Thank God that my fear of God is greater then my fear of man.

Proverbs 29:25 warns against the "fear of man." If I know Christ intimately, He will reveal His thoughts and feelings. These intimate revelations will often bring us into conflict with the world. Friends and family may not understand our passion for Christ. Even fellow Christians may resent us for our intensity, devotion, or worship. *"Do not love the world or anything in the world. If anyone loves the world, the love of the Father is not in him"* (1 John 2:15 NIV).

If the love of the Father is in you, it will cause your priorities, desires, and habits to change. The intimate relationship with Him will make you stand out. Your light will shine, and it will expose compromise, sin, and many heart issues in those you know.

The more you know Him, the more you will love Him. You can't help but fall in love with Jesus Christ. Jesus doesn't want a shallow relationship with you; He wants intimacy. He doesn't want a date; He wants a wedding. Jesus asked Peter three times if he loved Him. Each time Peter's response was the same, "I like you, Lord." Can you imagine how your wife or husband would respond to this type of answer?

"Sweetheart, do you love me unconditionally?"

"Yes, dear. I like you."

"No, honey, do you love me unconditionally?"

"Yes, dear, I like you sometimes." Would you finally give up and settle for a "like" relationship?

Many of us have settled for a "like" relationship rather then a love relationship with Jesus Christ. Have you set your heart to know Him abundantly? If you know Him more, it will cause you to love Him more, which will cause you to want to know Him more. John the beloved apostle had a revelation of God's desire to be loved. The Lord confronted the church of Ephesus because they had forsaken their first love. "*Nevertheless I have this against you, that you have left your first love*" (Revelation 2:4). They had an incredible church! The first and the last clearly saw the whole picture. He could see past all their great behaviors; He could see their hearts. They had lost their first love. It would seem natural for God to overlook this one matter.

First love is difficult to measure or quantify, but it is not hard for God. When He looks at your heart, what does He find? First-love passion for Him? Do you remember your first true love? Some of us married our first true love. Do you remember your first crush? Ladies, can you remember how you felt when the guy of your dreams only liked you as a friend? Guys, can you feel the pain and humiliation when the girl of your dreams shot you down? In a small way this is how God feels when we keep our distance from Him. Although this may sound embarrassing or uncomfortable (especially for the guys), Jesus wants to be the love of our lives. He wants us to be passionately in love with Him. The Song of Solomon is a candid display of the relationship we are called to have with Him.

Let him kiss me with the kisses of his mouth—for your love is more delightful than wine. Pleasing is the fragrance of your perfumes; your name is like perfume poured out. No wonder the maidens love you! Take me away with you—let us hurry! Let the king bring me into his chambers. (Song of Solomon 1:2–4 NIV)

How many times have we sought His power instead of His face? How many times have we gone to church or read His Word out of duty rather than love? Christians who served God faithfully in the second century were doing all the right things, but they had lost their passion. Deuteronomy 6:13–15 tells us God is a "jealous God" who wants to be known by us. A love based on deep knowledge is more resilient than one based on emotion or attraction.

My love for my children is based on years of care, prayer, concern, conflicts, joys, affection, and time. So many parents don't really know their children. They know what they want their children to become, but they rarely understand the children's motivations. Is it safe for your children to let down their guard? Do we listen to our children without interrupting or lecturing? "*To everything there is a season, a time for every purpose under heaven*" (Ecclesiastes 3:1), a time to dispute and a time to listen.

One of the greatest dangers of full-time ministry is the Ephesus Syndrome—a lot of dedication and hard work, but no love. How much time do you spend in prayer and study every day? Do you flirt with God once a week, or are you spending quality time with Him every day? There are no short cuts to knowing God. It takes time and good listening skills. Do you practice hearing God's voice? "*My sheep hear My voice, and I know them, and they follow Me*" (John 10:27). Can you hear God speak to your mind? He will speak in a quiet voice.

After the earthquake came a fire, but the LORD *was not in the fire. And after the fire came a gentle whisper. When Elijah heard it, he pulled his cloak over his face and went out and stood at the mouth of the cave. Then a voice said to him, "What are you doing here, Elijah?"* (1 Kings 19:12–13 NIV)

Some of us are proficient talkers in prayer, but few of us understand what God is saying to us. Paul was concerned about the believers in Ephesus; he deeply wanted them to fully grasp the love of God.

That Christ may dwell in your hearts through faith; that you, being rooted and grounded in love, may be able to compre-hend with all the saints what is the width and length and depth and height—to know the love of Christ which passes knowledge; that you may be filled with all the fullness of God. (Ephesians 3:17–19)

God helps us to understand the depth, height, and width of *agape*. If we can grasp the love of God, He will provide a safe place to grow.

Paul reveals that the secret of "being filled to the measure of the fullness of God" is knowing Christ intimately. The love of

Christ is not shallow or fleeting; it is four-dimensional—high, wide, long, and deep. Each dimension can be discovered through revelation.

Revelation only comes through

- being rooted by His *Agape* love,
- being grounded,
- having power, and
- being with all the saints.

We cannot hope to understand the dimensions of God's love without experiencing it in the context of the body of Christ. Knowledge of Christ can only come in the context of an intimate relationship with the Holy Spirit and the church. Paul knew more knowledge would not bring revelatory knowledge of God. Too many scholars have fallen in love with the pursuit of knowledge. Education is important, and degrees are fine; but they are worthless without relationship. Do you want to know about Him, or do you want to know Him? The second choice is more difficult, but it is worth every minute. You may never receive a degree for it, but you will bear much fruit.

Jesus confronted the Pharisees for the same condition that plagues the twenty-first-century church in America:

Woe to you Pharisees, because you give God a tenth of your mint, rue and all other kinds of garden herbs, but you neglect justice and the love of God. You should have practiced the latter without leaving the former undone. Woe to you Pharisees, because you love the most important seats in the synagogues and greetings in the marketplaces. (Luke 11:42–43 NIV)

In many of our churches, people love the positions they hold more than God's applause. They love entertainment more than worshiping the Lord. They love the approval of man more than God. They love numerical growth but not the people. They feed their sin rather than repent. They love idols of flesh, brick, people, and celebrities, instead of the one God who cannot be seen. They love comfort and hate sacrifice. They love ease and reject challenge. They love to receive but resist giving.

I have repented many times for these attitudes. I am grieved by the condition of our churches in North America. Can we all agree that we want Jesus Christ to enter our sanctuaries and confront the areas we need to change? I want to know Christ so He will not repeat, *"And He said, 'Woe to you also, lawyers! For you load men with burdens hard to bear, and you yourselves do not touch the burdens with one of your fingers.'"* (Luke 11:46). Can you agree with me in prayer to no longer settle for a "like" relationship?

PRAYER

God, please forgive us for our sins. We have grieved You many times with our lack of passion and devotion. We implore You to cleanse us from our compromising ways. Give us the power to know You intimately. May it give birth to a burning love for You.

ELEVEN

BE INTIMATE WITH HIS RESURRECTION POWER

I want to know Christ and the power of his resurrection and the fellowship of sharing in his sufferings, becoming like him in his death. (Philippians 3:10 NIV)

The apostle Paul continued his petition with a surprising request. He asked to know the power of His resurrection. It surprised me that the great apostle would ask to be intimate with this power. Didn't he already have it? Wasn't he the one who did not speak with eloquence but with the demonstration of God's power?

Many people have experienced God's power, but few have become intimate with it. During the great revival that is spreading around the world, millions have been touched by God. Prayer, healing, deliverance, emotional transformation, and signs and wonders have become quite common. People have been touched by the power of God, but have they been *transformed* by His resurrection power?

Paul was asking to become intimate with the power that raised Jesus Christ from the dead. The first time it was used was to raise the Son of God from the grave and to make Him the firstborn.

For those God foreknew he also predestined to be conformed to the likeness of his Son, that he might be the firstborn among many brothers. (Romans 8:29 NIV)

There was much more at work than raising a dead man or woman. The power Paul wanted was the *dunamis* that only Christ had experienced when He conquered hell and the grave.

I am the Living One; I was dead, and behold I am alive for ever and ever! And I hold the keys of death and Hades. (Revelation 1:18 NIV)

We still need this power to conquer hell and the grave. We need the same power that raised Him high and made Him victorious.

What does "he ascended" mean except that he also descended to the lower, earthly regions? He who descended is the very one who ascended higher than all the heavens, in order to fill the whole universe. (Ephesians 4:9–10 NIV)

Did Paul know what he was asking for? I believe he did. Would you have asked for it? God will examine the motive of your heart. Do you want to be intimate with this type of power? Then build an intimate knowledge of Jesus Christ, a deep relationship with the Son of God. Make sure that you have set a firm foundation for the manifestation of God's power. Many have been enamored by a powerful preacher, evangelist, teacher, prophet, or apostle. It is tempting to envy their power without wanting intimacy with Christ.

In Acts 8:9–13 we are introduced to a recent convert to Christianity who fell into this trap.

> *Now for some time a man named Simon had practiced sorcery in the city and amazed all the people of Samaria. He boasted that he was someone great, and all the people, both high and low, gave him their attention and exclaimed, "This man is the divine power known as the Great Power." They followed him because he had amazed them for a long time with his magic. But when they believed Philip as he preached the good news of the kingdom of God and the name of Jesus Christ, they were baptized, both men and women. Simon himself believed and was baptized. And he followed Philip everywhere, astonished by the great signs and miracles he saw.* (NIV)

Simon was a well-respected sorcerer who was saved, baptized, and followed Philip. The miracles and signs amazed him and all of Samaria. Simon seemed to be doing well, but one day his heart issues were exposed. He saw the power and wanted it. He was willing to do almost anything to get it.

> *When Simon saw that the Spirit was given at the laying on of the apostles' hands, he offered them money and said, "Give me also this ability so that everyone on whom I lay my hands may receive the Holy Spirit."* (Acts 8:18–19 NIV)

The end does not justify the means. Having the power to pray for the baptism of the Holy Spirit is wonderful. We need more people who have the faith to pray for seeking believers. I have noticed that most churches have done away with altar calls for baptism, healing, or deliverance. Many of our churches have become too "respectable"; they are afraid of the movement of God.

The natural reaction to this fear is a critical attitude to the supernatural or an envious spirit toward the few in power. Some anointed leaders are idolized and envied for the power in their lives. Some have been jealous of the accomplishments of great pastors, revivalists, evangelists, and leaders. These emotions betray a heart that does not understand this principle comes from God. Resurrection power is available to all who are willing to pay the price with their life.

I want to know Him and the power of the Resurrection. A firm foundation of knowing Him could give way to knowing the power. Some immature believers want the power without the knowing. They want the goose bumps without the romance. They covet the glory but despise the suffering.

PETER AND
SIMON THE SORCERER

Peter confronted the heart issues that spurred Simon to make this ungodly request.

> Peter answered: "May your money perish with you, because you thought you could buy the gift of God with money! You have no part or share in this ministry, because your heart is not right before God. Repent of this wickedness and pray to the Lord. Perhaps He will forgive you for having such a thought in your heart. For I see that you are full of bitterness and captive to sin." (Acts 8:20–23 NIV)

What can we learn from this example?

1. **You cannot buy the power of God with money.** You can only buy it with hunger, time, worship, obedience, and sacrifice.

2. **Simon's heart was not right in this matter.** God cares about our hearts. If they are full of sin and bitterness, then we cannot expect to be a conduit of resurrection power. God wants us to be clean vessels. David recognized the importance of a clean heart (Psalm 51). He saw the correlation between the condition of his heart and a steadfast spirit.

3. **Simon needed to repent.** The only way to deal with a heart of sin and bitterness is to ask God to change our ways of think-

ing. Repentance is the foundation for forgiveness. We must realize and admit that our condition is wrong. In order for an alcoholic to be delivered, he must first admit his problems.

4. **Simon needed to ask God to forgive him.** After we admit we are wrong, we can ask God to forgive us and cleanse us from our distorted thinking, disobedience, and rebellion.

5. **Simon was poisoned by bitterness.** How many people are poisoned with bitterness? This poison comes from hurt and anger. We must forgive the people who have hurt us or angered us.

If we don't forgive them, God cannot forgive us. If we are not forgiven, then we are separated from His love, grace, power, and protection. Do you know how to forgive? Have you often been frustrated with your inability to be freed from bitterness?

Perhaps these stages will help you as much as they have helped me:

- The act of forgiveness
- The process of forgiveness
- Walking in complete forgiveness

Simon was bound by iniquity. Do you know men, women, or teens who have been bound? Are you or someone you know bound by depression, anger, bitterness, lust, insecurity, loneliness, deception, addiction, or pride? Don't forget there is an anointing available to us to help set the captives free. The original mission statement of Jesus was clear: set the captives free and break the cords of bondage (Luke 4:18; 10:18; 1 John 3:8).

Do you want to know the power of the Resurrection? Make sure your heart is right in the sight of God. God *wants* you to experience this type of power. Are you ready for it? Prepare the altar for His great fire. It's explosive!

In His infinite wisdom and insight, God will not send 220 volts of power through men, women, and teens who can only handle 110. He doesn't want it to be a one-time experience; He wants to dwell in you every day. Can you become a semiconductor for the power of God?

On a recent trip to India, I realized a few insights about preparation. The electrical converters that I brought to convert 220-volt outlets to my 110-volt appliances did not fit the Indian outlets. I was not ready for a new environment. The anointing God has sent to our church is unique for Las Vegas. Someone once said, "New levels bring new devils." God has a unique anointing for every city and country. No more copycat programs. God has the right anointing for your life, ministry, and family, so don't envy someone else's. You don't know the price they have paid or the devils they have conquered. You don't know the years of preparation. It could be they are reaping generations of godly sowing. Grandparents and parents may have done much of the plowing, praying, and seeding in the past; they may be reaping the results of years of suffering and sacrifice.

Do not be deceived: God cannot be mocked. A man reaps what he sows. (Galatians 6:7 NIV)

This truth functions for both good and bad. In most cases great anointing and resurrection power are built upon years of the following:

1. **Impartation of a significant person by the laying on of hands, education, modeling, anointing with oil, counseling, and preaching**—I have dealt at great lengths with this issue in *The Power of Impartation* because this principle is huge. I have never met an anointed leader who did not have strong imparter connections.

   In my own life it is necessary to recognize the influence of Barnett, Freidzon, Dr. Lim, Annacondia, Dr. Dobbins, and many other wonderful leaders. Harry Chapin's song "Cat's in the Cradle" says it so well: "My boy was just like me. He turned out just like me." This is a gripping song that tells the story of a workaholic dad who neglects his son. As the son grows older the father wants to spend time with his son, but the son is now too busy to be with his dad. We do sow, don't we? The significant people in our lives sow seeds in us that bear fruit for the good or bad.

2. **The sacrifice of time, effort, prayer, fasting, and faithful service**—God doesn't haphazardly drop anointing or power on someone. He drops in on people who have prepared or have been prepared. In Asia, in order to make my appliances function on 220 volts, I needed to find an adapter to attach to my converter. Thank God one of the members of our mis-

sions board came fully prepared. He spent time and money to prepare for this need. He had over a dozen adapters in a leather case. Have you sacrificed the time and resources to become a conduit of His glorious power?

3. **No matter how much we prepare for true power and anointing, it only comes from God when He decides it is right**—The last lesson I learned about my appliances was that some of them were manufactured to handle 110 volts and some 220 volts. They were already wired this way by their creator. All I needed to do was find adapters to plug into the outlets. I firmly believe that we are all wired differently, some of us for 110 volts, others for 220 volts. Some of us are wired for the gifts of healing, and others for administration. We have all been designed by God to fulfill specific responsibilities in the body of Christ, the world, our family, and at work. Have you ever noticed that most administrators aren't great preachers? Most great preachers are lousy counselors.

There are different kinds of gifts, but the same Spirit. Now to each one the manifestation of the Spirit is given for the common good. All these are the work of one and the same Spirit, and he gives them to each one, just as he determines. (1 Corinthians 12:4, 7, 11 NIV)

Please do not be jealous of another person's ministry, gifts, or power. Seek to know Jesus Christ intimately, and He will entrust you with the power of the Resurrection. Be patient and realize

THE 5 POWERS OF GOD

God is working in you, preparing you to be an instrument of
His glory.

HOW CAN YOU BE INTIMATE
WITH HIS POWER?

- Read His Word.
- Meditate upon His Word.
- Worship Him daily, not only on Sundays. Develop a daily
  practice of worship and praise.
- Keep a clean heart.
- Serve the Lord by serving an anointed pastor. Become an
  Elisha to your pastor. You will receive impartation from
  key leaders whom you serve faithfully.
- Seek the Lord with humility and great hunger. In order
  to become intimate with the power of His resurrection,
  it will take time.

There are no short cuts to intimacy. God is looking for a long-
term relationship of impartation. He wants to work through you
like He did through Elijah, Elisha, Peter, and Paul.

Resurrection power will transform you and your world. As
you totally surrender to the Holy Spirit, He will flow through
you like a river. Do not be satisfied with a trickle; seek a river. Do
not settle for a touch; desire transformation. Do not just flirt
with the Holy Spirit once a week; let Him move in permanently
and take over.

If we make this choice daily, it will open up the next level of intimacy—suffering. We can't have intimacy without suffering. In fact, many people suffer without a sense of intimacy with Christ. Suffering is something most of us run from. Paul, on the other hand, asked to discover the partnership in it. I know this is frightening, but allow me to comfort you with this fact of life: everyone will suffer in his or her life. You might as well suffer for God, for a divine purpose and plan. Living for God yields fruit; suffering for God crushes the fruit to make a river of new wine.

I was recently studying a passage from the book of Amos. As I read Amos 9:9 God spoke to me clearly. He showed me how the suffering we had experienced as a family (a snowmobile accident, three car crashes, my daughter getting cancer, the loss of my dad, death threats, and many other things) and as a church was for a great prophetic reality. The shaking or sifting in Amos 9:9 must occur in order to loose the "river of new wine." *"For I will give the command, and I will shake the house of Israel among all the nations as grain is shaken in a sieve, and not a pebble will reach the ground"* (NIV).

"Behold, the days are coming," says the LORD, "when the plowman shall overtake the reaper, and the treader of grapes him who sows seed; the mountains shall drip with sweet wine, and all the hills shall flow with it. I will bring back the captives of my people Israel; they shall build the waste cities and inhabit them; they shall plant vineyards and drink wine from them . . ." (Amos 9:13–14)

Although the door of suffering seems unattractive, it is not. It is beautiful, purposeful, and bearable. We don't walk through this next door alone. Jesus Christ walks us through it.

PRAYER

Jesus, I want to be intimate with You when I go through trials and tribulations. I am even willing to suffer for Your church and the kingdom of God. Please help me follow through on this desire. Fill me with Your Spirit and Your power.

TWELVE

PERSEVERE THROUGH TRIALS, PERSECUTION, AND SUFFERING

On my recent trip to northern India, I preached on Philippians 3:10. I knew that several of the hundreds of ministers present at the General Council of Northern India had already experienced tremendous persecution; others would soon suffer more. Some would even have to give their lives for their faith. These dear saints were well acquainted with the partnership of His suffering.

In the twenty-first century, business partnerships are common. We can easily relate to the risks that partners share. If the business does well, they both do well. If there are losses, they both lose. If there are sacrifices to be made, they both make them. Each person takes a risk, and effort is shared in an equal partnership. Paul had come to be willing to experience more of the suffering for the sake of the partnership. It is not as if he hadn't already suffered; he had (2 Corinthians 11:23–26).

Paul realized he was a partner with Christ in ministry. He realized part of the risk was suffering. When two people suffer together they can either grow apart or be infused together by the fire. Paul wanted to be acquainted with the sufferings of Christ. He saw the purpose, but he also felt closer to the Lord as he fought side by side. Paul wasn't saying he wanted to suffer more; he wasn't a masochist. There is no glory in suffering for suffering's sake, but there is glory in suffering for the sake of the lost and hurting. Paul wanted to up his investment in the partnership with Christ. He wanted to take a larger share of the burden. Paul wanted to understand the responsibilities of the partnership and the intimacy that comes from suffering together for a greater cause.

> *The Spirit himself testifies with our spirit that we are God's children. Now if we are children, then we are heirs—heirs of God and co-heirs with Christ, if indeed we share in his sufferings in order that we may also share in his glory. I consider that our present sufferings are not worth comparing with the glory that will be revealed in us.* (Romans 8:16–18 NIV)

Suffering is a sign that we are co-heirs with Christ; it is not a sign that there is sin in our lives. Do you realize there can be a purpose in your sufferings? Do you understand that to be a real son or daughter of God means you will suffer? Paul wanted to place suffering in the context of a relationship. It had to make sense to Paul theologically. He was a theologian, a thinker who needed to understand and explain suffering to others. Have you ever tried to place your sufferings in the context of your relationship with Jesus Christ? I have been forced to do this in my past few years in Las Vegas. I would pray to be freed from suffering, but reality requires we all suffer in some way.

Consider it pure joy, my brothers, whenever you face trials of many kinds, because you know that the testing of your faith develops perseverance. (James 1:2–3 NIV)

In this partnership with Christ my sufferings have a purpose. (Not that they were part of God's perfect plan for us.) It seems crucial to underline the causes of suffering before we begin to misinterpret Paul's deep desire.

FIVE SOURCES OF SUFFERING

1. **People can hurt you.** Child abuse is a disease in our nation and the world. Young girls are sold into sex slavery in some Asian and African nations. Sexual abuse is constantly exposed in the media. The violence in our schools has reached epidemic proportions. The scenes of school shootings have brought this reality home to us. People can steal from you, lie to you, and try to use, abuse, intimidate, and hurt you in

many ways. God gave everyone a free will. You can use this gift to hurt or heal, give life or death. The first generation in the Bible illustrated how the gift can be misused: *"Now Cain talked with Abel his brother; and it came to pass, when they were in the field, that Cain rose up against Abel his brother and killed him"* (Genesis 4:8).

2. **You can hurt yourself.** Bad decisions, destructive behaviors, substance abuse, and personal neglect are only a few ways we can hurt ourselves. God gave you a free will. You have an active role in your health and destiny. How much of your suffering has been self-induced? Can you list the times when you have brought suffering into your life, home, or workplace?

But if serving the LORD seems undesirable to you, then choose for yourselves this day whom you will serve, whether the gods your forefathers served beyond the River, or the gods of the Amorites, in whose land you are living. But as for me and my household, we will serve the LORD. (Joshua 24:15 NIV)

3. **The devil and his demon forces are still dedicated to their mission.** Satan will use every tool and strategy. *"The thief comes only to steal and kill and destroy; I have come that they may have life, and have it to the full"* (John 10:10 NIV).

For our struggle is not against flesh and blood, but against the rulers, against the authorities, against the powers of this dark world and against the spiritual forces of evil in the heavenly realms. Therefore put on the full armor of God, so that when the day of evil comes, you may be able to stand your ground, and after you have done everything, to stand. (Ephesians 6:12–13 NIV)

The devil has limited power and ability, but he is still very cunning. We are in a life-and-death battle with the devil. We must put on our spiritual armor to fight him and turn back his schemes.

Be self-controlled and alert. Your enemy the devil prowls around like a roaring lion looking for someone to devour. (1 Peter 5:8 NIV)

4. **We live in a fallen world.** Sickness, earthquakes, storms, and other environmental tragedies are part of the curse.

To Adam he said, "Because you listened to your wife and ate from the tree about which I commanded you, 'You must not eat of it,' cursed is the ground because of you; through painful toil you will eat of it all the days of your life." (Genesis 3:17 NIV)

Insurance policies call many acts of nature "acts of God." I don't agree with this definition. God can exert His judgment on a disobedient race whenever He wants to. However, in most cases there are environmental causes for the problem. We live in a broken world that will one day be made perfect. That will be a real act of God. Don't blame tragedies on God. He is holding back His acts of judgment until the great tribulation.

> *For you know very well that the day of the Lord will come like a thief in the night. While people are saying, "Peace and safety," destruction will come on them suddenly, as labor pains on a pregnant woman, and they will not escape.* (1 Thessalonians 5:2–3 NIV)

5. **Our carnal nature is part of the problem.** The fallen part of our nature is unconscious. Paul speaks of this powerful force: "*But I see another law at work in the members of my body, waging war against the law of my mind and making me a prisoner of the law of sin at work within my members. What a wretched man I am! Who will rescue me from this body of death?*" (Romans 7:23–24 NIV).

There is a constant battle going on inside of us. Psychologists have tried to label it, understand it, and even mediate it. In many cases there is absolutely no logical reason for people's decisions and behaviors.

I have met with many leaders, pastors, teachers, and successful businesspeople who have fallen into immorality. When I asked them why they did it, the answer was always, "I don't know." Can you relate to this answer? It seems there is a dark force inside of us trying to push us to disobedience and bondage. This carnal nature lives in all of us. It is part of our emotions and is rarely rational, though most people can eventually explain it away. Addictions have their root in the heart and soul. Jeremiah 17:9 concludes: "*The heart is deceitful above all things and beyond cure. Who can understand it?*" (NIV).

This fifth element is so deceptive. We need accountability and honesty to overcome this force. Perhaps this is why James admonishes us: "*Confess your sin*" (James 5:16 NIV).

Many people confuse the causes of suffering with the purposes of it. God rarely causes suffering, but He can use it to perfect us, discipline us, or even test us. Hebrews 12:7–9 brings clarity to this issue. God disciplines us because He loves us, not because He is angry or frustrated. I have never enjoyed disciplining my children. It takes time, effort, and personal strength, but I know I must if I truly love my children.

> *He who spares the rod hates his son, but he who loves him is careful to discipline him.* (Proverbs 13:24 NIV)

This same principle holds true for our relationship with our heavenly Father. Through years of counseling and pastoring, I have concluded that it is rarely God who causes suffering; suffering usually is caused by our own poor decisions, sin, stubborness, or ignorance.

> *Do not be deceived: God cannot be mocked. A man reaps what he sows.* (Galatians 6:7 NIV)

> "*Come now, let us reason together,*" *says the LORD. "Though your sins are like scarlet, they shall be as white as snow;*

though they are red as crimson, they shall be like wool."
(Isaiah 1:18 NIV)

He sends us the Holy Spirit to deal with our sin and disobedience on a daily basis: *"When he comes, he will convict the world of guilt in regard to sin and righteousness and judgment: in regard to sin, because men do not believe in me"* (John 16:8–9 NIV).

He reaches out to us through pastors, friends, prophets, and rulers:

And in the church God has appointed first of all apostles, second prophets, third teachers, then workers of miracles, also those having gifts of healing, those able to help others, those with gifts of administration, and those speaking in different kinds of tongues. Are all apostles? Are all prophets? Are all teachers? Do all work miracles? (1 Corinthians 12:28–29 NIV)

Sadly, most people naturally blame pain on God. God, why are You doing this to me? God, what are You trying to tell me through these horrible things?

I will never forget the deacon's wife who was caught in a serious depression. After months of discouragement she came for help. The source of this darkness was quickly evident. She was mad at God for allowing her to experience three miscarriages. She was convinced He would keep allowing these miscarriages until she learned a lesson. Even though she did not say He was causing the miscarriages, she believed this pain was God's handiwork. Until she could discover the hidden purpose, she would continue to suffer. This interpretation of her circumstances is clear evidence of a distorted view of God.

God didn't cause her miscarriages, nor did He allow them for some hidden purpose. He allowed them because we live in a fallen world. People get sick; some couples can't have babies because their bodies aren't perfect. This woman did not need to learn her lesson; she needed physical healing. When you understand the cause of suffering, it is easier to deal with it. When we surrender our pain to a loving God, we can find His comfort, strength, grace, and even healing for our emotions. There are even occasions when God will do the supernatural by healing physically or delivering instantly.

SURRENDERED SUFFERING

And we know that in all things God works for the good of those who love him, who have been called according to his purpose. For those God foreknew he also predestined to be conformed to the likeness of his Son, that he might be the firstborn among many brothers. (Romans 8:28–29 NIV)

Even though God doesn't cause our suffering, He does allow it. Why would God allow sexual abuse, rape, murder, driving deaths, sickness, and so many more painful events? The answer is shockingly simple: because He gave us a free will. Not only did He give us a free will, but He gave us a free will in a world we defaced through disobedience. I know it brings so much more relief to blame it on Him, but the truth goes back to the fall of humanity: *"But you must not eat from the tree of the knowledge of good and evil, for when you eat of it you will surely die"* (Genesis 2:17 NIV). We cause relational problems, violence, sickness, injustice, and even environmental problems. We are a free-will people living in a broken world, but God still loves us. He can use us to spread His message of healing and reconciliation to a broken world.

> *All this is from God, who reconciled us to himself through Christ and gave us the ministry of reconciliation.* (2 Corinthians 5:18 NIV)

He can use us to alleviate suffering, not eliminate it. The final solution is not in creating a utopia through education, medicine, benevolence, or even religion. The final solution is Him.

> *How great is the love the Father has lavished on us, that we should be called children of God! And that is what we are! The reason the world does not know us is that it did not know him. Dear friends, now we are children of God, and what we will be has not yet been made known. But we know that when he appears, we shall be like him, for we shall see him as he is.* (1 John 3:1–2 NIV)

When Jesus comes into the picture, everything can change. Paul understood his sufferings in context of God's great plan of redemption. He understood his sufferings were staked upon Christ to reach more people with good news.

> Now I rejoice in what was suffered for you, and I fill up in my flesh what is still lacking in regard to Christ's afflictions, for the sake of his body, which is the church. I have become its servant by the commission God gave me to present to you the word of God in its fullness. (Colossians 1:24–25 NIV)

If you can learn to persevere through suffering, then you will be used by God in great ways. If you can see it from God's perspective, then you will learn to rejoice in it.

> You need to persevere so that when you have done the will of God, you will receive what he has promised. (Hebrews 10:36 NIV)

He persevered through temptation, tribulations, and trials. He became a vessel of honor and glory for His Father. How will you respond to suffering? Will you whine and complain? Will you get better?

My life has changed in the past few years. Prior to this time I had not suffered a lot of physical sickness or pain. We had experienced persecution and tribulation, but the experiences of suffering changed us. Four accidents in one year, one child with epilepsy, one teen rebelling, our eldest daughter with cancer, and I felt physical pain for years. These storms have been rough, but we have learned to surrender each one to God. Only He can redeem the pain and transform it into a gain.

Your attitude should be the same as that of Christ Jesus. (Philippians 2:5 NIV)

PRAYER

God, help us take the pain of suffering and place it in Your hands. Transform our tragedies into trophies. Make Romans 8:28 a reality in our lives. Not that everything bad that happens to us is good, but, Lord, You can turn it to good. Our pain can be someone else's gain. Our hurt can be the fuel to help us comfort someone else. Please, Lord, we don't want this pain to go to waste. Press the coal of our lives in the palm of Your hand and turn it into diamonds.

THIRTEEN

FIND A NEED AND FILL IT

I have had the privilege of attending Tommy Barnett's Pastors' and Leaders' School for several years. Denise and I chose to learn from this man early in our pastoral ministry. This book reflects what we learned from his philosophy of ministry. The anointing of God, the resources that we have, the power of prayer, and all our services are all designed to meet the needs of people. There are confused, broken, ignored, hurt, and bound people who have needs. The church body is called to reach them.

Bill Wilson of Metro Assembly in New York made a statement that challenged my thinking. Bill has built a radical life-changing outreach to thousands of inner-city kids and families. There was a need. It became his call, and God has blessed it. He was not called to the inner city, but he went because there was a need.

Then he said something that should shake all of us up: "the need is the call." Do you agree with this statement? At first I wasn't sure. I guess I am still not sure if this is always the case. I know that Denise and I were specifically called to pastor in Las Vegas. There is no doubt in my mind that call has kept us here during the tough times.

In fact, it was the only real condition I had before we came. I wanted to be sure that Denise felt as called as I did. It is incredibly dangerous for a couple to accept a ministry position when one of them does not sense God's call to that city or church. When the trials and tribulations come, it may drive a wedge of resentment that is difficult to overcome. If both partners agree, then one will not blame the other for "forcing them to move" or "missing God's perfect will."

You must be thinking that I totally disagree with Bill's statement. The truth is, I agree with him. Please let me explain. Through over twenty years of ministry I have discovered that many Christians remain inactive. They accept Christ and attend church, but they never lift a finger to help reach the lost, disciple the saved, change diapers, feed the poor, evangelize their city, pray for their pastors, or even give to the kingdom of God. Many have used the concept of the call as an excuse to do nothing. They don't do anything for people or God because they have not *felt* the call.

There is another repulsive abuse of the concept of a call. Many Christians feel called to a ministry until the fiery trials start. The call to a ministry has become a mere whim or emotional response to a plea for help. It is amazing how quickly God can call a person to a need, then call them out of it after a week or a month. We throw the term around so much that it has lost its significance. When we say we are called, we better make sure we are. A call should mean a commitment. It should include perseverance, sacrifice, and longsuffering.

At ICLV we challenge people to be true to a call. They cannot leave a ministry until they find a competent replacement. John Maxwell once said, "There is no success without a successor." We are trying to train our people to be successful. We are tired of Christians who use "God said" as an excuse. Weak Christians will never win their world. Are you a weak Christian or a world changer?

We can all be called to meet specific needs, but until we hear the call we need to find a need and fill it. Once you start meeting a need, it might become your call. So much of the body of Christ is apathetic to the needs of humanity. I am convinced the Holy Spirit moves on hearts to meet needs, but we don't respond. A lack of response to a Holy Spirit prompting leads to grieving Him. After we grieve Him a few times, He tries to find someone else who might respond. The Holy Spirit is always looking for people to accept a mission (Isaiah 6:8). How will you respond to the Holy Spirit?

And do not grieve the Holy Spirit of God, with whom you were sealed for the day of redemption. (Ephesians 4:30 NIV)

Do not harden your hearts as you did in the rebellion, during the time of testing in the desert. (Hebrews 3:8 NIV)

The pattern of the great imparters is that they were constantly meeting needs. Take Elisha for example; shortly after picking up Elijah's mantle, Elisha was faced with the crisis of a local city:

The men of the city said to Elisha, "Look, our lord, this town is well situated, as you can see, but the water is bad and the land is unproductive." "Bring me a new bowl," he said, "and put salt in it." So they brought it to him. Then he went out to the spring and threw the salt into it, saying, "This is what the LORD *says: 'I have healed this water. Never again will it cause death or make the land unproductive.'" And the water has remained wholesome to this day, according to the word Elisha had spoken.* (2 Kings 2:19–22 NIV)

The water was bad, and the ground was barren. Their people had a tremendous need; they had no water and no crops. Wouldn't it be incredible if city leaders came to church leaders asking for help? I know of one nation in Asia that has asked the local church to run a counseling center to help a troubled neighborhood. If this pilot program is a success, major funding will be provided. Praise God!

We need to be people who look for needs in homes, neighborhoods, businesses, and cities. If we meet needs, then we will take our cities for Christ. Unfortunately, so many churches and believers have become irrelevant. They are not making a difference. Who are they helping, healing, inspiring, touching, teaching, equipping, and transforming? If a believer is not meeting the needs of others, then he has fallen into a demonic trap. He may still get to heaven because of the grace of God, but his works will be burned in a millisecond.

Do you want to become an imparter? Then find a need and fill it! Don't make excuses. Don't allow fear to stop you. Serving God and meeting needs in others will unleash the flow of God's anointing and blessing.

"It is more blessed to give" (Acts 20:35), so don't be deceived by the enemy. He wants to take your blessing. Others need you; there is a place for you in the body. God can use you to fill the needs of hurting people.

PRAYER

God, help us not to be irrelevant. Fill us with Your Holy Spirit so that He can lead us to meet the needs of broken people and a hurting world. Hey, Lord, by the way, I really love You.

FOURTEEN

SERVE GOD WITH FAITH

Then a man came from Baal Shalisha, and brought the man of God bread of the first fruits, twenty loaves of barley bread, and newly ripened grain in his knapsack. And he said, "Give it to the people that they may eat." But his servant said, "What? Shall I set this before one hundred men?" He said again, "Give it to the people, that they may eat; for thus says the LORD: 'They shall eat and have some left over.'" So he set it before them; and they ate and had some left over, according to the word of the LORD. (2 Kings 4:42–44)

Elisha once again is faced with a need. Fear could have crippled him; he could have played it safe, but he didn't. He took a few loaves of bread and some grain and fed over one hundred men.

145

He believed the word of God: "*they will eat and have some left over.*" He took a step of faith because he had faith.

Impartation always involves faith. Faith requires some type of risk. Elisha risked his reputation when he told his men to start feeding the men with a little food. He risked being called a charlatan when the city leaders brought the water and he told them to put salt in it. Sounds like a crazy solution, doesn't it? God will often require imparters to live on the edge of ridicule and failure.

And without faith it is impossible to please God, because anyone who comes to him must believe that he exists and that he rewards those who earnestly seek him. (Hebrews 11:6 NIV)

As the heavens are higher than the earth, so are my ways higher than your ways and my thoughts than your thoughts. (Isaiah 55:9 NIV)

Elisha took a risk when he told the old widow to get all the empty jars in town, then start emptying her little flask of oil into them. Wow, that's faith. What kind of man would tell a widow to pour out her last possession into a sea of empty jars? A man of faith! What kind of woman would risk public ridicule and personal shame? A desperate one.

Imparters always seem to be at the bottom of their little flasks of oil before God does the supernatural. They live on the edge. God has called my good friend Dr. James Marocco, who pastors in Maui, to plant churches on the Hawaiian islands and elsewhere. With a congregation of about three thousand, they have started eight extension churches and they are presently in six building programs. God has recently called him to touch the islands of French Polynesia. Our church will help with this call. How would you like to be in six building programs? They customarily take up to three offerings a service. Their weekly budget is stretched to the last dime every week, but they keep moving forward in faith. The next miracle always seems to come with the next step of faith.

Have you ever been to the Dream Center in Los Angeles? Tommy Barnett had the vision to buy a 440,000-square-foot hospital and convert it into an inner-city church and a second chance outreach center. This man has immense faith. Even though he is at an age when many would consider retiring, Tommy took on this project and challenged other pastors, churches, and his Phoenix congregation to catch the vision. Several times a year they desperately need help to keep going or to meet the city's building requirements.

My faith is built every time I read their letters. Some people resent these men of great faith who take huge risks, but I admire them. Too many churches and believers have adopted a survival mode. We need to recognize that many have justified a spirit of fear by calling it caution or wisdom.

For God did not give us a spirit of timidity, but a spirit of power, of love and of self-discipline. (2 Timothy 1:7 NIV)

I am not advocating a wholesale dismissal of sanity and godly counsel. I am advocating being filled with the Holy Spirit. He will give us dreams and visions that will be bigger than our pro-visions or desires. The dreams will demand sacrifices, risks, hard work, prayer, and God. Have you ever seen the Mission of Mercy in Calcutta, India? I have. It is a memorial to the faith of Mark and Huldah Buntain.

I don't believe that you've lived until you attempted some-thing so great that if God is not involved, it will fail. So many leaders are so afraid of failure that they will never attempt a God thing. Are you afraid of people's opinions? What about God's opinion of your life? Is He waiting in heaven wondering whom will I send? Who will go for Me? Can you hear His voice? Do you sense His prompting? Has He deposited visions and dreams in your heart and mind?

Every service I have to make a choice, either to be an imparter or to play it safe. It would be easier for me to not have an altar call for salvation, to not pray for the sick, or to not ask the luke-warm to repent. Every time I pray for someone to be filled with the Holy Spirit or the baptism of the Holy Spirit, I take a risk. What happens if nothing happens? What happens if they are not healed? What happens if no one comes for salvation? What hap-pens if no one responds to the altar call? Many churches have done away with altar calls, anointing the sick with oil, and salva-tion calls. They are trying to remove the risk of offense or remove the risk of rejection. Do we want our churches to grow at the expense of obedience to God?

I am the type of pastor who wants to see people respond. I wonder if they are unable to respond to the altar call, how will they respond to the battles of faith? Putting fear and pride aside is not easy, but living a Christian life is a lot harder. How will they be able to withstand the opposition of their unsaved friends if they can't respond in a God environment? I don't want to sound like I am condemning these churches. They have to be obedient to their consciences and relationships with the Lord, and I have to be obedient to mine.

Our church is following the lead of its pastor. We are firmly evangelical, biblical, and Pentecostal. We are a soul-winning church dedicated to discipling believers. We are totally surrendered to the Holy Spirit. Our greatest concern is that we offend the Holy Spirit. I am sure we have frequently offended the religious sensitivity of some people. We have chosen our direction, and we have decided to please the One who is supreme, Jesus Christ. We are multilingual and multicultural, our building is multipurpose, and we often have multiple altar calls. Our faith has been stretched beyond reason many times.

We have planted churches during building programs and hired staff without cash reserves. We have started two building programs without money or a secured loan. We have started a Bible college in India and another one in Mexico. We have prayed for the sick, and we have seen people filled with the Spirit while the media took pictures. Our teams have gone into the most dangerous parts of Las Vegas. Our missions teams have ministered in dangerous places internationally (Rwanda after the genocide, the slums of Mexico, northern India's slums, on rooftops, in alleyways, fields, and streets). Our lives have been threatened many times, our campus has been vandalized, and two mission buses were destroyed by vandalism.

A demon-possessed person once tried to kill a staff member and our general contractor with her vehicle. After the two men jumped from the path of her truck, she drove into the front doors of the church. Perhaps she believed that we were a drive-thru church. Her pickup smashed through the glass doors right into the lobby. I can imagine the shock to those who were in the sanctuary when she backed up her vehicle in order to ram into the wall again. Joel Garcia, who was the director of our Bible Institute, confronted her as she stepped out of her stalled vehicle. He asked, "What are you doing?" She answered, "Satan sent me. I am dead, and you are all dead!" He then started to rebuke her in Jesus' name. It took four police officers to place her in their police car.

Real ministry requires real faith; real faith requires real risks. I have had the privilege of sitting with Pastor Lamb of China. This man of God pastors a house church of more than 1,600 people. He shared his life experience with us, which included twenty years of imprisonment for his faith. Hard labor and harsh conditions were his daily bread. Even though he had lost everything several times, he continued to risk it all for his faith. The ministry had cost him everything, but his joy was contagious. I will never forget the words he shared with me before we left his humble house. "Paul, tell the American church that: (1) everyone must suffer, (2) you must learn to love suffering more then money, and (3) Jesus is coming back."

Has the twenty-first-century church forgotten this risk of living a legitimate Christian life? Have you risked reputation, persecution, or ridicule for serving Christ? I hope so. When I played competitive hockey, I didn't feel like I was in the game until I hit somebody or they hit me. It was a disgrace to finish a baseball or football game with a clean jersey. We wanted proof that we were in the game. I can remember walking into a classroom after a game, full of pride and confidence. I was sporting a busted lip, my badge of honor. Jesus proved that He was in the game: "*Look at my hands and my feet. It is I myself! Touch me and see; a ghost does not have flesh and bones, as you see I have*" (Luke 24:39 NIV). Paul had proof that he took risks for the team: "*Three times I was beaten with rods, once I was stoned, three times I was shipwrecked, I spent a night and a day in the open sea*" (2 Corinthians 11:25 NIV).

Are you in the game? Where are your stitches, bruises, and breaks? Imparters are committed to full-contact faith and ministry; they don't play it safe. It is either God shows up or they look like fools. Either God starts healing people through your prayers or you feel worthless. Either God touches people through the laying on of hands or you are just going through the motions.

PRAYER

God, make me more like Tommy Barnett and others with huge faith. God, please give us a huge faith, a faith that will help us risk our reputations and finances for a cause greater than us.

FIFTEEN

FIND SOMEONE TO MENTOR

Now Joshua son of Nun was filled with the spirit of wisdom because Moses had laid his hands on him. So the Israelites listened to him and did what the LORD had commanded Moses. (Deuteronomy 34:9 NIV)

The greatest void in America and around the world is leadership. The world is looking for someone to lead them to the Promised Land. Unfortunately, people are so desperate for a leader that they will often settle for unethical and even immoral ones.

I once spoke at the Northern Indian General Council of the Assemblies of God. We met in the sanctuary of Mark Buntain in Calcutta. Mark and Huldah Buntain founded the church, hospital, feeding program school, and Bible College. Mark died, but

Huldah has valiantly picked up his mantle. As I preached out of 2 Kings, I was prompted to challenge their pastors to pick up the Buntain mantle. The fifty prophets that followed Elijah did not pick up his mantle, only Elisha did.

He picked up the cloak that had fallen from Elijah and went back and stood on the bank of the Jordan. Then he took the cloak that had fallen from him and struck the water with it. "Where now is the LORD, the God of Elijah?" he asked. When he struck the water, it divided to the right and to the left, and he crossed over. The company of the prophets from Jericho, who were watching, said, "The spirit of Elijah is resting on Elisha." And they went to meet him and bowed to the ground before him. (2 Kings 2:13–15 NIV)

You never hear about the other prophets. The only hint of their lives is the sad story of a prophet who died without leaving his family enough of an inheritance to survive. What a tragedy! Could it be that the fifty prophets were stuck looking for Elijah?

"Look," they said, "we your servants have fifty able men. Let them go and look for your master. Perhaps the Spirit of the LORD has picked him up and set him down on some mountain or in some valley." "No," Elisha replied, "do not send them." (2 Kings 2:16 NIV)

Isn't this an incredible illustration of what happens to churches and ministries during transition in leadership? How many great leaders have the ability to raise up other leaders? How many leaders can hand off the mantle of leadership when they face retirement or sickness? When a great leader steps aside or passes away, who will pick up the mantle? Who will stand around like the fifty priests watching from a distance? John Maxwell says it so well: "There is no success without a successor."

The truest test of our leadership is

- delegating authority to others,
- raising leaders, and
- training and raising up a successor.

Multiply the impact of your ministry by releasing the anointing through others. These are all risky ventures. Investing our lives in a few close mentors is frightening. You risk being hurt, betrayed, and misunderstood. When you mentor someone, you become vulnerable. Mentoring requires trusting and respecting the person. You will have to teach them your philosophy, the secret of your success, and your work ethics, and you must let them into your world. It is a tremendous sacrifice, but it is worth it. Jesus mentored His three, then His twelve. He successfully mentored eleven leaders who changed the entire world.

Then the eleven disciples went to Galilee, to the mountain where Jesus had told them to go. When they saw him, they worshiped him; but some doubted. Then Jesus came to them and said, "All authority in heaven and on earth has been given to me. Therefore go and make disciples of all nations, baptizing them in the name of the Father and of the Son and of the Holy Spirit, and teaching them to obey everything I have commanded you. And surely I am with you always, to the very end of the age." (Matthew 28:16–20 NIV)

We will all have our Judases, but we will also have our Johns. We may love a few Thomases, but there will also be Peters.

Who will follow the Buntains in Calcutta, the Pastor Lambs of China, the Barnetts in Phoenix, the Dobsons from Focus on the Family, the Chos of South Korea, the Mohans of Madras, India, the Annacondias from Argentina, and the Billy Grahams? The greatest achievement of these leaders is to have their work continue with even more fruit after their departure.

As I have passed the forty-year-old landmark and had a near-death experience, these issues have become very real to me. I am very conscious of my mortality.

You have made my days a mere handbreadth; the span of my years is as nothing before you. Each man's life is but a breath. (Psalm 39:5 NIV)

I have learned to pray like David: *"Show me, O LORD, my life's end and the number of my days; let me know how fleeting is my life"* (Psalm 39:4 NIV).

I am trying to prepare my church and children for the day that I head home. God has also forced me to think differently because of His call on my life. These two issues have caused me to focus my efforts on the following:

- Equipping leaders
- Releasing ministry
- Imparting through the laying on of hands and prayer, teaching, anointing in oil, and preaching
- Delegating authority and responsibility
- Giving vision to staff, Bible Institute students, Master's Commission, and our leadership
- Putting my thoughts in writing
- Improving the quality of our audio and video production
- Equipping and reaching people though our TV ministry
- Developing Bible colleges to train and release pastors, church planters, and pastoral counselors
- Starting Bible colleges and churches

All of our efforts are designed to raise leaders to touch the world. Once this is all in place, my final task will be to train and release the leadership to another Elisha: someone who has my spirit and vision; someone whom God can use to do even greater things for the kingdom.

My first target as a pastor is to pass my heart to my wife and children. If they have not yet caught the vision, then I am failing. One of my greatest joys is seeing my wife, Denise, minister with me at the altars, preaching, imparting, training leaders, and speaking at retreats and conferences. I have installed her as one of the executive pastors of our church because she knows my heart and the heart of the Father. God has used her to build a weekly ladies' Bible study with over seven hundred women in attendance. She is a tremendous woman of God.

My children are also growing in their anointing and ministries. Isabelle will be a great leader and preacher, like her mother. Christine is a talented singer, and I believe she will become a Holy Spirit–sensitive worship leader. Our Samuel is a tremendous athlete, student, and God-follower. He will either make millions playing basketball or join his father's staff one day.

I did not always consider my role as a developer of leaders. It is only since I received my impartation from Claudio Freidzon that I have embraced this privilege. My family has changed because of the impartation and focus to train up leaders in my home. Isn't this the greatest legacy a man or woman could leave? Not buildings or monuments, but leaders who can bear much fruit.

This is to my Father's glory, that you bear much fruit, showing yourselves to be my disciples. (John 15:8 NIV)

PRAYER

Lord, I know that my life should be all about raising up other leaders and even sons and daughters. Help me to renounce the fears and insecurities that hinder this generational blessing. By the way, I think that You are a great Dad.

SIXTEEN

SERVE THE ANOINTING

So Elisha left him and went back. He took his yoke of oxen and slaughtered them. He burned the plowing equipment to cook the meat and gave it to the people, and they ate. Then he set out to follow Elijah and became his attendant. (1 Kings 19:21 NIV)

Elisha served Elijah; this was the pattern of impartation that I have learned. Henry Hinn preached at our church about serving the anointing, if we really want the anointing. This concept rocked our church. After the service, it was late and we were all tired. It is uncommon to have deep conversation; our tendency is "let's get home and put the kids to bed!" It doesn't sound really spiritual, but it is reality. My son, Samuel, who was eleven years old at the time, surprised me when he told me on our way home, "Dad, I want to help you and mom more around the house; I

159

want to serve the anointing. If I forget what I just said remind me, OK?"

Praise God for Holy Spirit–filled services! Thank God that my children have been imparted into many times. Not only was my son changed by this concept, but our staff and several men from our men's ministries were touched by this also. Denise and I have felt a weight lifted as women have started to support her like never before. Men have started attending to my needs as well. Ministry can become exhausting; our schedule is so packed that we don't have time to take care of some daily necessities. Great armor bearers have come alongside to bear the burden. Our people caught this concept. They have seen our anointing and thought, *I would love to have that type of power.* Someone finally pointed out a way that they could get it.

Elisha washed Elijah's hands for years. Being that close to the anointing has to rub off. Jesus also teaches the principle of servanthood. He was not advocating it as a means to receive the anointing but as a road to glory and greatness. *"I tell you the truth, no servant is greater than his master, nor is a messenger greater than the one who sent him"* (John 13:16 NIV).

Servant imparters are on the road to greatness. They are great because they are touching lives. God loves servants; God loves people who pour into others. God gives more to these people. Have you ever committed to serving your pastor, mentor, teachers, or parents? Here are some Old Testament examples:

1. **Joseph served Pharaoh:** *"Joseph was thirty years old when he entered the service of Pharaoh king of Egypt. And Joseph went*

out from Pharaoh's presence and traveled throughout Egypt" (Genesis 41:46 NIV).

2. **Joshua served Moses:** *"Then Moses set out with Joshua his aide, and Moses went up on the mountain of God"* (Exodus 24:13 NIV).

3. **Jonathan served David:** *"And Jonathan made a covenant with David because he loved him as himself. Jonathan took off the robe he was wearing and gave it to David, along with his tunic, and even his sword, his bow and his belt"* (1 Samuel 18:3–4 NIV).

4. **David served Saul:** *"Whenever the spirit from God came upon Saul, David would take his harp and play. Then relief would come to Saul; he would feel better, and the evil spirit would leave him"* (1 Samuel 16:23 NIV).

5. **Samuel served Eli:** *"The boy Samuel ministered before the LORD under Eli. In those days the word of the LORD was rare; there were not many visions"* (1 Samuel 3:1 NIV).

6. **Ruth served Naomi:** *"So Naomi returned from Moab accompanied by Ruth the Moabites, her daughter-in-law, arriving in Bethlehem as the barley harvest was beginning"* (Ruth 1:22 NIV).

Every one of these servants was used mightily by God because of his or her servanthood. There is a direct correlation between serving and blessings. God honors the heart of a servant. Serving the men and women of God brings a very specific blessing. "*Let me inherit a double portion of your spirit,*" Elisha replied (2 Kings 2:9 NIV). In the New Testament, Jesus demonstrated and taught this principle throughout His ministry. He didn't come to do His will; He came to do the will of the Father.

> He went away a second time and prayed, "My Father, if it is not possible for this cup to be taken away unless I drink it, may your will be done." (Matthew 26:42 NIV)

Jesus came to serve His Father. He taught His disciple to serve each other by serving them: "*Now that I, your Lord and Teacher, have washed your feet, you also should wash one another's feet*" (John 13:14 NIV). We find that after His death and resurrection, Jesus imparted His Spirit into them. He also imparted to them their mission:

> Therefore go and make disciples of all nations, baptizing them in the name of the Father and of the Son and of the Holy Spirit, and teaching them to obey everything I have commanded you. And surely I am with you always, to the very end of the age. (Matthew 28:19–20 NIV)

The disciples then did what Jesus taught them: John and Mark served Barnabas, Silas served Peter, and Timothy served Paul. The disciples poured their lives into every corner of the world.

I want to encourage you to serve other people, to pour your life into others. Help meet people's needs. Find a good church to commit your life to. Don't just offer; get involved. There is a place for you to use your gifts and talents. Get to know the pastoral staff and leaders. Choose a mentor and serve that person. A mentor is someone who is spiritually more mature then you are, someone with whom you can enter into a mutually accountable relationship.

Serving is not a very popular model in our society. Everyone seems to be clawing and fighting for his or her advantage. Even in our churches, this concept is truly foreign. It needs to be taught in our homes, churches, and schools. Our entire society needs to reemphasize this moral principle.

Dr. James Marocco spent some time with our staff and taught us how service can function in a church staff; he calls it the platform of ministry. The platform of ministry is the ministry that God has given the senior pastor. Everyone on staff is there to serve the vision of the senior pastor. In exchange, they receive the benefits of the pastor's anointing, influence, reputation, skills, and character.

Staff members are not on the team to build their portfolios or to put in their time until a better spot is available. They are not supposed to build their ministry. It does not belong to them; they are serving the senior pastor. They are helping him reach the youth, touch the children, clear the property, reach the lost, heal the hurting, and disciple the believers. They must commit to serve the leader. Too many ministers and leaders have a spirit or an attitude. They are not there to serve; they are there to build their little kingdoms. There would be fewer church splits and rebellious staff members if this was taught in our Bible colleges and seminaries. If a staff member cannot serve his leaders with a clear conscience, he needs to resign and move out of the city. It would be unethical to build in the same backyard if his desire is not to build on someone else's platform.

As pastors and leaders serve their senior pastors, they will reap a tremendous reward. Even though David was serving a wicked leader, he never used his power to hurt him. He could've killed him, *"but the LORD forbid that I should lay a hand on the LORD's anointed. Now get the spear and water jug that are near his head, and let's go"* (1 Samuel 26:11 NIV). He could've cursed him, but he didn't. David served the anointing as long as he could, then he left. When it was no longer safe for him, he left town.

If you are on staff with a leader who has lost the spiritual or moral yearning, then resign and leave. Leave town and believe that God will give you a better place. He will reward you for serving the anointing in due season.

But he gives us more grace. That is why Scripture says: "God opposes the proud but gives grace to the humble." (James 4:6 NIV)

PRAYER

Father, serving others is not really easy, so please help me. I really want to get my eyes off of myself and my agenda. Help me live a life of helping others succeed. I will trust You with the rest. You're the best.

CONCLUSION

It doesn't sound really spiritual, but it is reality. The ministry of impartation is an incredible adventure that will take you into situations and locations you have never dreamed of. Each new day will offer opportunities to you to impart into the lives of others.

There are doors you must just walk through. Someday it will be the door of sufferings. Other days, it will be the door of faith or servanthood. Behind each door is a new world that will unfold before your eyes. We have discussed a few of the keys to open these doors. There are other keys and doors that you will discover on your own. You will need some help to get past some doors. This is why relationships are so important. Your friends, pastors, elders, mentors, children, relatives, counselors, coaches, and teachers will all play an important part on this journey. Please let them into your world.

Impartation is really all about relationships. We must recognize the impact we make on each other. We can improve these deposits. We can become more systematic and deliberate. We can strategically choose who will pour into us in the future.

THE 5 POWERS OF GOD

Some of these impartations may be destructive and ungodly. We need God's grace to work through these. Don't lose hope; your breakthrough is right around the corner.

The purpose of this book has been to introduce you to the concept of impartation, to help you prepare for impartation, then to loose you into a ministry of impartation. I hope and pray that we have achieved these goals. I want to conclude this book with an encouragement. Model your life and ministry after the poor woman who was about to lose her sons to creditors. She was a good woman, the wife of a prophet. It is unclear why she had come to this place in her life, but she needed a miracle. She did the only thing she could think of—seek the prophet Elisha. His counsel was stunning, even a little absurd.

> *Elisha replied to her, "How can I help you? Tell me, what do you have in your house?"*
>
> *"Your servant has nothing there at all," she said, "except a little oil." Elisha said, "Go around and ask all your neighbors for empty jars. Don't ask for just a few. Then go inside and shut the door behind you and your sons. Pour oil into all the jars, and as each is filled, put it to one side."* (2 Kings 4:2–4 NIV)

Be an imparter. Pour with faith and obedience until there are no more empty people. After all, Moses imagined the same thing (Numbers 11:29).

NOTES

Chapter 7
1. *The New Strong's Exhaustive Concordance of The Bible* (Nashville: Thomas Nelson Publishers, 1996), NT: 5486.
2. Ibid., 272.

HELL GATE

TWISTED LEGENDS COLLECTION

VERONICA EDEN

Welcome...

*Ten authors invite you to join us in the
Twisted Legends Collection.*

These stories are a dark, twisted reimagining of
infamous legends well-known throughout the
world. Some are retellings, others are nods to those
stories that cause a chill to run down your spine.

Each book may be a standalone, but they're
all connected by the lure of a legend.

We invite you to venture into the unknown,
and delve into the darkness with us,
one book at a time.

The
COLLECTION

Blurb

The first thing I'm warned about when I arrive at the girls' home is to stay away from the abandoned graveyard. Local urban legend claims it's host to a gate to Hell.

Then I was dared…

The legend is as real as the monsters I've summoned by activating the gate. Demons guard it, waiting for skeptical idiots like me to do the ritual. Three sinfully hot, dangerously powerful demons.

Valerian. Matthias. Alder.

Ruthless. Deadly. Terrifying.

The gate's three wicked protectors won't let me get away without paying their price.

Blurb

I'm at their mercy, fighting to survive them and the
supernatural world they drag me into.
But none of us are prepared for what is awakening
within me.

A long buried secret and hidden ancient magic will
change everything.
The match is lit and together we're all going up in
flames.

*Hell Gate is a paranormal reverse harem romance. Due to dark
themes, strong language, and graphic violent/sexual situations it is
recommended for mature readers.*

Content warning for mentions and brief depictions of past
emotional/physical abuse from a foster parent, themes of
abandonment and neglect, kidnapping, violence

Dedication

Kiss the villains…
they know how to make us scream.

Playlist

Gallows—Katie Garfield
The Tradition—Halsey
My Love Will Never Die—AG, Claire Wyndham
1121—Halsey
Bells in Santa Fe—Halsey
DARKSIDE—Neoni
Dancer in the Dark—Scratch Massive
Faith—CHVRN
All That I've Done—Levitate
Mumur—fantompower
please don't go—eevee
Strange Inside—Aimee Simone
dream of another way out—Visceral Design, anatu
Skin—Zarah Mahler
You—Lucy Daydream
i could be your goddess—CASHFORGOLD
Queen—CASHFORGOLD, Sidewalks and Skeletons
Lapse—Black Math
Royalty—Egzod, Maestro Chives, Neoni
Runaway—AURORA

As The World Caves In—Sarah Cothran

One
LILY

RAINDROPS SPLATTER THE WINDOWS OF THE ORPHANAGE matron's beat up station wagon, falling from the wet autumn leaves of sycamore trees lining the road. Mrs. Talbot, my new guardian, manages the girls' home we're on our way to. We haven't spoken for fifteen minutes since she picked me up in front of the tiny Amtrak station at the center of town. Dead air fills the car to the point I'm worried about suffocating.

The severely dressed woman took one judgmental look at my sharp winged eyeliner and thick thighs on display in a pair of fishnets beneath the black distressed shorts hugging my round ass and rolled her eyes.

Bitch. Sorry I don't subscribe to dressing in an

oversized shapeless sack to hide my body, because god forbid anyone else saw my curves. No one spontaneously combusts because they get a little self-conscious seeing a girl with big tits and a soft stomach confidently rocking short hemlines and low-cut tops. I wear what I'm comfortable in—screw anyone who has a problem with it.

My fashion sense is the one thing about me I still show the world.

It's not like I expected anything different, though. That's life in the system. Battered from riding the revolving door of foster homes to orphanages and never fitting in wherever I'm placed thanks to my history. They stopped sticking me with foster families years ago after too many...incidents.

Troubled, that's the word used most often in my file.

Lily is withdrawn...Lily is too much to handle...Lily got into fights at school...Lily started a fire again.

It's always the reason I ended up returned, like an unwanted Christmas present. A reject, that's me.

With stiff movements, I pull the cuffs of my burgundy sweater down over the scarred skin on the back of my clenched hands. The burns from the house fire healed, but they left my flesh ravaged by fine red and silver lines that run from my fingertips to my elbows. I don't remember everything about that night, only brief flashes of the worst parts.

The scars are my permanent reminder of it all—
that terrifying night surrounded by deadly flames,
the look on my foster brother's face, how there's
something not right with me.

An uncomfortable lump thickens in my throat
as I push my hands into my lap and trace the edge
of my thumb along one of the scar paths through
the sweater. For a moment, my vision blurs from the
sting of tears. Pursing my lips, I blink them away
and stare at the sad little town we drive through. I'll
never let them fall again.

I don't have any way to explain it, but whenever
I allow my emotions to get away from me, weird
things happen. I've trained myself to be less—dull
down everything about myself. This way I don't set
myself up for failure and the pain of rejection.

The strange oddities that follow me everywhere
scare people. Hell, they scare me. I have no
explanation for the impossible things that happen
around me when I'm out of control.

I've bounced from one group home to another
for two years. I liked the one in Philadelphia, but
thanks to overcrowding, I won the lottery to be
shipped out of the city to Brim Hills, PA to make
room for younger kids.

The town looks depressing as hell. One main
road cuts through it with old red brick buildings
sporting the cracked paint of faded business signs

from when this place was in its heyday. That's got to be at least sixty years ago.

In Philly there were things to do. Bumfuck Nowhere, Pennsylvania seems to offer the scintillating options of a library, a movie theater running two movies from months ago, and a pitiful looking diner. Great. This is about to be the most boring month of my life stuck in this dead town stalled in the past.

By now I've accepted I'm going to age out of the system. There's no happy ending in a forever home, not for me, not after the fire. Whatever. My eighteenth birthday is soon. This is one more little bump in the long pockmarked road of my miserable life.

A month in the girls' home here is my final stop before I'm kicked out of the last place that is required by the state to take me in.

Then I'll be on my own.

Sink or swim.

I swallow. The haunting memory of my foster mom's voice is like a gut punch out of nowhere. Anytime I remember her favorite phrase, all I taste is the earthy well water the tub was filled with. A shudder threatens to overtake me, and I struggle to fight it off.

Mrs. Talbot flicks her eyes at me and her austere frown intensifies. She probably thinks I'm a junkie

4

in need of my next drug fix. A lot of girls in the Philadelphia home have gone down that path. It's scary how easy it is to get your hands on any of it in Philly or the short train ride across the bridge to Camden. I won't touch the stuff. I'm already messed up and no amount of self medicating will fix me or numb whatever's screwed up about me.

We pass a sign stating the Brim Hills coal mines are permanently closed. It's a faded blue, tagged with graffiti.

"Why did the coal mines close?" I'm not sure what spurs me to ask. It's not like I really care. Simple curiosity to satisfy a bored mind.

She draws in a harsh breath and shakes her head, lips pressed so firmly together the wrinkled skin around her mouth pales. "Don't ask about the mines. Those damn death traps are cursed."

"Um, okay."

"Drove this town into Hell."

The hissed words seem to be directed at herself rather than carrying on normal conversation. She clutches the steering wheel in a death grip and her teeth grind.

I drop my head back against the seat with a sigh. "Sorry I asked."

She ignores me, which is fine by me. The main road ends and after a few turns, the station wagon pulls through a covered bridge onto a wooded road.

Tall, skinny pine trees reach high into the air like spindly fingers, connecting the canopy overhead that makes the eerie road dim and shadowed.

An overgrown abandoned cemetery catches my eye. The rusted iron gate declares it as Brim Hills Cemetery, but half the letters are missing.

It reminds me of a Japanese isekai manga I've read where the main character dies being hit by a car only to wake up in a different world entirely. The artist loved to use city ruins taken back by nature to contrast the main character's despair. I ended up enthralled by the story of discovering the hidden truth behind the world the main character was always meant to find. After reading it, I became addicted to isekai stories as my preferred escape from my harsh reality.

The cemetery disappears when we round the bend, then the tires hit a nasty pothole where the paved road is basically gravel. The car bounces and shudders through a turn down a driveway I almost missed.

"We're here," Mrs. Talbot announces.

Jumping for joy over here. Everything I take in on the short drive to the girls' home tells me the time I spend stuck here is going to suck. Creepy ass house in the woods? Check. Even more unsettling matching shed peeking out from beyond the house? Check. At least three miles to the nearest sign of civilization? Ding, ding, ding, we have ourselves a winner of a girls' home.

At this rate, I actually wish I could go back to live with the Clarks. Heat pricks my palms and I rub them on my thighs to stop the weird energy. Not now. Keep it together.

A brittle laugh catches in my throat before it can escape into the world. If I'd rather be there, it's official. I've finally lost it.

The car rolls to a stop in front of the three story house that looks like it was built by Wish-brand Quakers. One strong wind and this place could collapse. Weeds, ferns, and sapling sprouts create their own mini forest on either side of a damp mulch path leading up to the house.

"Get your bag and come inside. Don't dawdle," Mrs. Talbot orders as she exits the car and bustles away at a clipped pace.

One month. I scan the house again with a dejected frown. Absolute eternity.

Inside, I'm hit with a musty floral scent hanging in the air that I nearly gag on. I clap a hand over my nose and mouth. What is that, two decade old potpourri? Yikes.

Unaffected, she leads me to the second floor, down the narrow hall, then points to a door near the end. I pause in front of it, hiking the duffel bag stuffed with my meager belongings higher on my shoulder.

A piece of masking tape has *Lily Sloane* scrawled in marker beneath a more permanent black placard with white letters that reads *Marie Hawkins*. I stopped wishing for those cute little decorative name plaques for my door before I hit ten, but even this is a new low. A burning sensation stirs in my stomach. I rub it, yet it doesn't soothe the discomfort.

The matron raises her thin eyebrows. "It makes more sense to save resources and use something disposable. You're almost of age. You won't be here long."

Thanks, I don't say.

She opens the door to an empty room. It's set up much like a college dorm—two single beds pushed to opposite corners, matching desks, and two nightstands. My new roommate's side is tidy. There are a couple of posters pinned to the wall.

The sparse side of the room is mine. I dump my duffel on the faded floral quilt and wipe my clammy palms on my legs.

"House rules," Mrs. Talbot announces.

Oh boy, can't wait.

I keep my snarky non-enthusiasm to myself, as I do most things. People think I'm quiet and sullen, but I just prefer to play it safe. When I don't hold back, it's easier for me to lose my temper and things get away from me. When I lose control…

Well, it's not pretty.

I slump on the edge of my bed as Mrs. Talbot paces into the room.

"I was—informed of your need to act out," she begins with a hard glance in my direction.

Translation: she was *warned*. I'm used to it. Broken little Lily, desperate for attention. People stopped listening to me and looking for my side of things a long time ago. A wave of uncomfortable heat spreads across my chest. When my expression remains a bland mask, she continues.

"I'll have you know, I run a tight ship. Attitude and disobedience won't be tolerated here. You and the other girls are in my care, and I take pride in shaping each of you to the best of my ability during your time here." She assesses me with the same judgmental once over she gave me in front of the Amtrak station, lingering on the fishnets stretched over my legs. "Though you may not be under my roof long, I expect you to respect the rules here."

The weight of her stare follows another long pause. Begrudgingly, I mumble, "Ma'am."

"Good. In this house we wake at six sharp. First up is chores, then breakfast. After that, homeschool lessons." At the surprised sound that escapes me before I smother it, she turns from pacing to stand before me with her hands propped on her hips importantly. "You don't have your GED yet, young lady. Your time here is short, but you'll complete your lessons."

I cough in response and it seems to appease her. She drones on about lunch after homeschool. In the city, I was in my senior year for the second time, but what's the point? I'm not going to college. Once I've got the boot, I'm on my own.

My plan is to get out of here and find steady work. If I'm lucky, I'll land something that keeps a roof over my head and food in my belly. Too many kids are turned out onto the street when they age out, expected to fend for themselves with little help from the government funded program that cared for them up to that point in their lives.

"You're permitted to enjoy free time between lunch and dinner in the afternoons," Mrs. Talbot intones. "Do as you like, or work if you're inclined to seek a job. If you're home for dinner, we eat at six. If not, you're on your own. The fridge is stocked for such occasions and food is labeled accordingly." Her expression, if possible, turns even more strict as she speaks slowly like I'm an idiot. "Do not take from any container labeled for meal times. I specifically portion it out myself."

I nod dutifully, half-tuning her out. Jesus, Mrs. T. needs to get a grip. Or maybe let her bun down. From the corner of my eye, the door opens and my new roommate slips in. At first glance she's plain and lanky, but her fingernails are painted in a riot of color. She perches on her bed while our matron lectures me with the welcome speech.

Mrs. Talbot pauses again, scrutinizing my hair. I resist the urge to paw at my shoulder-length waves.

"If your hair is dyed that garish shade of red, you won't be allowed to use the bathroom for any home chemical kits."

"It's natural," I reply stiffly.

"I see." She sighs as if even my fiery red hair is an affront. "I've already told you about the mines. You're also to keep off the road that runs north of town. It connects to the underground coal fires still burning. Parts of the road disintegrate without warning."

Her words come out brittle and harsh. She flexes her hand, darting her glistening eyes to the window behind me. I look at the girl sitting quietly on her bed to get a hint if this is the norm with the matron or not. She's absorbed in her phone. It's a newer model than mine, which is so old it's practically a flip phone.

"Most importantly, stay away from the graveyard on the county road. It's the Devil's land. Poisoned ground. If I hear you've been there, you're out. It's absolutely forbidden." Mrs. Talbot stops talking, her face paling. She takes several deep breaths before she seems to regain her composure.

Her shaking hand motions toward my roommate. "Marie will help you for the next few days. Once you have your bearings, I expect you to be prompt, attentive, and obedient."

With that, she leaves, closing the door harder than necessary behind her. A skeptical frown tugs at my lips.

"What's up with that?"

Marie shrugs. "Don't worry. It's nothing—just an old wives' tale she likes to spread to scare us all into submission." She rolls her eyes. "At least you got The Talk, as we like to call it, at your age. I had to get it at twelve and was terrified she was going to give me a sex ed lecture."

My mouth slowly curves into a lopsided smirk. The shape of the barely there smile feels foreign. "Does that crone even know what sex is?"

She grins, hitching her shoulder. "Possibly. She had a son."

"Had?"

"Yeah, he died in some crazy accident when he was a teenager." She glances at the door. "We're not supposed to know about it, but she talks in her sleep sometimes and calls his name, begging him not to go somewhere."

Chills break out across my skin and guilt for laughing at Mrs. Talbot hardens into a pit in my stomach. Life sucks. I know that fact better than

12

most.

"Anyway, I just came in for this." She grabs her purse and heads for the door with a wave.

I don't ask where she's going or see if I can go with her. It's not my business. I've learned it's best to keep to myself. There's no point in making friends with girls who could forget about you tomorrow.

Flopping back on the bed, I wriggle to get comfortable on the lumpy mattress, turning my attention to the window outside. There isn't much of a view, only an old tree closer to death than life.

I can survive a month here. I've lived through far worse than a group home in the boonies with an uptight matron.

The second I'm on my own, I'm out of here. I don't know if I'll catch a train back to Philly, or head somewhere else. As long as I put Brim Hills behind me.

Two
LILY

TWENTY MINUTES AFTER MRS. TALBOT SHOUTS LIGHTS out and climbs to the third floor for the night, my new roommate shines her phone flashlight as she slips her shoes on. She's fully dressed in dark clothes.

I am too, but it's because I haven't mustered the motivation to unpack yet. I haven't moved from this spot all afternoon. Mrs. Talbot wasn't happy that I skipped dinner on my first night. I'm off to a great start with this whole punctual obedience thing she thinks she'll get out of me.

"Come on," Marie says when she catches me watching from my sprawl across my lumpy mattress.

"Isn't there a curfew?" I mutter.

She scoffs. "Yeah, you really seem like the type

of girl who follows the rules. Come on. We do this all the time." She crosses the room and tugs on my arm. "She sleeps like the dead and always goes to bed early so she can get up before sunrise. She's got a thing for the newspaper delivery guy, but don't mention it, or you'll piss her off."

My brows lift. That's a different picture than she painted earlier of our stern matron.

An owl hoots in the tree outside the window by my bed. At least I hope it's an owl. I'm not used to all this nature shit. The quiet stillness of this place is unsettling as hell compared to the constant noise, motion, and lights of city living. Without all that, I hear too many of my own thoughts. It'll take me at least another two hours to exhaust myself into sleep in this unfamiliar bed.

A light tap sounds on our door, followed by two slow taps, then a final tap after a beat of silence. Marie kneels next to her bed at the signal and rummages deep beneath it. She emerges with a long box and a bag.

Dusting herself off, she glances at me. "Seriously, last chance to come with us, or we're leaving you here."

I swallow, playing with the edge of the floral quilt beneath me. Left behind and left out, like always. No one asks me to go anywhere with them once they think they know my story. Mrs. Talbot

15

must not have told the girls here what's in my file.

Thanks for the solid, Mrs. T.

This won't last. As soon as they find out I'm a freak, they'll want nothing to do with me. Just like everyone else.

"Fine." I feign indifference while a bubble of anticipation expands inside me at being included.

"Wear something you don't mind getting dirty." She gestures at herself.

I examine my fishnets, shorts, and low-cut sweater. After mulling it over, I dig through my duffel for a zip up hoodie, throwing it on over my outfit.

Marie holds a finger to her lips once I'm ready and motions for me to follow her into the hall. It's empty. I guess whoever knocked on the door went ahead of us. At the stairs, she points to a step before skipping over it carefully. There are four more on the way down she avoids. They must creak.

We quietly sneak through the house until we meet up with the others outside on the mulch path. Marie hands off the long, thin box and her bag to the shorter girl.

The rain let up, but it left the air dense and foggy. Cold moisture clings to my legs and cheeks. I cram my hands into the pockets of my hoodie, eyeing two other girls I haven't met yet because I avoided leaving the room once I arrived.

16

"That's Jessica and this is Violet," Marie whispers, pointing to each of them.

Unlike Marie, Jessica has on a full face of makeup with dark winged liner like mine. A beanie slouches over her loosely braided black hair. Violet is shorter than all of us and is the only one in hiking boots and sweatpants. Both of them are around sixteen. Between the three of them and me on the brink of aging out of the system we make a nice little reject pack.

The only difference is they still have that look in their eyes, the one holding on to hope that someday they'll find a family to take them away from this. The hope I gave up on so many years ago, I barely recall what it felt like to wish for a forever family.

"Are you warm enough?" Violet asks.

"I'm fine."

"Seriously?" Jessica's eyes drop to my legs. "It's freezing."

Shoulders tensing, I burrow my hands deeper in my pockets and shift on my feet. "I run hot. Always have. Did you drag me out of bed to break curfew just to stand in front of the house, or what?"

"You'll see. Come on." Marie goes to hook her arm with mine and I startle, breath gusting from my lungs harshly as I use my elbow to break away from her side. "Whoa, sorry. I didn't know you weren't a hugger."

I almost laugh. Normal people aren't huggers. I'm far from normal. It's better if I don't touch people. It's not like anyone wants to touch me, anyway.

They might not know my story, but I'm doing a great job of letting them see what a head case I am. This might be a new record for me.

Without another word, I turn to go back inside, teeth clenched, crushing the bubble of anticipation that had no right to grow.

"Chickening out?" Marie cuts me off, standing in my way with her hands up and an apologetic smile.

I glance between the three of them with my guard up. She still wants me to go with them? I don't get it.

"We're wasting time," Violet complains in an undertone. "I'm leaving your asses. See you there."

For a girl so short, she's speedy, scuttling into the woods, high ponytail bobbing and weaving. The tension ebbs from my body, leaving me unsure how to act when I'm used to keeping to myself.

Jessica rolls her eyes. "Let's go before she trips again."

I follow silently, keeping my eyes on the path they take so I know where to step. All three of them make their way through the moonlit woods with familiarity. Even paying attention, I stumble a few times where it's too dark to see.

Not long after, the dense weeds and overgrowth opens up to a lumpy clearing dotted with trees. Wait, no, not a clearing. Squinting, I scan the ground until the stone shapes make sense.

Gravestones. My brows jump up. We're in the abandoned cemetery. The place Mrs. Talbot warned me to stay away from.

Moonlight pierces the clouds, illuminating the fog blanketing the graveyard. From here I see the gate at the entrance down a small hill. Violet is nowhere in sight.

"It circles behind Talbot House," Marie says. "It's huge."

"This is all there is to do for fun around here?" The unimpressed mumble isn't meant to be heard, but Jessica grins at me.

"Everyone comes here." She points to the remnants of a stone building at the top of the hill. "Think you've got the guts to enter the chapel? It's haunted. I saw a ghost last time we snuck out here."

I shrug. "Only one way to find out."

Without waiting for them, I trudge across the damp ground, not bothering to avoid headstones half-sunken into the earth. I pass a weeping angel statue with part of her face missing.

If the matron finds out about this little transgression on my first night after she explicitly told me not to come here, will she kick me out? She's state-appointed to act as my guardian for the next month. I don't care if she tries to get rid of me. It's the same old song and dance I've been stuck repeating for years.

My fingertips skim over thick ivy vines creeping up one of the few headstones that remains upright. A strange sensation swirls in my stomach. It's almost like recognition. For this spot. This person, maybe? Tilting my head, I attempt to read the engraving, but the elements have deteriorated the name beyond legibility. The best I can guess is the year this person was laid to rest, over two hundred years ago.

The longer I stand there, the stronger the nagging tug at the back of my memory grows. There's something about this place that feels oddly nostalgic. I can't put my finger on it and push the feeling aside with a frustrated noise, done with myself.

I've spent too long aching for a place to fit in that abandoned graveyards have started to feel downright homey.

A bitter snort escapes me as I skirt around a mausoleum. *Someone get this girl into therapy, stat.*

Why would I know this graveyard? That makes no sense at all. According to my file, I was abandoned as an infant in the Pine Barrens, left on a doorstep not far from the Leeds house—notorious home of the Jersey Devil, if you're a cryptid enthusiast. I'm not.

What's left of a small stone chapel stands on top of the hill, the bell tower caved in with the bell missing. A set of crumbling stairs to an upper floor hug the side of the ruins, ending abruptly in a short drop to the ground with no destination. A small archway sits beneath the steps, just tall enough for a person to fit through.

For a second I think the air inside the arch shimmers. I blink, trying to see it again. I shake my head. It's the fog playing tricks on my eyesight.

Violet emerges from within the chapel holding a lit candle when I reach it. "Did you feel it?"

"Feel what?" My tone is guarded and I watch her warily.

"I don't know, like something wants out?" She laughs, shrugging. "The others swear they can't, but every time we've come out here I get goosebumps."

"Maybe it's just adrenaline," I offer logically. "You're psyching yourself out and looking for something that isn't there."

Jessica and Marie come up the hill. They whisper to each other.

I turn to them. "What's the deal with this place? Why is it off-limits?"

Mrs. Talbot's warning about the cemetery being poisoned ground doesn't track. I haven't seen anything out of the ordinary tonight. This place is just old, and other than being rude to stomp all over the resting places of the dead, I don't see why she's superstitious about it to forbid her wards from coming here.

"It's where we commune with the beyond," Jessica drawls in a suspenseful tone. "Did you get everything set up?"

"Yeah. The board is ready to go," Violet says.

"Good." Jessica holds up a box and smirks. "Who's ready to get our seance on?"

"She's totally legit," Marie murmurs to me as we head inside the ruins lit by the candles Violet set up around the room. "She once did a tarot reading and that week another girl got adopted by the family in town that runs the hardware store she was working at."

Sounds more like the girl met her new family on her own to me. I nod, faking interest while glancing around the cramped room. The amber glow of candlelight paints sinister shadows on the damp stone walls. A chill lingers in the room that makes me shiver. It's warmer outside in the open air.

In the middle of the room there's a blanket and a ouija board. It's aesthetic—even my dead inside ass can admit that. It has a black background and white writing with an illustration of a badass reaper on it. The piece that goes in the middle depicts a sun and moon. The girls sit in a circle around it, then look at me expectantly.

I shift my weight on my feet before joining them. I'm not really into this kind of stuff. I might enjoy manga about reincarnation from a mundane life into fantasy worlds, but I don't believe in magic. Ever since the Clarks fostered me at a young age, I've been disillusioned of anything that classifies as occult or supernatural.

My foster mother's rotten voice echoes in my head. *You're unnatural. The Devil sent you to test me. I'll sink you before you pull me down.*

A bolt of searing heat shoots through my stomach at the memory. She's gone. She can't hurt me.

The girls touch the heart-shaped piece sitting on the board. I don't follow suit immediately, curling my fingers into my palms.

"Have you ever done this before?" Marie asks.

No. Do I admit that? Also no.

"Of course. Who hasn't?" My voice is stiff and forced as I mirror them.

Nothing occurs for several moments. The knot of tension eases in my shoulders. My hands brush Marie and Violet's, and absolutely nothing is happening. No one is getting hurt. No one is screaming.

I hold my breath, glancing up at them. "So...?"

Jessica closes her eyes. "Spirits, hear my call. If

23

you're listening, my sisters and I welcome you to communicate with us. We open ourselves as your vessels."

"You're moving it," Marie hisses.

"No I'm not," Violet swears.

Am I pushing the heart-shaped piece slightly? Maybe. I didn't mean to nudge it. We stare—them in awe and me in skepticism—as the four of us track it across the board in a suspenseful drag. I focus on keeping the pressure of my fingers light while one of them probably moves it. They each lean in as their anticipation rises until the whole thing seems to end.

Violet gasps. "No way."

"We've never had such direct activity with the board before." Jessica lifts her eyes to meet mine. "Usually the spirits here are shy. I knew I caught vibes off you."

"Okay?" I peer around the circle. "What do the deadbeats want? The Netflix password to cure eternal boredom?"

Marie grins. "Cute, but no. They spelled *go home* and started another word but stopped at L. They have to mean you. Your name is the only one that starts with an L."

Oh. I see. They're just messing with me. I play along. It's better than ending this now and spending the next month with three pissed off housemates because I couldn't take a joke.

"Cool," I say belatedly.

"Ask them something," Violet says. "Why do they want you to go home?"

Resisting the urge to roll my eyes, I turn my attention to the board. "You heard her, spirit dudes. What gives?"

Jessica clears her throat. "Spirits typically need you to be really specific with your questions. Communicating can be difficult for them. How would you feel if you were disembodied energy?"

Considering I feel like disembodied energy most days, I think these fake ghosts and I would get along great.

Letting out a small sigh, I try again to appease her. "I've lived in a lot of places. Which home should I go back to?"

The candles flicker, though no breeze moves through the stone ruins. Violet and Marie exchange a wide-eyed look. Again, the wooden piece we touch moves across the board. The girls hunch over to watch, spelling out the message as the heart tip points to each letter.

"O...r...i...g...i...n," Marie finishes with a pinch in her brows. "Origin? Where are you originally from?"

Officially? No idea.

Licking my lips, I give them a smirk. "Technically Child Protective Services was called when I was found in the Pine Barrens."

Jessica's gaze sharpens with interest. "The Jersey Devil is in the Pine Barrens according to urban legend."

I don't need her knowing I was basically found on Bat Boy's doorstep, so I play it off. "You know your cryptids."

She taps her chin as she studies me. "Did you know Brim Hills has its own legend?" At my blank expression, she grins. "We're sitting in the very spot where it was born. This chapel burned down because of it."

"I get chills every time you point that out." Violet hugs herself and shudders.

"Brim Hills is host to a gate to Hell," Jessica announces.

A sharp laugh punches out of me. "Sorry, a what?"

"A gate. A pathway to Hell. The legend marks this cemetery as the spot where the gate is located."

"Come on."

"I'm serious. They're all over the world. This one first earned its reputation during the Revolutionary War. It's said that the gate is hidden, but can be opened with a ritual to call on it." Jessica plays with the end of her braid, another proud smile tugging at her lips. "But once it's opened…your fate is sealed. There's a demon guarding the gate that claims the soul of anyone who dares to call on it."

I snort. "So why bother? That sounds like a really shitty deal."

"That's the history of the gate." Violet shrugs. "People come from all over to do it. It's a test of courage."

"Have you tried this dumb death gate?" I counter.

She shakes her head, then prompts, "So are you brave enough, Lily?"

"What?"

"Open the gate. We dare you to try it." Her tone shifts from challenging to simpering. "Unless you're too scared?"

Everything clicks into place. I purse my lips. This was why they wanted me to come out here. Why they made up all that stuff about the ouija board. Classic mean girl shit. Jessica wanted to ensure the pecking order remains in place with a new girl here. She's clearly top dog amongst these three.

Part of me wants to tell her to go screw herself, resigned to spending my time in Brim Hills labeled as the uptight bitch who can't take a joke.

Then there's the other side of me. The one so tired of always making myself less for others. What—they think they can scare me with this?

The acrid phantom taste of well water in my mouth makes me swallow hard. I've survived worse than some made up legend.

Climbing to my feet, I dust off my shorts and stand over Jessica with crossed arms.

"Fine. I'll open the gate or whatever." It's not like anything will actually happen. The legend they told me is total bullshit. "Tell me what I have to do."

Three
LILY

VIOLET LEADS US OUTSIDE AFTER GATHERING THEIR STUFF into Marie's bag.

"We'll watch from down there." Jessica points to the iron gate by the road. "Good luck."

I narrow my eyes, a bolt of heat simmering in my gut. "If I survive," I say with air quotes emphasizing what I think of all this, "what will you give me? Don't think I'm doing this for nothing. I don't give a shit about what you think of my bravery."

She considers me for a moment. "A hundred bucks."

I slide my lips together. Cash would come in handy. My own stash is dwindling from what little I've scraped together in savings from my time in Philly. A month won't be long enough to get a decent job around here. No one wants a flight risk. What she promises will go toward my ticket out of here when my time is up.

"Deal."

Marie lingers as they start down the hill, dancing between the headstones like fools. "Start at the top of the steps, then descend backwards while counting to thirteen. At the bottom, you go through the archway."

She hesitates and I grow impatient. "That's it? What's supposed to happen next?"

"Once you pass through, it opens the gate to Hell." She glances out at the cemetery and plays with the zipper on her jacket. "If you see into it, the legend says you'll die before the night is out. If you survive, then you'll suffer seven nights of misfortune to drive you to madness. From what I hear, no one has made it to the seventh night without going out of their mind or dying. Either way, the gate will claim what it wants."

I chew the inside of my cheek. "Ominous."

"You'll be fine." She sounds like she's reassuring herself rather than me.

"Anyone you know done this?"

"Well... Jessica dared me to do it when I got here four years ago." She ducks her head. "I told her I did, even though I didn't. But Mrs. Talbot's son. Supposedly he did it, and that same week he got in a horrible accident. A sinkhole opened up on the road north of town and his car crashed into the crevice. One of his friends confessed to her at his funeral service that they'd been out here smoking."

"That's a really sucky coincidence."

A niggle of sympathy for Mrs. T pulls at me. To live next to this reminder of her son's last activities before he died must be a heavy weight to bear.

"All I'm saying is, I won't tell the others if you pretend to do it like I did."

"Thanks," I shoot back, not bothering to hide the bite in my tone.

She offers to cover for me, but she's still part of this, still in on the joke against me. Jessica was whispering to her before they climbed the hill—for all I know, it was her idea in the first place to dare me to run around wiggling my ass at the ruins.

Marie pulls away from me with a spurned expression. Frowning, she trudges down the hill to follow the others.

"Time to get this over with," I mumble.

Surveying the stone staircase to nowhere with disinterest, I begin to walk up them. The worn stones are slippery with soggy moss. A breath punches out of me halfway up when I lose my footing. I catch myself on the wall of the chapel ruins, stomach churning. The drop from the top step isn't too far, but it would hurt to hit the ground and crack my skull open on the large stones dotting the ground below.

If other people tried this after a rainy day like I am, I bet they slipped and fell to their death. That's probably how the legend got started.

At the top, I scuff my boot over the crumbling edge. Tiny pebbles rain down. Sighing, I spare a glance behind me and start my descent with my arms out for balance. As I go, I count to thirteen in my head. Near the bottom, the trees stop rustling, the air going dead. I can't hear the girls or anything else. The graveyard is silent except for the thud of my boots hitting the last few steps.

My gut twists. These are the types of weird occurrences that follow me everywhere.

I don't know if I'm supposed to keep up the backwards thing to go through the arch, and my last fuck has just gone missing. I'm ready to get out of here. Spinning around, I lift both middle fingers while I pass through.

As I suspected, absolutely nothing happens. I scored a hundred bucks for doing it, though.

"There," I shout to the bottom of the hill. "I did your stupid test. Happy?"

Wait. I search the graveyard again, stomach tightening. The girls are nowhere to be found. I'm alone.

A sigh gusts out of me. I knew it. I bet they're

already back in their beds laughing about getting me to do the dumb ritual. Even Marie. I'm sure she's only been nice to get me to drop my guard, but being friendly isn't enough to deceive someone with zero ability to trust others. I burned that away long ago in the fire that incinerated the Clarks' house with Mrs. Clark still inside.

For a second, I thought things could be different.

Stupid. This is what I get for going out on a limb and thinking I was worthy of trying to fit in with people. What the fuck ever. I know better and let myself get played anyway.

An odd, faint sensation tugs at me as I step away from the gate, as if an invisible tether cinches tighter around my middle the further I move.

The strange sense of déjà vu from earlier returns, like part of me recognizes the mossy clumps I've trampled beneath my feet. It's unshakeable. Violet said she could feel it, too. That to her it was like something trying to get out.

As I glare at the stone arch beneath the crumbling staircase, the shimmering air I thought I saw earlier happens again. Small, barely perceptible silvery lines that look like static electricity flicker across the gap in the stones. Then all at once they disappear and my ears pop. My hands fly up to cover them and I blink slowly several times. I imagined that, right?

I've got myself half-convinced it's all in my head until the stillness breaks with a haunting cry that causes all the hair on my body to stand on end. It sounds like someone calls out to me.

I whip around. "Hello?"

The voice sounds again, but the words are garbled, almost sounding like a different language. It's not one I understand. The words drag like a needle skipping on a warped record.

"Marie?" Silence. "Guys? Okay, haha. Very funny. I hope you filmed my reaction, because that's the last time you're getting it."

A branch snaps to my left, jolting my heart rate. The breeze picks up, the trees overhead rustling. A low, monstrous growl pierces the foggy darkness, then a hot gust moves over the back of my neck. I dart down the hill, officially less than chill.

I catch a whiff of smoke and choke on the rush of fear that clogs my throat. Not again. Please. Not now.

My sweaty hands claw at my neck. Memories of the fire assault me in sharp flashes. There's no fire. I'm in control. I repeat it to myself with each rushed step until I believe it.

Near the base of the hill, I pull up short with a harassed yelp. Three guys step out to block my path. One seems around my age, the other two maybe a little older. The girls could know them from town.

Have they been hiding out the whole time, watching from the woods?

They're tall and give off an air of danger. The shortest of them with disheveled white blond hair props a foot on one of the headstones that came to just above my knee, making it seem like it's matchbox sized next to them. He gives me a cocky wave.

His companions have a couple inches on him, the biggest of the group also the most muscular. He screams military vibes with his stiff posture, though his brown hair is longer on top and trimmed on the sides.

The last of them has thick tousled black hair and tattoos that run down his neck, continuing beneath his clothes. He licks his lips, cocking his head to the side.

One thing stands out that they have in common—their eyes. They almost seem to glow in the darkness, each a different shade of blue, green, and gold. But that's impossible. I'm not sure how they manage the effect. Maybe special contacts?

Wait—that's it. They're part of this. The girls got them to jump out and scare me after the dare. A scorching buzz builds beneath my skin. Shit. No—I have to keep myself in check.

My heart thuds as I consider my odds of making a break for it. They said the cemetery grounds circle behind Talbot House. I could run past the chapel ruins and find my way back through the woods once I lose these jerks.

"Oh." The blond guy sounds pleased, checking me out with a lingering once over. He rakes his teeth over his lower lip with a dirty groan roughing up his tone. "A girl. It's been a while since the gate's been disturbed by a woman. Hi, pretty thing. I'm going to enjoy every minute with you."

He winks and my head jerks. Horny Fuckboy taps his buddy on one of his massive arms.

"Irrelevant," the big guy barks.

The force of his voice makes me shudder. I dub him Scary Asshole.

The third guy remains quiet. Observant. He catalogs me from head to toe with a fierce scowl. His baleful gaze moves past me dismissively, sweeping the cemetery with disdain. A muscle flexes in his chiseled jaw.

"You," the brooding man clips out in a smooth British accent that feels out of place in this area. His long dark coat sweeps over the ground when he steps forward. I press my lips together, not about to talk to any of them. "You are found unworthy of the gate's secrets."

Horny pulls a face. "Why is it always you who says it?"

"Shut up, brother." Scary cuffs the back of his head.

"How about you three stop, and I'll save you the trouble," I call. "I'm out of here."

Scary Asshole shoulders past the other two, stalking toward me like I'm a bug he's eager to squash. He looks like he could annihilate someone with his foreboding glare alone. His broad muscular frame is formidable, and I can't help falling back a step when he navigates the crooked decayed headstones separating us with inexplicable speed. He must know the area well. All three of them avoid tripping over the lumpy ground while I shuffle backwards, stumbling every other step.

"Your soul is forfeit," he grits out through clenched teeth.

Ice spears through me. I ball my fists. He's certainly committed to the act. This trio of dicks are out here to freak me out. As much as I hate to admit it, they're succeeding.

"Fuck you!" The yell flies free and I forget about my efforts to keep my thoughts to myself.

They exchange eerie smirks at my snarled response, then advance on me as one, Scowly Bastard and Horny Fuckboy flanking Scary Asshole. A tremor builds in my chest until my entire body shakes with each retreating step. I keep my wide eyes locked on them. My gut tells me if I look away, things will get worse.

"That's enough. Congratulations, you hazed

the new girl in town, and scared the shit out of her in the creepy ass graveyard. Can you just—"

My blustering false bravado cuts off with a yelp when I tip over a knee-high angel statue that's half-unearthed, my ass planting hard in a damp patch of weeds. I wince, grinding my teeth against the pain of a small pebble bruising my soft thigh. Fucking *ow*, that's going to be pretty tomorrow. Lifting my fuming gaze, I find the three chucklefucks studying me with interest.

"Can we just what?" The slow curve of Horny Fuckboy's full lips is downright sinful. So is the heat brimming in his strangely bright hazel eyes as he flicks them down to the swell of my tits.

He saunters closer and crouches beside me. The scent of a snuffed out campfire tickles my nose. I don't recall smelling any firewood burning when the girls led me out to the graveyard. Minus the douchebag behavior designed to frighten me, he's handsome with a square jawline, a mess of icy white hair that swoops across his forehead, and gold contacts that are luminous in the dark, foggy night.

I lean away when he hums and strokes a long, pale finger down my cheek. His touch should make my skin crawl, yet it doesn't, stirring a strangely pleasant burst of warmth in my chest—a warmth that doesn't make me frightened of losing control.

What the—?

His mouth stretches into a smug grin and he tosses his head with a raspy laugh that twists my insides. "Get on with it? Love to. I'm as eager to have a taste as you are to be eaten, lost girl."

My lip curls, unimpressed. I'm finding it hard not to let my true feelings out, my reactions slipping free without my permission.

I don't get what's so funny to him. What's up with these jerks? Is small town, middle-of-nowheresville Pennsylvania life so boring that preying on girls at night to scare the hell out of them is their only form of entertainment?

The big guy emits a deep growl and turns to Tall, Dark and Scowly. "We need to finish her and be done with it. I hate being in this realm."

My stomach bottoms out and a wheezing breath gusts from my lungs. Finish me? What are they planning to do with me? I picture myself enduring one horrible thing after another if I don't get away, ending up chopped to little pieces sent floating down a backwoods creek in a trash bag.

Before my racing thoughts get far, strong hands lift me to my feet. Horny helps himself to feeling up my ass as he pretends to sweep dirt and grass off my shorts. He hooks a finger in my ripped fishnets and snaps them against my thigh with a pleased hum. I smack his wandering hands away, forgetting about my effort not to touch others. It's his and his cohorts' fault I fell in the first place.

He's lucky. No freak accidental burns harm him when I touch him, as they have when others catch me off guard. I need to get out of here. I'm not in the mood to play games.

Undeterred, his arms circle my waist and haul me against his firm body. A gasp slips free at how warm he is, the heat of his body enveloping mine like an embrace. It melts through his flannel shirt into my hoodie and another answering burst of foreign warmth rises in me. I stamp out the weird flutter in my stomach.

No, body. We don't get the warm fuzzies for someone when we're in danger, dummy.

"You're never any fun, tough guy." He shoots a dismissive look over his shoulder at the other two, brushing off the comment to finish me. "I want to play first. It's been too long since we've been topside. She's ours for seven nights before duty calls."

"Your lack of respect for our orders is growing old, Matthias," Scary growls across the cemetery. "I'll make good on my threats to report you for it."

"I still get the job done." Horny—Matthias—dips his nose against my neck, inhaling. I flinch, squirming to get away. Despite being leaner, he's still way stronger than he looks, easily keeping my arms pinned in his hug. "Damn, you smell really fucking good. Like toasted cinnamon. Do you taste

40

as good, too?"

A strangled shriek works its way out of me when I feel the swipe of his hot tongue trailing a path up my throat. Is—is his tongue split? Another sinful groan rumbles out of him, vibrating against my neck. My stomach dips, clashing with my desire to get out of this. The strength of the mixed reaction leaves me dizzy and confused.

"Delicious. I love that shot of fear mixed in. It makes your blood sing." He lifts me up like I weigh nothing and I struggle, fighting him with my elbows and nails. It's futile as he drags me over to the others. "She tastes incredible."

My pulse rushes in my ears as they circle around me, closing me in on all sides. Ragged panting is making me lightheaded, draining my energy. My grip on my self control is fraying.

Up close, the other two are equally handsome. A short, hysterical laugh rips from me. Three sinfully hot assholes have me at their mercy.

Scary inhales sharply, tensing. "Valerian, she's—"

"Impossible." Even as Scowly mutters the refusal, he grabs at me, tugging sharply on my hoodie to pull me in his direction.

"I'm not done yet," Matthias says in a firmer tone, his languid joking around ceasing. "The first taste wasn't enough."

Three sinister growls reverberate around me. The sounds are gravelly and primal.

"Mine," Scary rumbles.

Horror twists my features as an answering noise like a goddamn pleased purr catches in my throat. I stop it before it escapes, snapping my wide-eyed gaze back and forth. Something in the air shifts and they cage me in until I'm bumping between three hard chests, their hands roaming my body as they please.

"Alder, hold her. I want to—" Valerian's order cuts off as a surging panic takes hold of me.

Sink or swim. Hands holding me down. Well water choking me, burning, burning, burning.

"No!" I scream.

The three of them fall back as if something pushes them hard and hot air swirls around me, leaving my skin buzzing. Oh no. Did I cause that somehow?

Valerian parts his lips, giving me a calculating once over. While his companions stare at me, stunned, he keeps his wits about him.

Before any of them have the chance to make a move, I bolt for the tree line. Heat billows in my chest and tingles in my palms. My lungs burn and overwhelmed tears prick my eyes, but I don't stop. A stray grave marker almost takes me out. I manage to keep my balance and run at full speed into the woods. Branches snag on my hoodie, my fishnets, and my cheek. I grit my teeth against the flash of pain from tiny scrapes.

The only thing that matters is getting away.

Once I'm deep enough, I hide behind a tree to catch my breath. Knees shaking, I peer around it, squatting to keep out of sight of anyone tracking me.

But they're not. No one follows behind.

With a heavy sense of foreboding, I make my way back to the house, my mind rejecting everything weird that happened tonight. Those guys were there to scare me by playing up the local legend. That's all.

Four
LILY

THE DAYS THAT FOLLOW ARE FULL OF ODD SHIT, EVEN by my skewed standards. While doing Mrs. Talbot's assigned chores, I swear hands and arms reach beneath the door to the cleaning closet to swipe at me, their limbs made of smoke and shadows that disappeared when I jumped back. Marie won't come on my side of our room, swearing I speak a freaky demonic language in my sleep. And I keep catching whispers that sound like my name. I'm sure it's Jessica being a bitch.

I haven't died or gone crazy yet, so it's a win in my book. Or maybe I'm just built different, too stubborn to let it all get to me like the other idiots in Brim Hills who mess with the supposed gate to Hell. It's all in my head. As long as I remember that, it will be okay eventually.

The weirdness will stop. I just have to ignore it like always.

On the third day after the night in the graveyard, I go to bed pissed off because Jessica refuses to cough up the hundred bucks she owes me for doing the dare. She'd better watch it; I'm not above stealing if I need to. Sleep brings no relief. As soon as I'm unconscious, I'm pulled into a terrifying prison my overactive imagination has cooked up every night since I ran from the cemetery.

The dream has been the same each night. It starts me inside the chapel ruins. Except when I leave, I'm not in the graveyard, I'm in a dark fairy tale realm.

Fire rages across the strange landscape surrounding me, yet it doesn't burn when I swipe my hands through it. The chapel sits on top of a rocky hill. Above the flames that can't hurt me, the violet sky is speckled with swirling clouds and a blood red moon. Across a ravine connected by narrow bridges made of ruddy clay and vines sits a city with architecture that pierces into the air above it. The heart of the city almost looks like a forbidden castle, the highest central tower emanating a bright orange glow.

There's something about this place that feels familiar. Maybe I've had this dream before. A different version where I'm closer to the underworld-like city

45

in the distance. Or maybe it's the effect this dream has on me, instilling a sense of history I remember when I'm stuck here.

I'm over the isekai my subconscious has made up. Lucky for me, all I have to do is step off the hill to leave the fake fantasy world. Unluckily, it sends me into another part of the dream that forces me to relive a version of the worst night of my life. I tug at the long, regal skirt of the gown I'm dressed in, scuffing my toe against a rock. I watch it tumble down the hill into the ravine. I can't stand dreams like this, being aware and retaining my memory of being through the dream before, but unable to change it or get myself out without moving forward.

Balling my fists in the fine material of the dress, I take a running leap into darkness. Uncomfortable pressure chokes me from all sides until I fight my way up from beneath the hot water in the tub. Mrs. Clark's fingers dig harder into my skin.

"It's not right. Unnatural. I have to fix it. Have to fix it," she wails before shoving my small head under again.

I splutter through frantic tears, limbs flailing to get her off me, clinging to my will to survive. Everything is too hot, burning, burning, burning. It hurts, the ache to breathe like a cavern dug out of my tiny chest.

At last, I'm out of the bathtub. The water

bubbles, steam filling the room. My skin is pink and I'm quaking all over. My foster brother, Mrs. Clark's son, shakes me by my shoulders, shouting unintelligible words my brain can't decipher while asleep. Then he freezes as his skin bubbles and puckers until it melts off his arms, leaving behind sinewy muscle tissue and exposed bone. He glares at me like it's my fault.

Then the dream shifts and I'm outside alone, watching the Clarks' house burn to ash, swallowed by roaring flames.

Jolting awake, I scramble to a seated position and scrub my flushed face with a trembling hand as ragged breaths scrape my throat. My heart races and I question if I really am going crazy. Three fucking nights in a row I've endured that hellish vision.

The way it plays out in the dream isn't what happened. He did stop her, but the fire was after. One minute I was screaming hysterically, the next fire spread out from my feet to swallow everything in its path. We made it out. She never emerged from the inferno. And he didn't glare at me. His look of fear is one of the only things permanently carved into my mind from that night.

Swallowing hard, I check the clock on Marie's side of the room. It's a little past four. My roommate sleeps peacefully like she didn't have a hand in fucking me over, her features lax and a string of drool trailing from the corner of her mouth. My brows flatten. There's no way I'll sleep after that unpleasant trip down memory lane. Might as well get up now.

Screw waiting the full seven days. I'm sick of getting myself so worked up I have to keep reliving my worst nightmare.

I keep myself occupied for the next two hours once I creep downstairs, the creaky steps memorized after that first night we all snuck out. The library doesn't open until eight. First I'll need to deal with Mrs. T.

She pokes her head in the kitchen with a suspicious squint at ten to six and finds me on my hands and knees scrubbing the floor with vigor. This is above and beyond my assigned chores on the rotation schedule. It's also the only way I can erase the feeling of my foster mom's bony fingers digging into my skin, the hard floor and stringent chemicals stinging my nose reminding me where I am.

"What are you doing?"

"Exactly what it looks like. Chores."

She allows a beat of silence. "Why?"

"Couldn't sleep."

She doesn't question me further, skirting around me to make coffee. She sets an extra mug on the counter and leaves it for me before she goes to make sure the other girls get up. I don't touch it. Not because I don't like it, but because I've learned time and again never to trust anyone's random acts of kindness. They don't exist. They're more myth than the stupid local urban legend.

Five
LILY

Mrs. Talbot lets me out for free time early with far less pushback than I expected. Whatever she saw in me in the early hours, scrubbing the floor so hard my arms are sore, she's left me alone today.

While the other girls are stuck in the house enduring the matron's homeschooling, I walk along the side of the sun-dappled road to head into town. I've skipped my fishnets today for knee high socks, a flared tan corduroy miniskirt with suspenders, and a black v-neck shirt that makes my cleavage look amazing. The sleeves are long enough to hide my scarred hands if I want to.

These are my comfort clothes, my own brand of armor that helps me feel empowered and in control of my life—what little control I can take for myself.

When I feel good about the way I look, it gives me the courage to take on the judgmental as fuck world.

I give the rusted iron gate to Brim Hills Cemetery the middle finger on my way past and cross the road at the next bend to walk through the red covered bridge. As far as I'm concerned, the night I met those three guys there after completing my dare was a cruel prank. I refuse to even acknowledge the strange things that happened as anything more than a psychological break born of the potent high of adrenaline combined with fear. The girls hyped up a legend and my mind played right into it to create a hellish night of terror. Same goes for the nightmares and things I've seen from the corner of my eye in the last few days.

Today I'm getting some damn answers to put it all behind me. I need reassurance to confirm my past troubles aren't returning to haunt me.

The main street in town is just as desolate and depressing when I arrive as it was my first day here. At least the early October crispness in the air feels good against my flushed skin. I haven't quite cooled down from my crack of dawn self care cleaning session, despite showering. My body has always run hot and once it warms up, it's difficult to regulate my temperature. One of my foster placements told me it must be a redhead thing, because no one else she knew would go around in shorts in the middle

51

of an upstate New York winter.

Crossing the road at the movie theater with more empty display posters than filled, I enter the library. It's a cramped, single-floor establishment that has a stale scent hanging in the air. One librarian sits at the counter by the door, though I'm not sure if he's a real person or a gargoyle statue. The temptation to wave a hand in front of his face for a reaction makes me pause.

I scan the shelves, wondering if they stock any manga. In a backwater place like this, I doubt it. If I'm lucky, maybe they carry Naruto. It's not my style, but since I'm stuck here I'll take anything. Pressing on my toes, I frown when I find the stacks only go three deep. Sighing, I go to the computer cubicles in the back corner, missing the city's bigger libraries.

There are three ancient desktops that look older than I am. I'm talking birth of the Internet-era hardware. I take the middle one, considering that it could be worse. At least they have computers.

Booting up takes forever. Once I'm logged into a guest account, I open a search engine and type in *Brim Hills Cemetery*. Results bombard me—news stories for disappearances that span decades, the graveyard being condemned, even a paranormal activity study. The link near the bottom of the page claims to be a full detailed history of the town.

I skim over the article's introduction explaining

the town was founded by Quaker settlers and the boring details about the small, close-knit population. It goes on to describe the town's notoriety centering on the urban legend that gained attention and earned its spot on the list of death dares like the legends of Bloody Mary and the Candy Man popular amongst teens.

Those said to disturb the gate to Hell in Brim Hills Cemetery will suffer fiery visions and psychological torment. Several deaths and disappearances are claimed to be linked to the condemned site.

"Yeah right," I mumble, reading on.

Brim Hills was originally named for the smell of brimstone early settlers claimed blanketed the town. They marked it as a bad omen, but remained in the area. In 1929, a sulfur pocket was discovered in the nearby hills. This underground pocket connects to the coal mine system.

Backing out, I pick another article that talks about local fires spreading across central Pennsylvania. This one talks about Centralia, a town not far from here.

The mine fire in Centralia is situated on a coal seam and has been burning underneath the borough since 1962. The fire's original cause is still debated. Many mines and roads have been closed due to the dangers of deterioration. This seam runs at least an 8 mile stretch and connects to the now closed mines of Brim Hills.

Well, that explains a lot. I haven't noticed the

sulfur smell, but I did pick up a smoky scent in the graveyard. These coal mine fires could be what inspired all of the stories about the Hell gate legend.

Getting an idea, I type *gates to Hell* in the search bar. Jackpot. At least ten other so-called Hell gates pop up and tout themselves as *the* doorway to the Devil. There's another version of the legend in Alabama, Colorado, Indiana, New York, and Washington. They're all over.

Some of the stories are way more fascinating and complex than the ritual I did. I get sucked into reading about the debate between the Devil picking one supposed spot because of witch hangings or because the graves of his children are there.

"Visitors are greeted by a ghost, then pushed down and left with the mark of the Devil? People are so imaginative."

I jump at the cool accented voice behind me. Angling my head, I find Valerian towering over me, tattooed hands braced on either side of my cubicle, looking very gothic prince standing in the middle of the small town library in dark clothes with his textbook bad boy trench coat sweeping the ground. His dark hair falls across his angular face, lips twisted in a mercurial frown.

"Do you mind? It's rude to look over people's shoulders," I snap.

He lifts a brow. "I do mind. You're wasting my

time."

I match my expression to his. When he doesn't move, I shoo him, growing agitated that he has the nerve to stroll up to me after what he did. "Then leave me alone. I don't want to see you or your asshole friends again."

I press my lips together. What is it about them that makes me unable to control my tongue or hold back my true thoughts and reactions?

He shakes his head. "I told you the consequence for opening the gate. You've sealed your own fate, just as others have before you. It's your price to pay."

His grip flexes on the cubicle walls and he leans over me to cage me in further. His handsome features shift from annoyance to something intense and hungry. God, those impossibly blue eyes are striking. In the light of day I can tell they aren't trick contacts, they're simply that brilliant, unique color. The raspy sound that catches in his throat makes my insides coil tightly. I hold my breath, pressing my thighs together against the flood of liquid heat.

This is different from the odd, instinctive sensations that teased my body the other night, less primal and wild. I'm in control. Yet I still don't want to feel any attraction towards this pompous bastard.

Shoulders tensing, Valerian moves one tattooed hand as if he's going to touch my hair, then drops it, his expression shuttering with precise control. "The sooner I'm rid of you, the better."

Damn him for being a total jerk because his British accent is like a smooth caress, even when he's irritated.

"The feeling's mutual," I grumble.

At least whatever weird Stockholm Syndrome I experienced at the cemetery isn't happening now. The heat from a moment ago fades as my anger at him returns. I'm glad. Out of everything, that was the strangest part of the night. I might not have any clue what I'm doing when it comes to guys, but I never expected to practically melt the first time one touched me. Seriously, yikes at myself for—for—I won't even name my reaction while faced with the precarious situation I was in.

"If you want to get rid of me, you can start by backing off. I'm leaving." I lift my chin, giving in to the urge to speak my mind instead of keeping my thoughts chained in place as usual. "In fact, just wait until Halloween in a few weeks. As soon as I turn eighteen, I'm leaving Brim Hills in the dust."

A dark, amused huff leaves him. "You think I'll let you escape? Go ahead. Run. Wherever you go, we'll find you."

Narrowing my eyes, I push up from my chair, satisfied when he inhales sharply and gives up his ground rather than touch me. That's more like it. I sock him in the arm, shoving aside the flash of fear that tells me bad things happen if I touch others. He makes another humored sound. It's creepy to see him laughing, his brooding sneer turning into a vicious smirk.

"Was that feeble attack meant to hurt me?" He tilts his head so his tousled dark hair falls in his face. "None of you ever learn."

"That's for the other night. Fuck you and your buddies for the trick you played on me. Did the girls at Talbot House put you up to it?"

I shut down the computer, ignoring the press of his eyes on my back. In the reflection of the monitor, I find his attention locked on the swell of my round ass. Gritting my teeth, I shove past him and make for the exit. I got the explanation I came here for. No more nightmares for me. The corner of my mouth lifts until I register Valerian's smoky, slightly bitter scent and the thud of his boots.

"Are you still following me?" I imitate his accent and moody tone. "I thought you wanted to be rid of me."

He waits until we're on the cracked sidewalk in front of the building, almost sounding like it costs him to admit, "You…smell different than most humans. It's the only thing that's earned you our mercy so far. A mere curiosity we wish to satisfy before fulfilling our duty."

Great, now he's insulting me. Is he kidding me?

I smell?

"Sorry for offending you," I sneer. "The deodorant provided by group homes is the cheapest the state budget can skate by with."

His brow furrows as he stares at me. I get the vibe that he's the brains between the three of them, the type who doesn't get surprised easily because he's already thought of every possible outcome of a situation. For all I know, I've crossed a small-time gang that believes they run this town. A bit out of place for middle of nowhere Pennsylvania, but the powerful way he holds himself fits, like he doesn't believe anyone can go up against him and win.

"You're impossible." His mutter seems to be meant more for himself than in response to me. "Such a strange black cat. I will figure out what you are."

Impossible. The same thing he said in the graveyard.

Oddly, the word resonates, colliding with me like a brick to the chest. I swallow past the lump that lodges in my throat and whirl to tell him off for being the world's biggest douche. Except—he's gone.

The words die on my tongue as I glance around. How did he muffle his footsteps? Whatever. I don't care.

I smirk, continuing down the main road while picturing him scurrying away to keep the mysterious illusion that he can simply vanish. He probably squeezed his sexy, emo ass down one of the tight alleyways that run between the shops.

A curiosities storefront catches my attention. I missed this during the drive in. Stopping, I peer at the items on display. It's interesting until I spot something that makes me roll my eyes—a homemade pamphlet on the cemetery. The headline reads *open the gate...if you dare*. Ugh, stupid legend crap.

"Hey, pretty thing," a charming voice says behind me. "I missed you. Couldn't stand watching from afar anymore. Are you on an adventure today?"

I spin to face another guy from the graveyard. Matthias, the flirty fuckboy with handsome boyish features. He leans against the brick exterior, messy white blond hair moving in the wind and full lips curved in an easy, lopsided smile complete with a damn dimple.

Small fucking town. I resign myself to the torment of running into the guys who pranked me for the next few weeks until I ditch this place.

Unlike his morose counterpart, Matthias wears a distressed band t-shirt that looks vintage and stretches perfectly around his biceps, black jeans with the knees sliced open, and a flannel shirt tied around his hips. It gives me a good view of the tattoos decorating his arms. The ink is a collection of styles and trends, everything from a badass lunar moth to a bright blue dolphin that would seem random if the rest weren't also such an eclectic mix.

Shit. If I didn't hate him for taking part in the prank on me, I would totally be into him. Compared to the others, he gives off a more approachable vibe, and the mischief dancing in his golden eyes entices me.

This day is shaping up to suck big time. What have I done to deserve this?

Existed, a poisonous corner of my mind whispers.

I huff to dispel the sting piercing my throat. "Watching from afar? Stalker. Why are you following me, too?"

The side of his mouth tugs higher as he checks me out without bothering to hide the sensual drag of his gaze. "Why wouldn't I? You're a knockout."

"I know I look good." I lift a brow at his grin. No, not every curvy girl spends her days lamenting her body image, thanks very much. "How about the real answer?"

Matthias strokes his chin, his playful demeanor sharpening to seriousness. He glances around as if he's making sure we're alone before he murmurs, "I'm drawn to you. The taste I got wasn't enough. It will never be enough."

When the words leave him, my heart gives a strange flutter and my chest tightens. His gaze holds mine, those gold eyes brightening as if they're glowing. But that's impossible. A trick of the light reflecting off the glass. I can't look away, my heartbeat thudding.

The moment passes when he pops off the wall, relaxed once more. "It must be the thrill. I haven't been topside in years. Come on." He plucks on the suspenders of my skirt with a cheeky wink and nods down the street. "There's a record shop at the end of this block. Every time I go in, I find gold."

No. I should definitely turn around and go the other way.

He can't win me over with that cocky smile after pranking me with his friends. Even if he did, it would end. He's definitely a player that can't be tied down, and I'm not keeper material. *Lily the reject.*

Yet I go with him, because I'm a glutton for punishing myself with the things I'll never have. Has it come to this? My desperation for any scrap of attention someone's willing to throw my way is so bad, I'll go along with a cute boy—one that was mean to me—just for a moment of *what if*. Whatever, I have to, anyway. Talbot House is that direction.

He ducks into the record shop and I hesitate on the threshold before following, expecting him to flip the switch and be a dick again any second. At least with the other two it's easy to hate them—with him, his open flirtatiousness with a dash of golden retriever energy throws me off from how he acted in the graveyard. I watch him carefully, waiting for the switch to flip back to asshole mode.

"Does anyone even listen to records anymore?" I trail after him, tapping my fingertips on the cardboard sleeves while he eagerly thumbs through a punk rock section.

"If they don't, they're idiots. Vinyl is the superior medium." He picks one, flipping it over to scan the back. His broad grin steals my breath. "It produces the best sound. Here. Like this."

He captures my wrist and tugs me to an old school record player set up with headphones. The side of his full lips curls up and he flashes me an impish glance, disheveled blond hair covering one of his eyes as he sets up the record. When he puts the headphones on for me, his gold eyes bounce between mine, nimble fingers moving through my hair. I'm trapped in his stare while the record starts, my pulse thrumming.

The song he picked is about a pair of runaways looking for something to make them feel alive. His grin grows while I listen, eagerly watching my reaction.

"See? It's unbeatable. The lyrics, the melody, it all sounds better and makes you want to hit the road." He brushes his fingers over my chest, and I let him, not pulling back when I'd usually jerk out of reach. "It resonates here."

I push the headphones off, skin still tingling from the contact. "Or I could just listen to as many songs as I want on my phone instead of keeping this cumbersome stuff."

He mutters something about MP3 players until I take my phone out. The thing is ancient, the touchscreen cracked, but it works. I don't get a data plan, so any public wifi is a blessing. After three days here, I've learned that this town barely understands what wifi is.

My phone catches his attention and he grabs it from me, ignoring my miffed protest. He turns it back and forth, tapping the apps and making a delighted noise with each one he opens. I slide my lips together, fighting off the thought that he's kind of adorable. Each one of those excited sounds causes something to unfurl in my chest.

"These things have come far. Last time I was here, they folded in half."

Clearing my throat, I raise a brow at the strange remark and snatch it back. "Well, everything about this place seems stuck in the past. There's nothing to do, the wifi is nonexistent and—" I squash the expanding sensation in my chest and give him an unimpressed glance. "—the people are pretty shitty. Basically, it blows here."

"Welcome to Brim Hills, lost girl." Matthias

chuckles darkly, swiping his tongue along his lip. I don't know why I thought it was split before. It seems normal now.

My eyes narrow as he returns to flipping through the bins of records in the musty shop. "Why the hell do you keep calling me that? You and your buddies each decide on a nickname to keep hazing me with?"

He shrugs lazily. "Dunno. You feel lost."

It hits too close to home, leaving me unsettled. I worry my lip with my teeth and back away. I should go, but each time I take a step toward the door an odd instinct stops me, pulling me back.

There's something about him that makes me think he would understand what it's like to feel so lost all the time. I don't know why, but watching the way he lights up at little things like finding a record by a band he likes makes me want to know more.

Toying with the edge of a record sleeve, I grapple with the urge to drop my guard, to give up something about myself. When I do that, I leave myself raw and vulnerable, and every time I end up hurt. It's why I've learned to keep my walls up and dull myself for self preservation.

The minute I start to respond, Matthias stiffens with a frown. Setting his jaw, he shoots a glare through the window of the shop. I don't see anything on the street to put him in a mood.

He nods curtly. "Fine." With a tetchy sigh, he abandons the records he picked out and heads for the door. "Sorry to cut this short."

The corners of my mouth tighten, holding in what I was going to say. There's the flipped switch. It comes every time without fail.

I follow him out. "Yeah." My voice is back to being flat. "I have to go, too."

"See you soon, lost girl. I wish…" The smile he gives me this time is tinged with a hint of regret. He laughs, shaking his head. "Nah. Never mind. It's a shame it's not meant to be. Alder would maim me. And then Vale would finish me off."

A beat up truck rolls by with its sad excuse for a muffler rumbling. I watch it chug down the road, gathering my courage. It's the first time in so long I've wanted to keep a conversation going. I open my mouth to ask what he means, but just like his broody partner in crime, he gives me the slip by the time I turn around.

This time it leaves an empty feeling hollowing out my chest and a burning sensation in my stomach. Always left behind. Always unwanted.

Not meant to be, like he said. At least the others are upfront with being shitty. He's more dangerous because he made me think for a second that I could actually let my guard down. He's still toying with me, the prank in the cemetery not enough to entertain him. Fuck them all. And double fuck him.

I blink away the tears that blur my vision, bitter hatred reigniting not just for Matthias, but for everything and everyone that's ever come and gone in my life.

The walk back feels twice as long, everything less vibrant than this morning—the autumn leaves on the sycamore trees, the red paint on the covered bridge, the satisfaction of finding the answers I wanted.

The entire way it feels like someone— some*thing*—watches me.

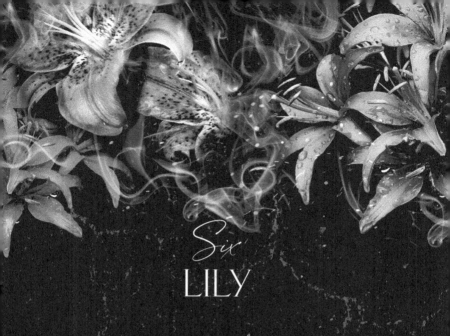

Six

LILY

WHEN MY EYES SNAP OPEN IN THE MIDDLE OF THE night, my pulse races. I lay still beneath the floral quilt in the dark, trying to get my brain to work. I wasn't having a nightmare. After I went to the library two days ago, I stopped having the same dream of the fake fantasy world my mind invented.

So why…?

Movement from the corner of my eye makes my heart stumble violently. A gasp catches in my throat as the huge shadow moves into the moonlight.

A large hand covers my mouth before I release the scream building in my lungs.

"Hush."

It's Alder. The last of my shadows.

I grab his wrist and squeeze hard, digging

my nails in. He brings his face close to mine, near enough that I can make out his unaffected smirk in the faint light filtered through the curtains. Forcing out a pissed breath through my nose, I react without thinking, attacking hard enough to break skin.

He flexes his grip, giving my jaw a little shake before he lets go without even a grimace of pain. I want to scream just to spite him. Sitting up, I press my back against the wall, bringing my knees up.

"What. The. Fuck?" I hiss. "Are you psychotic? How did you get in here?"

How long was he there watching me before I woke up?

Alder emits a gravelly rumble, jerking his chin at the window. I gape, eyes sliding from his massive build to the tiny window.

"You've got to be shitting me," I whisper-shout.

Across the room, Marie snuffles in her sleep and rolls over. My death grip tightens on the blanket. Oh god, if she wakes up—

"She will not wake," he mutters. "No one will while I'm here."

Is that a cryptic and creepy way of telling me he killed everyone else in the house? Dosed them? What is wrong with him? This is taking their odd obsession with messing with me too far.

My chest tightens. Even if I report him for breaking in, no one believes me when I'm in trouble.

68

Sharp sensations prickle across my palms.

Licking my lips, I fight to control my rapid breathing. He can't hurt me. He *won't*. If he tries anything…I'll lose control, like I always do when I let go of my emotions.

"How did you even find me?" My eyes widen. I knew I felt someone's gaze on me the other day. "Did you also follow me? Have you been watching me?"

He crosses his arms, making his rugged muscles appear bigger. "I tracked you by your scent, little stray."

My shoulders go rigid. What the fuck?

Pursing my lips, I subtly run my fingers through my hair and angle my head to take a sneaky whiff, checking if I stink. His friend insulted the way I smell, too.

"What are you?" he rasps. "Vale was right, your scent is…"

His gruff words trail off. Leaning in, he touches my hair, thick fingers sliding through it until he gives the short ends a light tug. Nothing about it is threatening. It feels sort of nice, which pisses me off. With an uneven breath, I lift my hand to bat him away. He grabs my wrist, his touch hot against my skin.

"Scars." I shudder at the fierce way he says it, the deep, angry rumble vibrating through my body.

"Burns," I correct harshly, even though scars is right.

Clenching his jaw, he examines my hand and follows the old wounds from my childhood up my arm. His piercing green gaze is intense and inescapable when it meets mine once more, even in the dark when I shouldn't be able to discern the vibrant color.

Each tiny movement I make, Alder tracks with the hunger of a predator, a hunter. If I run...he'll chase me until he catches me. Maybe push me face down into the dirt, wrap his huge hands around my hips and—

I slam down on the direction of my thoughts, chest heaving. When Valerian dared me to run, it sounded sinister, a challenge I would accept just to piss him off, but thinking about being hunted by Alder sends fire into my veins. The idea of doing anything with a man I hate should repulse me, but it has the opposite effect, my nipples pebbling beneath my camisole. He watches that too with a gleam in his hypnotic eyes and a ghost of a smirk tugging at the corner of his mouth.

"Stop it." I wrench my wrist from his firm grip. Screw my last few weeks as a ward of the state in the system. I don't want to stick around if it means living in close proximity to them. "I'm over this game. If you guys don't stop stalking me, I'm out of here."

"I'll always know how to find you. I'll enjoy it every time I have to hunt you down until we fulfill our duty and take what's ours." He frowns, backing away. He holds my gaze a beat longer, as if he wants to memorize me before tearing his attention away. "Time is almost up."

A shiver races down my spine at his deadly tone. I search for something to throw at him without taking my eyes off him. Marie's clock is too far, and my pillow won't make a satisfactory weapon. Phone it is. Gritting my teeth, I reach for it beneath my pillow. He watches, completely unthreatened.

Oh yeah?

With a vicious grunt I lob it right at his head, crowing in triumph when it clocks him across his brow. His head jerks and he allows my phone to clatter to the floor. Regret fills me immediately when he's unharmed. I probably just broke my phone for nothing.

"Shit," I bite out, scooting to the edge of the mattress to rescue my phone.

When I look up, Alder has vanished, melting into the shadows like a fucking creeper. Just like the others. I sit up all night, unable to go back to bed in case he comes back and decides to smother me in my sleep after all once he's finished sniffing me.

The seventh day comes and goes and I'm still here, so take that legend. I knew it was all fake.

Each day that passes helps me breathe easier.

It's not until halfway through the following week that I realize between my encounters with all three of them that I talked more to those assholes—and didn't hide the sarcastic remarks I'd normally keep to myself—more than I have in years. It's noticeable because I've spent the last four days practically silent around Mrs. T, Marie, and the other girls in the house. A new girl arrived this week, the youngest out of all of us, and Mrs. T is already marking the days on the calendar until I'm gone so the newbie can have my bed instead of the pullout couch.

The sooner my birthday comes on Halloween, the sooner I can get out of this town. Two more weeks. I can make it through that.

It's dark when I'm done poking my head in every single shop on the main street looking for part-time work. They all turned me down. I figured, but I had to try. I really need money to get me started once I age out.

"That hundred bucks you're gatekeeping is mine, Jessica." I cross my arms over my chest and ignore the sidelong looks from an older couple passing me.

I mull over my options. I could try the diner again. Diners always need help. I'd rather do that than hustle home to make it for Mrs. Talbot's house dinner.

When I turn to head back the direction I came, hands grab at me, yanking on my cropped hoodie and my high-waisted shorts. Before I so much as flail or scream, they cover my mouth. I'm lifted off the ground and carried down one of the narrow alleys between the buildings with my legs kicking. I suck in stinging, forceful breaths through my nose and aim a merciless elbow jab at the guy holding me. He grunts.

"I warned you, Lily Sloane," Valerian growls in my ear. "Time to pay the price. For all the trouble you've caused us, your soul is going to taste so fucking sweet. No more mercy, no matter what you are. You're done."

Oh shit. Oh *shit*.

My struggling becomes more frantic, survival mode kicking in. He sounds way too serious, making me uneasy. This doesn't feel like it's about a stupid prank. I thought I'd escaped and they'd knock it off. We're well past the seven nights crap they mentioned in the graveyard to freak me out. The anxiety I kept at bay when they taunted me for a week floods back in a dizzying rush.

How does he know my name? Alder creeping into my room in the middle of the night last week springs to mind. I bet anything he scoped out my name taped to the door.

No matter how hard I kick and flail, I can't get free. Valerian holds me with minimal effort, moving further into the shadowy alley. Once he's satisfied, he dumps me on my feet and slams my back against the wall. I wince, smothering a pained sound.

"Fucking bastard," I spit.

"Hold her," he commands.

I freeze when he steps away, Matthias taking his place when he melts out of the darkness. He grasps my waist, pinning me in place with equally little effort while Valerian leans against the brick wall beside us, watching with an infuriating cunning gaze. It probably helps that I stopped struggling, too stunned to process what's happening like a dumb bitch inviting death and worse things by not fighting my way out of this.

Snapping out of it, I blurt out the first thing that comes to mind. "What about vinyl?"

"Duty calls." Matthias' mutter is detached, void of his typical carefree spirit. The hard glint in those gold eyes that were so warm when he looked at me in the record shop squeezes my heart. "Even though your scent's got us curious, you opened the gate. That's not a fate I can save you from. It is what it is, lost girl."

What, are they part of a cult that kills people and covers it up with the urban legend of the gate?

"No." I shake my head, flinching as he massages my waist. "No, it's not real. You're being crazy. It was a dare. A stupid fucking prank."

He nods with a sigh, pressing a quick kiss to my forehead. I pound my fists against his chest, hatred welling in me until it feels like I'll burst. My palms prickle with a needle-like sensation and I swear the ground beneath us tremors. Fear rockets through me, making it difficult to breathe.

"You're sure? No take backs." Matthias directs the question at Valerian, studying my face in wonder. "You feel that, right? Because that's not me."

"I knew I should've brought Alder instead," Valerian grits out. "Just end the girl, collect her soul, and be fucking done with it. This fascination has run its course. We're over the limit. If we don't return to our guard posts, we're in a heap of shit with the council."

End me. Take my soul. Those are not euphemisms.

This is definitely not a mean joke to haze me. They're serious. Who the hell are they?

"I know how this works, Vale. Shut up."

"Then stop stalling."

They argue as if I'm not here and the topic isn't

take Lily's miserable soul. I guess it doesn't matter if I hear.

"My vote is hell fucking no," I screech. "Get off me!"

Matthias closes his fingers around my throat and croons to me like I'm a frightened animal. It's not as soothing as he thinks because I'm still riding high on terror and adrenaline.

I gulp as he buries his face in my neck and inhales. "Mm, toasted cinnamon. Double shot of fear." He licks, the sensation of his tongue being split back, just like that night. "Delicious."

Releasing a shrill yell, I aim a shot at his groin with my knee. He deflects it with a low chuckle, pinning me to the wall with his body so I can't move. My heart beats so fast my head swims. I gulp for air, mind racing for a way out of this.

Valerian bats Matthias' hand away, replacing it with his own. He wrenches my face to look at him. Out of the corner of my eye, the ink covering his skin moves of its own volition along his forearm, slinking beneath his pushed up sleeves. Freaked out and sure my brain has broken, I try to look at his tattoos. Both of them hold me in place, pinned between the wall, Matthias' body plastered against mine, and Valerian towering at my side to block my view of the alley.

"I told you, darling." His dangerous rasp fans over my lips, those haunting blue eyes dipping to my mouth. Transfixed, he drags his thumb along it. "There's no escape. Be a good girl and die for me."

His command sends a shiver through me, my fear sliced through by the shot of arousal ignited by his crisp, domineering order. Twisting free of his grasp, I spit. Saliva splatters his face, hitting him across his mouth and chin.

He stills. Trapping me in his penetrating gaze, he licks his lips, tasting my saliva. I gulp at how wrongly attractive it is when he does it. He lets go of me and swipes the rest away. The veins on his hand stand out prominently against his tattoos.

"Slit her throat," Valerian orders.

"I have a better idea." Matthias' teeth scrape my neck, making me jolt at how sharp they are. His words take on a musical quality that echoes around me as if I'm in a dream world. My rapid pulse slows from a frantic rush, my fear overtaken. His voice sounds so nice, it makes me want to do anything he says. "What if I fuck her to death? You can watch."

The arousal intensifies at his suggestion, spilling through me. My mind short-circuits and a strained gasp tears past my lips. I hate them, but—

"Look at you, pretty thing. You like that idea? Your cheeks turned such a delicious shade of pink." Matthias' eyes are so bright, the gleaming gold ensnaring me so I can't look away. I need to fight him off, but I can't remember why. All I'm aware of is how much I want is his devious mouth on every inch of me. "Which part? Vale watching? Riding my cock until your very last breath?"

With each lilting, oddly echoey question, he brushes a kiss lower and lower down my throat until he reaches the crook of my neck. A dizzying inferno of desire builds inside me. Yes. *Yes.* I want to do what he suggested. He swipes his tongue out to taste my flushed skin, then brings his lips to my ear to release a rough, filthy groan of pleasure that makes me shudder.

"You taste so good," he murmurs.

This is insane. I need to get away. Scream. Run. Anything.

My limbs don't obey. Why can't I move? Why am I so into this? Do I have a death wish after all?

Darting a look at Valerian, the corners of his mouth twist with a sinister smirk like he can read every thought flitting through my head. The press of his gaze has me burning up while Matthias drags his hands down to my hips and grinds the hard ridge of his dick against my stomach.

Matthias buries his face in my neck again, lips brushing my sensitive skin. "Fuck, I want to split your pussy apart with my cock, lost girl. Split you in pieces."

My core throbs. I smother the cry that tries to escape me, arching into him. His sinful, smoky words have the opposite effect on me than I expect when I'm not sure if he's talking in the literal sense or not. They ignite an inexplicable need in my veins stronger than I've ever known, one as strange as that purring noise I made in the graveyard when the three of them circled me. It comes on hot and fast, intensifying when he chuckles in approval. Hooking a hand beneath my thigh, he wraps it around his body and angles his hard bulge between my legs, right against my center.

Stars explode and my head tips back against the brick at the divine friction. What he's doing to me feels amazing. My hips move, my throbbing clit seeking more as my insides wind into a tight knot.

"Oh god," I choke hoarsely.

"No gods here, darling," Valerian says. "Only demons."

He's transfixed on my exposed neck. He brushes his tattooed knuckles down my overheated skin, eliciting another embarrassing, needy whimper from me while Matthias slides a hand beneath my cropped hoodie. He licks his lips with measured precision and I swear the tip of his tongue is forked like a snake. Matthias latches his mouth onto one side of my neck and Valerian dips his head, hot breath coasting over my thrumming pulse. He pauses before his lips connect with my skin and my body is hyperaware of the small distance he keeps between us.

For the first time ever, I'm burning up without being afraid of the explosion, without being afraid of whatever freakish thing will happen. I don't care, all I need is more of this. The world around me can burn to ash if I can have more of this.

Lifting his head, Valerian catches my chin and watches the shift of pleasure across my features, the parting of my lips and fluttering of my eyelashes as Matthias torrents my neck.

"Are you going to come for him?" Valerian asks.

"Please." I crave what comes next, needing more. I don't want this to stop.

A wild thought crosses my mind that sends another wave of heat spiraling through me—both of them touching me. Matthias taking me against the brick wall, but instead of watching, Valerian's mouth claiming mine in a heady, heart-stopping kiss while Matthias fills my pussy.

The cry that bursts from me is out before I can stop it. There's no fighting what I'm feeling, nothing to stop this crazy pull winding tighter. Matthias' touch is like a drug and with Valerian watching intently, I'm close to shaking apart, the tightly-wound coil of need about to snap and tip me over the edge into oblivion.

My heavy-lidded gaze drops to Valerian's lips. He emits a rough, dominant rumble, hovering his mouth over mine. Another rock of Matthias' hips makes my breath hitch. I'm so close.

"Christ, I can smell how wet you are. How much you need it, pretty girl. Doesn't she smell incredible, Vale?"

"These need to come off." Valerian tugs at the waistband of my shorts.

I gasp at how sharp Matthias' fingers feel against me beneath my hoodie, his fingertips becoming points that tease my bra. The same sharpness traces my hip. Dropping my attention to Valerian's hand, I freeze. His fingers shift before my eyes, lengthening into coal colored talons. When Matthias pulls away from my neck to grin at me, I gape at the pointed teeth in his smug, hungry smile.

Fangs. Glowing eyes. Absurd strength. Moving tattoos. *Claws.*

My heart beats hard, awareness slicing through some of the thick haziness keeping logic at bay.

"What the fuck?" I whisper.

There's no way to fool myself to explain what I'm seeing. These aren't magic tricks. I just watched them transform, changing from human to—to—monsters. I was about to fuck a legit monster.

If monsters are real, that means the legend is true. All those things I didn't want to believe I saw actually happened.

No gods here, darling. Only demons. Oh god. An

unpleasant tingle spreads across my body. Demons. That's what they are.

"Matthias." The curt urgency in Valerian's tone erases the last of my daze.

"Damn it," Matthias grumbles. "Now? It was just getting good."

My head pounds as the aftereffects of whatever hypnotic shit he did to me ebbs away. I screw my eyes shut to block out everything I don't want to handle right now. One of them—Matthias, I think—murmurs goodbye and caresses my cheek.

When I open them, I'm alone—again. They let me go, vanishing into the night.

This time, I don't know if I hope to never see them again, or if I wish they'd finished what they started. They didn't kill me. Doesn't mean they won't try again.

My jaded, scarred heart gives a painful throb. It's not like anyone would miss me if they succeeded. The world will be glad to be rid of troubled, difficult Lily Sloane. Maybe I'll get a cool do-over in a different kind of world like in my favorite isekai manga.

I sag against the wall to remain upright. The comedown from whatever Matthias did to me with his glowing gold eyes is a bitch, leaving me dizzy and thirsty. My mind is still twisted up in how into it I was, how I was moments from letting them do anything they wanted with me. Why do weird as fuck things have to follow me everywhere I'm bounced around?

A scuffle against the concrete makes me jump. I whip my head to the other end of the alley. A shopkeeper with a grizzly beard dumps trash at the back end of the alley and peers around. Spotting me in the shadows, he takes a step in my direction.

"Alright, miss?" he asks.

"Yup." Nope.

He takes another step. "Why don't you come inside?"

Are his eyes a little too bright, or am I still reeling from the adrenaline rush from an encounter with demons?

"No thanks. I've got to go."

Gathering all my strength, I push off the wall and hurry back to the main road. My heartbeat doesn't slow down, my thoughts a racing mess I can't make sense of.

I never should have gone to the graveyard and done the dare.

Seven

LILY

MY LONG SKIRT SWISHES AROUND ME AS I MAKE my way down a long hall with pillars and an arched, intricately carved ceiling. The obsidian floor reflects the flickering orange flames dancing in my palm. I smirk at my pretties, curling my fingers around the fire. Double doors open at the end of the hall, and someone inside calls a name that isn't mine.

Wait.

This isn't right. Am I dreaming again?

The thick dark fog surrounding me shifts once I'm aware of it. I come out of the vision of another world, waking up to a dark room with a muffled yell.

What the—? My mouth is cottony and I gag.

unable to swallow, unable to close my mouth because there's something stuck in it that makes my jaw ache. I want to rip it out, but my hands are stuck behind me, tied to the chair. Yanking, I get nothing but stiff limbs.

What's going on? Was I drugged?

Lifting my head, I blink several times, taking in the unfamiliar room. This is wrong. I went to bed at Talbot House, finally passing out after staying up for twenty-four hours reading the books on demon lore I borrowed from the library. I should be in it right now. It feels like I've barely been asleep, though my breathing turns harsh when I spot the date on the busted, flickering clock. Two days? No way.

Disorientation leaves my mind like sand pouring through an hourglass. It's the same unpleasant comedown I had after the hypnosis in the alley wore off. Bit by bit, the thick, abnormal fog seeps away, allowing flashes of what happened when I went to bed to rise to the surface of my memories.

They melted out of the shadows. Grabbed me. I fought, my elbow throbbing with the tenderness of crashing against rock hard muscles. My captors argued. Then came the order to knock me out.

If I close my eyes, I can still sense the large warm hand brushing my forehead with his thumb before the unnatural darkness claimed me.

Grinding my teeth against the fabric gag tied

around my head, I recap what I've learned in the last sixty seconds since waking. I don't know where I am, but I'm guessing it's a shitty motel going off the hideous, dated furnishings and the faint stench of nicotine hanging in the air. I'm bound and gagged, still wearing the oversized t-shirt I went to bed in. Judging by the twinges in my stiff body, I've been like this for most of the two days missing from my mind.

Alder, Matthias, and Valerian are dead for fucking kidnapping me. Chest heaving with fury, I squirm against the restraints to loosen them. My muscles are sore from being locked in the same position, but I savor the throbs of pain, feeding each one to my hatred. Once I get out of my bindings, I'll kick their teeth in.

The door opens and I catch a brief glimpse of a dark parking lot lit by the neon glow of a motel sign. Then my three asshole stalkers stride in.

Demons, my mind supplies helpfully. My stomach clenches. There's no denying what I saw in the alley. Their fingers that changed into long, terrifying claws. It's not normal. Not human.

I can't believe the gate to Hell is real. I can't believe I convinced myself they were going to leave me alone after that shift from danger to…something far more potent in the alley. They've each said they can't let me go. But kidnapping? Seriously?

Drawing in a deep breath, I launch into a tirade that's unintelligible with the gag blocking my mouth. They don't acknowledge me, too wrapped up in their own conversation. I rock back and forth on the chair, yelping when I nearly overbalance the damn thing.

Alder comes close enough to right my chair prison before it topples, scooting me with a forceful shove so I'm wedged between the ratty bed and the nightstand. Once he ensures I'm not going to tip the chair over, his focus returns to the other two men without sparing me another glance.

That's how we're playing this? Fine. Fuck. Them.

Huffing, I drop my head back and stare at the ceiling.

"Killing her was a total fail. We couldn't—hurt her," Matthias argues in a confused tone. "She looks the part, but I don't think she's human. Not completely. You felt it, didn't you? The pull is intense."

Fuckboy say what? I tune back into their conversation, no longer ignoring them out of spite.

Valerian waves dismissively. "We have more pressing problems and need to act quickly before we entertain our theories. The demon council won't buy it much longer with only one of us posted at a time. It's a risk for all three of us to come here."

"We have to make a decision," Alder cuts in. "We've made her disappear, but it's not enough."

"Uh-m, heh-oh? Ahh-hullth!" My agitated words come out completely garbled by the gag. I go for the loudest scream I can manage instead, satisfied when two of them turn their attention to me.

Alder takes a step in my direction first, but it's Matthias who beats him to me and touches the gag.

He lifts his brows. "No screaming. Deal?" I narrow my eyes. He huffs in amusement and holds up his hands. "If you scream, Alder will have to put you under again. You can punch me as much as you want if I take off the gag. Does that sweeten it for you?"

Put me under. It was definitely his large, rough hand that caressed my head before the darkness trapped me in that vision.

After considering, I nod curtly, flexing my jaw in relief when the soggy material leaves my mouth. I tense as he massages my cheeks before undoing one of my arms.

He gives my arm the same treatment, working the sore muscles with his skilled hands. "Sorry for this. You almost woke up twice already, so it had to be done. Better?"

Without missing a beat, I wrench my arm free, ball my fist, and drive it into his arm as hard as I can.

He barely moves, humming a little laugh that rakes across my frayed nerves.

"For the record, it was Alder who felt up your fantastic tits when we had to knock you out," Matthias adds.

Alder's expression darkens with outrage. "I carried her. I didn't—"

"Enough." Valerian interrupts Alder's response.

I shoot Alder a death glare, mouthing *I hate you, shithead*. In turn, he glowers at Matthias, fists flexing with the promise of violence.

"Why did you kidnap me?" I spit venomously, the ire for my enemies giving me courage to stand up against demons.

I've faced plenty of vile people. Demons can't be much worse.

"I don't see the need to repeat myself endlessly," Valerian says.

"People will know I've gone missing. The matron at the girls' home will call the police."

With a rough, scornful rumble, he stalks over and grabs my chin, giving me a glimpse of the whorls of ink that move across his knuckles before he angles my head up. "Think. You're close enough to the age humans cast you out of the system that grants you shelter. It was quite easy for us to stage your disappearance. Will anyone care to look for you, or will they believe you ran off on your own?"

Even I know it would be a stretch for anyone at Talbot House to bother. I only had another week and a half left there. Mashing my lips together, I level him with a scowl that gives the broody bastard a run for his money. He narrows his eyes and cocks his head, grasping my jaw with more force.

"Not such a mouthy little thing now, are you?" He serves me a cruel smirk. "If you didn't want to be captured by demons, you shouldn't have summoned us by calling on the gate."

Demons. My mind still attempts to shy away from the truth.

I push out a tight breath and jut my chin against his hold. "You still haven't killed me. What do you plan to do with me?"

Heat melts down my spine and coils in my core when I think of what happened when they tried to murder me in the alley. Valerian's nostrils flare, his blue eyes sweeping over me.

"If only it were that easy," he says with caustic bite. "We'd all be better off without you."

I try to hide my flinch at his callous remark, my walls against the constant rejection the world throws at me no longer as strong with splintering cracks in them. One little taste of being wanted and my heart can't withstand his dismissal.

He works his jaw, cutting his gaze away. "There's something about you. Something we can't stay away from."

Every word of his admission sounds like he's fighting to hold it in and keep it to himself. Matthias told me right away, much more open about what made him curiously fascinated by me. For some reason, they're drawn to me. Something that feels like a faint thread pulling in my chest echoes when I have the thought.

"You dragged me into this mess. You could've just left me alone." My throat clogs. "Or if you were worried about people wondering if the legend was still real, you could've just told me to get out of town. It's not like I was planning on sticking around."

"Humans missing you aren't the problem. The demon council is. They expect a soul."

"But you won't kill me," I say slowly.

"*Can't,*" Alder cuts in with a glare. He scrubs his brown hair. "And we want to know why. We've never failed."

Valerian strokes my chin with his thumb, the tip barely edging against my lower lip. I lift my eyes to his, stomach dipping at the way the bright blue darkens. After what I know now, and what happened the other night I should be disgusted by his touch. Except disgust doesn't describe the way my insides flutter. His mouth curves, showing the hint of fangs.

"Perhaps once we understand what's different

about you, then we'll find a way to feast on you," he croons.

I shiver, picturing their sharp, monstrous teeth against my bare skin. Okay, so maybe I'm down to fuck monsters. I would never trust them, but a whisper in the back of my mind wonders what it would be like. The way it felt when Matthias touched me, when I wanted Valerian to kiss me, was unlike anything I've ever experienced.

Valerian's cunning gaze is inescapable, watching as my lips part and my cheeks flush. A gravelly sound vibrates in his chest when he leans over me, tipping my face up.

"Let's fake it."

Matthias' suggestion breaks the moment between us as he sprawls on the bed to my side. He winks at me, trailing a finger down my arm and teasing the bottom edge of my shirt, unbothered by the way Valerian invades my space while he does it.

"Fake it?" Alder questions, posting himself with his bulky arms crossed by the nightstand at my other side.

"Her death," Valerian clarifies, his eyes narrowing in thought.

With all three of them crowding me at once, the air grows thick and hot around me. I strain to draw breath. The alley was bad enough with two of them caging me in, but this...I squeeze my thighs together, mortified by my reaction to their proximity. What is wrong with me? Why am I getting so turned on by the three men I hate? By my kidnappers? By demons?

Get it together, I scold myself. These are my enemies.

Shaking my head to clear it, I ignore Matthias' cocky stare. Whatever sinful, dirty thought is in his head, I don't want to know it.

"Would that work to fool your overlords or whatever?" I ask. "And how?"

"Demon council," Alder corrects with pride coloring his tone. "They oversee the different factions of demons. There are many like us—warriors, guards, hellhounds, and soul reapers. Those that can cross between the realms. Our king, Lucifer, rules the underworld and the council is like his right hand." His proud expression turns conflicted. "Disobeying our sworn duty to the council is as good as spitting in the king's face."

Color drains from my cheeks. "Don't piss off the Devil's lackeys in Hell. Got it."

It feels weird just saying that with a scrap of seriousness. Demons are real. The Devil rules over Hell in the underworld. Yeah, not getting used to that anytime soon.

"You oversimplify our realm. It would be too difficult for you to understand," Valerian mutters.

"This is why humans have such skewed knowledge when it comes to the underworld. Hell is only one part of our realm."

I scoff. "Politics suck no matter what. Doesn't seem that hard to grasp."

The corners of his mouth tighten. He starts to respond, then they all freeze, heads cocked like they're listening. One of them curses.

Matthias slides off the bed, his languid nature replaced by someone that moves with efficiency. He slinks to the window, flicking the curtain carefully to peer out.

My shoulders tense at seeing him so serious. "What is it?"

Alder and Valerian exchange a glance.

"Too late," Valerian says. "They've come for you."

"What?" I yelp in alarm.

Matthias closes the curtains. "They're circling the parking lot."

"It's a scout group," Alder says.

Without another word, Valerian kills the lights. The three of them take up positions in the shadowy corners around the room to conceal themselves while I'm left out in the open. I snap my head back and forth. What's the plan?

"Hello! Tied up still over here!" I jerk against the restraints, using my free hand to yank on them. I can't reach the knot. "I'm not playing bait!"

"You are," Valerian shoots back. "You'll only get in the way or run off the first chance you get because humans are all stupid, fragile creatures. Stay there."

"Are you fucking kidding me?" My muscles strain with my attempt to wriggle free. "I hate you. I hate all of you so damn much."

None of them are listening.

I freeze as the doorknob glows red-hot and melts, dripping down the door. It swings open with an unsettling creak and a tall figure steps inside, silhouetted by the lights from the neon motel sign and from the parking lot that stream in. Thick horns curl back from his angular face, his skin is stretched tight over cheekbones, giving his features a gruesome appearance. There's no mistaking him for human—he's a demon.

He speaks to the dark room in another language, chuffing in croaky amusement when no one responds. With each step he takes toward me, my heart climbs higher in my throat. Sharp pains cramp my stomach and stab my palms as terror ratchets higher.

Any minute now, guys.

They don't move from their hiding spots.

Don't let me die, assholes.

The light from the open door illuminates his face better when he turns toward me and I suck in a breath. His eyes snap to me, intent and eerily bright. I know him. I've seen him somewhere, without the horns.

My eyes widen when it hits me. It's the same grizzly beard. He was in the alley! "Wait—aren't you—?"

The not-so-human shopkeeper releases a horrible, ear-splitting screech and flings a ball of fire at the spot I last saw Matthias. With a grunt, Matthias dodges and the curtains ignite, the burst of flames licking up the fabric to reach the ceiling in a matter of seconds. Putrid smoke chokes me, the fast-spreading fire flinging me back into all my worst memories.

Alder charges the demon from behind, his huge arms encased in fire. Before he catches him, two more gremlin-like monsters rush through the door, one going high and the other sinking low, their leathery red clawed hands splayed to attack. While Alder is forced to split his attention to defend himself, the shopkeeper's fists bloom with more flames and he launches himself at Valerian when he darts out of the shadows.

They clash together, sending another burst of fire and ash into the air. The darkness flickers away with collisions of their dueling fiery fists grappling for the upper hand. My heart plummets when the shopkeeper gets hold of Valerian's neck and lifts him off the ground. He spits something in another language and flames erupt from his hand, burning Valerian's neck. Valerian lets out an awful, choked sputter, struggling against the vicious move.

Matthias comes to his aid, jumping on the shopkeeper's back and shooting fire into his face from the hand he slashes across it. The shopkeeper's fire sputters out. Growling, the demon reaches back and flings Matthias off. He turns while holding Valerian by his throat and punches a fireball through the air.

"No!" I scream.

My heart seizes as the blow knocks Matthias against the wall before he collapses to the floor. He doesn't get back up.

Valerian's chiseled features morph in rage, his transformed hands dragging across the shopkeeper's face while planting his feet in the demon's chest and forcing a gust of smoke and hot air with a push of his palms to break away. His opponent doesn't give up ground, raking a flaming hand down his side before he lands on the floor. He lets out a roar that makes me want to fly out of my chair and do something to help.

Alder isn't faring much better. Even with his massive size, he doesn't have much advantage over the two demons double teaming him. They're faster, using their quick moves to get in his blind spots and swipe at him. What's left of his shirt hangs in tatters from his body, showing the angry red welts and oozing cuts from their attacks no matter how many volleys of fire he blasts at them from his clenched fists.

Each panicked breath I drag in is tinged with smoke. I cough, tears welling in my eyes. I can't get out of the chair no matter how hard I struggle.

One of the demons Alder is dealing with peels off and jumps on the bed, peering down at me with a sickening fanged grin. The demon's claws recede and he grabs me by my hair. Gritting my teeth against the searing pain in my scalp, I shrink away instinctively, knowing it does nothing to protect me. Instead of worrying about how I'm about to get sliced to pieces, my focus shifts to the others.

This is bad. The fierce desire to help them screams at me. I hate the three of them...but they're better than the monsters attacking us.

If I hadn't done the dare, we wouldn't be in this mess. I would go on living my miserable life and they would still be guarding the gate to Hell.

Valerian was wrong. The demons haven't come for me. They've come for all of us. To kill me *and* them.

Eight
LILY

MY THROAT CLOSES AS I ACCEPT DEATH. THE DEMONS beyond the gate I opened expect a soul, and they're succeeding. At least my shitty existence will end in an epic way. No isekai hit and run or falling down the stairs, I'm going all out with a paranormal attack. I close my eyes.

A fierce, guttural roar across the room makes them snap open again.

"No!" Alder bellows. "Don't touch her!"

He has the other demon he's fighting incapacitated in a hold, brawny muscles flexing. He snaps the demon's neck with inhuman force, dropping the crumpled body before barreling across the room to stand between my attacker and me. There's barely any room for his huge frame, but he wedges between us, acting as my shield.

My heart clenches painfully. No one has ever cared about my safety. Never, not even as a small girl.

The demon on the bed screeches, fisting my hair tighter and yanking hard. A pained scream tears from me.

Seething, Alder slams his bright red smoldering fist down on the demon's arm to weaken the hold on my hair. The fucker doesn't budge, tearing some strands from my scalp. I grit my teeth while Alder grabs the demon's limb, digging in hard. From the corner of my eye, I gape in disbelief as the demon's arm melts, the leathery flesh bubbling and oozing pus as Alder's unyielding molten hot grip burns through tissue until he reaches bone. Once he does, he bares his fanged teeth with a growl and closes his fist with a stomach-churning *crunch*, destroying the bone with insane strength.

Holy shit.

The counterattack earns him a few seconds. Instead of pressing the advantage while the demon is down, writhing in pain, he reaches back and grabs my restraints, putting my safety before his own. With a sharp tug, his claws slice through them, freeing me from the chair. I spring to my feet and back away, fighting the urge to hug the guy who was prepared to kill me the night we met for saving me.

"Stay down and behind me." The second the clipped words leave him, the demon is up on his feet, ready with another attack despite missing an arm. "You won't have her."

Something cinches tight in my chest at his protective tone. His back muscles ripple as he takes up a fighting stance. The Henley shirt is nothing but scraps of fabric dangling from his body. My gaze flies down his body, taking in the wounds he's sustained. Something else catches my eye, illuminated by the fire eating away at the motel room. Markings cover his torso and arms.

Scars.

The air in my lungs punches out of me. They look similar to my burn scars. Is this why he was mad I had them? Because he knows? An ache pangs in my chest, questions tugging at me. I wonder how he got them, if they bother him.

An ugly painting decorating the room crashes to the floor from its hanging spot on the wall, snapping me out of it. The room is still very much on fire and we're still in the midst of fighting demons that want to kill us. I don't have time to think about this now.

Focus.

Darting a look over my shoulder, I'm relieved to find Matthias on his feet again, swiping his mouth with the back of his hand. His playful boyish features take on a brutal edge to match the callous glint in

Valerian's eye as they circle the shopkeeper. An icy chill arrows through me when the shopkeeper gives them a hideous smile in anticipation.

Flames spread down Valerian's arm in a coil almost like a whip. His gaze flicks to Matthias. Signaling him with a nod, they both move together, Valerian using his fire to encircle the demon and hold him in place. He fights against the binding while Matthias forges the fire springing from his palms into a pointed tip, using it like a dagger. The demon throws up his arms to block, then grabs hold of Valerian's coil.

A niggling sense bolts down my spine out of nowhere with some kind of recognition of what's about to happen when he yanks Valerian closer with it.

"Watch out!" I shout.

They both fall back from the burst of hot hair the shopkeeper puts off with another screech that pierces me to the bone. I drop to a knee, slapping my hands over my ears.

By the time my head stops pounding and I scramble to my feet, the fighting seems dire.

None of the guys can get an edge over the shopkeeper or the other remaining demon. Blow for blow, they're matched and overpowered. Matthias takes a hit to the side that slows him down, pain written across his contorted face. Alder can't catch the smaller, quick demon keeping out of his reach before darting in when he can't block to carve his claws into his skin. Valerian is backed against a wall, glaring at the shopkeeper pining him with a rush of fire shooting from his hands.

No, no, no.

Oh god. It's not enough. They're all going to die because of me.

As the harrowing thought enters my mind, I gasp from the sensation of being squeezed by an invisible force.

The pressure becomes unbearable. I reach for Alder, gasping for air. My vision blurs. Shit, I can't breathe. Panic trickles over me, my senses bombarded by smoke and heat. I feel as though I'm being compressed from all sides. Is the shopkeeper doing this?

Sparks prick along my nerves, racing down my arms. The energy builds in my palms, growing hotter. Static blocks out my hearing, then a sharp *pop* makes me wince as the sensation ceases, flowing away in a rush. It leaves my hands tingling with the aftereffects.

Bright electric sparks rain over the open door to the parking lot, followed by a loud explosion that shakes the building from outside. It distracts the attackers. I think a transformer blew because the lights outside cut out, leaving the room lit by the orange glow of the fire.

Everyone freezes, glancing suspiciously at each other. Valerian uses this to his advantage, recovering while the shopkeeper isn't paying attention. His merciless uppercut snaps the shopkeeper's head back and he grabs him by his horns.

"Now," he barks.

Matthias crosses his hands in front of him, gold eyes flashing bright. He tears the demon's throat with his claws while Valerian traps him. The shopkeeper's black eyes bulge and he gurgles. Dark, tar-like blood seeps from his ravaged neck, staining his chest.

"Oh my god," I choke.

Alder finally grabs the smaller demon and releases a chilling growl. With one forceful yank, he rips the demon's body in half like it's made of paper. Blood and other gross innards spill from each severed half, coating Alder and the bed. My pulse thunders and inexplicably I think of beefy lumberjacks who rip tree logs in half with their bare hands.

When the shopkeeper's body slumps to the floor, the blaze engulfing the room sputters out, leaving it stinking of sulfur. Part of the drywall has burned away, the beds are destroyed, and the TV is cracked in half, toppled to the floor.

"I don't think you're getting your security

deposit back." The mumbled words are the first to jump in my head.

Matthias smirks, rubbing his side. "Not our problem." He winces. "Damn, we're out of shape. Alder, you good?"

He grunts in response, dumping the demon remains on the trashed mattress before shredding the scraps of his shirt clinging to his glistening muscles. I swallow thickly, unable to move from the center of the room.

We won. My demons beat the other demons, each of them reveling in their violent triumph. Valerian slowly wipes away the shopkeeper's blood, lips curling into a ruthless smirk. Matthias releases a laugh that's more than a little unhinged, grabbing the shopkeeper's slack face and shaking it. Alder's chest heaves with rumbling breaths, more beast than man at the moment.

My heartbeat thrums with relief, fear, and something warm and fluttering I don't want to name as my gaze moves between the three of them.

When I move, my limbs feel stiff. My hands skitter over Matthias' side first. "Are you guys okay?"

"I'm better now," he murmurs.

I ignore the brash smirk he gives me before I move to Alder, hovering my fingers over the fresh welts covering his existing scars. Valerian clenches his jaw and gives me his back.

"Not now." Alder takes my wrist and tugs me with him. "We need to move before more come."

Outside, I spot the smoking transformer that blew, the plume of smoke rising high into the night sky. My palms tingle with the phantom sensation I felt before. Rolling my lips between my teeth, I curl my hands into fists to dispel the tingles.

Valerian is the last to leave the destroyed motel room as we circle the long strip of rooms to the edge of the building. A sleek, black muscle car is parked there. Matthias pulls out a set of car keys. Before I learned the truth, I wouldn't blink twice. Knowing he's a demon, it trips me up.

"This is your ride? Where did you get a car?" I blurt.

Matthias grins. "Stole it."

"Get in," Valerian demands as he takes the keys.

"Where are we going?" I question as Alder hustles me into the backseat.

"Our gate," Valerian says. "We need to contact the demon council to find out what's going on."

My brows pinch. "Is that a good idea?"

Alder distracts me for a moment while Valerian pulls onto the road. He pets the top of my head with a big palm. My breath catches. Whatever he's doing helps soothe the dull throb lingering from having my hair ripped out. I want to melt against his warm side and beg him to never stop running his hand over my head like that.

Biting my lip to smother a sigh, I focus on my questions. "I mean, did the council put out like a burn notice or something for not killing me?"

Matthias twists from the passenger seat with a smirk. He understands human references much better than the others.

"They don't operate on whims without a deliberation to pass judgment," Valerian says. "Even if a human escapes death by a gate guard's hand, there's an order to these things."

"It's not just that they attacked us unprovoked that's a red flag," Matthias explains. "They broke our laws by potentially exposing our kind to humans. Big fucking no-no."

I smack the back of his headrest. "Then what about people like me who fuck with your gate? You revealed yourself then."

"Humans who summon the gate fall under a different classification than the general populace," Alder says. "They are destined for death, so it's not necessary to hide our true nature from them."

The car falls quiet as I process what they've told me. According to the dash, it's almost three in the morning.

"That guy spoke to you before he attacked us." I frown. "It was in another language. What did he say?"

Alder shakes his head. "He accused us of being traitors to our king. It doesn't make any sense."

Unease churns my stomach. "So why send scouts if they think you're traitors?"

"That was not a fucking scout group," Valerian grits through his teeth. "Who gave the order to the warrior guild to come topside? The council would never go to such extreme measures for a mere human."

"And us," Matthias reminds him.

Valerian's grip tightens on the wheel and he steps on the gas. The sign for the Brim Hills town limits comes into view.

Nine
LILY

I f I were a mere human, this would be over already. Before their kidnapping plan went tits up because of the attack on the motel, Valerian said there was something different about me. The impossible thought clangs around in my head as the car rolls to a stop in front of the abandoned Brim Hills Cemetery. I've been told there's something wrong with me my whole life and have fought to run from it.

"I saw that demon in town before all this." Valerian and Alder freeze at my confession, turning expectant gazes on me. I avoid their eyes. "Um, in the alley. Without the horns, obviously. Before you and Matthias left."

Heat spreads through me when I recall what they were doing to me, how close they had me to exploding in pleasure before something made them leave.

"That was the scent I picked up." Valerian mutters a curse and slams the car door when he climbs out. "Stay alert. If they've been watching that long, something isn't right."

"Got it," Matthias says.

I poke my head out of the car and Alder blocks my path. "Stay here."

"Um, how about fuck no. You three kidnapped me. You're not leaving me behind to sit in the car with potential murder demons on the loose." I point at myself. "I'm not bait."

"Very well."

Sighing, he stands aside and allows me to enter the cemetery, keeping close behind me. The dead grass crunches beneath my bare feet. My gaze drifts to the woods that lead to Talbot House. If I run, he'll catch me easily. Part of me wants to test them to see, but it's fleeting. My curiosity keeps me moving up the hill with everyone.

I haven't stepped foot inside the graveyard since my first night here. It's not lost on me that the last time we were all here together I was running from them in terror, believing they were playing a cruel prank on me. Now the three of them position themselves around me while we navigate the headstones as if they want to keep me safe.

At the top of the hill, Valerian approaches the chapel ruins. He recites some kind of lilting incantation, frowning when the air crackles. The others tense. If I squint, I can make out the static electricity in the stone arch beneath the staircase, fainter than when I thought I saw them before.

"What's supposed to happen when you do that?" I ask.

"Not that," Matthias mutters. "As guards of the portals between realms, we have a connection to our gate. It's like a unique key."

"So the door is locked?"

"They've been here," Alder says.

"Yes." Valerian blows out a breath. "They've blocked our exit back to Hell. We have to abandon our post."

Without another word, he starts down the hill. Alder lingers, touching the side of the arch. The tightness at the side of his mouth and eyes draws a pang of sympathy from me.

I place a hand on his arm. "Are you okay, Alder?"

"Fine," he responds gruffly.

"Roadtrip. I call shotgun." Matthias drapes an arm over my shoulder, steering me back to the car. I don't miss the cautious glance he sweeps the area with as we walk through the cemetery. "Give the big guy a minute. He takes his orders seriously. Vale's been guarding this gate the longest, but Alder's the one who lives to serve our king. Abandoning our post is as good as treason to him."

I peer back at Alder. "I mean, they did try to kill us. I think we're past that."

"It will be difficult to prove we aren't traitors by leaving," Alder says behind us. "We've never failed our duties before."

"Better than dying," Matthias says.

"I could just go back to Talbot House." I motion to the trees with no intention of stepping off the path I've been dragged down to return to my miserable life. "It's right there through the woods."

Matthias drags me closer. "Nah. We've captured you. We're not letting you go yet, lost girl." He plays with the ends of my short hair. His tone shifts, becoming more intense. "You're ours."

I huff, grasping for sarcasm to cover for the weird tug low in my stomach at his words. "I guess I'm stuck with you. Woo. My safe word is meatloaf."

He snorts, but this reference seems lost on him. I explain the lyrics being the perfect fit for when things are over the line and his golden eyes light up. I want to kick myself for ever thinking they were special effects contacts as a way to convince myself otherwise and ignore everything I saw, because that luminous flare of color is pure magic.

His knuckles brush my cheek and my stomach

dips. "Clever little thing."

The wind rustles through the trees, making me shiver. My gaze darts to the woods again. "So, uh. Do I have time for some B and E? I don't want to go around barefoot in the t-shirt I wore to bed. Hopefully Mrs. T hasn't donated my clothes yet."

His crooked grin stretches into something wolfish and he tugs on the hem of my shirt, sending a cool breeze higher up my thighs the more he exposes them. "I dunno, I'm really digging this on you. It has easier access than that hot little pair of shorts you had on."

Alder smacks the back of his head as he passes us with long strides. "We took your bag when we stole you. Made it look like you ran off on your own. It's in the trunk."

"How thoughtful," I say cynically. "Thanks for leaving me unconscious for two days without pants on."

The warm, rich scent of woodsmoke and maple tickles my nose. I glance between Matthias and Alder, trying to decipher which of them it belongs to. Matthias' expression is too open, but a muscle in Alder's jaw jumps and he flexes his hand at his side.

Valerian is behind the wheel and has the car idling by the time the rest of us reach it. Alder lifts me without warning and carries me to avoid broken glass at the edge of the road. He deposits me in the backseat, then goes to the trunk and thumps his fist on it twice. Valerian pops it and Alder brings me my beat up duffel bag held together by duct tape and a prayer.

"Thanks." I quickly rummage for a pair of leggings and shimmy them on while the car whips around to head back the way we came.

"You're the source of the power surge we felt during the attack." Valerian's accusation slices through the silence in the car.

I glare at the back of his head. "Excuse me?"

"It wasn't power from the three of us." His haunting blue eyes flick to the rearview mirror to meet mine, narrowing. "We've been together long enough to recognize the feel of each other's power signature. It came from you. Care to share what you haven't told us?"

"You're crazy. That wasn't me." I cross my arms. "I don't have powers. It could've been the demons that attacked us."

Matthias barks out a sharp laugh from the passenger seat. "They couldn't take out a transformer without touching it."

Alder shakes his head. "The warrior's guild is powerful. Yes, those demons were high ranked, but no one in the guild is capable of producing that surge of energy without more demons to pool their powers together."

"No way," I insist hoarsely.

My breathing turns shallow and strained as flashes of memories assault me. The haunting pieces of my past I've run from and ignored.

Fires I've never been able to explain.

Flickering lights when I got yelled at. My palms prickling with sharp pains when my emotions were too much to cage inside me.

Even the time the whole street went dark, the street lights bursting on my way home after a teacher kept me late. The touchy feely old bastard thought that because I was a group girl no one would believe me. Except, when he went to grope me, I grabbed his wrist and burned the hair right off his arm. He took me to the principal and had me expelled.

"I believe this is why you've triggered these strange instincts in us." Valerian says instincts like it's a curse. He works his chiseled jaw. "Why you don't smell like a human should. Instead it's more like a scent escaping through the cracks, like something is masking what you really are."

Not human. I feel human. How could I not be?

With a thick gulp, I tuck my hands between my thighs, as if hiding the worst of my scarred flesh makes it disappear. "It's not like I hit puberty and sprouted horns I never knew about. My body is normal."

"Your body is gorgeous," Matthias chimes in.

"One hundred out of ten would smash."

Alder strokes his chin, studying me intently. "Still, what we felt… It was far more powerful. Something on the king's level almost."

I blanche. "The king—as in like, Lucifer? The Devil?"

"Smooth motherfucker himself. I've seen it firsthand. About a century ago, at an orgy at the palace." Matthias bites his lip, his chuckle depraved. "I swear he was commending my form. Anyway, his power feels like that, like it could choke you and you'd thank him for it."

I smother the angry pinch of jealousy in my stomach and skip right over the tossed out *century* comment. "I don't have powers."

"Whatever you say, pretty girl." Matthias winks over his shoulder, reaching back to squeeze my knee.

"We'll discuss it later when we get somewhere safe," Valerian mutters.

The sharp, bitter smell of smoke chokes the car. It's coming from one of them. Their scents seem to shift with their emotions.

Plucking at the seatbelt, I slide my lips together. More questions burst free after a short silence. "What are the gates? Why do they exist if you're not supposed to show yourselves to humans? You look human enough, until you go all Wolverine hands and Human Torch with the fists of fire."

Valerian's expression shutters and his grip tightens on the wheel. There's a beat of tense silence before Matthias breaks it.

"They weren't always a secret. Humans used to know about them." He ignores the severe scowl Valerian shoots at him, acting like he's setting the stage for an epic tale. "Not as urban legends, but as altars."

"Altars?" My stomach clenches.

"For sacrifice." Alder's no-nonsense confirmation doesn't make me feel any better. "The humans sacrificed an agreed upon number of souls willingly to feed the demons and keep the king of the underworld from razing the mortal territories to the ground when we all existed as one realm."

"Oh god," I whisper.

Valerian scoffs and catches my eye in the mirror. "God," he mocks. "Humans have told themselves such twisted lies. What you understand of Hell and the underworld is mostly wrong. Your folklore is born out of an ancient war that split the realm between the demonic fae beings in the underworld and the humans."

My fingers tighten on the seatbelt and my voice shakes. "I'm not a religious person, but I know the Bible doesn't talk about anything like that. I don't think any other religion does either."

What he's saying is nothing like the books I read

on demon lore.

"Exactly," he sneers. "The humans are left to have their own ideas. There is only a semblance of truth when in reality, our kind has existed far longer than yours, descended from the primordial gods of the heavens and the underworld. Humans wouldn't be able to fathom the truth now."

I wait, disbelief ricocheting around my head, but he doesn't elaborate. "Okay, so why do you guard the gates if you're just going to kill the people who find one?"

"To keep humans from wandering into the underworld on their own, as they used to. It's part of the treaty between fae and mortals in the aftermath of the war that divided the realms," Alder says. "The gates are still used for hunting grounds as part of the old sacrificial quota."

"And bridges between the mortal and underworld realms," Matthias adds. "They're our only access points. We can't just blip back and forth wherever we want. There's a barrier that separates our realms."

"Yes. But they've become a secret, another myth," Valerian interjects in an acidic tone, his hatred unmistakable. "To ward off humans too smart to meddle where they should keep away from predators. The number of souls consumed has dwindled because of this change. Don't look so nauseated. This is how the world works. There's nothing you can do about it, no saving the humans from what awaits them. It's not as though your kind are endangered. They are the prey and we are the predators."

I hate that he's right. The world sucks—I know it better than most.

"Humans can't be your only food source." I hope they're not.

"No, we eat and drink regular food." Matthias laughs, tipping his head back against the headrest. "Most demon fae aren't all like blood suckers and incubi that need to feed on specific things to survive, though we're definitely the best looking of the bunch. Souls bolster our strength. We're closer to our hellhound cousins with the ability to shift some of our appearances. Only difference is they can fully turn into beasts to hunt for damned souls marked for Hell."

"Vampires are real?" I choke. "What's next, aliens?"

My love of fantasy and isekai manga has only helped me process the existence of more than one world with magical beings so much. I rub my pounding temples. Alder reaches across and pinches the back of my neck, his fingers warmer than normal as he massages a pressure point that helps with my stimulation overload headache.

Between the three of them, Alder and Matthias can't stop touching me, finding little excuses to brush against me or put their hands on me. I'm not used to the feeling at all, but it's...

Well, I don't hate it. No one will catch me admitting it out loud, though.

Maybe I'm already addicted to the odd tingling thrill that runs through me whenever they do it. I tuck away the thought, not willing to unpack how pathetic I am for buckling to the first sign of attention after going so long without it. This is temporary. It's not like they'll stick around when their place is in the underworld.

Needing another distraction, I ask, "Do you have horns? Is this just some skin suit you put on for my sake to blend in?"

Matthias snorts. "This is how we look. Most of us stick to a fully human appearance when we're topside. Makes humans easier to hunt. Demon fae aren't all red little monsters humans depict us as. Different bloodlines have different traits. Tails, horns, scales—there's a she-demon I know with wings. The three of us just have claws, fangs, and these ears." He rakes his blond hair back and his ear shifts, extending into a pointed one like an elf's. He smirks, eyes dancing. "It means our dicks are huge."

"Matthias," Alder grouses impatiently. "It's a mark of our strong bloodlines, you imp. Different appearances like horns come from crossing bloodlines with other underworld beings. The original demon fae were made in the old gods' image."

"That's enough," Valerian says. "We still don't know what she is. Until we do, we can't trust her."

His callous words slice into me, leaving a hollow space in my chest. He's the only one who stops himself from creating a connection between us when he reaches for me. It shouldn't upset me because I hate him right back, yet I can't stop the flood of disappointment.

"I'm right here, dick."

He ignores me. With a huff, I lean against the window and stare at the town we're leaving in the dust. Leaving Brim Hills was my goal, though I never planned to do it with company.

My heart skips a beat when we pass the faded sign that says *now leaving Brim Hills, come back soon*.

They've pulled me into a world I never knew existed. Somehow in the span of a couple hours I've gone from reject orphan to kidnapping victim to a fugitive soul on the run with my enemies, bound together as allies until we find out what's different about me, and why it matters to the demons beyond the gate.

Ten
LILY

WE DRIVE UNTIL SHORTLY BEFORE DAWN, STOPPING AT another motel outside of Manhattan on the New Jersey side. I wake with my head pillowed on Alder. All he says in response to my raised eyebrow is that he didn't want my neck to cramp from how I fell asleep. When I ask why we're stopping here, Valerian says he wants somewhere to lay low and blend in with human scents. The denser population of the cities masks their distinct scents.

They let me sleep until early afternoon in the stuffy motel room. I'm surprised I managed to sleep at all, not used to letting my guard down around those I can't trust. As I peel my eyes open groggily, I groan at the dull ache throbbing in my temples.

"I told you I should've helped her sleep."

Alder's deep, rumbling voice comes from the corner of the room. "She needs rest."

"She'll be fine. It wouldn't have worked anyway. She came out of it on her own when you knocked her out." Valerian stands over me. "Up."

I give him the finger. There's something about his pompous attitude that pisses me off even more when he's being demanding in his crisp British accent. "Are your manners crammed up your ass next to the barbed stick stuck there?"

He disregards my snarky remark, his chiseled features impassive. "It's time to test what you are, if not human." Leaning over the bed with a hand planted on either side of me in the sheets, he narrows his eyes, his smoky scent changing from sharp to something smooth and spiced. "Stop being a petulant brat. Get out of the fucking bed, or I'll drag you out myself."

I freeze, trying not to breathe in his scent and failing spectacularly. It's alluring, making my mouth water. An ache builds between my legs. Oh god, his scent is turning me on. I have to hold on to my hate for him, not wish for him to close the distance and crash his full lips against mine.

His blue eyes flash brighter, then the color disappears, his eyes darkening with unmistakable, heady lust. He clenches his fists in the sheets as his gaze searches my face like he's savoring the flush of my cheeks, my parted lips, the movement of my throat when I swallow thickly. His face lowers another inch, his mouth practically touching mine. My stomach dips and I rub my thighs together, barely aware of anything outside of his inescapable stare.

"Get out of bed, Lily," he rasps. "Now. Before I—"

"Fine. I have to pee anyway." He continues caging me for another beat before backing off. Huffing, I fling the covers away, tugging my sleep shirt down from where it rode up to my soft waist. I use the excuse to fly through the motel room, pushing past a smirking Matthias into the bathroom. Locking myself in, I brace against the door. "What is wrong with me?"

Crap, I'll have to walk back out there in just a t-shirt. I ditched the leggings on the floor between the beds when I crashed.

A knock sounds on the door.

"I brought your bag in from the car. I'm leaving it here," Matthias says. "Alder went out for breakfast."

"It better not be another human," I mutter through the crack in the door when I open it. "If any of you assholes try to kill someone, I'll stop you."

"Donuts and coffee."

I press my lips together. Begrudgingly, I admit to myself that while Valerian is still an asshole, Alder and Matthias are tolerable. Sometimes. It's hard to hate someone that brings you donuts.

"Fine. How do any of you have money to pay for the motel and food?"

His face appears in the small opening as I grab my bag. His attention flicks down like he's trying to see if I'm naked yet. I glare and he holds his hands up with an amused tilt to his mouth. "I told you. I love coming topside. A human I met a long time ago insisted on investments being the way to go. He opened a bank account for me and now I apparently have a lot of money."

I shower in record time under ice cold water that makes me groan in relief from how overheated my body is. I resist the urge to play with my hardened nipples and relieve the thrumming pulse in my clit. No way in hell will I touch myself while thinking of Valerian's sharp jaw, piercing blue eyes, or his demanding accent whispering filthy things to me with his fangs grazing my skin. Nope, nope, nope.

The harder I try not to think about it, the more my mind drifts down a dangerous road contemplating if demon dicks are different. Am I getting into the tentacle porn arena? A delirious laugh bubbles out of me. These demons make themselves appear human-like, yet I've seen their claws, their fangs. I've felt their forked tongues.

Pushing my face into the frigid spray, I shudder,

my hand gliding down my torso, slipping between my thighs. At the first touch, my eyes fall shut. I bite my lip hard to keep silent while I indulge my fantasies.

By the time I dress in a killer pair of red leather shorts I found at a secondhand shop and a black cropped bleach-dyed t-shirt, Alder has returned with food. Matthias pushes the box of donuts across the small table we congregate around, his gaze intent, almost as if he can somehow see what I did in the shower written all over me. I avoid his smoldering stare and dig in.

"What's the game plan?" I ask once I've downed two sugar dusted donuts and half a cup of coffee.

"We'll stay on the move for now in case scout groups are tracking us." Valerian props a shoulder against the wall, folding his arms. The black button down shirt he changed into stretches taut against the curve of his biceps and defined forearms, his abstract tattoos peeking out from the collar and sleeves. "Once you're finished, Alder found an alley we can use to test you."

"I didn't know there'd be a test," I deadpan. "I didn't study."

The corner of Matthias' mouth hitches up. "Not that kind of test, lost girl."

"Quit it," I grumble. "I'm sick of you calling me that."

It hits too close to home, picking at all my insecurities of being rejected and left alone. Their theory that I'm not even human exacerbates those feelings. I don't want to think about having powers because then it validates every horrible thing ever said about me. *Sink or swim.*

"Do you prefer pretty girl instead?" He chuckles at my blush.

"We talked while you bathed. We believe the reason you smell so damn g—" Alder cuts off and clears his throat gruffly. "Your scent could be different because you truly belong to the underworld. A demon trapped inside a human body. It's the only thing that fits. These instincts to protect you wouldn't be triggered otherwise."

He doesn't mention the way the three of them nearly fought over me the first time they caught my scent and circled me in the graveyard, or bring up what happened with Matthias and Valerian in the alley, assuming he knows. Protecting me isn't the only thing they're interested in.

We're not talking about it. The thing that happens whenever they're too close to me, like earlier with Valerian, or when one of them touches me for too long. The invisible pull that I don't understand. A force that defies logic and overrides any hatred we harbor for each other, almost like fate forcing us together. I shut down the ridiculous thought. It's an off-limits topic and I'm happy to keep it that way.

I purse my lips to the side. "I've lived here in the—the mortal realm my whole life. I didn't even know all this supernatural stuff was real outside of the books I like to read."

There's the strange things that happen when my emotions are out of control. The buzz of energy beneath my skin. The inexplicable incidents. Everything I've ignored and run from.

"I think there's some kind of seal blocking you to make you and everyone you encounter believe that. Both your power that is seeping through the cracks and possibly your memories." Valerian surveys me, stroking his chin in thought. "If there is one, I want to know why. We'll break it to see if it gives us an answer to what you are."

"Great," I say dully around a mouthful of a third donut. The burst of sugar on my tongue is the only thing keeping me from going insane at this conversation. After licking the remnants of sugar from my fingers, I wiggle them at the guys. "Let's get this over with so you can let go of the idea of me with powers now."

Three sets of otherworldly, luminous eyes are trained on my mouth.

Our motel is situated in an industrial district with the New York skyline peeking over the top of the squat warehouses. I pause to look at it. I've been bounced around this area, but I've never been to Manhattan.

Matthias catches my hand. "If we had time, I'd take you to the Lower East Side. There's a killer burlesque club there. It's an unforgettable experience."

"You've been to New York?" My attention shifts back to the towering buildings across the river.

"I've been all over. I make a point to see as much as I can when I'm in the mortal realm." He shoots me a smirk. "I love humans. They're all so fascinating and inventive."

"But you also kill people."

He shrugs. "Death is a fact of life."

"Yeah, if you get sick or in an accident."

"I'd say summoning demons and challenging the power of Hell is in the same category of people that die climbing mountains. There's an acknowledged risk involved."

"Not if they don't know the danger, like me."

Matthias ruffles his hair, making it more disheveled. "Not our fault if people are nonbelievers."

"No, just some dumb ancient treaty that stole the knowledge this world used to have, according to you guys. That's not fighting fair."

129

"Life isn't fair, baby."

"Don't I know it," I mutter.

The guys lead me down an access road behind the motel to a wide alley between the buildings backlit by the afternoon sun. It has a gravel lot at the back of the dead end road.

"This will do. Stand over there, Lily," Valerian instructs.

"This is a waste of time," I mutter while I stand in the middle of the alley.

After Valerian does a strange circular gesture in the air with his hand toward the mouth of the alley, he positions himself beside Alder a short distance from me while Matthias moves to the stairs jutting off from one of the warehouses.

Voices drift over. Two men in utility uniforms pause at the end of the alley as they talk. They haven't noticed us.

"They don't know we're here," Valerian says dismissively.

"Barrier." Matthias props his elbows on the metal railing and leans back. The sun makes his messy white blond hair shine. He wiggles his fingers. "They can't sense the ward magic. And if they did, I'm very persuasive. They won't bother us."

I wonder if he means like Alder's ability to put people in a deep sleep, remembering when his big hand brushed my head before the strange fog overtook me. Matthias seemed to hypnotize me in the alley. Do all demons have a unique parlor trick like that up their sleeves on top of the fire they control? I have no idea what else these guys are capable of. If he can pull tricks on the mind, I bet he's the one who fed me all those visions that tormented me the week after I called on the gate.

Everything I've ever thought about demons is wrong. They're real, for one. Instead of twisted souls of humans or fallen angels, they're actually supernatural beings from a different world with magic.

And they believe I have powers sealed away in me. Because they think I'm not human. That I could be from the underworld somehow.

It's difficult to wrap my head around. I've spent a lifetime rolling with it for the sake of shoving down the weird stuff that happens around me. I've never wanted to face it. Stuck on the run for our lives with them, I have little choice other than to go along with it all.

I flex my hands at my sides. "What am I supposed to do?"

The three of them exchange glances. Alder speaks up, extending his arm. "Visualize what you want. The energy will build." A swirl of fire and smoke dances in his palm before he closes his fist to snuff it out. "You harness it with your will."

Oh, good. Just will it, even though I wasn't aware I was capable of it. Piece of cake.

"Here goes nothing."

I hold both hands in front of me, imagining a fireball expanding between them. My fingers strain as I stretch them as far as they can reach and my tongue sticks out from the corner of my mouth. I feel like an idiot trying to follow Alder's advice.

After several minutes, it's clear it's not working.

I scrub my face, my words coming out muffled. "Look, I don't know, guys. I have no clue what I did before."

"Don't sweat it, petal."

My head jerks up at the new pet name from Matthias. At least he listened about not calling me lost girl anymore. He saunters over and stands behind me, tracing his fingertips up my arms. I suppress a shudder.

The curve of his grin presses against my ear when he dips his head. "No one gets it on their first go. Here, put your hands on mine. I'll show you."

Sighing, I allow him to lift our arms in front of me, palm to palm. His skin is warm against mine, then grows warmer as he emits tiny sparks between our hands.

"Oh." I startle. "That kind of tickles."

He chuckles and leans his head against mine. "See? It doesn't have to be a big power move. Start small."

He lowers his hands and the sparks ignite into flames. I start to yank my hands away but he stops me.

"Wait. I won't hurt you. It's a bit strange, but I feel like I could never consider hurting you again. The thought of you hurt is…" He pushes out a stilted laugh, unlike his usual relaxed nature. "Painful."

Angling to glance at him from the corner of my eye, his flirtatious smile tinges with regret for a moment before he pulls it back. As open as he's been with me, this feels like the first truly genuine glimpse he's allowed me to see. Ducking my head to hide my smile, I keep my hands in place, surprised when the fire doesn't burn me. Biting my lip, I swipe my fingers through it.

"How are you doing that? It doesn't burn."

He pauses in consideration before answering. "It becomes instinctive, like breathing. If I focus on it, then I can picture the well inside. Once you tap into that, you'll be able to do it, too. Try it. Give me some sparks, baby."

I huff sardonically at the double meaning he injects into his request. "I don't think we need to pour anymore gasoline on those sparks. Things already get out of control with the barest provocation."

Like me being fully okay with him fucking me in the alley, if it got that far. I smother the urge to press my thighs together and give myself away, though he seems to know the direction my mind goes.

"I disagree." His voice lilts and he brushes the top of my head with his lips as he steps closer so I can feel every firm line of his body against my back, the hardness he nudges against my ass. "I think you'd ignite the hottest inferno. I want to burn up in your fire."

An unsteady breath hisses out of me. Licking my lips, I try not to think about the flutter of need he stirs in me and try to replicate the sparks he showed me. Come on, internal well. Help me out here.

Nothing. Again.

I blow out another sigh. "This is pointless. I can't do it. I don't have the powers you think I do."

Matthias snuffs out his flames and wraps his arms around me. "We'll figure it out. Don't worry."

His embrace is tight and comforting, the calming scent of a campfire surrounding me. He hugs me like he never intends to let me go. My chest constricts.

Don't get attached. Temporary, I remind myself. I don't get to stay with them. I shouldn't even want that.

"Let me try to help you." At Alder's offer, Matthias returns to leaning against the railing. "Young demons coming into their powers often need exercises to assist them until they understand how to control their power on their own. Give me your hands."

My fingers rub together for a beat in hesitation before I place my hands in his. A jolt of energy shocks me when we touch. His grip tightens with a forceful rumble when I try to pull away. When the feeling fades, he turns them over.

"Stay still. When I pass hellfire to you, just maintain it."

"Easier said than done," I say.

"Focus."

With no effort at all, his hands glow like molten heat flows beneath his skin, then fire engulfs his hands. His thumbs stroke the sides of my palms and his green eyes catch mine, holding my gaze.

"Look, you're doing it," he says with a hint of pride and wonder.

My eyes widen. Oh my god, I'm doing it. The fire he transferred to me dances above my skin without scorching me. I have power. Which makes me not as human as I believed. This is unreal.

I can feel the energy constantly shifting, swaying as it seeks freedom. It challenges my feeble control, wanting more, wanting to explode.

In the few seconds I manage to hold his fire in my palms, my stomach rolls as reality overlays with the buried memory of my childhood resurfacing from the tight mental prison I locked it away in. I drop my hands and the flame dissipates. It doesn't take my harrowing memories with it.

I remember that feeling, the sensation of something taking control of me, to stop the pain and fear of my small head being pushed under the bath water. That night, after my foster brother pulled me from the tub, it whispered to me and promised to take away my hurts. While he yelled at his mom, it erupted from me before I understood what would happen. It lied.

People were right to fear me. Those strange things that follow me...I cause them all.

My shaking scarred hands cover my face. I'm unable to stop hyperventilating. An awful noise of despair tears free.

All three demons rush me.

"Breathe, sweet blossom." Alder keeps murmuring to me, his lips brushing my forehead as he gathers me in his arms before my knees buckle. "Breathe for me."

Within a few minutes, he helps me calm down. I sniffle, listening to the steady beat of his heart until I stop trembling. His embrace feels safe, wrapping me up and sheltering me from the world. He won't let the fire or anything else hurt me. I can fall apart and for once there's someone there to catch me.

"You know it won't burn, so why panic?" Valerian scrutinizes me. I bury my face in Alder's chest. "You've done that before."

It's not a question. Alder strokes my back. Gritting my teeth, I nod.

"You're blocking yourself," Valerian says. "Instead of panicking over whatever your mind is telling you, you need to face it. Access that side of yourself."

"Enough testing your theories for one day, Vale." Alder plants himself in front of me to shield me. "We confirmed her power. She needs a break."

I step around him, shaking out my hands as I pace. "I'm fine. Just—give me a minute."

Valerian gets in my face, moving too fast for me to track. I gasp at his proximity, aware of the intense press of Matthias and Alder's gazes. They don't stop him, despite Alder's admonition a moment ago.

"Come on, Lily."

His growl is demanding, the rough way he says my name making my mind snap to this morning when he practically covered my body with his in bed. He grabs my waist and hauls me closer. My hands fly up on instinct and rest against his chest. His heartbeat is thundering like mine. I should push him away, but the feel of his hard body against mine makes me hesitate.

"Fight me off," he commands, then lowers his voice to a sensual rasp as his nose grazes my cheek. "Blow us away again like you did last night, little flower."

A strangled cry lodges in my throat. The tight hold I keep on my emotions shatters, already shaky from facing my memories and unable to withstand the way my chest blooms at his words, leaving me caught between anger—at him, at myself because some part of me wants him to keep pushing me, to take this further—and the force of my desire.

My forbidden thoughts that taunted me, tempted me in the shower an hour ago flood back without my willpower to compartmentalize it all. They're the absolute last thing I should be thinking about in this situation.

A burst of hot air and a blinding stream of sparks knock him back when I shove against his chest with a fierce yell for making me face this. The familiar tingling in my palms lingers. My eyes grow wide. I did that. That—that power came from me.

Valerian regains his footing several feet from me across the alley. Staggering back another step, he swipes at his mouth with an intrigued glint in his eye. "I see. Strong emotions allow you to get past the seal. It's a start."

Shit. It's true.

My dazed attention falls to my scarred hands. They turn blurry before me as overwhelmed tears gather in my eyes.

All those incidents that frightened my guardians in the system, the fire at the Clarks', the things they brushed under the rug and explained away as me being a troubled, dangerous, uncontrollable kid.

I have powers. And I've been running from them all my life.

Eleven

LILY

THE NEXT WEEK BLURS TOGETHER AS WE STAY ON THE move from those hunting us while they work with me to use my powers. To think that only a few weeks ago I was counting down the days until Halloween. I'm pretty sure it's this week, though now I'm not sure if my birthday is even real. If I'm a trapped demon caged by some magic seal, I have no idea how old I really am. For all I know, being a demon could make me hundreds of years old, like the guys seem to be going off their casual comments talking about centuries like they're nothing.

I'm losing track of where we are and where we've been from the constant cycle of motel hopping, and training to connect to my powers. Since the first moment I accessed them, an uneasy worry sets up camp in the back of my head. I haven't got a decent night's sleep since. That could also be because we don't stay in one place for more than a full day, and when we do stop, the guys rotate guard shifts, one of them resting in the second bed while the other two keep watch.

Though they eat regular food, they don't need as much sleep as I do, my practice sessions leaving me even more drained. They assure me once I learn how to wield the power hidden within me that it won't tire me out so much every time I call on it.

I squint at the overcast sky behind today's training grounds. The condemned roadside pizza shop provides cover while Alder and Matthias encourage me to set a pile of sticks on fire. My boot nudges the pile I haven't succeeded in igniting. Not even a sizzle.

"I'm not your walking, talking matchstick," I complain. "And being here makes me crave pizza."

If I focus on that instead of the large pond behind the building, I don't have to think about Mrs. Clark. Letting the past in leads to me losing my shaky hold on the magic fire I manage to produce.

"Stop deflecting. You'll never gain control if you're not serious." Valerian is a tyrant during these little training sessions, impossible to fool. Every time I get frustrated, he pushes my buttons to throw me off before I can compartmentalize my emotions. He pushes off the counter and circles me, the long black trench coat he wore the first night we met sweeping my legs. "If you continue to cower in fear every time you use your power, it will only fail you. That power is yours, Lily. Take it. Use it. Bend it to your will."

Working my jaw, I prop my hands on my hips. "I'm getting tired of these lectures."

He stops behind me, hot breath fanning over my exposed shoulder from the cut of my flowy shirt tucked into my fitted high-waisted skirt. "Tough shit. I'll keep giving them until you show me you can do it."

I roll my eyes and try again when he steps away. Reaching for my powers is finicky at best. I don't know if young demons deal with this, but it's annoying as fuck to feel so inept at the simplest tasks.

"You can do it, babe." Matthias gives me a supportive smile from his cross-legged perch on top of a table.

Okay, inner power well thing. Time to make you my bitch.

Concentrating on the pile of sticks Alder crouches beside, I picture the flow of energy, the build of heat from smoking to the first spark to the flame catching, visualizing the odd sensation of painless fire twisting around my fingertips. It's close, but not there yet. I shift my stance, sinking to one knee across from Alder, holding my hands above the sticks.

Wrong move. The pond snags my attention when it enters my periphery through the open door. My mouth floods with the imagined taste of metallic water and a gasp rips from me. *Sink or swim.* That awful, deranged voice taunts me from my memories even though she's gone.

I lose it as a burst of erratic power knocks me on my ass on the dusty, dirty cracked tile. The pile of sticks implode, burning hot and fast until they're nothing but cinders.

Controlling this is a struggle. I either produce inconsistent spikes of energy that are too much power, or end up with a sputter that's far too little.

"Damn it."

"Better. Again." Valerian's order brooks no room for opposition. He makes a demand and expects me to obey. "Get out of your head next time. You're the one holding yourself back."

The laugh that punches out of me isn't humorous. I wipe soot from my arms and frown at the snag in my fishnets. They caught the edge of a busted tile. Better my tights than my pencil skirt, I guess.

Alder offers a hand to help me up. I smile in thanks. He doesn't let go, drawing comforting patterns on my scarred skin. His musky woodsmoke scent surrounds me.

"You will learn to control this, but it only comes with practice." He dips his head. "Understand?"

"Yes."

At my determined exhale, he smiles, hypnotic green eyes hooding. "Show me what I know you can do."

His steadfast belief in me feels like something I stole. It makes me want to get this right.

Clearing my mind, I shut my eyes to visualize better. Instead of following every change in the energy that tingles beneath my skin, I picture their displays of power. Their faces spring into my head. Their gazes, smoldering, predatory, and penetrating.

The heat in my palm expands with an incandescent rush that spreads throughout me with insurmountable speed, touching every part of me.

I hold my breath, staring in awe at the perfectly formed flame cupped in my hand. It's beautiful.

"I did it! It worked this time!"

I beam at Alder first, then Matthias. Their smiles, both proud and happy, fill me with a glow I've rarely experienced. I seek out Valerian last, and my heart thuds at the way he looks at me, the satisfaction and hunger sending a bolt of excitement down my spine.

"Well done, little flower," Valerian praises in a smooth tone.

The approval washes over me, opening me up

further. It makes my heart drum, pushing me to go to him.

I take a step toward him, unsure why, but giving in to the intense tug drawing me closer. One of them rumbles as I take another. He pins me with his gaze and my nipples harden, every inch of my body strung tight. I want—

A splash in the pond outside snaps us all out of the heady trance. I blink, mortified at how badly I wanted to close the short distance between us to throw myself at him. It worries me that the onset is happening quicker and without us touching now, like an invisible force pushing me together with one of them. With all of them. Thanks for the save, duck.

The three of them don't relax, their stances tense and alert. Valerian nods to Alder and he takes up a position at the back door. Matthias unfolds himself from sitting on the table and moves to my side in seconds, wrapping a protective arm around me.

"Be ready to run if I tell you, okay?" he murmurs, expression guarded.

Oh crap. Was it not a duck? My stomach turns.

"No matter what happens, get her out," Valerian commands. "We'll meet you at the car. If we're not there by the time you get it started, go."

"Wait—"

Before I get out any protest, an attack strikes the window, shattered glass raining across the floor.

145

Matthias yanks me against him, shielding me as his arm sweeps through the air to send a fiery burst slashing through the air at the demon. Valerian doesn't give the tall, vicious-looking woman the chance to retaliate, punching a continuous streaming blaze like a flamethrower. Her slicked back high ponytail whips around as she spins to block it. They trade blows back and forth, neither of them landing a hit.

Alder's grunt of pain wrenches my focus to him. At the back of the small abandoned building, he grapples with another demon. She's mid-shift, but instead of the claws and fangs I expect, her jaw lengthens into the maw of a beastly, black dog-like creature that snaps her terrifying teeth at his neck.

"No!" I fling my hand out before the decision fully forms. The badass torrent of flames I visualize comes out of my fingertips as nothing more than sparks. "Fuck, not now. Come on!"

I hate not being able to help him, my gut churning as he jerks his head away from the beast's jaws. It knocks him off balance, massive paws pinning him to the floor.

Before the demon Valerian fights shifts her form, he catches her around the throat. His fingers lengthen, claws sprouting forth.

"She'll never be queen," the demon garbles. "You've already lost."

Valerian growls, gouging his elongated clawed fingers deeper into her throat, ripping it out mercilessly. Her body slumps to the ground, choking and spluttering as her blood pools around her and her hands slip against her skin to stem the bleeding.

"What are you waiting for? Get her out of here," he snaps.

Matthias' arm tightens around me. "Time to go."

"Wait—no! Not without them!" I push against his chest, but it's futile. The three strong demons have no trouble manhandling me. Matthias lifts me when I drag my feet. "Not yet! We can help!"

"Sorry, Lils." He doesn't sound too sorry.

I yank on his hoodie and pummel his back. It's futile. Before I know it, his long strides reach the spot we stashed the car. He stows me in the back seat, grabbing my chin to force me to look him in the eye.

"You won't leave this car." His voice has a musicality to it that sounds so good. "Okay?"

That sounds like the best idea. I nod. With a relieved sigh, he gets behind the wheel and starts the car.

Wait. My face scrunches. There was a reason I wanted to get out of the car. It's important.

Alder and Valerian aren't in the car. My ears pop and I grab a fistful of Matthias' hoodie.

"Don't leave without them," I scream.

"How the fuck did you break through that quickly?" Matthias grits his teeth, revving the engine. "Petal, it's to keep you safe."

"No! I'll—" I trip over my threat to kill him if we leave the others behind, the word sticking in my throat. A sharp pain stabs into my chest, pricking my racing heart. I claw at my shirt, panting. "Don't fucking leave yet."

"Two minutes. Max, baby. They're my brothers, but protecting you is more important."

I grind my teeth, plastering myself against the back seat to watch. Every second we're separated while they face danger feels like an unbearable eternity.

At last, Valerian's dark tousled hair and sweeping trench coat come into view, followed by Alder, his muscles straining as they sprint toward the car. A plume of smoke rises into the treetops behind them.

"Go!" Valerian shouts once he has the passenger door open. "The second one won't be down for long in her shifted form."

Alder barely has time to throw himself into the back with me, the car rocking with the force as it rolls into motion.

"Fucking hellhounds," Matthias snarls as he floors the gas, the tires kicking up dirt in our wake.

"If the hounds are tracking us, it's bad." Alder surveys his scraped up arms. "There could be anyone hunting us."

Heart twinging, I touch his forearm, careful to avoid where he's hurt. "Shit, are you okay?"

"It's nothing." He pauses to smirk at my fussing. "Truly, I'll be fine. Are you alright?"

She'll never be queen. The fuck was that supposed to mean?

I tuck my hands between my thighs and the seat. "Yeah, just rattled."

"They won't get you," he says fiercely.

"We need to put miles between us and them," Matthias says. "If we're lucky, they'll lose our trail."

The car ride knocks me out, surprisingly. I didn't think I could sleep after we were discovered, but I wake up warm in a drowsy daze as we pull into a rest stop. Closing my eyes again, I snuggle further into the charcoal-scented pillow. It shifts beneath my cheek, then an arm cinches tighter around me. I lift my head so fast I almost crack my skull against Alder's jaw.

He pulls back with a soft smile, watching me. "I was just about to wake you."

"Let me guess, you were worried about my neck

cramping again." I surreptitiously check the snug fit of his t-shirt for drool spots.

The scrapes he sustained have vanished, his defined, veiny forearms back to normal with the faint red and silvery scars that crisscross across his skin.

He caresses my hair and cups my cheek. "Sleep on me whenever you need."

My lips roll between my teeth and I try not to nuzzle my face into his palm for more of the sweet touch. "Thanks."

Matthias parks at a gas pump in front of a convenience store. "Let's stock up while we're here."

"Is it safe to stop for that long?" I ask.

"As long as we're quick," Valerian answers. "They're pack creatures. First they'll wait until they've recovered enough to hunt together. They won't catch up on foot, even in their hellhound forms."

Once Matthias sets up the gas pump, he grabs my hand, dragging me inside. He heads straight to the snack aisle. He plucks packs of powdered donuts, gummy bears, and cheddar potato chips from the shelves. I watch, twisting my fingers, not wanting to assume he'll help me when I have no money to pay for any goodies I might want.

"Don't you want snacks?" He nabs the pack of chocolate-covered pretzels I've looked at three times while he saunters up and down the aisle.

Damn him. He plays up the carefree act, but he's perceptive.

I pat invisible pockets on my skirt. "No money."

The few bucks I scraped together before leaving Philly for Brim Hills are back there, stashed between the mattress and box spring of my bed. I never keep money in my bag when I have it, too conditioned by life in group homes.

He shoots me a wink. "Get anything you want. If you don't pick something, I'll pick for you." Putting the bag of pretzels in my hand, he grasps my chin, leaning into me. "Anything you want, I'll give you, Lily."

Excitement flickers to life gradually until it drowns out my skepticism. Matthias wants to treat me. To take care of me.

Putting my trust in someone else to care for me after a long, hard life of only being able to rely on myself for survival is foreign. The hurdle shouldn't be so easy to overcome, yet something instinctive tells me I can trust him.

Picking out the first colorful package that catches my attention, I swallow back the lump that forms in my throat. No need to get so emotional over some snacks. No one's going to steal them or tell me I can't have any. I get into it the more I scan the selection. A bag of spicy nuts with a cute flaming pepper character calls my name.

"These sound good."

He pauses, watching me with a tender, charming smile that makes me glow inside. "What do you like better? Salty or sweet?" He grabs some beef jerky. "Maybe a little bit of savory to break it up so you don't get a stomach ache. Why limit ourselves, right?"

"I...don't really know what I like," I mumble. "I've never really tried any of this because there wasn't a point."

Matthias halts. "A Twinkie?" I shake my head. "Sour gummy worms? A cherry-raspberry mixed Icee? Why?"

Even a demon from another realm knows more about this than I do. "My foster placements were all frugal, and any time I was on my own in a group home, it was harder to find money. There was a bakery in Philly that donated day-old stale donuts, but that's about as wild as things got for me."

Matthias' smile tightens at the corners of his mouth, his golden eyes shifting over my shoulder. "I'll go get you one. We'll split up, cover more junk food bases. Sound good?" I nod and he plants a quick kiss on my forehead. "Remember, anything you want."

I laugh, my heart swelling. "Got it."

A shadow moves into my peripheral vision

when I go to the next aisle. I angle my head to look back at Valerian lurking behind me.

"Still a stalker," I joke.

His lips twitch. My eyebrows shoot up in surprise.

The amused expression drops off his face as quickly as it appeared. I smirk. He must have realized I made him show a sign of humor before he shut it down.

With a growl, he pins me to a pillar halfway down the aisle. It effectively tucks us between the shelves, hiding us somewhat from anyone passing by unless they came down this aisle. His sharp, narrowed gaze cuts back and forth, searching for something. His guard is up.

"Wh—? Vale," I breathe. "They found us?"

"No, different scent," he clips out. "Definitely demon, though. There are too many people in here to fight them. Play along. We need to blend in."

"People don't really, uh, do this in convenience stores." I grip the lapels of his trench coat so I don't wrap my arms around his neck.

"They won't know that."

"What about the people here who do?" I hiss.

"Christ, Lily." His grasp on my waist flexes.

I hold back a shocked cry as he leans in, gaze intent like he might kiss me. He diverts at the last second, burying his face in my neck. It could appear like we're kissing to anyone that spots us.

He speaks against my neck in a gravelly voice that shoots heat straight to my core. "For once, just do as I say without arguing about every little thing."

"You're infuriating," I shoot back hoarsely.

"Likewise, little flower." He nips my neck, the prick of his fangs teasing my skin. A strangled noise tries to escape me. "If I could be rid of you, reject you somehow, I would." I flinch, the sentiment of rejection cutting me deep. He soothes me with a rumble, petting my sides, pressing us closer together in contradiction to what he's saying. "Then I could kill you, perhaps. Rip this pretty throat out with my teeth and enjoy the sweet taste of your blood on my fangs. Maybe that would end this obsessive need to keep you near, to keep you for myself."

I forget why he pinned me to the pillar in the first place, too overcome by the needy ache pulsing between my legs. A faint groan sounds from him, his fingers sinking into my hair. I crave the feel of him crushed against me, but he keeps some distance between our bodies.

Warm, smooth hickory twines around me, the same as I picked up on in the motel room near New York. Is this his scent when he's aroused? I know the threat is empty since they admitted they're unable to kill me. Instead of fear, I'm captivated by his dark allure, wanting to learn if his touch would be as rough and intense as his callous words.

"Don't move." His fingers dig into me. "Sell it."

Oh. Demons, right. My head swims. Focusing is nearly impossible when everything in me is screaming to wrap my legs around the tall, brooding bastard and beg him to fuck me in the middle of a rest stop. The fact that sounds so wrong doesn't even register to my clouded brain.

Then I smell it—sulfur. Brimstone.

I strain my ears, squeezing the material of Valerian's jacket. He moves his head like we're locked in a passionate kiss. I mimic him with stilted, clumsy finesse. For good measure, I fake a moan. His grip turns bruising, a deep, sexy rumble vibrating against my neck.

My eyelashes flutter. Oh, shit. Okay, moaning was too much. We're both dancing on the precarious edge of control as it is from our close proximity. Faking intimacy is only fanning the flames.

The unpleasant scent drifts closer. Shit, it's not working! The demon's on to our act.

"Hey! The machine is on the fritz back here. It's spitting frozen drink everywhere, man." Matthias' voice sounds from the back corner. The demon changes course. "Is anyone around to fix this?"

"Move." Valerian nudges me in the opposite direction, toward the exit.

Seconds after we exit, Alder pulls the car up.

Valerian herds me into the back seat, keeping his grip on my nape. Matthias bursts out of the store, whipping off his blue-stained hoodie. He takes shotgun.

"Floor it. Blue raspberry isn't going to distract him for long," he says. "Too many humans around to kill him. I just made it look like he slipped and hit his head."

"Was it another hellhound?" I ask.

"No," Valerian says. "This was a low-rank reaper. Possibly one in training.. It was a bad coincidence he wandered in at the same time. We need to change tactics. If there are so many demons in the mortal realm, it will be difficult to avoid them in populated areas while you learn to use your power."

His bitter smoke scent chokes the car, blending with the sharp and musky scents the other two put off as Alder drives away. I pick his out as the same scent the last two times we were under attack, using it to read his frustration. It's far different than the warm hickory scent whenever he has me pinned at his mercy.

Valerian's grip on my nape doesn't fall away, even several minutes after we get away.

Twelve

LILY

NEAR DUSK AND TWO STATE LINES LATER, WE FINALLY stop when we find an abandoned theme park Matthias knew of in Maryland. Alder melts a hole in the fence for us to slip through. Past the *KEEP OUT* signs, the rusty attractions with chipped-paint inside the park are partially swallowed by wild overgrowth.

"I've always wanted to go to an amusement park. I walked by a small carnival one summer when I was growing up." They stop when I linger in front of a kiddie coaster. My reminiscent smile falters. "That foster placement was one of the few I thought would stick. The following week, they sent me back because I had another nightmare and they decided I was too much to deal with. Just like the others."

The three of them flash me fierce looks that stir a flutter in my chest. It expands into a hum in my blood that wants to split me in three different directions. Shaking my head to clear it, I move on, craning my neck to look up at the ferris wheel.

"Think any of these still work?"

"Doubt it." Matthias scratches his stomach, pushing up the black t-shirt he threw on when we were far enough away from the last demon we encountered. While it was off, I got an eyeful of his trim, tattooed body. I watch while trying not to. He catches my eye with a dirty smirk. "But I'll take you on as long of a ride as you want, babe. We won't stop until you're screaming."

"Matthias," Alder growls.

He dodges with a cocky laugh when Alder swipes at him. We continue walking through the park. I picture it lit up and bustling with people rather than the eerie silence interrupted by the tread of our feet on the pavement.

"Think we'll be safe here?" I ask.

"Long enough to rest and regroup," Alder says. "We'll remain on guard until then. No training while we're here. I think the hellhounds found us because of the strength of your magical signature. The more you use your power, the stronger it is to sense. Let's not find out if I'm right tonight."

"Good with me."

I press my fingers against my eyes, rubbing weariness away before raking my fingers through my hair. I'd kill for a shower, my short red locks feeling too greasy for my taste. We've been on the go nonstop and I didn't expect two demon encounters in the same day throwing us off our planned course. I'll have to endure it because I doubt there's running water here, and I'm not touching any standing body of water.

Alder motions to a faded striped tent. We duck inside, taking in the worn wooden floor strewn with straw and the tiered benches that circle the space. It must have been used for a small circus show.

"Rest," Alder says. "I'll go set up a perimeter to ward off anything that could be in the area."

I sit on a bench, plucking at the snag in my fishnets from when I fell in the pizza shop earlier. Hard to believe that was this morning. "Never thought I'd miss the shitty motels you guys picked out. We don't have to go full off-grid, right?"

Valerian studies me with a sidelong glance. He's kept close after we got out of the car, hovering over me. "We need to plan out our next move. You're not in control of your powers, so we can't go to the underworld yet."

"We're going there?" My head jerks up. He towers over me, the corners of his eyes tight.

"Eventually. We can't run forever from those hunting us. We don't belong here. Neither do you."

I twist the material of my fishnets around my fingers. The one thing I've kept at bay in my mind after learning I have a secret power hidden away inside me is that they were right about me. I'm not human. If I'm not human, then the mortal realm isn't my place. It's not like I've ever fit in. I never imagined it's because I wasn't part of this world to begin with.

Matthias sits next to me, offering one of his charming dimpled smiles. "You'll like it. Our home is unlike anything you could ever imagine. The shifting mountains of the Whispering Highlands that reach so high you can see for miles across the realm when they appear. Vast caverns lit by magic gemstones that create kaleidoscopes on the cave walls. Midnight falls that spill into pools of starlight beneath the blood moon." His eyes crinkle at the corners and he covers my hands, stopping me from worrying my ruined fishnets. "After we've sorted this mix up with the demon council, I'll take you there."

My heart stutters, then beats harder at the way he says *our home*. Like I could belong there without question. A long-buried wish for my own place to fit in rises from the depths where I hid it.

There's also something familiar about what he

describes, like in the dreams I had the week after I opened the gate.

I tuck my hair behind my ears, peeking at both of them through my lashes. "How will we get there? The Brim Hills gate is blocked."

"First, we must find out how to break the seal that's kept your power buried away." A muscle jumps in Valerian's cheek when he clenches his jaw. Some of his dark hair falls in his face as he gazes down at me. "There are many gates. It's harder to access them without being the guard with the incantation key, but we'll deal with that when we get to it."

I take in the troubled shadows in his drawn face, resisting the desire to reach up and smooth the rigidness in his features until they're gone. "Do you miss your gate?"

"No." His curt response is immediate and for the first time since he pinned me to the column in the rest stop, he turns his back on me, his spine rigid.

Something Matthias told me when we were first flung into our life on the run surfaces in my mind. "It's okay to grieve it. You guarded it for a long time."

"There's nothing to miss about a cursed assignment to punish me for my mistakes," he growls. "I'm going to check the perimeter is secured with Alder."

I jump to my feet as Valerian stalks off.

Matthias catches my hand to stop me, grip firm. "Stay with me." His gaze cuts away, the bright gold color dimmed. "Let the broody bastard go. He gets like this sometimes without Alder around to distract him from getting lost in his rage. They used to be at each other's throats when Alder was appointed to keep him in check. By the time I was assigned to guard the gate with them, I was sure they'd kill each other and I'd wind up with a sweet gig all to myself."

I watch the tent flap, wishing to go after him, but not wanting to leave Matthias' side when he asked me to stay. "Why?"

"The three of us have been together a long time. Over a century for me, even longer for them. In all that time, we've never really forged friendship. We tolerate each other at best." He chuckles, ruffling his hair. "Alder used to say it was because he had no respect for a disgraced knight and a guy like me who doesn't take anything seriously. He's a buzzkill yes-man who follows his orders no matter what. Guarding the gate isn't what he wanted, though. I think he was just pissed he was taken away from a warrior guild to become a guard."

"Valerian was a knight?" I picture him as if he's a character from one of the fantasy worlds in my manga, cutting a brooding yet handsome figure with a cloak and armor.

I can see it, though I prefer the trench coat I first teased him about in my head. There's something more roguish and dangerous about him now that's far more appealing.

"Yeah, highly decorated, one of the top fighters among Lucifer's knights. The king trusted him implicitly. He was lined up to become commander of the demon knights until he screwed up and lost the charge he was supposed to protect."

"Oh."

It helps me understand why Valerian got so uptight about today's encounters. He doesn't want to fail protecting another person he's promised to keep safe.

"The council decided instead of paying for his failure with his life, he would spend eternity guarding the borders between the realms."

"So if Alder only took the guard position to follow orders and Valerian had no choice, how did you end up there?"

"The urban legend was drawing too many people for them to handle alone. The only good part was free rein to discover how interesting the human world is, and even that was starting to lose its appeal. This is much more exciting. Being on the run with you." His mouth tugs up at the corner and his fingers thread through mine. "You came along and somehow you're the glue that makes us work together."

"Come on," I scoff. "We're all dysfunctional. Forced together because the alternate option is dying. I'm sure you'd all survive just fine without me."

He steps past me, tugging on my hand. "Let's go explore. You said you've always wanted to go to a theme park." Some of his upbeat energy returns. He's been odd since our close call at the rest stop. He shoots a kid-in-a-candy-store grin over his shoulder. "We're not passing up the opportunity."

I laugh and allow him to lead me out of the tent under the twilight sky. My worries and stress slip away as he lifts my spirits.

When we reach the carousel, he helps me untangle myself from a thorny vine that snags my clothes. I rest a hand on his shoulder for balance. "A pencil skirt is definitely not the right outfit for exploring abandoned rides."

"Want to trade?" Matthias' smirk is mischievous. He pinches the hem of his t-shirt to flash me his abs. "You'd look way better in my shirt."

I fight back a smile at his flirting, glad that he's back to his normal self. It breaks free anyway, and he hums, offering me a hand to help me step onto the carousel platform. I spin around when elastic snaps against my thigh, lifting my brows at his mask of innocence. He hooks a finger in one of the holes of my tights and flicks his gaze up to meet mine.

"I'll get your bag from the car when we go back to the tent so you can change."

"Thanks," I say sardonically. "My hero."

His teeth rake over his lip and he waggles his brows. "As long as I get to watch, babe."

A soft, husky laugh leaves me. Grabbing the pole of a faded white horse, I swing away from him. "It sucks we can't get this thing working."

"Pick one." He follows me as I weave through the carousel. "We'll close our eyes and imagine it."

It's like I have permission to let go of everything that weighs me down when we're alone. He reminds me I deserve to have a good time rather than the bitterness I've internalized for years. I have more fun with him than I've ever had.

I circle the entire first tier of the ride, ending up back at the horse where we climbed on. Matthias brushes against my back, grabbing my hips. A squeal slips out of me as he boosts me onto the chipped seat.

"Here, beautiful." He has a small wildflower he twirls between his fingers. "I found this on the other side for you. A flower for my petal."

Cheeks flushing, I accept it. "Thank you. What's this for?"

"Because I love your smile and I'll do anything to earn it," he murmurs.

The carousel horse puts me eye to eye with him. A warm glow fills my chest that breaks through the walls I built up around my vulnerable heart when the world made me believe I was troubled, difficult, and unlovable. He always accepts me without judgment.

"I get the sense you haven't done a lot of smiling while you've been stuck in the mortal realm."

I tear my gaze away. "Not really."

"Then it's my job to make up for all the smiles you've missed out on. I promise to make you smile every day."

He braces a hand on the horse's rump and caresses the outside of my thigh. The fear that used to make me wrench myself away from allowing anyone to touch me vanishes around him. I bite my lip as his touch trails up to my hip, his eyes bouncing between mine when I'm brave enough to meet them.

"You're the perfect height now."

Matthias dips his head and captures my lips. My stomach bottoms out and my fingers twist in his shirt.

The press of his mouth is sweet. He cups my cheek, swiping his tongue along my lips. Startled by the feeling of the fork in his tongue, I gasp into the kiss. He swallows it, deepening the kiss with a groan. I follow his lead clumsily until kissing him becomes natural. That devious tongue wraps around

166

mine and he *sucks* it into his mouth, ripping a moan from me. Things go from sweet to sensual and wild, heating up with the filthy way he claims my mouth.

He ends it before I'm ready. I chase him, eager for more. He swoops back in with a depraved chuckle, kissing me until my lips feel swollen. Stroking my hair, he breaks away, leaving me breathless.

My heart thuds as I bring my fingertips to my tingling lips. That was my first kiss. And my second.

He gives me a soft, crooked smile. His golden gaze brims with affection as he traces the corner of my mouth with his thumb. My stomach dips and a shaky breath leaves me. I'm not used to anyone looking at me like this, like I'm the only thing they need in the world.

"Wow. You're even more stunning after you've been kissed, petal." His eyes roam every inch of my face greedily. "I've wanted to do that for weeks."

"You have?" I breathe.

"Since the first moment we met. One hit of that toasted cinnamon scent and I was a goner. Vale ordered us not to touch you after we let you run away. He doesn't think we should let the pull your scent has on us control us, but fuck that." His forked tongue peeks out to trace his lower lip, captivating me once more with the split shape. Sinking his fingers in my hair, he rests his forehead against mine and groans. "Your scent is so intoxicating, Lils. It's euphoric. Even just holding you like this makes me want you. All of you."

My chin quivers. I don't have any experience with this. He's so good at getting past my defenses, making me want to trust what he's saying. Wanting to believe he won't rip away at any second and reveal it's all a joke, because how could anyone want me, the reject?

"When I saw Vale all over you at the rest stop, all I could think was *mine*." His embrace tightens and his hot breath fans over my lips. I strain closer, hoping for another kiss. "I don't care what Vale or Alder want, Lily. I'm fighting for what I want—fighting for you. I'm done holding back when everything is screaming at me to make you mine."

His. I like the sound of that, my heart beating faster.

"I want to take care of you no matter where we end up. It's not just that I find everything about you sexy as hell. This pull I feel—" He puts my hand over his heart. He's breathing almost as hard as I am, his tone heartfelt. "It means something important. That you're mine to cherish, if you'll let me."

Every time I've felt a moment of tension between us and held myself back from more was because I've been setting myself up for disappointment and loneliness as usual. A lump forms in my throat as I struggle not to fall apart at his promise that this isn't temporary, that someone could want me. My heart swells, echoing the sentiment. I want that, too. I want to be with him.

Guilt at choosing passes over me for a moment, but I'm happy as long as I get to stay with one of them. It's not like Alder or Valerian have feelings for me outside of the strange thrall of sexual tension my scent triggers in them. Something inside me fights against that belief, but I push it down. In a short span of time, they've each become important to me. I can't imagine what life would be like without them. When we've figured all of this out, at least I don't have to go back to being alone.

"I feel it, too," I stammer.

His head lifts, surprise written across his face. "You do?"

I nod, throat constricting. "I've felt it for a while. In the alley, when you…" I trip over my words, sliding my lips together. "I wanted you to. Even though Valerian was right there watching, even though you were threatening me, all I wanted was more. I needed you to kiss me, to keep touching me, or I thought I would die before you could make good on your threat. Isn't that insane?"

A rough noise falls from his lips. "Right here?"

His other hand covers my heart and my eyes fall shut. The invisible tug around it at his touch draws me closer to him. I don't admit I've felt this sensation for all three of them whenever they're close or touching me, terrified that if I do, he won't want me anymore.

"Do you know what that means?" At the shake of my head, he presses his lips to my forehead. "That's a bond you feel. They only happen when you're near the connection it wants to make. It means I'm your fated. That I'm yours and you're mine. In the underworld, a fated bond with your demon mate is considered a sacred gift."

When he says *mate*, I cry out, clinging to him as something cracks open inside me, sending a strange pulse thrumming all over my body.

This is crazy. The kind of thing that only happens in the fantasy stories I read, not real life.

It's an instinct I've ignored and shut down until now. The whisper at the back of my mind I've pushed aside because I didn't understand it and it overwhelmed me. Yet it feels so right once I acknowledge it. He's someone who would never reject me, the one meant for me. My soulmate.

"Damn." He sways against me, dipping his nose to rest in the crook of my neck. He inhales, wrapping his arms around me, his erection grinding against my legs. "I think I'm literally high on your scent right now."

I snort at his slurred observation. It helps cut through the frenzied need that crashed over me a moment ago. The ache between my legs doesn't quiet completely, though I feel more in control of myself.

"Mine," he repeats in a smoky rasp.

I shudder, my head swimming from his enticing scent. "Yours."

Matthias grasps my chin, tipping it up. The bright gold in his eyes darkens to a warm, sultry shade of honey. "If you look this gorgeous after a kiss, I have to know…"

"What?"

His hands drag down my back, trailing down the sides of my skirt before he pushes beneath the hem, massaging my thick thighs. "What you look like when you come. I have to get another taste of you. I'm going insane imagining it all the time."

An acute, heady fire spreads through me once more, burning hot in my core as he slides my skirt up my hips, exposing me to the chill of the night. I nod, wrapping my arms around his shoulders. A sinful, pleased rumble vibrates in his chest and he rips a new hole in my ruined fishnets to get at me.

He kisses me again, each swipe of his tongue and nibble of his teeth dizzying and addictive. His fingers trace the edges of my panties, teasing me. I squirm, desperate for his touch on my pussy.

"Please." The breathy plea comes out mumbled between kisses. "I need—"

"I've got you, petal," he swears in a sinful tone. "I'm going to make you feel so good. Fuck you with my fingers and eat your sweet cream from them when you come. You taste so perfect everywhere. I knew you would."

I moan, digging my fingers into his shoulders. His mouth moves to my neck, sharp fangs scraping my sensitive skin, followed by the flick of his forked tongue. My hips buck, my clit throbbing with the rush of pent up desire. I've only allowed myself quick relief in secret when I shower. It's not enough. I need him.

His fingers slip into my panties, wrenching the material aside. My thighs squeeze together on instinct, and he blocks me, pushing my legs wide for him to step between. He glides his fingers through my slick folds and presses a filthy sound against my ear.

"So wet already, petal." Matthias leans back, encouraging me to look at him. His gaze burns into me as he lifts his fingers to his mouth, tasting me. "Mm, so damn sweet and perfect. I can't wait until your pussy soaks my cock."

My lashes flutter, panting breaths tinged with little moans of pleasure when he circles my clit. I open my mouth to tell him what I like, but the words die out, his touch skilled perfection. The tingling sensation of sparks bursting and causing vibrations against my clit and folds rips a startled cry from me.

"Oh my god." I whimper. "What are you doing? That feels... Oh, shit."

"You liked it when I showed you these sparks before. This is what I was imagining doing to you," he rasps. "Oh yeah, you like that. You're grinding on my hand, baby. Making such a gorgeous mess, getting my fingers all wet and sloppy. You need them filling your pussy?"

"Yes," I hiss.

My head falls back, spine arching as he teases his sparking fingers around my entrance. We've barely done anything and I'm already close to shattering, faster than any time I've made myself come.

"Tell me, Lily. What do you want right now?"

A ragged breath rushes out of me. "Please, Matthias."

"Tell me and I'll give it to you."

"I want—I want your fingers inside me. Fuck me with them."

His hooded gaze traps me. "You want to come all over my hand?"

I nod. "Please."

A whimper spills from me as he pushes a finger inside. I've only ever touched myself, and this feels like so much more, so much better than when I do it. The further he sinks inside, the more my core throbs, the tight coil ready to snap.

"Christ, you look good like this."

I like the roughness tinging his voice, like he's seconds from losing control. Illuminated eyes flashing brighter, he adds a second finger, curling them deep inside my pussy with each thrust. His thumb circles my clit.

The sparks grow more intense and I can't hold on. His power sends me over the edge with a shudder. I bite my lip, burying my face in his shoulder as the eruption of oblivion ripples through my core.

"Fuck, pretty girl. Look at you coming for me." Matthias kisses my temple. "Such a good girl."

He keeps going, still amplifying things with his sparks, thrusting inside me until the sound is obscene. It tips me from one orgasm right into the next.

"That's it. Cream all over my fingers. Give me a good taste."

Once my body stops shivering, he pulls free, making sure I watch as his forked tongue licks his fingers clean. His wicked gaze ensnares me. *Mine.* The thought echoes in my head and the corners of his mouth hitches up.

"What about you?" The words slip out before I'm able to stop them.

I duck to hide my blush as I reach for the bulge in his jeans. I came twice and still clench around the emptiness without his fingers inside me.

Am I being too greedy to want more? Too much too soon? I don't know what I'm supposed to do, only able to follow the thrumming instinct of the bond. Using my palm, I map the thick hardness of his dick and rub him.

"Shit, babe." He grinds against my touch for a moment, features slack with pleasure.

My brows furrow when he pulls back. "Don't you want to come?"

He grins, cupping my cheek. I lean into his palm, savoring how good it feels, the affectionate touch filling me with a warm glow.

"I do, baby, so badly. But I can sense the others making their way back, and they'll be pissed if they find out I've stolen you away to ravage you. You should get some rest. Let's head back and take a nap to recharge before we have to hit the road again." He winks. "You can use me as a pillow. I can't promise I won't feel you up while you sleep, though."

"Okay." It comes out through a laugh. I've never laughed so much in my life, but with him I feel light and free.

Matthias helps me down from the ride and fixes my skirt before stepping away. My heart gives an unsure, panicky thump at the distance. The worry that he's done with me rears its ugly head, despite everything he promised.

It calms down when he reaches for my hand. My

world feels a little less askew as I take it, quieting the fear that I'll be discarded.

Thirteen
LILY

AFTER OUR SECRET NIGHT TOGETHER, I FEEL TORN IN two. The pull I feel with Matthias settles after he claimed me as his fated mate a couple days ago, yet it doesn't go away around Alder and Valerian. If anything, it's more intense, stronger without them coming as close. If they look at me, the sensation acts up, begging me to go to them. When Matthias wraps his arms around me and brushes kisses along my neck, the unruly thing within me calms, content in his embrace.

I'm happy with him. I shouldn't want more, yet…

Can someone have more than one soulmate? I thought it would go away after what happened with

The confusion has today's training session off to a rough start. I have yet to successfully block Alder's mild ranged attacks and Valerian's patience is growing thin. The next one catches me off guard and knocks me to the dead pine needles covering the sandy floor of the woods we're in. They sizzle as I stare up at the tall trees.

It's been eighteen years since I've been back to the Pine Barrens. Jersey Devil territory, where I was found as a baby. If this is where I was, I wonder if there is a gate to Hell near the Leeds house. I prod at my mind, searching for a memory clouded by the magic that trapped my powers until they broke free, but there's nothing there to tell me how I got from the underworld to here.

"Are you going to daydream the next time a hellhound or warrior attacks as well?" Valerian mutters coolly. "Because you'd be dead by now. Pay attention, or you'll never learn to defend yourself in combat."

"I am. This is still weird for me." Climbing to my feet, I wave my hands. A burst of wild steam rises from them into the trees at my untamed emotions. "I didn't grow up knowing I could do this. I was terrified every time a fire was blamed on me because it meant I was a freak and I'd be booted from a foster home placement again. It's hard to tap into this when I haven't been doing it as long as you all have."

It's still a lot to wrap my head around—a demon trapped inside a human body. I don't even know how I can withstand my powers in this form, unsure if this body is mine or if I'm like the others, able to shift to a true form behind the human appearance. I flex my smoking scarred hands. If I'd known how to control this, maybe I wouldn't bear the mark of the horrors I've been through.

Before I admit more than I want to about my past, I snap my jaw shut. Valerian narrows his eyes, gesturing for me to go again before crossing his arms, his rolled up sleeves straining around his strong forearms inked with tattoos that shift with his moods.

Arms wind around me from behind and Matthias surrounds me with the scent of a campfire shot through with warmed chestnuts and maple. The frustration that consumed me a moment ago melts away at his soothing embrace. I hum, my pleased smile slowly curling the corners of my mouth.

"Hey."

"I'm attacking you, babe." His breath tickles. "Fight your way out of my arms. I like it rough, so don't hold back."

"Matthias, get the fuck out of here," Valerian grits out. "You're distracting her. Go check the wards along our perimeter."

Alder and Valerian have doubled up on the

179

magical barriers they erect around us when we stop. They believe it will help mask the magnitude of my power and keep us from being tracked. It's worked so far while we keep moving.

Matthias presses the curve of his smile against my ear. "Turn around, baby."

That tone is all mischief. I spin to face him, sucking in a breath when he cradles my face and kisses me deeply. I meld against him. It's over too soon and I already crave the next one.

The other two growl, their stances rigid. Valerian scowls and Alder glares at Matthias. Both of them shift their focus to me and I gasp at the desire filling their penetrating gazes. It's almost like they're jealous. My stomach tightens at the thought, the pull confusing me again when it wants me to do the same with them even though I love kissing Matthias.

We haven't hidden anything from the others, though this is the first time he's kissed me in front of them. For the most part, we've spent the last two days holding hands and sticking close together once we moved on from the amusement park before dawn.

"I'm not hiding or stealing moments with you," Matthias says. "You're mine. They'll learn to deal with it."

Biting my lip, I nod, the tiny glow inside my

chest expanding every time he claims me like that.

"Matthias," Alder pushes out through clenched teeth.

"I'm going. Check the wards, got it." He smacks my ass affectionately and takes my chin between his thumb and finger. "I promise to keep you safe so you can figure your shit out."

I huff, rolling my lips between my teeth to keep from snickering. Giving the others a challenging stare, he saunters off through the trees.

"Get back in position," Valerian says roughly.

Sighing, I follow his orders. After Matthias shed some insight on his past, it's not hard to miss that he's used to being in command of those around him.

"At the ready," he says. "Though in a true fight, you won't have the heads up. It's best to remain prepared."

"Oh shit!" I throw my hands up too late when Alder's next attack—a spiraling stream of steam and flames—barrels at me with more force than he's used all morning. The fire singes a hole in my sweater, plunging the neckline deeper where the yarn melts away to reveal more of my cleavage. I flick at it, then glare at him. "What's your deal?"

"Training," Alder grumbles. "If you didn't want to ruin your clothes, you should've worn something else."

"Maybe I'll borrow one of your shirts and see if

you still want to fuck up my clothes."

Alder quiets, his green eyes gleaming with the silent promise that he definitely would as his focus dips to my chest. I falter, picturing it. His oversized t-shirt hanging off my curves, the way his fire would burn through it, leaving me bare for him to devour me.

"I've removed the dalliance driving you to distraction, so what's the problem now?" Valerian stalks toward me, ignoring the daggers Alder glares at his back when he doesn't stop until he's in my face, drowning me in his spiced smoky scent. I stand my ground, fighting the heady stir of lust at my forbidden fantasy. "Or do you think this is a game we're enjoying?"

"Fuck you."

Valerian smirks when I push against his chest. The pull inside me becomes taut, almost unbearable. Both of us breathe hard, our scents mixing together. Hickory and cinnamon. It's the first time I smell what they sense. His eyes are almost black, blown pupils swallowing up the blue as he grips my elbows to keep me in place.

"Vale," I choke out.

A deep rumble vibrates in his throat at his name falling from my lips. "Do I have to keep pushing you until you break, little flower? I will. If that's what it takes, I'll keep pushing until you beg me."

His head dips closer. I strain, caught between closing the little distance left between us and remembering that I belong to another.

Alder grabs me by the arm and breaks us apart. Valerian sighs, releasing me as Alder draws me away. I find no relief from the invisible force inside me, struggling with the same insistent push toward him.

"Step away." I flinch at the hardness riding his tone. His fingers dig into my arm almost to the point of bruising, contradicting his words. "Do it, Lily. Please. Before I do something you don't want. I can't—when you smell like this, it's difficult to resist."

Thinking of Matthias' affectionate smiles and how much I need them, I wrench free with a pained cry. Alder's fist closes around nothing as I stumble away, scrubbing at my face. This bond shit isn't fair. Why is it tormenting me like this after finding my mate?

Once I no longer feel like ripping my clothes off and demanding one—or both—of them take me, I lean against a tree. Valerian has stalked far away, his attention locked on me. Alder sits on a rotted out log, bracing his forearms on his legs, veins prominent when he clenches his fists.

We need a break. I call on a small fire, pushing the limits of what I've learned to control without my power failing me or exploding free. It dances in my palm, not scorching me.

"Why doesn't it burn my skin?" I ask without looking away from the orange glow.

"Our own powers don't hurt us," Alder says. "It's innate, a part of us. It comes from within you."

"Then why…" I force out a tight breath. Talking about this terrifies me, but I have to know. He would understand. It gives me the courage to let them in. "There was a fire when I was little. It burned down my foster home after something bad happened. I think—it came from me."

"Is that why your hands are scarred?" Valerian's dangerous voice is closer.

I nod. "I was in the hospital for two weeks once I was back in the state's custody." I pass the flame back and forth between my marred hands. "I don't know exactly what happened. I blocked a lot of it out. After that, I learned to suppress my emotions. If I didn't feel too much, I would be safe."

Valerian's boots enter my peripheral vision. "Do you know what a changeling is?"

"They're in fairy tales and mythology. A stolen child swapped for another." My eyes widen. Oh. I was found as a baby. "Is that what I am? How I appear human, but…I'm not?"

"I believe so. Your demon was magically sealed in this form. You're trapped. It's possible that the

184

force of your mature powers were too much to handle before your human vessel aged to adulthood." His voice hardens. "Whoever brought you here and sealed you like this most likely expected your powers to kill you."

My shoulders sag. So this might not be my body. Lily Sloane doesn't exist. I'm nothing.

I smell smoke before I sense something—off, like a strange shift in the air. It's not a familiar scent from one of the guys. Alder and Valerian tense, searching the woods. The three of us whirl to a rustling bush. Alder rushes to guard me, pulling me behind him.

Matthias tears through the bush, alert, fanged teeth bared. "Do you sense it?"

"Someone's approaching," Valerian confirms.

A deep laugh echoes around us, seemingly from all directions. Valerian instinctively reaches for his hip, closing his fingers around air. He curses under his breath.

A moment later, a demon materializes out of thin air on a small incline above us with a broad grin. "I see it's still impossible to sneak up on you, Vale."

"Rainer," Valerian says flatly, still on edge.

"Hello, old friend. It's been a long time."

"Almost three centuries," Valerian mutters.

Rainer looks every bit like a knight, his dark leather attire outfitted with a sword hilt attached at his hip beneath his cloak. He has thick sandy hair that reaches past his shoulders, half tied back, and a trimmed beard. Like my demons, the only indicators he's not a human messing around cosplaying a fantasy knight in the woods are his glowing eyes and the serpent-like tongue poking out from the edge of his smile, keeping his other demon features hidden. His friendly eyes are a deep amber that match the shade of mine. He said three hundred years, but only looks in his late twenties at most.

He jumps down from the incline, surveying us. "I found you. As soon as I heard, I set out to search for you. I have news—"

Valerian cuts him off. "Not here." He sweeps our surroundings with a calculating gaze. "If you can get past our perimeter without tripping it, so can others."

Alder keeps himself positioned between Rainer and me as we head for the dinky motel we're staying at on one of the isolated backroads that cut through the Pine Barrens. Matthias puts his arm around my waist, almost lifting me off my feet from how tightly he holds me. Even Valerian serves as a barrier when Rainer glances at me.

The walk to the motel isn't far once we make it to the road from the trail we took into the woods. Valerian remains alert until we're inside the dim, musty room.

I crinkle my nose, looking forward to getting out of here. I grab the first stray shirt I find— Alder's, making my stomach dip—and slip into the bathroom to change out of my ruined sweater. His shirt reaches the ripped knees of my jeans. Tying it in a knot at my hip, I dust the sand and a leaf stuck in my hair before returning to find my three demon companions blocking Rainer from entering the room further than the small chair posted by the door.

Smirking past their shoulders at me, he takes a seat.

"So what the fuck is going on?" Valerian folds his arms. "It's been a shitstorm up here. Demons are crawling all over the realm."

"The underworld is in chaos as well." Rainer sighs, gesturing flippantly. "No one can get to the king to seek an audience and find out his wishes. The council is acting on his behalf. You've been labeled as traitors. It's come down directly from the council."

"The council?" Alder barks. He pushes his large hands into his brown hair. "How? What did we do that warrants this?"

"The official report is grim. It details your plot to harbor a fugitive to overthrow the crown and take the throne for yourselves."

Valerian scoffs. "That's ridiculous. If I was going to do that, I would've been better off doing it with Lil—" He cuts off, sharp jawline working as he collapses to sit on the end of the bed I'm standing beside. It's the first time I've seen him so weary. He glances at me. "I was in a better position to stage a fucking rebellion when I was a knight. I don't have any interest in that. My loyalty has always been to Lucifer. Why would I wait until now, festering away guarding a gate portal?"

"I'm only telling you what the council claims. I don't believe them for a second. Though it's been a long time, I still know you, Vale." Rainer shifts his curious gaze to me. "They say the girl is powerful."

The three of them close rank around me with feral warning growls. Valerian pulls me into his lap while Matthias and Alder square off with Rainer. My heart thuds, startled by the speed they moved. Valerian's arm slides around my waist, his palm spread on my soft stomach to keep me in place.

"Don't look at her," Matthias says viciously.

The force of Valerian's answering growl vibrates against my back, his chin dipping over my shoulder. In my periphery, I can see his fangs as his lip curls back. Alder's fists are poised to punch, his tense knuckles smoking with his impending flames at the ready.

Rainer sniffs the air and laughs. "I see. Quite the predicament you've ended up in, old friend."

"Why are you here?" Valerian demands.

Rainer holds up his hands. "To repay the life debt I owe you. And because you still have people's trust. Allow me to be your eyes and ears in the underworld."

The three of them exchange glances. Alder stares at my shirt, seeing me in it for the first time. Matthias lingers on the way Vale holds me, but doesn't show Rainer any cracks in our unified front.

Alder nods in agreement. "We need to understand what's going on instead of running blind."

"Very well." Vale's fingers twitch, giving my stomach the barest caress. "Update us when you can."

"I will." He holds out his hand.

Valerian seems reluctant, like he's torn between letting me go and allowing Rainer any closer. His exhale blows my short hair and he shifts me off his lap, rising when Rainer does. They clasp arms, Valerian's tattoos swirling across his forearm.

"Thou who seeks to bind in loyalty and allegiance. *I consentio relligo*," Valerian intones.

"Thine pledge is my fealty, given in honor. *I conveniunt ad nervo*," Rainer responds.

Their skin glows with an intricate red design that matches up where they touch. The magic light becomes brighter, then burns off in a flash of smoke and ash. The only evidence left behind is a small circular mark with the same pattern on both of their wrists. Rainer mutters something in another language, dragging two fingers across the mark. It vanishes, melting into nothing on his skin.

"Whoa." I lean forward. "What was all that?"

"A masking spell and a Demon's Pledge," Rainer explains. "It's a binding promise forged between your brethren. It'll allow me to communicate with Vale across vast distances."

My brows jump up. "Even across the realms?"

"That's more difficult, but possible. Only bonded mates and very strong demons are capable of such feats."

My gaze seeks Matthias. He's already watching me, gold eyes hooded and a dimpled smirk playing at the edge of his mouth.

"So we don't have to keep running? We can do something about this. Fight the council."

Alder frowns. "It's suicide to go against the council."

"They're the Devil's right hand," Valerian says.

"We have to try. Otherwise we'll be running forever. I don't want to run." I slide my lips together, shocked by my own fierce burst of confidence. "If we can get Lucifer to listen, we can convince him to call off this hunt."

A muscle jumps in Valerian's cheek. "You think you hold so much sway that the king of Hell would grant you an audience, little flower?" His cold gaze cuts away. "He is merciless."

I narrow my eyes. "Then we'll go without you."

"You'll do no such thing," he grits out.

Matthias pulls me away from Vale by my hand, wrapping me in his arms. Alder reaches out, touching the shirt I stole from him.

Rainer chuckles, patting Valerian on the shoulder. "I should be off before my presence upsets the balance among you. Be careful, old friend. I only tracked you because I understand how your mind works after fighting alongside you, but the hellhounds are circling the area. Witches are keeping them at bay."

"What do you know of the local covens?" Valerian slides into strategy mode. "I'm seeking them out to find one that can break a powerful magic seal."

"They're to the east along the coastline. Ask for Juniper."

Valerian nods. Before Rainer leaves, he clasps his shoulder. "It's good to see you. After so long."

"And you." Rainer gives him a smile that's sad and fond. "It will not be so long next time."

Valerian nods, his throat bobbing. A pang hits me in the chest at the display of emotions he keeps locked up tight. It makes him look younger when he's not scowling.

Fourteen

LILY

Aafter Alder brings back lunch, Matthias takes my hand with a mischievous glint in his eye. He gives me a playful wink.

"Come on."

"I thought I had to finish learning how to block?"

Valerian left shortly after his knight friend to look for any witches nearby, leaving orders for me to continue the interrupted training session. Alder expects me to follow him back out to the woods in fifteen minutes.

"Skip it. You deserve a break and I want to take you out." He draws me closer, kissing me. "I can see you're about to go crazy if you don't get away from this for a little bit. You think you're hiding it from us but you're not as good at it as you think."

It's odd that he can read me so well when I've spent my life hiding my thoughts and opinions, dulling myself for the sake of others. Odd and nice. With the guys, I don't have to do that anymore. I can be my real self, the girl I've never fully shown to anyone else.

"I won't let anything hurt you." He traces my nose with the tip of his, white blond hair brushing my forehead. "I might not be a warrior like Alder and Vale, but I know how to fight."

"Always trying to slide in as my hero," I tease. "You already got the girl."

"That's right, baby."

"Fine." My beaming expression gives me away. "Let me change first."

I take my bag into the bathroom, hesitating with my grip on the bottom of Alder's shirt. If I'm going out with my demon boyfriend, my—my mate, I shouldn't be wearing another man's clothes. His shirt smells so good, woodsy with hints of charcoal. Shaking my head, I peel it off. Instead of leaving it for him to find, I stuff it deep in my bag and pick an outfit I think Matthias will like. Once I'm dressed in the leather miniskirt that hugs the curve of my wide hips and a loose crop top with skull hands that appear to hold my breasts, I swipe on some mascara and red lipstick I stole.

"Bombshell." Matthias rakes his teeth over his lip, taking me in with a heated gaze. His arm drapes across my shoulders and he leads me out to the car Valerian didn't take, swinging the keys around his finger. "I want to make it up to you that we missed out on your first rest stop junk food feast. I found a spot nearby I think you'll like."

I tilt my head curiously, brushing my fingers against his chest as an excuse to get closer. "What is it?"

The corner of his mouth lifts. "It's a surprise."

"Surprises generally aren't a good thing for me."

With a hum, he brings his lips to my ear. "Then I'd better get to work on showing you how enjoyable they can be."

The shiver I attempt to hide makes him snicker. He opens the passenger door for me with a grand sweep of his arm. A laugh bubbles out of me at his antics and the spark of excitement flickers to life as he pulls away from the motel with the windows down. The cool autumn air blows my hair back from my neck and shoulders. He rests one hand over the wheel and stretches the other out to thread through my hair before he drops it to my lap, tucking it between my legs. The casual, possessive move makes my insides twist pleasantly.

"When Alder finds out we bailed on him, he's

194

going to kill us," I say.

Matthias squeezes my thigh. "He'll be more pissed he didn't think to take you out first."

As much as I like how that sounds, I bite my lip. "I don't have a lot of experience. Well, none, if I'm honest. And I'm pretty terrible at expressing myself because I've spent a long time keeping quiet. But I'm yours." It leaves me breathless every time I say it, feeling more important and permanent each time. I placed a hand over my fluttering heart. The invisible cord around it hums with a gentle squeeze. "I'm yours."

He smiles, thumb stroking the top of my leg. "I know, petal. I love that you're mine."

The back roads of the Pine Barrens almost make it seem like we're the only two people in the world. More houses and farms break up the trees as we reach a main road. We're not on it long before he pulls into a farmers market stand.

"Here's our first stop." He takes my hand and urges me to the faded blue and white stand boasting fresh fall pies and cider donuts.

"Is it open? We're the only customers."

"It is. Do you like apple or pumpkin?" He holds up two different pies. "Or both. We don't have to choose between them. You can have everything you want. Everything your heart desires. If you feel the urge, take it."

There's something about the way he says it that makes me pause, looking up from the basket of fresh apples. The bond stirs in my chest, the faint tug in the opposite direction ever-present. Are we still talking about pie?

"Both? I don't know, I've never had any."

For a moment, his mouth tightens and his golden eyes flash. He covers with a nod. "We'll have to fix that, won't we? Both it is. Anything to spoil my pretty girl."

I blush, moving along to the huge pile of pumpkins. "The cider donuts sound good, too."

"You know we're not leaving without donuts, Lils. Some for now and some for later."

I play with the bottom hem of my top. This date isn't grand or fancy, but it's perfect. Once we're stockpiled and Matthias pays, we get back in the car.

"This was fun." I rub my fingers together before reaching for his hand. He twines our fingers together and kisses my knuckles, drawing a soft smile from me. "I don't think the others would care, but this is more than anyone has ever done for me. Thank you."

He watches me from the corner of his eye. "They would care. And we're not done yet. The best part about getting pie is enjoying it."

"We're driving in the opposite direction from the motel."

"It's just up ahead. Found it while I was scouting past our perimeter last night."

I shake my head. "Do any of you actually sleep?"

"We can go a long time without it." He shoots me a wink. "We have excellent stamina."

Heat bolts through me at his sexy tone and I lick my lips. Matthias grins without looking at me. He lifts his chin and inhales, eyes hooding.

"Fuck, you smell good. When you're wet, my mouth fucking waters and I can't wait for my next taste. Just hold on a little longer, petal."

"W-what?" I cover my mouth, hissing through my fingers. "You can smell when I'm—turned on?"

His grin stretches. "That's right, mate. Your scent is better than the sweetest sin."

"Oh my god." I press my legs together while the bond practically purrs in my chest from the praise of my fated mate.

The car pulls into a parking lot with a sign for hiking trails. He hops out of the car and produces a sheet from the trunk.

"Is that from the motel?"

He waggles his brows. "Yeah, I swiped it. We're having a picnic."

I bite my lip around a warm smile. "I've never had a picnic."

We grab the donuts and pie, strolling along the wide sandy trail. Matthias teases me by bumping against me and pretending he didn't do it. He switches sides, blowing on the back of my neck, avoiding my eye with a playful smirk. I get him back by flicking sand at him with my boot. He retaliates by smacking my ass with a deep laugh.

"I'll get you back for that," I promise.

"Don't drop our pie," he taunts.

My attention falls to his tattooed arms. He has a geometric wolf and a badass lunar moth on his biceps. The one that makes me most curious is the random dolphin.

"How does a demon have tattoos? The ones you got here, I mean."

He smirks. "Who says I got them in the mortal realm?"

"Come on, I can't picture a demon tattoo artist inking butterflies and swallows on people. Plus, Valerian's aren't like yours. His move."

"You're right. He got his in the underworld." He shrugs. "I like these."

"I like them, too." The charming crooked smile he gives me makes my chest expand with a soft glow. "What about the random ones?"

"They're my expression of self. None are random."

"The bright ass dolphin?"

He laughs, cheeks coloring as he scratches his nose. "Ah, it was the nineties. It was the thing to get."

The trail opens up and my good mood evaporates. I freeze in terror at the edge of the trees. The lake would be beautiful and peaceful to anyone else. To me, it makes my stomach cramp and my limbs turn to statues. The pie box crinkles between my death grip.

"Lily?" Matthias turns serious, scanning the area for a threat. "What's wrong?"

"The lake," I whisper hoarsely.

"Did you see someone there? A demon?" He moves in front of me, fingers lengthening into claws.

"No." Fuck, will I ever escape this? I press my face against his back, trembling. "I'm sorry. I'm ruining this."

"Tell me what's got you so spooked?" Realizing there's no actual danger, he turns and wraps me in his arms. His claws recede and he strokes my hair. "It's okay."

I take deep gulps of his scent. "I…" My throat constricts. I hate this stupid fear. "I don't like water."

His embrace tightens, the pie probably getting squished between us. "I didn't know. I'm sorry." He rests his cheek on top of my head. "I wanted to surprise you and show you a good time."

"It's not your fault." I squeeze my eyes shut.

"Will you tell me why you don't like water?" he murmurs.

I try, but the words won't come. I blink away tears and soak in his gentle touches. "When I was a kid I had a bad experience."

It's an understatement, a mere shadow of the truth, yet he doesn't push me for more. He just holds me, helping me breathe easier. "I'm sorry." He presses his lips to my forehead and speaks against my skin. "Let me make it better."

"How?" I've tried so many things to get over my fear.

"We'll overwrite your bad memories of water with something good."

My lips slide together. The fact he wants to erase my bad memories touches me, calming the racing beat of my heart. The bond tightens with the hug he gives me.

"Do you still want to have our picnic?"

I lean back, frowning at the pie box. "It got kind of crushed."

His expression softens and he massages the back of my neck gently. "It's okay. Or we can go. Anything you need."

Matthias only wanted to take me on a date. He did this for me and I ruined it.

"I don't want to go. I want to stay here with you."

His tender, protective gaze bounces between mine. "I'll be with you anywhere we go. You never have to worry, mate. I'm with you."

At my nod, he guides me along the edge of the tree line, keeping us separated from the lake. I can still see it, but it's better we're not on its banks. We find a spot with a small clearing and he spreads the stolen sheet.

He kicks off his boots and sprawls across it, patting the spot beside him. "Come here, pretty girl." I follow suit, accepting his encouragement to lean into his side. "Is this okay?"

"Yeah. This is nice." It's a relief that I haven't messed up our date and driven him away. As long as he's with me, I can survive sitting near the lake.

"Good." He kisses the top of my head and we sit like that, listening to the rustle of orange leaves overhead until my heart stops beating so hard. Sensing I'm more relaxed, he plays with my hair. "Ready to try your first bite of pie?"

"Yes."

"Close your eyes."

I tilt my head back and do as he asks. The scent of a campfire and maple gets stronger, winding around me like a phantom caress from my mate. I swallow thickly, waiting. A low, pleased rumble sounds right in front of me and his fingertips touch my lips.

"Open for me, Lily," he rasps.

I part my lips, gasping at the first buttery sweet taste melting on my tongue. It's so good, the tartness of apple spiced with cinnamon and the sugary flakes of crust making me moan. He traces my lips reverently.

"You like that." His mouth captures mine, kissing me deeply. "Keep your eyes closed. Now try this."

Matthias feeds me another piece, this one smooth, less sweet, but just as delicious. "What is that?"

"Pumpkin pie." I lick some of it from his fingertips, mouth quirking at his groan. "Hold on. I want you to taste this."

His sugar coated fingers bump against my lips and his breath fans across my cheek as I accept it, sucking on his fingers. The cider donut is good, but his skin tastes even better. His lips trail across my jaw, his searing, open-mouthed kisses moving down my neck as he grasps my waist.

"So good," I murmur.

"Yeah? Not as good as you taste." He nudges me until my back hits the sheet, covering my body with his. "Like here." His forked tongue swipes between my breasts. "Mm, so sweet."

I open my legs and he settles between my thighs, rocking his hardness against my core. He grins at my gasp, guiding my arms overhead. Pinning them there, he nips at my neck, grinding against me until the tight coil inside me snaps, sending a ripple of pleasure through me.

"That's it, baby. Let me make you feel good."

"More."

The whisper feels illicit, yet I don't want to stop. Not with him. I want everything.

I want to squash my fears and remember the divine sensation of his lips on my skin instead. Overwrite the bad memories with his touch.

Matthias slides his hands beneath my shirt, groaning when he finds no bra. Going without was worth it for this. My back arches as he plays with my nipples, pushing my shirt higher to expose me.

"Watch," he rasps.

With effort, I snap my eyes open, meeting his heady gaze. He closes his mouth around one and sucks, tongue swirling. A gasp tears from me and I wrap my legs around his hips. I'm burning up, filled with a delicious, frenzied heat that I don't want to end. I need to feel him, my core aching for it.

"I want you," I choke out.

"Shh, I've got you," he murmurs, kissing his way back up my neck to my lips, speaking between kisses. His tone shifts to something filthy and rough. "Is this what you want?"

He grabs my hips and thrusts against my pussy, making me cry out. Panting, I nod. With a feral sound, he shoves my skirt up and all but claws my underwear down. When he strokes his fingers through my folds, I buck my hips. He spends a moment teasing me, then sinks a finger inside me.

"So wet, pretty girl. I want to worship you. Take my time and savor every sound you make. Taste you all over." He growls as I clench around him and spears me with another finger. "I can't promise to go slow right now. Your scent is driving me crazy. I'll be gentle later. Right now I need to claim you and make you feel me after."

"I want it. I want to be yours," I beg, as swept up as he is, the heat overtaking my body. My hips move with his fingers as he fucks me with them, heightening my pleasure by giving me jolts of his power with small, sparking vibrations that push me to the edge. "Please, Matthias."

Removing his fingers, he braces over me, pinning me under his sultry gaze as he licks the slickness from them. Without breaking eye contact, he reaches back to peel his t-shirt off, then drops his hands to pop the button on his jeans. He takes them off and I gasp at the sight of his cock.

The curiosity crossed my mind before. My imagination didn't prepare me and my chest collapses with my exhale.

His cock is big—longer than a human's, enhanced with two rows of ridged bumps along the top. The ache in my core intensifies and arousal spills through me.

Matthias watches me with a primal glint of amusement in his eyes, circling his fingers around the thick base. He strokes it, spreading the precome leaking from his tip until his length is slick with it. He settles between my hips, the big tip of his dick teasing between my folds.

"Oh," I breathe. "It's big. Will it fit?"

His rumbling chuckle is downright dirty. "It will fit. This pussy will take it all and beg me for more."

He concentrates his power, hitting my clit with tingling sparks from his cock. A moan slips out of me and my back bows as pleasure races through me. My fear of the lake is completely forgotten, swallowed by my need for him, for my mate to claim me as his.

Lining up, he kisses me hard. "Burn with me, petal."

His cock sinks into me with a long thrust, somehow fitting every dizzying inch. My lips part and he swallows the cry that escapes. He stills, allowing me to feel him inside, bracing on an elbow to roam my face with primal hunger for my reaction. I wrap my arms around his shoulders as he claims me, the size of him overwhelming as the ridges rub deep inside me, filling me, stretching me to the brink. It's intense, the sensations making me lose control.

"Oh god," I whimper. "Matthias, it's too much."

"Fuck, your pussy was made for my cock." He drops his head to mouth at my neck, nibbling on a sensitive spot that makes my vision hazy. "You take it so well. Listen to those pretty sounds you're making."

I moan, half-delirious as an orgasm hits me out of nowhere, the ecstasy exploding from my core. My nails scrape his back as his pace picks up. A strangled noise catches in my throat when he slides his fingers into my hair, then maneuvers his other hand between us to rub my clit, fingers releasing intermittent sparks, echoing them inside me each time he buries his cock inside me. He keeps me riding the wave of pleasure, extending it each time I'm about to recover.

"Fucking gorgeous," he praises. "Gorgeous and mine."

The possessive growl against my neck comes as a blaze spirals through me, sending me over the edge once more from the heat building between us. With a ragged groan, his cock throbs inside me as he comes.

Something expands in my chest, bright and hot, the light touching every part of me and engulfing him. He covers my heart with his hand and kisses me.

I feel him everywhere as I'm shattered and remade, no longer a broken, unloveable girl. Inside me. In my heart where the bond connecting us thrums. Holding me. Marking me as his forever in every way.

"You belong to me, petal," he breathes against my lips, fingers tightening in my hair. "I've claimed you as mine. You'll always be mine, mate."

Those words burn into my very soul with the promise I'll never be alone again.

Fifteen
LILY

WE TAKE OUR TIME GETTING BACK, LINGERING IN the moment while we giggle about feeding each other slightly squashed pie. When we finally get dressed and return, Valerian waits outside the motel room with a surly expression. I steel myself for his anger, not in the least bit sorry for enjoying the afternoon with Matthias instead of training. I can still feel him between my legs, inside me, the glowing warmth in my chest at his claiming vow emanating from within me like a beacon.

The anger doesn't come.

Valerian stares at me for a long beat, something unreadable shifting across his chiseled features. He inclines his head, his black tousled hair falling in his face. "Get back in the car. We have to go south."

Alder comes out of the room with my bag and heads for the car. He pauses halfway there, spine rigid as his head jerks in my direction. There's no way he or Vale can tell that we had sex, right? I hope they can't smell it on us like Matthias said he could smell when I was aroused. I avert my eyes from Alder, heart pounding.

"Did you find the witches?" Matthias steers us around, rubbing my back in soothing circles.

"Yes, but they couldn't do what I want without calling on other covens to join them at their sabbath. We can't wait that long. They suggested another coven and contacted them on my behalf. It's a long drive."

So much for showering. Not that I'm in a rush to wash away what happened.

Once we're on the road, my mind has free rein to roam. I curl against the door in the back, watching the scenery speed by. Alder and Valerian mutter to each other up front while Matthias dozes, arm outstretched across the seat so his fingers brush against my hip.

An hour into the drive as we're leaving the state, my stomach tightens at the thought of what awaits me when we find a witch powerful enough to undo the binding trapping me as a human.

What will happen if it's broken?

The guys think I'm a changeling, my true

demon form locked away. But what if that demon is different? What if the person I am now disappears, erased once the memories of my demon life are free?

A harsh breath blows past my lips as I wring the hem of my loose skull hands crop top.

If I'm not me, will I still be Matthias' fated mate? I bite the inside of my cheek to stave off the panicky beat of my heart. No. I felt it earlier by the lake—his words touched me to the core of my being.

Yet the niggle of worry only grows, as it always does once the thought enters my head, the ugly whisper that I'll be alone.

I don't even know what it means to be a changeling. There's a chance that breaking the magical seal might destroy this body to reveal my demon. It occurs to me again as my thoughts turn in circles that I might not be the age I think I am depending on what my life was before I was brought to the mortal realm from the underworld. My head jerks with a bitter snort. All the years I've spent dreading and hoping for my eighteenth birthday to escape the system that never helped me, yet I might have aged out ten times over.

She'll never be queen. The hellhound's vicious snarl surfaces in my head along with Rainer's report about the council labeling Valerian as a traitor for the treasonous rebellion he's plotting.

They can't mean me. I'm no queen.

"Come here." Matthias moves to the middle of the seat and pulls me into his lap. "I can hear those gears turning in your head. Steam's about to blow out of your ears from thinking so hard. What's bothering you?"

The panicky internal crisis slows down once I'm in his embrace. I focus on the calm beat of his heart against my back.

"I'm fine. Just nervous I guess." I twist my fingers in my lap. He covers my hands, squeezing them comfortingly. "We don't know what will happen if the witches can break the seal."

"Let me take your mind off it." His tone lowers and he shifts against my ass so I feel his erection. "You still smell like me."

My cheeks flush and I dart my eyes to the front. Can they smell it?

"It's making me want you again," he whispers against my ear. "Can you be quiet?"

I angle my head to give him a *what the fuck* look. Smirking, he releases my hands and slips his fingers beneath my shirt, tracing the edge of my breast. I smother a shaky breath as he ignites a new burst of heat in me.

He lifts his brows in question—continue or stop? Rolling my lips between my teeth, I give a small nod.

This is wrong. We shouldn't, not when Alder

and Valerian are right there in the front seat. Yet I don't stop him from caressing my hips and teasing the hem of my short skirt with a barely there touch. Part of me wants them to see, wants them to hear what it sounds like when I come. A pulsing hum fills my chest at the thought, urging me on.

He brushes light kisses along my shoulder, tracing maddening circles on the inside of my thighs. Then he stops until I wriggle, rubbing them together to help the throb in my clit. His mouth curves against my neck and he massages the softness of my legs, encouraging me to open for him. When I do, he rewards me by sneaking his hand up my skirt to stroke a knuckle along my pussy through my panties.

"So wet still," he breathes against my ear so the others won't hear.

My heart stutters as he pushes past them and strokes me. My legs spread wider and a soft sigh rushes out of me before I realize it. I swallow thickly as he slowly tortures me.

"Can you stay quiet while you take my fingers?" he whispers. "What about my cock? Do you think you could ride my cock without them knowing?"

A strangled noise catches in my throat as he pushes two fingers inside my pussy with little resistance, my body still loose from when he claimed me in the woods. Cursing under his breath, he curls them deep inside me, making my chest rise and fall as my hips roll, seeking more.

I forget about staying quiet when it becomes too much, clamping my legs around his wrist as my pleasure implodes in my core.

There's no hiding what he's doing to me anymore. We're going to get caught. The bond wriggles in my chest and I clamp down on the dirty little thing dancing in excitement at the idea of Valerian and Alder watching this.

"S-stop," I hiss. My head tips back on Matthias' shoulder and my eyes slam shut against the sensation of his fingers stroking my folds. "Please. This is—they can hear…"

"Not just hear. Your scent is telling them everything about how good you feel right now," he murmurs against the side of my neck, mouthing at my flushed skin with a hint of his fangs. His fingers circle my clit and I feel the curve of his grin branded into my throat when I shudder. "I'm not stopping until you're soaking my hand, petal. I want you dripping for me, baby. I want you so wet you ruin the leather so none of us ever forget it."

"Oh god." I arch into his sinful touch, lost to the headiness of his filthy demand.

The game is over. It was over before we began. We both knew there was no way to hide this, no way I could be quiet. I forget about stopping, shuddering as he rubs the spot inside me that lights me up.

A rumble catches my attention. I look at Valerian, but he's glaring ahead at the road, knuckles white on the wheel, the ink that normally covers them retreating up his wrists. My gaze slides to Alder and I gasp. He's staring between my spread legs like I'm a feast waiting for him, intently fixated on every movement of Matthias' hand. He reaches out and hesitates before placing his big hand on my knee, encouraging me to open my legs wider. My body quakes and another cry escapes me.

This is insane. I'm letting Matthias fuck me with his fingers in the back of the car while Alder gets a front row seat to the show—literally. But god, I can't stop. It's too good, too intense, too hot to ever stop.

"Slow down." Alder's deep rasp causes a pulse in my clit until his words register.

Matthias stops and I nearly whine. He soothes me with a sweet kiss to my jaw. "Hush, petal. I've got you."

"She's too close. Draw it out. Tease her." Alder lifts his hypnotic green eyes to meet mine and my stomach clenches. "Make her beg for it."

Fuck. Oh *fuck*.

Matthias' mischievous laugh vibrates against me. "You dirty fucker." He follows Alder's directions, fingers playing with my pussy almost absently. "How many more times do you think I can make her come? I already wrung one out of her."

"Don't stop until she's crying."

Air punches out of my lungs and I bite down hard on my lip when Matthias thrusts a third finger into me without warning. The sound they make from how wet I am is obscene. In the mirror, Vale's nostrils flare, but he remains silent while his demonic buddies have me at their complete mercy.

Instead of feeling ashamed and wanting to hide, a powerful thrill shoots through me. I feel beautiful, the sense chasing away the horrible voice in my head that whispers I'm not enough and makes me believe everyone will leave me alone.

But my demons won't. Matthias claimed me, swearing I belonged to him. Alder watches me with desire filling his gaze. Valerian promised I'd never escape him.

They won't leave me.

I don't stop the moan that bursts from me as Matthias' power vibrates inside my pussy while he teases my clit. He murmurs praise in my ear, taking me higher to teeter on the brink of falling.

"The whole fucking car smells like her." Alder growls, his fingers shift and his claws dig into his seat.

"Smells like a beautiful sin," Matthias purrs. "Ready to come again? C'mon, you can do it." I shake my head, panting raggedly. It's too much. If I come, I'll split apart at the seams. "Yes you can. Do it for me. For us. Come for us, petal."

His thumb presses down on my clit and he plunges his fingers deep within me, hitting the spot that makes me shatter with a stronger burst of sparks that ignite into a flame stroking me until I fall apart. The noise that tears from me doesn't even sound human. All I know is sweet oblivion and the pleased murmurs from Matthias as I shake apart with another orgasm.

"Good girl," Alder rumbles.

"Mm, so good for us," Matthias says.

The heated flush spreads like wildfire across my skin, engulfing my body in the erotic flames of ecstasy from what they're doing to me. My fantasies are overlapping with reality.

Matthias pulls his fingers free. They're glistening and he chuckles, curling his tongue around them to taste me.

The serpent-like forked tip still sends a jolt through me and a rush of air hisses past my lips. How would that devious, otherworldly tongue feel buried between my legs? In me? The thought drives me crazy. As if he can read the sensual places my mind goes, his warm gold eyes flare, the radiant flecks glowing to make them brighter.

Alder watches with hunger burning in his hardened green gaze. His own forked tongue flicks his lower lip, sending an answering thrum of desire to my core.

Another low laugh vibrates against my back and Matthias hikes my leather skirt higher, bunching it around my hips. I'm completely exposed like this. Alder's chest collapses with the breath he forces out, focused on the way Matthias strips my panties the rest of the way off. He flings them and my face is seconds from spontaneously combusting because they arc through the car, landing up front.

"Where'd they land? Please tell me I got the gear shift. Twenty bucks if I did."

Vale mutters something in an acidic tone I can't decipher, too caught up in the depravity pricking my senses. I don't want to stop though, lost to the aching need for *more*.

"Prop her foot on the seat," Alder demands. He yanks on his seatbelt, the distinct sound of the taut material tearing audible as he shifts around for a better viewing position while Matthias complies, hitching my leg up.

"Not done yet, babe." Matthias presses a trail of hot kisses over my jaw, teasing my ear with his wicked tongue. He uses the heel of his palm against my swollen folds, groaning when I rock against it for more. "Fuck. You make me want to drive my cock into you again and make you scream."

Alder growls from the front seat. I guess he's

fine with watching his friend finger me, but he doesn't want to see how Matthias fucks me.

"Fine, fine. But christ, I'm going to fuck you so good later. I'm going to rearrange your goddamn guts, baby."

Matthias' hard cock digs against my ass as he buries his fingers inside my pussy with a thrust that tears a frayed gasp from me. He fists my hair while he grazes his fangs over my throat. I arch against him, riding his fingers.

He nips my skin. "You want that, petal? You want me to bend you over and split you open on my dick?"

"Yes!" I'm too delirious to manage any coherent response other than begging for everything he wants to give me.

Somehow my eyes flutter open and lock with Vale's in the rearview mirror. His eerie blue gaze burns into mine. My core spirals tighter with his eyes on me, piercing through me as senses are overwhelmed by the smoky scents filling the car from all three of them.

Is he picturing what Matthias said he'll do to me later? Does he imagine it's him bending me over instead? Liquid heat fills my core as my own imagination takes off with that thought. My heart stammers just as Matthias presses deeper and triggers another orgasm that shakes me to the bone.

I'm lost to wave after wave of heady, mind-blowing pleasure, the thrum in my chest going crazy. For a moment, my world isn't tilted off its axis, the echo of rightness panging inside me.

When I stop quivering, Matthias uses the corner of his shirt to dab at the beads of sweat on my face and fixes my skirt before nestling me on his lap so I'm sideways, resting against him. His lips brush my forehead.

"Does she need water?" Alder asks.

Whoever decides to answer, I miss it, but no one shoves a drink in my face. I'm grateful for it because I don't want to move. Matthias is comfortable and I'm pretty sure I'm a puddle. A chill moves over my leg and I feel the remnants of his ministrations dripping down my thigh. A tired smirk pulls at my lips at the thought of the car permanently stained with this memory.

"You did so good for us, pretty girl." Matthias' tone is affectionate and proud. It envelops me, igniting a glow of happiness in my chest. "Sleep now, petal."

"We'll wake you when we get there," Vale says.

His voice is strange. Rougher and thicker than the detached iciness I'm used to from him. I like it.

Low murmurs fill the car, but I drift in a hazy toneless cloud, too wrung out to even worry about what had my thoughts racing before Matthias and Alder's wicked game. I burrow further into Matthias' arms and smile when they tighten around me. This is where I belong, the place I've searched for my whole life.

Sixteen
LILY

"So… Can I have my underwear back?" I keep my voice low, but Alder hears my whisper to Matthias anyway when we climb out of the car later that night somewhere in Virginia.

"If you continue to taunt us because you're the one who gets to have her, I'll kill you," he growls.

"No!" My outburst is loud and fierce, cutting through the night.

Fire springs forth to cover my hands, his threat to kill my mate the only thing that registers.

The precise control over my powers startles all of us. I've never managed to call something of this level on my own.

Matthias tucks me under his arm and kisses my cheek. My fire snuffs out at his touch, smoke rising from my arms. "It's okay. He's not serious."

Valerian pockets my underwear and goes into the motel office. A heated flush pricks at my cheeks and my stomach twists with the illicitness of his actions. Did that asshole seriously just—?

It should piss me off that he stole my panties, yet the thrum circling my chest likes the idea of him carrying them around, knowing I'm bare beneath my miniskirt.

He returns a few minutes later with keys to a room. "Don't go anywhere unless it's to work on your defensive moves."

"Where are you going?" Alder prompts.

"The coven. They're expecting me. I'm going to find out if they have a witch that can access the seal, or at least tap into her memories to find her true identity."

"This late?" I question.

"It's the witching hour," he says plainly.

His gaze falls to the possessive arm Matthias has around my shoulders and a muscle jumps in his cheek. A sting spears through my chest when he turns his back on me without another word.

Once he drives off, Alder catches my wrist, tugging me away from Matthias' side. "We're not done. You're finishing your training for the day."

"What? Are you kidding?" My skin warms beneath his firm hold, tingling pleasantly. I bite my lip, his gruff words while he watched Matthias finger fuck me filtering through my head. "It's late. All I want to do is shower and go to sleep."

"I'm not joking. You're not escaping this."

His grip presses into my skin, unwilling to let me go. A thrill shoots through me, much like the way I felt when he touched my knee to spread my legs wider to expose my body for his own devious pleasure. I make no move to free myself.

Heat throbs between my legs. I'm bare beneath my skirt.

He tosses my bag at Matthias, dragging me across the damp pavement reflecting the purple neon glow of the motel sign. "Meet us out back. I'll find a spot to work."

We head around the side of the motel. A small slope leads down to a narrow creek. I suck in a breath at the sight of murky water trickling across dead leaves and sticks. Alder pauses, giving me a sidelong glance.

The fear isn't as potent as it usually is. Closing my eyes, I picture Matthias' kisses in the woods by the lake earlier until I breathe easier, a relieved smile twitching my lips. His effort to replace my bad memories with a better one worked.

Alder shifts directions, heading for a copse of trees. "Here will do. There's not as much room as we had at our last location. We'll work on close range."

He finally drops my wrist, only to wrap his arms around me from behind. "Breaking a hold is about understanding balance and reserving your energy to utilize against your attacker efficiently."

The circle of trees feels as though it blocks us off from the world, interrupted only by the faint sounds of cars passing on the nearby road. His palms skate across my stomach, toeing the edge of decency when he moves up and takes the hem of my shirt with him, dangerously close to revealing the bottom curves of my tits. My chest rises and falls, my awareness shrinking to the feel of his rough hands on my body and the drum of his heartbeat against my back.

"Alder," I whisper.

"When you can't protect yourself, I will be there to keep you safe." Sighing, he locks his arms around my shoulders, effectively pinning my arms at my sides. He speaks against the top of my head. "But I'll teach you to fight like a warrior. I sense she's within you."

My stomach dips and I brush my fingertips against his sides, the heat of his embrace captivating my senses. His gravelly rumble reverberates against my back, surrounding me. I know he's teaching me, but I don't want to move from this spot, from his steadfast embrace.

"To get out of this, you have two options. Drop your center of balance lower than mine, then use the force of your power to push the advantage by attacking the inner knee or groin. I want you to focus on this method."

"What about the other way?"

"Your other option is if your hands are pinned like this, call on your fire to punch up through the hold, then turn and drive with all your might toward your attacker's chin. With enough strength behind your counter attack, you can knock them back and even blind them. We'll run through it so you understand the basic maneuver first, then do it with hellfire in the mix."

He mutters gruffly, talking me through what he wants me to do, guiding my movements. Once I have the basic idea down, he instructs me to try on my own.

My attempts only lead to him tightening his hold. "How am I supposed to break out of this if you know what it takes to do it? When I go to drop low, you just hold me tighter."

"Escape," he urges, his low tone fraying. "I won't go easy on you and let you go."

An insistent pulse echoes inside me.

Slow down. Make her beg for it. Don't stop until she's crying.

My lashes flutter as I try to clear my head. Licking my lips, I rein myself in. The car was a fluke. It was the pressure of life on the run living in close proximity with them blurring the line. A dirty fantasy come to life that we're not likely to repeat. I should focus on what he's teaching me instead of getting horny.

The problem is that I don't want to get out of his hold, enjoying the feel of his firm chest plastered to my back.

I barely let myself look at other boys growing up, too worried of how much deeper their rejection would cut. I have no defenses against this deep well of desire I've uncovered in myself, too addicted to these stolen touches healing years of isolation that have left me starved for any touch.

"Do it, Lily," he orders roughly, as affected by our proximity as I am.

Gulping, I get it together. His directions run through my head. I fake dropping my weight, then drive my elbow back hard. He grunts. I doubt I actually hurt him, but it's enough of a distraction to catch him off guard when I drop a second time. Crouched low, I charge my shoulder against his knee until he stumbles backwards a few paces.

I freeze, a smile breaking free. Getting up, I launch at Alder. He catches me and I hug him. "I did it."

"You did." He hesitates, then returns the hug with crushing force. "Well done, sweet blossom."

A laugh bubbles out of me. "Let's do it again."

He releases me and I turn around.

My concentration is occupied by repeating the moves he showed me. I don't hear the swift footsteps moving through the trees until Matthias appears before me with a mischievous smirk. Before I react, he pushes me back against Alder's chest, pinning me by my shoulders.

"What are you going to do, Lils?" he murmurs. "Now you're trapped between the two of us."

My brain short circuits, everything Alder showed me flitting away as they press against me, sandwiching me between them.

"Hold her," Matthias says.

Alder growls in warning, yet he grabs me by my upper arms with more strength than a moment ago. Escaping this hold is too difficult. I don't attempt it, not interested in moving from between them, drowning in their smoky scents blending together. An intense throb thrums in my clit.

Matthias swipes his tongue along his lip, then kisses me. It's not sweet or soft. The kiss is urgent and sensual, scorching me in a matter of seconds with each slide of his tongue against mine. He owns me with it, reminding me I'm his. He doesn't let up, sweeping his palms down my sides, pushing beneath my shirt to caress my skin. I forget about training, chasing his wicked tongue for more.

"Mm, petal, I love it when you smell like this. So

fucking delicious, so needy." His touch skates down, nudging between my legs, cupping me beneath my skirt. "You have no idea how much I want to feast on you until you can't stand without Alder holding you up."

A hoarse cry escapes me. I feel Alder at my back, grinding his hard cock against me at the dirty picture Matthias paints of him on his knees before me while I melt against Alder's embrace. I struggle for air. He feels even bigger than Matthias is.

"Oh, damn. You just got wetter," Matthias murmurs against my lips as he teases between my legs. "Is that what you need right now? Alder helping you ride my face until you make a gorgeous mess?"

I blink as shock filters through my arousal. It's almost like he wants me to be with Alder, too. Is he serious? If he is, could it mean he wouldn't be mad if my heart was pulled in another direction than only him? My pulse speeds up at the possibility.

"You want that?" I push out.

"Baby, I want everything," he croons. "I know you'd look so beautiful coming apart, submitting to your pleasure. Just like earlier while he watched. You liked that?"

I nod, my stomach dipping pleasantly. "Yes."

His eyes flare. "I want to give you all of that. Let us take care of you. Both of us."

Both. My head swims from the force of the bond trilling in my chest.

Alder stills, then presses against me more insistently. My head tips back and he dips his face to my neck with a feral sound, his touch searing with a divine heat that spreads across my body. I arch as Matthias kisses a path down my throat.

"This isn't defense training." Valerian's cutting tone penetrates the sensual fog of desire I'm lost to. If Alder wasn't supporting me, I'd tip over and collapse. Valerian steps out from behind a tree, jaw clenched. "Enough. Time for her to rest. Matthias, you're on watch."

Matthias pulls away, smiling at me unapologetically as he tucks my hair behind my ears. "I'll finish this later." He plants a quick kiss on my lips. "Sweet dreams, my pretty girl."

Alder is more reluctant to release me, keeping me in place when I try to step away. His nose grazes the top of my head, inhaling faintly. A beat later, he lets go. I hug myself, but it's not the same.

"Tomorrow you're coming with me to meet the witch," Valerian says.

My demons surround me on my throne carved from jagged obsidian in a large room with high stone arches and burning sconces. Alder kneels before me, taking my hand, and Matthias perches on the arm, brushing a knuckle along my cheek while Vale grasps my chin to guide my eyes to him on my other side. Contentment fills me as they dote on me. I don't want this moment to end, happy to stay like this forever with them by my side.

But something is wrong.

One by one my men are stolen from me by cloaked figures with gruesome claws. They fight to escape, and I'm powerless to help, a chain locked around my ankle to keep me on the throne. I don't want this. I never wanted to be the queen ruling Hell.

Hellfire explodes from my hands to destroy the chain. As soon as I'm free, I run, searching the long halls, my crimson gown getting in the way. I fling off the crown atop my head, the studded spiked halo weighing me down.

"She will never be queen!" The demons hunting me shout it over and over.

"No!" I scream.

But it's no use. They capture me without my handsome demon knight to guard me.

Their claws slice into me, shredding my gown, pushing me down to the gleaming dark floor. Their red eyes spew fire and they bare their fangs at me. The floor swallows me, the water sloshing over my head. I flail hard, unable to break free. I sink further into the abyss and death calls to me.

The stale air in the dark motel room chokes me as I snap my eyes open with a harsh gasp. I press a trembling hand to my throat, my lungs searing as I drag in air. I'm not drowning.

Squeezing my eyes shut, I wrench the neck of my sleep shirt—the one I stole from Alder and put on after a shower—up to my nose, dragging in deep gulps of his scent.

My bed shifts, drawing another freaked out wheeze from me. Who the—? Matthias has been sleeping in bed with me, but tonight he's out on watch. I went to bed alone when Alder and Valerian stepped out to talk.

Large hands grab me as I struggle, a deep voice hushing me. The scent of smoldering charcoal and woodsmoke registers when I'm pulled against a broad, muscular chest. *Alder.*

"Shh, sweet blossom." He pets my hair. "What's wrong?"

It takes me a moment to calm my harsh breathing and find my words, the horrible tendrils of the dream clinging to my mind. "Nightmare," I choke out. "You're here?"

"I'm here. You're safe," he promises. "You were tossing and turning. Something agitated you. When I laid next to you, it seemed to settle your restlessness."

"I feel better like this," I admit. "Your scent is nice. It makes me feel protected."

A brief pang of guilt plagues me. I shouldn't say it, even if it's true. I belong to Matthias.

He gives a gravelly hum in response, his embrace cinching tighter. My heart swells. Why does it feel so right in his arms?

"I'll hold you as long as you need," he promises. "Nothing can hurt you."

My throat stings and I burrow against his chest, tucking my nose into the crook of his neck. His strength and support are everything to me. From the first time we were attacked after they kidnapped me from my bed, he's guarded me with unwavering dedication. He's stopped my training whenever I'm too tired or over emotional. He makes sure I rest.

When I feel like I'll fall apart, he lets me. I don't have to hold myself together on my own as long as he's there to catch me.

"Thank you," I mumble.

Alder cards his fingers through my hair and massages my neck and shoulders with power warming his touch. I melt against him, allowing him to ease away my nightmare. He's patient while he comforts me. We exist in a bubble, just the two of us.

After a while, he traces my scars. He's not as relaxed as he was a few moments ago.

"Who hurt you?" The jagged demand slices through the quiet. He guides my chin so I face him instead of hiding. His mouth presses into a thin line. "Tell me what humans did to make you lose control and let your power out like this?"

I freeze. My throat constricts and I shake my head.

"I want to hunt them all down and rip them limb from limb for hurting you. Since I first saw them, I knew you had known pain no one should suffer," he growls. "They don't deserve to live another day for this."

My heart beats harder, a band tightening around my chest. I don't talk about this. He squeezes my hand and I think of his own scars. If he can turn out so strong and bear those scars, maybe I'll grow strong, too. Gulping, I tell him the truth.

"She's dead. She died in the fire I started." I close my stinging eyes as he brushes the pads of his thumbs across my marred skin. "It's only her memory that hurts. I was a monster all along, just like she always believed."

He makes a fierce noise refuting my words. "You are not a monster. I've known many monsters and you aren't one of them." He doesn't stop me from touching the red marks that crisscross his forearms. "My father. I descend from a line of demon warriors with a long-standing reputation. He wanted to uphold it. Forced me through harsh training, not understanding the importance of control."

My throat closes in sympathy and the cord in my chest draws me closer to him. I want to shield him from the pain of his past. Without a second thought, I lift his hand and press a kiss to his knuckles.

"You're nothing like that."

Our eyes meet and something snaps taut within me, tethering me to him. I can't fight the pull anymore. There's no way to resist what every part of me wants—him.

"Ald—" I begin to murmur his name urgently, but he captures my lips in a searing kiss.

It's over far too soon when he breaks it off. His harsh exhales fan over my skin in the small space that separates our mouths while his hands roam. He traces the shape of my jaw, down my neck, his inescapable gaze reverent.

My breath hitches when he traces the collar of the shirt I wore to bed, tugging on it. Neither of us acknowledge that it's his shirt, his scent wrapped around me that I slept in rather than the other clothes in my bag.

His hand trails lower, brushing my pebbled nipples through my shirt, mapping the softness of my stomach, my hips. At the edge of the shirt draping over my thigh, he keeps blurring the line. He takes a meandering path along my thigh, skimming higher.

I can't help squirming, silently urging him on, too afraid to speak and break this spell.

He stops short of where I'm aching, not going any further. Lowering his head, he mutters against my temple. "I should let you sleep."

The simmering heat in my body is unbearable and the pull in my chest won't be silenced.

"No," I whimper. "Please. Please touch me. I need you—"

I don't finish before he releases a rough noise and destroys the line drawn between us. The first stroke of his fingers against me makes me quiver and bite back a moan. He rubs my clit more firmly, with more purpose than Matthias' teasing. I like it just as much, writhing in his arms. It's exactly what I need right now.

"More," I demand.

He wrenches my underwear aside and sinks two thick fingers inside me. My back bows and he holds me steady. His fingers alone fill me, stretching my body to accommodate him.

"Matthias got to have you first, but I will be the first to taste you here." His fingers curl inside me. "The first to feel you come on my tongue."

"Wait." It bursts from me. He goes rigid, then begins to pull away. I put a hand on his chest, pressing closer as my pelvis rolls to grind on his hand to chase the pleasure he's giving me. "Ngh.

No, not—I don't want to stop. Please. I want to taste you, too."

His hypnotic green eyes gleam, cutting through the darkness to capture me. "Have you ever done that?"

I shake my head. The corner of his mouth lifts, the curve of it belonging to the same predator that once promised to chase me until he caught me. My heart stutters and my thighs clamp around his forearm, enjoying that look on him, a spark of pride racing through me because I put it there. The muscles flex as he plunges his fingers deeper inside me.

"Lay back," he says.

I watch while he peels my underwear down and discards them off the side of the bed. He wastes no time stripping out of his clothes, kneeling before me naked and unashamed, every inch of his muscular body on display. I stare at his huge cock, eager anticipation spiraling through me as liquid heat spills into my core. His hungry gaze tracks my tongue as I lick my lips.

Like Matthias, his cock is lined with two rows of ridged bumps, the tip leaking a copious amount of fluid that he spreads down his endless length while he works himself. If possible, his dick thickens more while he leers at me. Jesus. There's no chance of fitting even half of it in my mouth, let alone inside me. Still, a sensual thrill runs through me at the thought of trying and an answering thrum pulses in my chest to encourage me.

When I reach for the hem of my shirt, he catches my wrists. "Leave it. I want you to come wearing it."

I bite my lip. He's going to make me come while I wear his shirt.

Alder lays on his side next to me, his body turned the opposite way. His thick, long cock strains toward me. He hooks a hand under my knee to draw my thigh closer, nibbling a path up my sensitive flesh. Again he stops before he gets to where I want him so badly. A whimper escapes me.

"Open your mouth."

Bracing on an elbow, he cradles my head, threading his fingers into my hair. When I part my lips, he rumbles, attention fixated on my mouth as he guides the tip of his cock inside. Closing around it, I give a tentative suck. The velvety skin is hotter than the rest of his body, the tip smooth against my tongue when I press against it. I like the weight of it and the shape of the ridges, angling my head to take more in my mouth.

"Fuck. The sight of you with my cock in your perfect mouth will be permanently seared into my mind." His smoky scent grows muskier. Tightening his grip on my hair, his hips give a little jerk when I tongue the underside of his head. "I'm going to fucking devour you."

He lowers his face between my thighs, covering me with his mouth. The first swipe of his forked tongue makes me release a garbled cry. He pins my hips, sucking on my throbbing clit. I try to focus on sucking his cock, but what he's doing is too much, too good. Before I know it, I fly off the edge while he laps at my pussy, my core clenching as the ripples erupt from deep within me.

"Oh god," I hiss. "Oh my god, Alder. It feels so good."

"Not done yet." His tone is feral, stoking the wild flame within me.

With a deep growl and a yank on my leg, he pulls me on top of him, spreading my thick thighs wide and squeezing the globes of my ass while his mouth and tongue bring me the sweetest, most sinful pleasure imaginable. With his grip on my backside, he encourages me to rock on his face. He licks and sucks me without care for his need to breathe, entirely focused on heightening my pleasure. I'm consumed by the simmering heat spreading through me.

My fingers wrap around the base of his thick cock and I suck on it, moaning each time his tongue flicks across my clit. He's leaking into my mouth and I swallow his taste. Fitting his entire hard length is impossible, but a determined part of me that's high on this moment, enthralled in erotic abandonment wants to give him as much pleasure as he's giving me.

He tenses, fingers digging into my flesh. With a filthy groan, his cock twitches and come floods my mouth. It's all I can do to swallow some of it, the rest leaking out of my mouth when he doesn't stop eating me until I shatter again.

"You are every dream I've ever had come true," he whispers against my thigh while I tremble. "My stunning blossom."

My heart drums as I collapse on top of him. I'm distantly aware of him petting my thighs and tracing my spine. Time feels strange inside the hazy cloud of passion being with him has left me tangled in.

Once we catch our breath, he rearranges us so we're beneath the covers, dragging me back into his arms. I can barely function and I'm grateful for how he takes care of me.

All I know is how right this feels, my head on his bare chest as his thumb caresses my cheek, catching the remnants of his release I didn't manage to swallow. Drowsiness takes over, keeping my thoughts at bay. This is all that matters—the safe warmth blanketing me in Alder's arms.

"Sleep now, sweet blossom," he says gruffly. "I'm here. I won't let you go."

The bond feels more at ease in my chest as I drift off, my off-kilter world shifting closer to alignment.

Seventeen
LILY

I<small>T'S OFFICIAL</small>—I'<small>VE CRACKED</small>. I'<small>M SURE OF IT</small>. B<small>ETWEEN</small> being dragged into a supernatural world I'm somehow part of, life on the run from other demons, learning to use powers I didn't know I had hidden inside me, and finding a demon that is my fated mate I've grown greedy, wanting to live my life instead of watching it pass me by. Maybe it's Matthias' encouragement and determination to ensure I indulge and live in the moment.

This girl who doesn't tamp down on her emotions, who won't let what she wants slip through her fingers is unrecognizable. But I think I like her.

I want more.

Specifically, I still can't stop my heart from fluttering or my pussy from throbbing every time

Alder or Vale are near. And last night I gave in to the tempting desire, letting the pull I still feel towards my other demons have what it wants.

It's not possible to have more than one fated mate...is it? I'm still getting used to the idea that one person is destined to love me. The idea—the fleeting, impossible hope—that there could be more than one fated match for my heart is too good to be true.

Alder is still asleep, though another part of him is very much awake and pressed against my stomach. I admire his features, his stern practical nature softened in sleep. Despite his habit of getting the minimum amount of rest they need and taking the most watches, he stayed with me, holding me close the rest of the night. My heart pangs. I allow myself one more moment of resting in the cradle of his strong arms before I slip free.

I sit on the edge of the bed, reliving a dream where I didn't have to choose between the three demons who stole me away. They surrounded me in the dream, all of them touching me without hesitation, as if I'm someone they cherish above all else. It was like last night, Alder's head between my thighs, devouring me while Matthias held me in his lap, pinching my nipples to get me to arch as Vale grasped me by the throat and kissed me for an eternity. The three of them sharing me, devoted to me.

Want crashes over me so fast and strong that it steals my breath away, the insistent thrum in my chest expanding like it needs to break free.

My thighs slide together and a husky sigh leaves me. I wait for guilt to tarnish the incredible fantasy that played out in my dream, to berate me for what happened last night without stopping to think of Matthias, but it doesn't plague me. The bond purrs in my chest, wrapping around my heart like a supportive hug.

Maybe in Hell and the other underworld realms it's not a big deal to be with more than one person. I twist my fingers in Alder's shirt as hope rushes through me. I should ask Matthias and tell him about what happened with Alder last night while he was on guard. He let Alder watch in the car, and if Valerian hadn't interrupted, things might have gone further while I was pinned between them. I hold onto my suspicion from yesterday that he almost wants me to be with Alder, too.

Still, maybe I shouldn't have allowed the insatiable pull urging me on last night to control me without asking my mate if he was okay with it first. Things happened so fast, the pull so demanding that it was impossible to withstand. I don't want Matthias to decide that I'm not worth the trouble, fated mate or not.

My grip on the shirt becomes rigid. He won't hate me or decide he's done with me. I know he won't. I repeat it to myself until the side of me so ready to accept that people will throw me away fades into the depths of my mind.

"It's time to go."

Valerian interrupts my thoughts, making me startle and fall off the edge of the bed. I rub the plump curve of my ass, glaring at him. He lurks in the small alcove leading to the bathroom.

"Why did you have to sneak up on me?"

He lifts a brow, melting out of the shadows to stand over me. I squeeze my thighs together, remembering I'm bare beneath the shirt. My underwear is on the floor between us.

"You were the one enjoying a languid morning lie in." His smooth accent carries a bite to it that makes me hot all over. His eyes flick to the bed, the corners of his mouth tensing. "Both of you."

Cheeks prickling, I scramble to my feet. "Not that I have to explain myself to you, but I had a nightmare. He helped calm me down."

He doesn't answer, his cunning gaze moving over Alder's shirt hanging off my body in a sensual slide. His eyes flare, then he scoffs. "Calming you from a nightmare. That's why you stink of him." Expression hardening, he folds his arms, the abstract black swirls on his exposed forearms shifting in agitated movements beneath his rolled up sleeves. "Shower. I'm not getting in the car with you smelling like that again. You have five minutes."

Rolling my eyes, I shove past the broody bastard.

The ride to the witch is strained and silent. I'm miffed Valerian forced me out the door before I got to see Matthias, stating that we'd be late if he allowed me to get distracted again. It's the first time we're truly alone together. Since we first crossed paths, Vale's been careful to avoid being alone with me other than the one time he tracked me down at the library.

His demanding words stick in my mind, refusing to leave me alone. There's no way he was jealous to find Alder naked and holding me in bed, but the more his crisp accented words repeat in my head, the more I'm struggling to refute the jealousy in his tone.

The animosity between us has waned, yet it's not truly gone. It's no longer rooted in anger and contempt, but neither of us give up an inch when it comes to fighting with each other. Mainly because he knows exactly how to get under my skin and make me fly off the handle whenever he pushes my buttons and prods at my weaknesses. I don't despise him anymore, but when he challenges me I have a tendency to fight back before thinking. It's not like that with Alder and Matthias; with Vale, I think he finds enjoyment in trading barbs with me.

Looking at his scowling brows, the sharp slope of his nose, the shape of his frowning lips, I can't deny he's handsome. Devastatingly so. The side of me that allows him to get to me, that goads him because I enjoy testing him, does it on purpose because I think I crave his attention. The thought of those haunting blue eyes looking at anyone but me pierces my heart.

My attention slides to Valerian's pocket. I think he still has my other pair of underwear. I couldn't find them anywhere, not in my bag or left out in the room when I snatched up the pair Alder all but ripped off me last night. Vale's wearing the same dark pants and black button down he wore yesterday, the sleeves rolled up, tempting me with his tattooed forearms on display.

Warmth creeps up my neck as I picture my underwear draped on the gearshift between us. I wonder how debauched I looked spread on Matthias' lap, bared for Valerian and Alder. Peeking over my shoulder, I scan the leather for any inkling of what happened, for proof that I had all three of them contributing in some way to my orgasms.

If things had been different and Valerian had my

245

body spread and at the mercy of his whims, would our passion feel different?

Yes. I sense the truth of it without a doubt.

When I fight with Vale, the fire he ignites in me is hotter, the burn more intense. I know it would consume us both if we gave the tension between us free rein.

As the journey continues, I judge the distance to our destination by Valerian's shoulders growing tenser and the sharpness of his smoky scent pressing in on me from all sides. The wheel begins to smoke beneath his rigid grip, fingertips glowing with smoldering embers of his power leaking out. He never lacks this much control over himself. It sets me on edge that he's worried enough for it to show, his brooding no longer able to hide his emotions.

"What will happen if the witch succeeds and breaks this seal binding me in this human body?" I bite my lip as soon as the words are out, stomach cramping at letting him witness my vulnerability. It's worth the risk because the nerves are about to eat me alive. "Will I still be me?"

He takes a long beat to answer, eyes narrowing on the winding road leading up the rolling hills. "I can't say for sure. You're the first changeling I've encountered."

The lack of reassurance that this version of me—Lily Sloane, a stubborn girl learning there's

246

a fighter within her wanting to be let out and take on the world—won't be destroyed to make way for the demon I truly am doesn't bode well. Is anything about me real? A bitter thought surfaces. My love of isekai manga might even be born of some part of me longing for another world I'm meant to return to. Anything I've ever liked in life could be attributed to the person trapped by the magic seal.

I could be temporary. Fleeting and easily forgotten. Replaceable.

Acid churns in my stomach and I shift uncomfortably. I should be used to it by now. I've been rejected, returned, and replaced my whole life. A hot sting slides down my throat. I don't want to go. Don't want to leave Matthias or the others. Don't want to be forgotten and left behind.

Vale studies me, his dark blue gaze penetrating. "No matter what, keep your guard up. Don't divulge information unless I give you permission."

I cross my arms. "It's my body. My power trapped inside me. Why are you suddenly the boss of it?"

He gives me a hard look. "Because it's my duty to protect you and I won't fail it. Demons and witches have a shaky relationship in the mortal realm at best. We are natural enemies. They summon us through rituals and trap us within their sigils to siphon our power."

My mouth drops open. "Then why is the witch agreeing to help?"

Before responding, he turns into a mulch driveway under an ivy-covered arch of woven sticks and vines. The air here feels different. Even inside the car, it seeps through the steel and glass, twisting around me.

"Hallowed ground." His mouth flattens. "She's blessed her land to ward off those that mean her harm. It's testing you."

Stones capped with dried moss line the driveway and damp dead leaves blanket everything. A small creek runs alongside us and circles around a cottage. When we stop, he gets out, scanning the area with a calculating sweep.

"I thought demons couldn't step foot on hallowed ground?" I stretch my stiff legs and adjust my distressed shorts from rolling up.

"Another myth humans adapted to convince themselves they were safe from the predatory fae who hunt them. One the priests borrowed from the very witches they burned at the stake, if I'm not mistaken." He steers me by his grip on the back of my neck, halting before we enter the covered porch. "If I give you an order, follow it. Understand?"

My nape tingles where he squeezes firmly, leaving me slightly lightheaded as my stomach dips. "Fine."

He pounds a fist on the door. "Witch!"

The door opens a few moments later and an unimpressed woman with crow's feet at the corners of her freckled face eyes us, giving Valerian a shrewd once over. "Demon." She narrows her eyes, then waves an arm in invitation. "My name is Lane."

"Hi, I'm Lily. Thanks for your help."

I glare at Valerian when he clamps on my neck hard, ignoring the burst of heat throbbing in my core. What harm is there in giving my name? It's not world-ending information.

Lane's wavy brown hair is tied back and shot through with streaks of silver, though she doesn't appear burdened by age. She moves spryly through her house as we follow to a kitchen with a worn round table and dried herbs hanging from the exposed beams. Like the rest of the cottage, her kitchen is cluttered at first glance, every worktop covered in repurposed tea tins, candles, and an eclectic mix of knickknacks. I get the sense she's a woman who enjoys spending her time in nature and working her land.

"My sisters assured me you'd pay well for my help." She wipes her hands on an apron and gestures to a chair. "Sit."

"And they assured me you're the best at dealing with spells of a binding nature." Valerian positions himself behind me, bracing his hands on the high back of my seat. "Your payment depends on that skill."

"Best on the east coast," Lane says airily. "Let me get a sense of you, Lily."

She lights a stick of cloying incense and brings it to the table, wafting it around me. Vale releases a low growl in warning when she grasps my chin. She ignores him, turning my face from side to side before taking my hands and closing her eyes.

"Oh," she murmurs.

"Is something wrong?" he demands.

"No, it's just—the pain. It's overwhelming."

I duck my head, face flaming. He didn't mention the witch would be able to see through me in under thirty seconds.

"What about the seal?" He presses closer, his torso brushing against the back of my head. There's an urgency I've never seen from him bleeding through his sternness. "Can you sense if her memories are there?"

"I need to put her in a meditative state to get a better sense of the binding. It's strong. Though I'm able to discern that she's stronger." Lane hums and creases her brow. "This feels as though she was forced into a rebirth. If that's true, there's a chance there aren't memories to find locked in her head. She may only have echoes and fragments left of her past life."

I exchange a glance with Vale when she moves away. The corners of his mouth are downturned in thought. A knot forms in my stomach. What's rebirth for a demon? Did someone kill me and reincarnate me?

Another awful thought pops in my head. He seems to care about the demon inside more than me. If I don't live up to his expectations, he'll abandon me as a lost cause that upset the balance of his life as a guard for nothing.

"Here." Lane returns with a tray of crystals, a small green bottle, and a hammered bronze dish stacked with orange marigolds. "Drink the potion."

Before I bring it to my lips, Vale snatches it, giving it a whiff. He glares at Lane. "Poison."

"No. It's a small dose of belladonna to encourage the meditative trance. It's not enough to poison her." Lane places an amethyst in one of my hands and clear quartz in the other, sitting them face up on the table. "The quartz will act as a vessel to take on the energy scribed to it, keeping you grounded. The amethyst will promote mental clarity to help us navigate your mind and find the path to the magical seal binding you. And for distrustful demonic minds, the calendula flowers are for me. They bring positivity to the spell."

"Sounds legit," I say.

She huffs in amusement, casting a baleful

glance at Valerian. "That's because it is. Now, take the potion and close your eyes while I chant the incantation to guide you into the trance state."

"Bottoms up." I toast Vale and down the slightly sweet concoction.

The trickle tingles down my throat, spreading outward gradually until my fingers and toes feel numb. Everything is heavy. Lifting a finger takes effort. My head lolls back and Vale stares down at me with concern, cradling my face. He strokes my cheeks, mouthing my name. I can't hear him clearly over Lane's chanting, like I'm underwater. The thought sends a spike of panic through me, and he brushes his knuckles down my cheeks when Lane waves a hand at him.

The last thought to cross my mind before the darkness at the edges of my vision takes over is that he looks nice with his tousled black hair falling in his face like that.

Eighteen
LILY

"Vale," I mumble.

"—here. Right here, little flower."

The soft touch to my cheek feels so good. I nuzzle into it, seeking more.

A bright flickering light to my left distracts me. I'm not in Lane's kitchen anymore, but the hall from my dream with obsidian floors and stone arches. I turn my back on it, not interested in visiting the throne room. Although—the guys could be there. The need to see them crashes over me.

My demons, my heart tethers, my home.

I pick up the gauzy material of my skirts and hurry down the halls, passing columns lit from the floor by pools of eternal hellfire flames. The closer I get, the longer the hall stretches. That's not right. I know this wing of the demon king's castle.

"Matthias?" I call. "Alder? Valerian!"

My voice echoes off the high walls. An inky swirl of black smoke rises from the floor to my right, circling faster in a churning frenzy until it forms a portal. The king—?

Red eyes glow within the magic and the demon's clawed hands snatch me. Something pushes me back hard.

When I blink my eyes open with a wheezing gasp, Lane's face is pale, her attention locked on a bowl of water that bubbles and turns black.

"My wards." It's the only thing she gets out before Valerian wrenches me from the seat, sending both of us crashing to the floor as the back door blasts open in a rain of fire.

"Go!" he commands.

Four terrifying cloaked demons charge through the door with impossible speed, short, deadly black horns, and white hair. Two of them converge on Lane. Horror traps me in place when they grab her by her hair and slash her neck before she can do any magic to counter them. The sachet clutched in her hand falls to the ground and her eyes bulge in shock. Then her body drops to the floor, severed from the head the demon grips by her hair.

An ear-splitting scream rips from my lungs.

Grunting viciously, Valerian pushes to his feet.

His tattoos shift as hellfire erupts from his fists. He punches the first demon he rushes, throwing up an arm to block the second that goes for him. He's a sight to behold when he fights, his speed and ruthlessness unmatched. His black elongated talons spear one of his opponents under their wide jaw while he holds the other back with a wall of firepower.

The other two turn their attention on me, dropping Lane's head. Opening their fanged maws, they both let out chilling growls. They advance on me and I scramble back, banging my head on a cabinet. My flames spark along my arms and sputter out at my fingertips, blocked by the fear coursing through my veins.

Valerian's demanding voice fills my head. *Don't panic. Control it.* It's followed by Alder's gruff encouragement. *The power is yours, blossom. It's not something you need to fear.* Then Matthias' warm tone wraps around me. *You're more amazing than you realize, pretty girl.*

I can do this. I can help fight against our attackers.

This is my power. My life that's been toyed with, stolen, and locked away from my access. Whoever the hell the demon is trapped inside me, these fuckers don't get to kill her or me.

They come for me as a unified force, undeterred by the ball of flame I morph between my palms. I fling it and curse when the one on the left dodges while I scramble to my feet. The demon's yellow eyes flash like he's mocking me. As I gather tingling energy in my hands to form another blast, they draw swords, dragging their claws along the blade with an awful screech. Fire licks along the weapons and they raise them.

Oh god. I'm not as fast as them. How do I block a fucking flaming sword?

"Lily!"

Valerian's hoarse roar cuts through the terror freezing me in place as the demons' swords arc down. He throws himself in front of me, directly in the line of attack. My mind splits in two, the scene overlaid with a strange vision—instead of his black shirt, he wears a knight's attire like Rainer's.

The swords find a new mark, slashing into his sides as he blasts them back with a strong wave of flame and hot air before he staggers on his feet and falls to one knee with a groan.

"No! Vale!" My chest aches as if the blades pierced my heart.

This is my worst nightmare come to life. The sight of him hurt, crouched on the floor in pain because he protected me unlocks a fathomless well inside my chest that demands retribution. It's the same fierce feeling that erupted from me when Alder threatened to kill Matthias.

A savage noise bursts from me and my power explodes like a furious star. Bands of fire lash out from me, my arms spread and my head thrown back. They whip around the room, claiming the neck of each demon. I choke them, my flames forcing down their throats. Their legs kick as I lift them into the air, their strangled sounds of pain not enough to pay for what they've done. Baring my teeth, I eviscerate them, burning their bodies to ash from the inside out.

Blood rushes in my ears and I collapse, the power retreating. I gasp for air from how much it drained my energy, taking in the destruction surrounding me—Lane's wrecked kitchen, her dead body, and what little remains of the demons.

My heart leaps into my throat when I lock eyes with Valerian. He's propped against the cabinets, intense gaze trained on me. Straining against my dizziness, I rush to his side.

He stares at me in astonished reverence. "Lili—" He cuts off, gritting his teeth and pressing a hand to his side. His hand comes away bloody. "Damn it."

Grabbing his wrist, an agonized breath catches in my throat. His dark blood soaks the tattered black shirt, the deep gashes visible through the holes. "You're hurt. Don't move."

I swallow the painful lump clogging my throat and scrounge around the kitchen in search of medical supplies, casting an apologetic glance at Lane. This is my fault. Her death, the attack, Vale getting hurt.

"Sorry Lane."

There's nothing I recognize, only herbs and unmarked bottles. A floral tablecloth in the next room catches my eye. With a sweep of my arm, I knock the contents from the table and shred strips off the tablecloth. Kneeling at his side with a bowl of water and the makeshift bandages, I grimace at how much blood there is. I've never seen any of my demons this badly injured.

"There's no first aid kit. This will have to do." I shove aside everything around us and focus on him.

He remains surprisingly quiet while I fuss over him, obliging without argument when I unbutton his shirt and help him out of it. I wet my lips, sparing a moment to admire his physique while I carefully dab a damp cloth to his sides to clean them.

The abstract ink on his arms moves in reaction when I brush my fingertips over his abs for balance to reach his other side. Intrigued, I repeat the touch, lower and the tattoos shift faster. I keep working diligently until it's clear he's not going to die if I don't stop the bleeding. Curiosity gets the best of me and I trace the whorls covering his arms, the smoke-like ink morphing into shadowy outlines. The tattoos respond to me, fascinating me when they seem to curl around my touch.

I tilt my head. "What does that feel like? Can you control the movement, or is it just part of magic tattoos?"

He remains silent, nostrils flared as he scents the air. There's an unreadable look in his eye when I chase one of the smoky shapes to the inside of his elbow, a thrum echoing inside me when I catch it. His chest expands with a deep, shuddering breath. I tear my hand away, worried I've hurt him. Biting my lip, I resume tending to his injuries.

"This is pointless." Other than the mild interjection, he does nothing to stop me, tracking everywhere I touch him like he doesn't want to miss a second of it.

"Why? Don't tell me some bullshit about being too stubborn to accept help." I drop the bloodied cloth in the murky water, frowning at how bad the wounds look. "Just shut up and let me repay the favor of saving your life, asshole."

His lips twitch at the almost fond way the derogatory term comes out. I clear my throat, busying myself with wrapping his torso with bandages.

"I'm not going to die. Demons have the ability to heal. This drained my energy, that's all." He rests his head against the cabinet. "It will take some time to replenish my strength."

"How can you replenish your strength?" I pull a face. "You don't strike me as the bed rest type.

Should I get you Powerade or something?"

The smile he gives me is feral, fangs peeking out. He leans closer, erasing the small distance between us. "When in the mortal realm without access to the natural power that sustains us in the underworld, two ways. One, consuming souls."

Usually the thought pisses me off, but the way he traps me in his stare sparks a wildfire that grows from an ember and quickly engulfs me. Gulping, I whisper, "And two?"

Vale's hand skates over my hip, traveling up my side, thumb brushing the edge of my breast while his attention falls to my parted lips. This time I'm the one that inches closer, our hot exhales mingling.

"Feeding on another kind of energy," he rasps, tracing the curve of my breast maddeningly slow. His fingers dig in. "Like what you feel between you and—your mate."

Matthias. Or does he mean Alder? My mind flickers between both of them. He lifts his hand and wraps his fingers around my throat, wicked gaze promising me sinful bliss if I give in to the temptation. It's happening again. The invisible force tied around my heart drawing me closer, and in different directions. I want this. I want to kiss Valerian.

No, I need to kiss him. More than I need my next breath. My entire being urges me to close the scant gap.

Before our lips touch, he stills, then glances around. *We need to go. We should get back to the others. I smell the blood of the witch's coven on these demons. They're from the assassin's guild.*

I blink. His voice filtered through my head, but his mouth didn't move. "Did—Did you just talk inside my head? Like, telepathically?"

Shock flits across his face before he nods sternly. "Alder can control consciousness. Matthias has the ability to persuade the mind. My gift is communicating without speaking aloud. Come on. It's not safe to stay here."

"Wait, can you read my mind?"

"It doesn't work like that." He takes my hand to help him to his feet, clenching his jaw. "Only with a special bonded connection, like the one between fated mates, is capable of creating a true mental link."

He pauses at the door to pass a devious look over me. A moment later, my mind floods with the mental image of exactly how I looked from his point of view in the back seat of the car, riding the fingers Matthias buried inside me with abandon.

"Dude," I hiss.

He smirks. "As you can see, I can push thoughts into your head." He stops me from patting him down for the keys. "No. I'm driving. Get in."

I'm too occupied with the buzzing warmth spreading through me at the image he put in my head to argue. Once we get off Lane's property, he floors it. I'm not a religious person, but I glance back and offer another silent apology for getting her killed.

"Why didn't you talk to me that way before?"

His hand moves from the gearshift, reaching for me. It falls short and he balls his fist. "I had no interest."

The curt brush off feels forced. This hidden skill explains how the three of them seem to get by with few words sometimes. When they've fought off the demons after us, they move as a unit despite how different they are.

As we race away from the cottage, part of me wishes we could have stayed in that stolen moment longer so I could know what it's like to kiss him.

Nineteen
LILY

Once we reach the others, we don't sit around. Valerian decides motels aren't safe anymore. Within minutes, we're in the car speeding away in a winding path to the nearest city, circling around and trailing in a different direction. At certain points of our meandering journey, he makes us get out to purposely leave a trace of our scents before we're on the road again.

Then at random, he directs Alder to pull in when we pass a remote cabin in the middle of the Appalachian Mountains. It looks like a vacation home. The quaint house has a dead garden and stale dust coating everything when we get inside after me and Matthias find a rusty spare key hidden under

The garden makes me think of Lane again. She didn't deserve to die because of me. I hug myself, wishing I could've saved her.

"There's practically no human scent here," Matthias says. "Should be safe enough with the scents we left to throw them off. We'll triple the barriers on our perimeter to be sure. The gates in this area are far off. The nearest one feels like it's at least two hours away."

"As long as they're unable to track us after we doubled back to the mountains from the opposite direction. They're not likely to expect us to return to the same area near where they attacked you," Alder mutters. "Now, tell us what the hell happened? Did the knight set you up?"

We only gave a brief picture of what we went through at Lane's cottage, Valerian unwilling to divulge more details until he was sure we were safe.

He sets his jaw. "No. Rainer owes me a life debt. Besides that, he wouldn't betray me. He's one of the few that believed losing my charge wasn't my fault."

His gaze seeks me out. It's the same strange look he had in the cottage. I cover the insistent thump of my heart with a hand.

"We were attacked by assassins. The Shadow Vanguard, going by their white hair and swords," Valerian says. "They have to be tracking the witches because I could smell the blood of the coven I met with that sent me to this witch."

I cast my eyes down. More blood on my hands. Alder said I'm not a monster, yet I'm feeling the label fits right now.

"Damn. That highly classed? They only go after the priciest bounties." Alder scrubs the top of his head, tugging on the longer brown locks on top. "That was smart since the hellhounds haven't been able to keep on us. How did you fight them off?"

"Lily. It makes more sense to me now." Valerian studies me. "She has an incredible amount of dormant power at her fingertips. More than we sensed. She took all four assassins down with one attack. Her demon is someone important, high ranking—high *value.* Someone that others would benefit from by getting rid of her with the level of power she has. It's more than enough to rival the Devil's and must be why the demon council has every faction hunting us to protect their seats."

The reverence and respect coloring his tone recounting how powerful my counterattack was when he was injured catches me off guard.

"Do you know who?" Alder asks.

Valerian hesitates. He covers it quickly, but I don't miss the flicker in his eyes. "Not yet."

"Did the witch break the seal?" Matthias grasps my chin, bringing his face close to study me. "You don't look any different, pretty girl."

Needing him, I close my fingers around his wrist and press on my toes to kiss him. *Oh.* My heart swells at the swipe of his tongue. I missed this. Missed him. He wraps me in his arms with an affectionate hum that chases away my guilty sadness for the witches.

As long as my demons are okay, I'll be okay.

"No," Valerian answers. "The only answers we got are that she might have been forced to reincarnate."

Alder releases an unhappy rumble, pressing against my back while Matthias strokes my hair. Between them I'm safe and warm. Could it be this easy to have them both? To share their love and fit them both into my heart? An empty void tells me I still have room for more in my hungry heart.

"No demon I know would challenge our laws like that." I lift my head and Alder elaborates for me. "It's forbidden. Reincarnation is a gift from the fae gods demons descend from. Forcing it is sadistic torture, keeping the demon from healing, on the edge of death until they trigger the regeneration."

I shudder, picturing the swirling black portal that swallowed me whole. Is that what awaited me on the other side?

"The witch put her in a meditative spell to access the seal, but we were interrupted before we could find out for sure," Valerian says.

"It felt like something pushed me out." I frown.

"I thought maybe it was because her concentration broke, but could it be the seal keeping me out?"

"Yes." Matthias touches my temple. "The mind is a complex thing. Like when you broke free of my persuasive thrall to stay in the car. It can be swayed, but for the complete block of a binding seal, the magic has its own layer of protection to convince the mind to stay away."

"What did you see when you entered your mental plane?" Valerian asks.

"I was in a castle. It had an eerie gothic vibe, like Dracula would definitely live there." Matthias snorts, kissing my forehead. "It also felt...familiar. I knew the hall I was in would lead to a throne room."

The three of them exchange a glance. Alder squeezes my shoulders. "That's Lucifer's castle at the heart of Hell in the Towering City."

I nod slowly in acceptance. There isn't any running from this or ignoring it.

"I've dreamed of it before today. I knew my way around. At Lane's, I was going to the throne room to see if you guys were there like in my dream. Before I got there some kind of—portal, I think? Smoke gathered from the floor and swirled around. Someone grabbed me through it."

Valerian braces against the back of the sofa, staring out at the sun setting behind the mountain view through the door that leads to the deck.

"Alder."

"Right." His nose touches my crown and he inhales. "I do not wish to leave you, sweet blossom."

"What?" Whirling around I grab two fistfuls of his fitted t-shirt. "Don't go."

"We need to set the protective wards so we can settle here for the next few days," Valerian says. "After that, I need to find Rainer."

Alder nods. "We should check if the demons hunted the other witches down. We can keep muddying our trail so we're harder to track, too."

Valerian pushes off the couch with a faint flinch of pain. "Agreed. Matthias, you'll guard Lily."

"With my life," Matthias says.

"Are you insane?" I release Alder, ignoring the crack in my heart to block Vale's path. "You're still hurt!"

"I'm fine. It's faster if the two of us go alone." The tip of his serpent-like tongue traces his lower lip. "You can play nurse later. Stay put. I mean it."

He uses his most demanding tone and cups my face, throwing me right back to the moment we almost kissed. The tether in my chest strains with the desire to crash against him and taste his lips. His blue gaze flares brighter.

The tense beat breaks when he nudges me into Matthias's waiting arms. The scent of maple and roasted chestnuts surrounds me.

"I'll take care of you, mate," Matthias says against my ear in a rough tone that makes me shudder.

Vale holds my eye. "We won't be gone long. Before the night's out, we'll return."

The pull in my chest tugs as I watch two of my demons leave me behind. Even Valerian's promise doesn't soften the fractures splintering my heart.

It's been too long. I'm sick of pacing, my stomach tying itself in knots. Matthias isn't faring better, his usual easy nature tinged with restless agitation.

"I can't take this." I scrub my face. "I don't like not knowing what's going on or if they're okay."

"I know. Come here, petal." He pulls me into his arms and flops us on the thick chaise cushion of the L-shaped couch with me resting on his chest.

Guilt clangs around inside me for a moment. Matthias hasn't left my side, indulging my need to keep moving. He's done everything to keep my mind occupied to steer me away from spiraling into an anxiety-induced panic. As soon as the guys left, he suggested we explore the house and check if the hot tub on the deck worked so we could try to relax. It didn't, unfortunately. We did find a questionable shrine to Mothman in the basement, complete with totally Photoshopped blurry photos of the cryptid, a hand-sewn costume, and some sexy Mothman fan art.

"I just hate waiting," I mumble into his neck.

He plays with my hair, combing through it soothingly. "Want to see if there are any movies? I didn't see a VHS player, but hopefully they've got something."

"It's all on disc now. DVD. It's more compact."

He makes an inquisitive sound. "Such clever creatures. So what do you say, babe?" He claps his hands on my plump ass and squeezes. "Let's pretend the world doesn't exist for a minute and we've escaped for a lover's holiday. We'll act like we're watching the movie until we can't keep our hands off each other. I'll eat your pussy until the credits roll and you're crying for me to stop because it's too much."

"That's called Netflix and chill now." I giggle at his quirked eyebrow.

"There's that smile I love so much." He kisses me, keeping my laughter going when he attacks my face with more light kisses.

This is what I like about being with Matthias. He does everything to make me smile and make me feel worshiped. He also reminds me life doesn't have to be so serious. With him, I can laugh even when the world around me feels like it's about to fall apart.

"Sometimes I forget you're older than you seem until you remind me you're basically stuck in the 90s." I give him a wry smile, shyly tugging on a lock of his hair. "How old are you really? You seem younger than the others."

"Not by much. Vale is the oldest, but age is relative to us. Demons don't celebrate the way humans do." He pretends to chomp on my finger, grinning around the digit and coiling his tongue around my knuckle until I squirm. "If I seem young, it's a personality flaw for a trickster demon like me. Chaos is addictive."

"Yeah, you give off that vibe." I smirk. "When we first met, I called you fuckboy in my head."

He waggles his brows. "Before I became of age, I kept sneaking through the gates. The demon academy had a hell of a time controlling me. It was decided that I'd be assigned as a gate guard. They thought it was a lesson in restraint, but I lived my best life every time I got to go topside."

I shake my head, smiling easier than I have all night. "You showed them."

"You know it, babe." He cups my face. "I think I was so drawn to this realm because I've been searching for you."

Our bond hums, twining around my heart in contentment.

"Okay, so if not a movie, what would you do,

then? Pretend we're not on the run. Hit me with your ideal day." The corner of his mouth lifts. "I promise to make it happen because you deserve the world, my pretty girl."

A warm glow fills my chest when he talks like that, like he cherishes me. I guess a fated mate is wired to love the one they're bonded to, but I still have trouble believing he feels that way for me.

I blush, licking my lips. "I doubt Vale and Alder would let us do that."

Matthias brushes my cheek with his knuckles. "Pretend the underworld isn't in chaos and our lives aren't at stake. What would make you happy?"

"I don't think anyone's ever asked me that," I admit. "People in my life were always more focused on how messed up they believed I was."

His smile falters and he draws me down for a kiss. "You never have to face that again. I'm asking you now, so tell me."

I roll my lips between my teeth as I open up a part of my mind I've kept closed off and neglected. What I want... Scenes from my isekai manga pop into my head.

"I've always dreamed of seeing the world. The foster system bounced me around, but I've never been to the beach. If I could do anything, I'd want to do that."

"And swim in the ocean?" he asks cautiously.

"I'm surprised after your reaction at the lake."

"Oh. Well, I know the ocean is saltwater. I think I would be okay. It's just freshwater that makes me think of—"

I blow out a breath. I can tell him. It's scary, but I have him and the others to protect me now. I'm not alone anymore.

"Of the well water. The taste, the smell. It makes me relive what I'm afraid of."

"We'll rewrite all the bad memories with good ones. I promise."

Relief spills through me at his lack of judgment. "You'd really take me to the beach?"

"I'd take you anywhere you want to go." His serious expression clears and he winks to lighten the mood. "Plus, I love sex on the beach."

I pinch him. "Matthias!"

He smirks. "I could put on the costume we found downstairs and we could indulge in a sexy role play game to cure ourselves of going stir crazy."

"I'm not a monster fucker, you dick."

"Just demons, then?" His dimpled grin is unapologetic. "You do bring out the beast in me, mate. I can be more monstrous for you. Anything you need, baby."

When I sock him in the side, he snickers, forked tongue poking out from the side of his mouth. I kiss him to cut off his laugh, chasing that mischievous tongue. He threads his fingers in my hair and rolls us over, pinning me to the couch while he claims my mouth. The kiss turns hot fast, fueled by our anxiousness and uncertainty. We both need to feel right now.

Matthias slides a hand under my shirt and we break apart so he can whip it off. My bra follows and I arch with a moan as his mouth captures my nipple while he palms my other breast. He trails his way down my body, worshiping every curve, every dip and fold with sultry kisses, murmuring how beautiful and soft I am.

I gasp as he drags my shorts and panties off. "I need—"

"I know, pretty girl." He gets on his knees and tugs me to the edge, settling between my spread thighs. Blond hair falling across his forehead, he peers up the length of my body, snaring me in his sultry golden gaze. "I can smell how badly you want my cock, and I'm going to give it to you, baby. But I'm fucking starving for you. I need to feast on your first."

"Oh god." The first swipe of his tongue is heaven.

Like the kiss, the glide of his mouth on my pussy heats up quickly. He doesn't draw it out to tease me with sweet torture, but insists I come on his tongue. He devours my pussy. When his tongue pushes inside me, I whimper, grabbing hold of his hair. He groans against my slick folds as my hips undulate.

Then I shatter for him, the tidal wave of pleasure rolling through me for long moments. He releases a gravely noise as he positions his thick cock at my entrance and thrusts inside, filling me with his dizzying length. I gasp, nails scrabbling on his back. The ridges on his cock rub the sensitive spot still throbbing from my first orgasm, another one racing up to steal my breath as he sets a hard, wild pace.

"Fuck, your pussy feels amazing, petal. So good for me, squeezing my cock so tight. Is this what you needed? My cock destroying your pussy, making you come all over it?"

All I can do is push out a breathy moan and hold on, engulfed in the molten heat between us. His thrusts have so much divine force, each one scoots me up the chaise until he climbs onto the cushion, covering my body with his. He hooks an arm beneath my knee and wraps my other leg around his hips, positioning me so I feel him even deeper when he drives his cock inside me. My mouth falls open on a scream of pleasure.

It doesn't register that the door opened until the blended scent of woodsmoke and rich hickory hit my nose.

They're back.

Matthias doesn't stop, pinning my wrists over my head. There's no break in his pace as Alder and Vale come into view past his shoulder, the hot press of their gazes making me writhe in sinful ecstasy.

Alder's eyes darken with desire at the sight of Matthias fucking me with wild abandon without stopping. I meet his fiery green gaze and cry out, clenching on Matthias' cock. Matthias groans, burying his face in my neck, nibbling at my flushed skin.

He braces over me, giving me a filthy smirk. "You like the audience, petal? You're getting wetter by the second. They're watching you, Lily." A hot, dirty chuckle falls from his lips as my core throbs and tightens around him. He glances over his shoulder at the others, then looks at me with a challenge in his hooded golden eyes. "Show them how gorgeous you are when you come on my cock."

Alder rumbles, coming closer. Valerian hangs back, leaning against the wall. God, he's staying to watch instead of leaving. A strangled moan catches in my throat as Alder kneels next to the chaise, his breath ghosting over my neck before his lips connect. Matthias grins, adjusting to give Alder room to fondle my tits as his tongue licks a stripe up my pulse point, taking over pinning my wrists in one big hand as they wrench pleasure from me.

"Show us, Lily," Alder rasps. "I want to see you

come. Soak his cock."

With a choked gasp, I flutter my eyes open and seek out Valerian, burning up from the intensity of his attention locked on every move I make. I tear my eyes away with effort, meeting Alder's smoldering stare as he drinks me in and teases my nipples. Then Matthias grasps my chin and steals my focus, his eyes flooding with lust at the obscene sound of his cock driving into me from how wet I am, the slickness dripping down my thighs.

This is so much more intense than what happened in the car. The thrum in my chest sings in harmony as I come hard with all three of their gazes trained on me.

"That's it, petal. So beautiful when you cream my cock like that." Matthias reaches between us, touching where my body is stretched around his hardness. He brings his glistening fingers to his mouth and groans. "You taste so fucking sweet. Here, you need to taste her right now."

Matthias grabs Alder's arm and guides him to do the same. His thick fingers skate over my folds, rubbing my clit. A low growl vibrates in his chest as I tip my head back, lips parted. I pant under his unwavering stare as he brings me to the brink again. When I fly off the edge into oblivion, my pussy fluttering around Matthias' dick, Alder swipes my wetness and sucks his fingers clean without breaking eye contact.

He dips his head to capture my lips, letting me taste my own pleasure when his tongue pushes into my mouth to glide against mine in a searing kiss. I wrap my arms around his shoulders, clinging to him while they both stoke the inferno blazing within me. He swallows my gasp when he surprises me by shifting his fingers into claws, grazing my skin. Matthias does the same, teasing my hips with light scrapes that have me shaking apart with a breathless moan.

If it's this unbearably good with two of them, what would it be like if I was with all three of them at the same time? I wish Vale would come kneel on my other side and give me the kiss I wanted so badly earlier.

Movement in the corner of my eye snags my attention. Valerian moves to the kitchen, ignoring the depraved scene at the edge of his periphery. He raids the cabinets with meticulous focus, pulling down a forgotten, half full bottle of whiskey. He doesn't bother with a glass, swigging straight from the bottle.

My chest clenches, then loosens at Matthias' croon in my ear. "Do you think this pretty little pussy could take two of our cocks at once if we shared you?" He hums when my core flutters. "Good girl. Soon, petal. Soon we'll both fill you at once and show you that you belong to us."

"Yes," I whimper.

The orgasm that crashes over me at his possessive, claiming words is intense and all-consuming, pulsing through my body in time with the thrum of the bond in my chest. Matthias braces above me as his dick throbs, swelling even thicker inside me on the next thrust. I lose my breath at the full sensation, the stretch overwhelmingly good. My head lolls and my vision swims as sparks of ecstasy race through me.

"Are you knotting her first after you also had her first, you bastard?" Alder growls.

"Can't help it," Matthias grits out. "Fuck, she feels so good."

I'm aware of Alder smoothing my hair back, of Matthias brushing his lips across mine, the place where we're connected, and the shivers of blissful passion racking my body. Everything else fades away as I drift in and out for a long stretch, my heart beating hard and the bond in my chest reverberating with an incandescent glow.

"It's okay, sweet blossom. We've got you," Alder murmurs. "You're doing so well. Taking your mate's knot is intense the first time, especially for a human body. Just let go and let us take care of you."

Twenty
LILY

W E PLAN TO MOVE FROM THE CABIN AS SOON AS
Valerian heals. The morning after, I was
surprised by how much better the wounds looked
when I caught him shirtless, a towel wrapped low
on his waist while he made coffee in the kitchen.
He turned at my sharp inhale, meeting my eye with
a smirk when I muttered I was glad he wasn't on
death's door.

Neither of us brought up what happened when
he returned with Alder and caught Matthias fucking
me.

The memory of how it ended is still hazy. I
came back to myself in a warm bath, resting against
Alder's hard chest while Matthias gently washed
away the mild soreness between my thighs. The

adoration in his bright gold eyes made my heart float all day.

But it doesn't dull my frustration that the answers are out of reach because of the attack. It eats at me. I throw myself into training while we're at the cabin, determined to improve. I'm at it day and night, pushing my powers to obey my command until my legs shake, ready to buckle from draining my energy. Alder tries to stop me the first day, but Vale intervenes and tells him to let me do what I want. I've lost track, the hours bending together, sunsets becoming sunrises.

I'm getting sick of running. I have to get better so we can stop this insane hunt for our heads before it gets us killed.

Training this hard also means I have an excuse not to talk to Matthias about Alder and Vale. It's shitty of me, but when I see his affectionate smile, my chest constricts. I'm terrified my mate will look at me with hatred like every other person that was supposed to love me. Choked by the fear he'll be angry because I have feelings for the others. I couldn't bear it, but I'm powerless to stop what I feel.

It's not just Alder and Matthias I'm torn between. It's Vale, too. Almost losing him made it clear that I don't want a world without him in it, challenging me, pushing my buttons, igniting my need to fight back.

Matthias said I belonged to both of them, yet I can't quiet the fear lurking in the back of my mind that he'll reject me.

I shove everything stressing me out from my mind, bracing my hands on my hips as I catch my breath. My panting clouds the night air in the woods behind the cabin where I've cobbled together my practice area.

Gritting my teeth at the ache in my arms, I lift them and force my hellfire to spill into my palms. The lid I pulled off the broken hot tub—my makeshift target—has holes singed in it. This time I'll hit a bullseye. My focus zeroes in on the spot I want to go. I push with all my might, the fireball bursting from my hands.

The force knocks me back and my twinging legs give out.

"Fuck!" The fireball skews to the left, taking out a bush as I tumble backwards, landing on my ass in the dirt.

"Stop shifting your center of balance to compensate for pushing yourself to the point of exhaustion." I jump at Alder's stern tone. He steps out of the trees behind me, shirtless, wearing only a pair of gray sweatpants that make my mouth water with the memory of his dick filling my mouth. "You're training too hard. Control isn't just about hours of practice, Lily. It comes when you learn to rest, too."

I climb to my feet, rubbing my sweaty face with the back of my hand. "How long have you been watching?"

"Every night you've snuck out here after pretending to fall asleep." He frowns at my crappy form when I prepare to try again, nudging the inside of my knee for a sturdier center of gravity and tucking my elbows. "I didn't appreciate the sight of you leaving me alone in bed. I'm sure Matthias hasn't enjoyed it, either."

I falter, screwing up my fireball blast before the flames have swirled into a mass. They sputter out as I whip around, my throat stinging.

His stoic expression softens and he smooths his hands over my shoulders, massaging the aches and pains from my overworked muscles with magic heat emanating from his touch. I wobble on my feet with a feeble moan, ready to sway into him. He hushes me, working out the kinks in my tired body until blissful tingles spread throughout it.

"Why are you so stubborn?" He doesn't seem to expect an answer, talking more to himself. "You don't have to do this alone. You have me. Matthias. Vale, in his own way. We'll take care of you, blossom. You only need to ask."

I give up my fight with gravity, leaning against him. He supports me without question, adjusting his embrace to keep me upright while massaging the back of my neck. My eyes flutter. God, this feels incredible. Safe, warm. All the things he reminds me I have now.

"I'm sorry," I mumble with my head against his chest. "I just want to get better. I don't want to fail again if it means any of you getting hurt trying to protect me."

"It's alright. We swore to protect you, Lily. I understand your desire to be your best." My heart thumps with his promise. I wind my arms around his waist, hugging him. He sighs. "I don't want to see you push yourself as hard as my father pushed me. You'll only end up hurting yourself. I won't allow it."

A smile twitches my lips, cutting through my waning exhaustion. "Yes, sir," I sass. "Are you going to punish me for being such a brat?"

He stills, then adjusts his embrace. His woodsmoke scent grows thicker, snaking around me with a heavy swirl of charcoal mixing with it.

The air between us shifts, crackling with tension as he catches me in a hold we've been practicing. Our bodies are plastered together, his grip tightening on my arm to tug me against him, making the invisible tether in my chest flutter. The hard ridge of his dick grinds against my spine.

"Get away," he challenges.

"I thought I needed rest?" My words are light and breathless, too distracted by the throbbing heat building in my core.

"You need something else. No more holding back."

His nose grazes my neck, inhaling with a low, pleased rumble. I rub my thighs together. Can he smell how wet I am? How much it turns me on to be trapped by him?

"I've grown tired of Matthias' teasing. He doesn't get to keep you to himself anymore," he rumbles. "I won't wait around for him to share you."

The flutter in my chest ricochets around my heart. "Alder—"

"Break out of my hold, Lily." His gruff tone makes it hard to deny his wishes.

Focusing on what to do is a struggle with the distraction of his scent and every place we touch. I drag in a breath, wanting to earn one of his proud smiles when I get things right. Wriggling my shoulders to fake a struggle, I wedge my hands into position and drive them up in the circle of his arms with a tight spiral of flames to add to my force while stomping on his foot.

Breaking away, I whirl with a satisfied grin. It feels badass when I execute these moves. Size and shape don't matter. Only technique and understanding balance. Alder taught me that and with his lessons, he's giving me something even more powerful—the ability and confidence to defend myself.

I open my mouth to go off about my success, but the words never come.

Our eyes meet. My breath hitches at the primal darkness in his piercing stare.

"Run," he orders.

I fall back a step, eyes widening. Is he serious? I can barely stand. He'll catch me in no time and—*oh*. I lose my breath in a rush. He'll catch me, like the wicked promise he gave me at Talbot House in the middle of the night.

A thud drums against my ribcage. I want Alder to catch me. I want to be hunted by him until he pins me in the dirt and takes what I desperately want to have with him.

His chin dips, his predatory hooded gaze trained on me. "Run, sweet blossom. *Now*."

My pulse races as I take off, stumbling on a root. I feel it everywhere—my heart, my neck, my clit. Every pumping beat sends lust and a thrilling shot of anticipation coursing through my veins.

At first he crashes through the trees behind me, a deadly beast on my trail. Then as I brace a hand against a tree to catch my breath, I can't hear him anymore. His scent drifts on the air, tickling my nose, letting me know he'll never stop. My stomach twists into a pleasant coil of desire. His hunting becomes silent, stalking his prey for the right moment.

A threatening growl echoes to my left. The dangerous sound should strike fear in me, but all it does is steal my breath and make me crave the moment he'll catch me. I push off again, circling around to double back.

"I would've thought catching me would be easy, big guy," I call teasingly. "You said you'd always be able to hunt me do—*oof!*"

A heavy mass of brawny muscle and alluringly scented smoke collides with me, catching me off guard from the opposite direction I expected him. His strong arms lock around me, taking the brunt of our fall. His sweatpants are gone, discarded somewhere while he hunted me.

Rolling over, he pins me face-down beneath him in the dirt, gathering my arms and pinning my wrists at the base of my spine. I writhe, not willing to give in so easily. He grinds his cock into my ass the size of it spreading between my cheeks. I gasp, twisting to rest my flushed cheek against the cool ground, then press back against his erection with more purpose. My core clenches, aching to feel him inside.

Alder releases a feral sound, digging his fingers into my hip to keep me still. "I don't care that Matthias claimed you first. All that matters is that you're mine."

"Yes," I whimper.

He fists my pants and shreds them with a brutal yank. I squirm beneath him in the dirt, small needy sounds slipping out. My shirt goes next, the back of the tank top split from the neckline. The chilly night air teases the sides of my breasts as he caresses his palm down my bare spine. His grip around my pinned wrists flexes, then he destroys my panties, tearing the material like it's paper to bare me to him.

"Beautiful girl."

He guides me to kneel with a jerk of my hips, leaving my chest against the ground. Cupping between my thighs, his thick fingers glide through my slick folds, using it to massage my entire pussy.

"So wet," he praises gruffly.

My legs threaten to give out as he torments my clit with firm rubs that make me race to the edge of oblivion. "C-close," I whine. "Alder, please. I want to come."

"I know. You will." His lips brush the small of my back with a tender kiss. "You'll come so hard on my cock you'll never forget."

"Forget what?" I breathe.

He stops playing with my clit right before I reach my orgasm and I cry out, wriggling against his uncompromising hold to seek out the friction I need. He chuckles when I shut up at the feel of his thick head rubbing against my entrance. "Forget that you're mine."

My nipples tighten to hard peaks at those words falling from his lips in a jagged and steely tone. At the same time, he grabs my hip and pushes inside with a forceful thrust that makes me see stars. My breath comes in ragged puffs as he fills me so deep, stretching my body to accommodate his massive size, the ridges on his length lighting me up with each inch he buries further within me.

It's so intense, awakening the raw need inside me for him to make me irrefutably his, to carve his name into my very soul and claim me in every way.

"Please." It's the only word I can form, my core ravaged by our passionate flames.

"So fucking tight." He strokes my back, giving me a moment to adjust to his size once he's buried to the hilt.

His fingers trace down to dip between my ass cheeks. They disappear for a moment, then return wet with spit as he circles the hole with a teasing lightness that grows more insistent until one of his thick fingers sinks inside to the first knuckle.

"Oh!" My back bows at the sensation of his cock filling my pussy while he plays with my ass. He starts to move, his thrusts growing sharper as my body opens for his huge cock. "Fuck, that's—that feels really good."

"Yes, blossom." The rough possessiveness in his tone sends a shiver down my spine. "I'll have you in every way imaginable."

I moan at the promise, flooded with want for whatever he'll give me.

A savage sound rips from him and he releases my pinned wrists to wrap his arms around me, lifting me against his chest. A scream catches in my throat as the position seats him so deep it pushes me over the edge without warning, the eruption of ecstasy exploding from my core. I scrabble at his muscular arms banded around me as he fucks me harder, our scents blending and heightening my pleasure.

"Mine," he growls.

All I can do is nod. More than anything, I want it to be true. I want to be his too, because this feels too good, too right to be wrong.

My nerve endings burst all over my body, the insistent thrum in my chest singing in harmony with my aroused moans. His forked tongue swipes at the crook of my neck and his lips close on my pulse point, sucking hard on my sensitive skin. As I reach oblivion again, he slams deep inside my fluttering pussy, rugged muscles tensed as a feral sound tears from him. His cock pulses within my core as he comes.

His release leaks from where we're joined, dripping down my thighs. My lips part and I tilt my head back, angling to kiss him. He captures my mouth, hips pumping with tiny movements that make me gasp into the kiss. He swallows every sound, lips curving against mine.

As his hand coasts down my soft stomach to splay across my lower abdomen, his chest reverberates with a rumble. My eyes pop open and I break our kiss as something urgent occurs to me.

"Will I get pregnant? I don't think there are condoms big enough in the human world for you and you definitely didn't pull out."

Not that I wanted him to. I love the feeling when he spills inside me. I gulp, realizing I haven't used protection with Matthias, either.

He shakes his head, sighing. "Though I would love nothing more than to see your belly swelled with our child, beautiful, you won't be able to conceive like this. The seal that binds you keeps your true form trapped."

I sag against him. "Okay. I'm not ready for that."

I might never be. After the life I've had, I'd no doubt screw a kid up. My heart twists, thinking of how many kids in the system go for so long wishing for a family to pick them.

"We would never push you to do anything you don't want," he assures me. "But I do like this."

His hand dips lower, caressing my swollen pussy and touching my stretched entrance. Gathering his come leaking out of me, he pulls out slowly and uses his fingers to force his come back inside. I clench around them, feeling empty without his cock buried in me.

"Next time I want to knot you," he rasps. "Then after it's gone down, spend the rest of the night pushing my come back into your pussy with my fingers before I fuck it back into you with my cock."

My thighs clench and a ragged breath hisses out of me. His chuckle is warm and tinged with a dirty air he's kept hidden from me. I like this side of him. He continues playing with me, fingering me gently until I'm writhing once more. He's not satisfied until he wrenches another orgasm from me, leaving me fucked out and on the edge of delirium.

"It's time for bed." He kisses me deeply again, laying his claim and possessing me with his mouth. "This time you'll stay put by my side. If you try to sneak out again, I'll chase you, sweet blossom."

"I don't know if that's a bad thing." I laugh at his warning look. Biting my lip around a smile, I nod. "I want to stay with you."

Alder sweeps me into his arms, leaving my tattered clothes behind. I'm glad, because this time I really am past my limit. I'd never be able to stand after that. We're covered in dirt and worn out, a sweet ache lingering between my legs. He carries me through the woods, back to our cabin.

His lips brush my forehead and his comforting scent twines around my heart as it bursts with the unfamiliar happiness of being completely taken care of.

Twenty One
LILY

MY HEART SITS IN MY THROAT ALL DAY FROM THE moment I wake up in Alder's arms near noon. Last night, I was powerless against my desire, influenced by the strong pull to him. I have to tell Matthias. Fear ingrained from so much rejection locks around my heart.

After I snuck into the shower, then found my bed empty, Matthias convinced me to take a break from training. We walked a nature trail he found, weaving around the cabin in the cool autumn breeze while he conjured dazzling little light shows with his illusion magic and pretended to be a tour guide to get me to smile. I opened my mouth at least a dozen times, the confession about last night ready to burst free, yet unable to escape. Each time he cast a worried look my way when he thought I wasn't paying attention, my heart wedged tighter into my throat.

He treats me to the sweetest day, showing me consideration no one's ever given me before. It underlines the fact I can't hide from him any longer.

Our day-long date ends with dinner on the balcony watching the moon rise.

We sit on a blanket overlooking the moonlit Appalachian mountains, surrounded by candles and the dinner he put together for me. It's a beautiful night and I'm with the one my heart is fated to. He's done everything to spoil me today and I can barely taste the food because my stomach is in knots. I'm a terrible mate.

"Okay." Matthias wipes his mouth and draws me against his side beneath his arm. "You have to tell me what's on your mind, or I'll—"

"I had sex with Alder." I blurt it out with way less tact than the million other ways I thought of to tell him. Closing my eyes to avoid seeing his disappointment, I push the rest of my confession out. "Twice. Alone. Not like—not like what we've done before. It was last night, and at the motel last week."

I tense, waiting for his rejection. My heart fractures at the thought of my mate rejecting me. Even fate doesn't save me from the eventual moment everyone leaves me behind because I'm not enough.

Matthias chuckles. "Is that all, petal?" My eyes fly open and he lifts my chin. "Did his cock make you cry out in that beautiful way I love so much?"

My lips part. He grins at my flustered expression.

Raking his teeth over his lip, he sighs. "Fuck, I wish you'd let me watch, mate. Bet it was so hot. I want to see him fuck you and hear every sexy sound you make while you take his cock."

I sit in stunned silence for a beat, heat spreading through me. "You're not mad?"

"No, baby. Trust me, if I wasn't willing to share you with my brothers, I'd never let them see you. But they're the only two I'll ever let touch my mate. If anyone else dares to look at you, I'll carve out their eyes with my claws." He kisses my forehead when I shiver at his casual possessiveness. "I'm relieved you followed your heart. I was worried you'd deny yourself. Tell me this, did you want him?"

"I—yes." My cheeks are inflamed. "I did. I… do."

"Then that's all that matters. Your happiness is what makes me happy." I swallow the lump in my throat. He covers my heart with his hand. The bond reacts to his touch, emanating a soft glow. "You feel it? You belong to me. But you also belong to Alder, too."

"How?" I breathe.

"The bond's magic doesn't allow us to look at anyone who isn't our fated mate. If you didn't feel it for him, he wouldn't be able to seduce you away from me."

His explanation opens a whole new world to me. Reawakens the hope I hardly allowed to take flight—that I could have more than one fated mate. The tugs I've felt in three directions aren't trying to tear me apart. I didn't betray the bond with my mate and he's not casting me aside after finding out I was with Alder. The stress I've battled all day ebbs.

I cover his hand with mine, my lashes brushing my cheeks at the feel of our bond filling me. "That's really possible? I could have more than one bond?"

"Of course, petal." He frowns at me in concern. "We thought you knew once your bond with me took shape. I'm sorry. I would have explained it better to you instead of dropping hints."

I shake my head. "It's okay."

"It's rare. We're as shocked by it as you are, but I told you we feel it, too. Your scent is what triggered the bond and helped it form. Outside of hellhounds, only powerful demon lines have more than one fated mate."

Relief spreads through me. "I was so afraid you would hate me when I told you."

"Never, Lily." He cradles my jaw, tilting my face. His eyes gleam with affection. "You don't have to choose between us. You're our mate, and we're yours."

I shudder at those words. The truth in them echoes through me, my bond growing as I stop fighting my feelings out of fear of rejection.

Matthias kisses me deeply. Every brush of his lips and tongue feels like a promise to love me. The cracks that formed in my heart with my worries mend.

"Did you like your birthday dinner?" he asks when he ends the kiss.

"Wait, what?" My brows pinch. "You told me demons don't celebrate birthdays. Besides, mine isn't even real."

"You grew up here. We wanted any excuse to celebrate you, Lils. Birthday girls get spoiled in the mortal realm and I want to spoil you forever, mate."

I gasp against his mouth when he swoops down to give me another scorching kiss.

"It's belated. I think the mortal's Halloween was a week or two ago." He pulls a face, then shrugs. "But we put this together for you. The day off, this dinner. The rest of tonight is up to you."

My heart skips a beat. "We?"

"All of us." He winks. "It was Vale's idea and I ran with it. He saw you training so hard. He'll be back later when Rainer relieves him from watch to guard us all tonight."

For the longest time, I thought I'd spend my eighteenth birthday walking away backwards from the group home with both middle fingers raised. One final *fuck you, goodbye* to the system that screwed me over time and again.

Instead, I spent it on the run and forgot about it. Tonight has turned into the most perfect one I could imagine out of all the times I wished for someone to celebrate me growing up. My real age as a demon doesn't matter right now. What does is that they did this for me. They gave me today—gave me permission to exist. It's the greatest gift of all, the one I've longed for the most.

Tears of gratitude well in my eyes. The way the three of them meet my needs heals me from years of crushing abandonment.

"Thank you," I whisper. "This is... No one's ever done this for me. I've always spent my birthday alone."

"You'll never be alone again." He traces the shape of my lips with his thumb. "For now, why don't we go inside and find Alder?"

"Yes." My breathless answer makes Matthias chuckle.

As soon as he suggests going to find my second mate, need arrows through me. I have to see him. Have to tell him how I feel.

We find him sitting on the first step, rugged

arms braced on his thighs and his stare locked on the door as we come back inside. He sits up straighter and my heart gives a drumming beat when our eyes connect.

"Any longer and I was about to come out there," he grumbles. "I shouldn't have agreed to your plan. You just wanted her to yourself all day."

"It's what she needed. I'll put her needs first above any of ours every time." Matthias takes me by the shoulders from behind and brings his lips to my ear. "Go to him."

My breath comes in short bursts. Each inch of distance between us is unfair. *Mine.* The rough, feral tone he used last night crashes over me, knocking the wind from me.

"Alder." He shoots to his feet at my strained murmur. I rush him when he opens his arms, squeezing my eyes shut when he catches me and lifts me off the ground. "Mate."

"Yes, sweet blossom," he rumbles into my neck. "You're mine."

"And mine." Matthias makes no move to intervene in our moment. "Ours."

"Ours." Alder's embrace tightens.

It feels so right, the tender light in my chest brilliant, more settled. When he lifts his head, I kiss him, my heart opening for him. His chest reverberates with a deep, gratified rumble and he braces my back against the wall. The ardent, claiming kiss is full of smoldering heat that burns me with the sweetest passion.

I pull back with a gasp. "Can we go upstairs?"

Alder grabs me beneath my thighs and hauls me higher, wrapping my legs around his ripped torso. His strength leaves me lightheaded. I rest my hot cheek against his shoulder. Matthias follows as Alder carries me upstairs, kneading my ass the entire way.

In the bedroom, I glance between them, then strip until nothing separates me from them. The burn of their gazes on my body fills me with confidence and makes me feel incredibly beautiful. Alder reaches back to tug off his shirt first, then Matthias does the same. They leave their boxer briefs on while I'm bare.

It's not that I want to have sex with both of them right now. The bond is making me crave skin on skin contact. The intimacy of feeling their heartbeats directly against mine.

"Whatever you want," Matthias reminds me.

I nod and take both their hands, inviting them to get in bed. They sandwich me between them, their arms draped over my waist and stomach. I face Alder and Matthias drags my hips back, my ass snug against his erection. Neither of them push me, allowing me to take this bond with them both at my own pace.

Tucked between them, I feel like I've found my place for the first time in my life.

I'm at a loss for what to do next, reluctant to end this blissful moment wrapped in their arms. It could've been like this from the first moment we felt the bond if I hadn't resisted what I was too scared to hope was real.

Part of me is glad we could take it slow. If I'd realized they were my fated mates in the abandoned graveyard, before I knew I'm really a demon, it would have freaked me the hell out. I wouldn't have believed it, too broken to think the demons who threatened to kill me were destined to love me, the unlovable, troubled orphan.

"What's going through your head?" Alder cups my cheek with his big hand.

A soft sigh leaves me at the touch and I rub my face against his palm. "Imagining how this would've gone down between us if we realized the night we met in Brim Hills." I smile wryly. "Not only would I not have believed for a second you wanted me, but the whole we're here to kill you thing would've made it awkward."

Matthias snickers. "We resisted the pull, too. None of us understood why it was happening. It was hard to focus because you smelled so fucking good."

302

I marvel at how easy this is now, to be free to map the hard planes of Alder's chest while Matthias traces teasing circles on my stomach. "When did you realize what it meant?"

"For me, the moment we were attacked. When the demon was going for you, I couldn't bear it. I needed to protect you without regard for my life or my brothers'," Alder says.

"At the rest stop when I saw Vale all over you." Matthias huffs. "Vale's probably known this whole time. I bet it's why he was so resistant to letting us seek you out alone."

A comfortable lull stretches. I bask in their soft touches and indulge the urge to touch my mates. Each exploratory caress opens a bottomless well of hunger in me, leaving me starved for this to stretch on forever, to always feel the profound joy that glows in me at their touch.

"God, this all had me so stressed." I press my face into Alder's chest. "I'm sorry I didn't say something sooner. We could've had this instead of me keeping us apart because I was afraid."

He pets my hair. "As long as you know you're ours now. You'll always be ours, sweet blossom."

"I'm not used to having anyone to rely on. I don't know how to do—this. Love. Relationships, magically ordained or otherwise. Even friendship is foreign to me."

The vitriol people have directed at me my entire life runs across my mind. Perhaps it's because they sensed the demon hidden in me that instinctively terrified them, but I endured it all, focusing on making myself less and less to keep my emotions from lashing out at their hatred.

My teeth sink into my lip and I push myself to be open with them. "I've spent a long time keeping my thoughts and emotions to myself. Trust in others doesn't come easily for me when I've been feared and rejected all my life by the people who believed I was different. That girl couldn't dream of finding one person fate chose to love her, let alone more than one."

When my choked words break off, Alder growls, holding me closer. Matthias echoes the fierce sound. Both of them show me with their embraces that I'll never face that kind of cruelty again.

Alder speaks against the top of my head. "I want to destroy any human who has ever made you feel this way."

Matthias kisses my shoulder, squeezing my waist. "And the ones who stole you from the underworld and put you through this. They'll pay for this."

A shuddering breath leaves me. Their acknowledgement alone that I shouldn't have been treated the way I was, shouldn't have been made to endure the abuse of the people that were supposed to shelter me splinters the thorns I grew around my heart.

Alder catches my hand and kisses every burn scar, then does the same to my other hand. He showers each marred expanse of skin that I've always hated with tender brushes of his lips.

"Every mark you bear is proof of your survival," he rasps. "You made it through that. It didn't break you permanently, and you'll never be alone again. Our hearts and souls will never be separated now that we've found you, Lily."

"You have us forever," Matthias adds.

I sniffle, burrowing against Alder and reaching for Matthias' hand. He scoots closer so there's no space between the three of us. The only thing that would make it better would be if Valerian were here, but for now this is enough. Understanding that I'm not being forced to choose by the fated magic connecting us is enough.

They cocoon me in their warmth and devotion. Every loving touch is a balm directly to my battered soul. It's almost overwhelming how the simplest caress of their fingertips following the roundness of my cheek or their fingers carding through my hair lights me up with an incandescent glow, almost drunk on their affections because I've never known the kindness of a hug. Between my mates, I'm enveloped in tenderness that makes my heart swell with euphoria.

The tears that spill down my cheeks aren't born of sadness. Neither of them say anything, maybe understanding how I feel better than I can voice myself. They simply hold me, showing every curve, every scar, and every invisible crack in my heart that they cherish me.

Twenty Two
LILY

AFTER I DOZE FOR A WHILE, I WAKE FROM MY NAP with a soft whimper. A sinfully delicious heat engulfs me, and when I open my eyes, I find Alder's head between my legs, massaging my thick thighs as his tongue plunges inside me.

Matthias smooths my hair back and grins when our gazes lock as I dance on the edge of falling. He traces my lips, then presses more insistently until I grant him access, allowing him to slip two of his fingers into my mouth, arching against Alder's divine ministrations as Matthias strokes my tongue.

I catch the rich scent of hickory and seek Vale out, my chest constricting when I find him seated in a chair by the bed. Watching. Out of the four of us, he's the only one fully clothed, the others stripped as bare as I am.

They're all here with me. All focused on me. A harmonious hum reverberates in my chest. Valerian's scent teases me while Matthias bends to capture my lips, swallowing my moan when Alder pushes me over the edge, crashing into a sea of pleasure.

"So gorgeous when you come." Matthias' golden gaze darkens, fixated on my mouth as he pushes his fingers in again, keeping my tongue occupied. My cheeks prickle from how much I like it. He pulls free and grasps my chin. "What do you want, pretty girl? We're going to take care of you."

Clashing emotions clog my throat. Gratitude, desire, and my newfound confidence that these men treasure me chase away the nasty voices in my head that have spent my lifetime telling me I'm unworthy of this. Of being loved and taken care of. It's not true, not anymore. Because I have my mates.

It's difficult to think, the pleasure about to pull me back under as Alder continues devouring my pussy with unwavering concentration. Not yet— this is important.

"D-don't go," I say to Vale.

Whatever he hears in my plea, he nods. I relax against the bed, relieved he won't ignore me again.

Alder's rumble vibrates against my sensitive folds and he buries his face harder against my center, drawing a ragged sound from me.

"Like that?" Matthias smiles, kissing my forehead. "Like when Alder feasts on your sweet pussy? Come for him again, petal. Soak his tongue and give him a good taste before he fucks you."

A deep pulse beats in my core at his sultry croon. Alder looks up the length of my body, the pupils of his hypnotic green eyes blown. He spreads me wider and spears me with his wicked tongue, then makes an obscene slurping sound as he sucks and laps at the slickness coating my pussy.

"Ah!" The coil in my core snaps and I ride the waves of my orgasm, hips rocking against his face.

Alder soothes his palms up my sides, then crawls over me, kissing his way up my body. "I want to be inside you."

I nod eagerly. His arms slip around me and he rolls us, grinding his hardness against me. I spread my legs to straddle him, planting my hands on his chest to push up. Reaching between us, he lines up and my head falls back as I sink down his enormous length.

He grips my hips and guides our pace. Matthias stretches out beside us, watching with a heated gaze as he strokes his cock. The press of his gaze and Valerian's makes my blood sing as I ride my mate.

"Fuck." Vale's wrecked mutter cuts through my haze of pleasure.

His legs fall open and his hand squeezes the

hard bulge tenting his pants. The evidence of his arousal turns me on even more.

A pang of sadness hits me for a moment. I know what I feel for him is the same as what I feel for my mates. I wish he'd join, melt me with his touch. But he's here, watching. He's not leaving. As long as he doesn't leave, it's okay.

He catches my eye and holds my attention. "Alder. Turn her around. I want to watch her tits bounce while you fuck her on your cock."

I shiver. He smirks, his hooded blue gaze smoldering as it slides over every inch of me straddling Alder's hips.

Alder props on his elbows, grasping the back of my neck to drag me down for a searing kiss before he lifts me off his lap and repositions himself to sit on the edge of the bed. We'll be facing Valerian, giving him a complete show. My chest collapses with a dizzying exhale and Alder tugs me into his lap, mouthing at my nape. He grips beneath my thighs and spreads me wide open. Vale's gaze is a sinful caress while Alder lifts me with ease and lowers me onto his length once more.

My eyes flutter as he fills me and sets a pace that makes me moan with each thrust. I reach back to hold on to his head and clutch one of his muscled arms supporting me with my free hand.

I swallow as Valerian takes out his cock. It's

310

big—not as thick as Alder's, but it has to be about as long, also enhanced with the row of ridges that feel incredible stroking my inner walls. A shiny dribble of precome drips from the tip, rolling over each tantalizing ridge along his length. He makes sure he has my attention as he takes himself in hand. My core clenches as I imagine what it would feel like inside me and Alder grunts.

Matthias stands in front of me and dips his head to kiss me, making me gasp as he teases my nipples. He skates his free hand down my soft curves to circle my clit with his fingers.

"You look so gorgeous riding Alder, Lils," he murmurs. "Mm, I want to know how tight you'll be if you take us both at once."

"Both? I don't know if I could," I push out. "You wouldn't fit, you're huge."

Alder slams me down harder, his chest shaking with amusement at my scream. I lean back against his broad chest, pussy clenching around him. The erotic sound of how wet I am is obscene.

"You were made for us," he says. "Made to take our cocks."

His praise arrows through me. The thought of taking both of them is enticing.

"Our pretty girl," Matthias says.

His fingers sink into my hair and he kisses me, nipping at my lips. I chase his kiss when he pulls away. He gives me another, smiling into it before leaning back.

His grip tightens in my hair and his eyes hood. "I need to fuck these tits, baby."

Biting my lip, I nod, arching my back. He plays with my breasts, thumbs teasing my nipples in maddening circles that spread electric tingles to my core.

"Please," I beg.

As Matthias holds the base of his cock and trails the leaking tip over my skin, Alder licks a stripe up my throat. The weight of Matthias' hardness rests between my breasts and he gathers them, squeezing around his length. I gasp at the friction when he snaps his hips. The slide of his hot, velvety skin as he tightens his hold on my tits stirs a throb deep in my core. His precome slicks the tight channel he makes thrusting between my cleavage until he secretes so much he glides against me as easily as he sinks into my pussy.

With Alder fucking me and Matthias using me for his own pleasure while Valerian watches the three of us, touching himself, I lose myself to the sensual experience.

Matthias curses, head tipping back with a grunt. His come splashes across my tits as his hips keep bucking, his dick sliding through it. I moan as some of it hits my chin, wishing to know what he tastes like.

I feel utterly marked, *claimed* by his come coating my skin while Alder fucks me and sucks another possessive mark into my neck.

"Mine." Eyes gleaming, Matthias draws a heart on my messy cleavage, then catches some of it and flashes me a mischievous grin before he smears it across my lips with his thumb and pushes it in my mouth.

I suck it from his thumb greedily, enjoying the tangy taste of him as much as I enjoyed Alder's.

His. Theirs. And they're mine. The thoughts bowl me over. I never thought I could be so happy.

Alder slows down his pace, dragging out my pleasure with even more intensity as he makes me feel every inch of his huge cock each time he guides me down on it. My eyelids fall to half mast, my lips parting as he lifts me and drives into me again slow, slow, slow, the ridges on his length sending heady shocks of pleasure racing through me.

Matthias falls to his knees before me, working around Alder. He gets Alder to hold my legs open even wider, my back bowing at the new angle the slight change causes as he spears me on his thick length. Then Matthias flicks his forked tongue across my throbbing clit and I shatter, one orgasm drifting right into the next when he sucks on it with a filthy chuckle, enjoying every second of ecstasy he wrenches from me.

"Oh god!" I whimper.

Alder groans, his grip flexing on my thighs as my pussy clenches. "So tight."

"Keep going, Matthias," Vale orders. "Make her cream his cock so much that it leaks out of her cunt from having her clit sucked so good while she gets fucked."

A choked gasp slips out of me as Alder and Matthias match their pace, the rhythm of Matthias' tongue synced with Alder hitting a spot deep inside me that is so overwhelmingly good, tears spring to my eyes as I come hard, dropping a hand to grip Matthias' disheveled white blond hair, overtaken by a greedy, primal desire to keep him *right there*.

"That's it, little flower. You're fucking beautiful like this, taking what you want," Valerian croons in his smooth accent. "Ride his face. Grind your needy little clit on his tongue while you take your mate's cock."

"Fuck, fuck, fuck," I hiss.

I collapse back against Alder's broad chest. He buries his face in my neck, his fangs grazing my sensitive skin. How would it feel if he bit me? Marked my skin with a lasting reminder of this moment, of his claim on me? My head spins with how much I want that.

As though they sense my thoughts, Matthias

rises from his knees. He sits next to us and threads his fingers through my hair, tilting my head back to expose my throat. Three approving rumbles sound around me. Lips and teeth move on both sides of my neck. One of them mutters *mate*. I can't pick out who, though an answering flutter beats in my chest.

"You feel it, sweet blossom?" Alder laps at my throbbing pulse point.

I nod, unable to verbalize the sensation thrumming in the bond. A purr escapes me. I'm trapped in Valerian's sensual stare, his blue eyes burning bright and hot as he strokes his cock.

"You're ours," Matthias rasps.

"Yours. All yours," I echo with a cry, needing my mates to know.

Alder's fangs scrape my neck again and Matthias brushes my cheek with his knuckles. Swallowing, I wish for Valerian, the bond snapping like a vibrating chord in my chest.

"Please."

Vale makes a rough sound from his spot, watching intently. He staggers over, tracing my parted lips.

A glow lights me up from inside. "All yours."

"Yes," Vale whispers raggedly, his come spilling over his fist.

My vision grows hazy when Alder groans and tenses. Part of his cock swells thicker, stealing my breath. His chest shudders with a wild exhale and he gently lets my legs down, wrapping his arms around me as our bodies lock together with his slower, rocking thrusts. Every small shift of his hips brings me unbelievable pleasure and I exist in an endless tide of orgasmic bliss.

"I've got you," he says. "You were made to take my knot, my beautiful blossom."

The intensity leaves me in a daze. I'm distantly aware of Alder's fingers touching the place we're joined, tracing the edge of my pussy stretched around the swollen base of his dick buried inside me.

"Look at you, petal." Matthias splays his palm across my soft stomach. "So pretty and full. Shit, I can't decide if it's sexier to knot you myself or watch you take my brother's."

Valerian grasps my chin, his thumb tracing the shape of my lips. I press a kiss to it and my heart stutters at the reverence shining in his eyes. My name falls from his mouth in a hoarse whisper. "Lily."

Alder's arms tighten around me and with another low groan, his cock throbs deep inside as he finishes. The pulse of his come filling me makes me clench around him, shattering once more with a frayed, overstimulated whimper.

I don't fully return to earth until Alder and Matthias have me cleaned up and nestled between them in bed, surrounded by their warmth. Their gazes are full of devotion that touches me to my soul. The thrum in my chest is a quiet, content hum, no longer constantly pulling in different directions.

The chair near the bed creaks, the sound stabbing through my chest.

My head pops up and a sound of distress snags in my throat. Valerian catches my hand and sits back down, his chair scooted closer to the bed.

"I'm not leaving, little flower," he says. "None of us will ever leave you."

Tears blur my vision. "Okay."

Alder and Matthias draw me back to rest between them. Once again, the bond is at ease, settled knowing I have the three of them with me.

My past in the mortal realm is painful, and I can't remember my life in the underworld. Those memories might be lost forever. I focus on who I am now because it feels like after everything I've endured, I have a real future as long as I can stay with my three demons that have stolen my heart piece by piece.

I needed each of them more than I knew. With them, I have someone who understands my painful scars and protects me from getting hurt, someone who makes me smile and reminds me to be myself, and someone who challenges me and sparks my fighting spirit to life.

For so long, I've suppressed my ability to love because the world didn't want me. I learned not to open up and give myself to others because I only ended up spurned and hurt. Opening up for my mates is like opening a floodgate. My wounded heart expands bigger than I ever thought it was capable of, no longer afraid of being abandoned.

Somewhere along the way, my enemies became my lovers. My fated mates. I've fallen for them. My heart is irrevocably theirs. Every broken, damaged shard of me belongs to all three of them because with them I've found the thing I've always longed for—my true home.

Twenty Three
LILY

In the morning, I smile without opening my eyes, sandwiched between Matthias and Alder in bed. It's a tight fit, yet I wouldn't change a thing. As long as I'm surrounded by them, I'm happy.

The bond dances in my chest. I trace my fingers over my heart, so relieved to understand it better. Now I get that it was never about making me choose between what I feel for my three demons, but attempting to guide me to the fated connection I share with each of them.

Stretching, I savor the pleasant ache between my legs from Adler's knot. His stoic features are softened in sleep, I gaze at him, my heart brimming with the rightness of being his. A soft snore at my back makes me roll over to snuggle beneath

Matthias' chin, smiling fondly at his smoky maple scent. They shift to accommodate me, even in sleep they naturally drift closer to wrap around me.

It's so simple to just lay here and feel high on absolute bliss.

"You're awake."

I twist and pop my head up to see past Alder's wide shoulders, blinking at the sight of Valerian in the same spot as last night. He didn't go. "How long have you been there? All night?"

"For most of it." He smirks at my blush. "I relieved Rainer of his watch at dawn. No demons have tracked us here. It seems we remain safe for the time being, so I can be indulgent."

I bite my lip, wondering if the indulgence he means is watching me sleep. Hope trickles through me.

As amazing as last night was, I don't know where we stand. The bond is happy when I'm near Vale and I know I want to be with him, too. He stayed all night, but I'm not sure if I'm allowed to touch him as freely as I can with my other two demon mates.

Before I gather the courage to ask, he stands. "Come on. I need to talk to you."

My stomach clenches. Leaving the safe bubble of this room is daunting.

"What about…"

"They'll wake soon and join us. For now, let me have you to myself." He pauses at the door. "I know who you are. Your demon."

My heart stops, then thuds hard. Reluctantly, I leave Matthias and Alder in bed, grabbing one of their discarded shirts to slip into. I duck into the bathroom quickly, halting at the sight of my neck covered in hickeys. My lips twitch as I prod at them.

Downstairs, Valerian offers me a steaming mug of coffee and leads me out to the balcony. The early morning sun cascades through the trees. We lean against the railing side by side, his wrist ghosting against my arm.

"I've suspected who you could be for a while," he starts. "Part of me might have always known, but I thought it was my own past mistakes twisting my mind into seeing you. I told myself it was impossible. That I'd lost you."

"You knew me?" My eyes roam the sharp lines of his profile, wishing he'd look at me. "This is from when you were a knight."

It's a guess. He nods stiffly, blowing out a breath.

"Since I had myself convinced it was wishful thinking, I've ignored the other signs. I should've recognized your hellfire right away. And only the most powerful demon lines are known to have more than one fated mate." A tingle spreads through me when he says *mate*. "I should've known from the moment I first caught a hint of your faint scent seeping through the cracks in the seal binding you. You've always smelled of toasted cinnamon."

My brows furrow. "At Lane's cottage, did you know then?"

"It was when I first let myself believe. Even without your memories to confirm it, I know you. I feel you where I thought I never could again." His throat bobs and he rubs at the center of his chest. "The forbidden bond that almost formed between us doesn't lie. It didn't fully form before, but now…"

"Forbidden?" I swallow and pull his hand to my chest by his wrist. His fingers fist the material of my shirt, yanking me closer. My coffee sloshes over the edge of my mug. "Whoever I was, I'm not letting anything come between us."

The corner of his mouth lifts. "Always so stubborn. I'm glad your fiery spirit isn't lost."

Before I demand he stops dragging this out, he pushes an image into my mind—a memory that isn't my own playing out. It's…me, but not. The way my dream self is me, though slightly different. In the memory, I have pointed ears, small black horns peeking from longer red hair, fangs, and vibrantly glowing amber eyes. Familiarity tinges the scene as I get in a demon knight's face, jabbing a pointed, bright crimson claw in his chest.

"You think you get to boss me around and keep me

contained? Tough shit. If I wish to go somewhere, you can't stop me." I smirk. *"And if you think you can, by all means, challenge me. I have no qualms fighting the king's knights. I relish whooping your asses every chance I get."*

Valerian laughs. "Are you tormenting my knight's guard yet again, Lilith?"

My smirk stretches into a playful grin when I realize he's there. "Always. It's only my favorite pastime. They think they can order me to stay within the castle's boundaries when everyone knows I prefer to spend my time adventuring throughout the underworld."

"Dismissed," Valerian says to the guard who tried to stop me from leaving the courtyard. Once he's gone, he offers a smirk to match mine. "If you sneak off on one of your adventures, it's my duty as the knight assigned to guard you to follow."

My eyes flash with mischief. "Then catch me if you can, Vale. I won't go easy on you."

"Always." He glances around to check if we're alone before stepping closer. "I like it when you give me a challenge."

I blink as it fades away. *Always.* The warmth in his tone echoes through my mind.

He inclines his head. "Lilith."

My lips part. "That feels like I know it."

"It should. It's your name." He steps closer, repeating it in his crooning accent. "Lilith."

The way he says it makes my knees go weak. I

clutch at the railing. His gaze darkens with a hint of deviousness at my reaction.

"Your disappearance three hundred years ago was shrouded in mystery. You were just—gone." He clenches his teeth. "On my watch. I thought you were just out exploring the realm, but I couldn't find you. No one could. We never thought to look in the mortal realm. The king was furious. You were meant to become the queen of Hell and rule alongside Lucifer as his bride."

Everything in me revolts at the thought of being married to the Devil, the bond bucking uncomfortably. *She'll never be queen.* I inhale sharply. That's what the demons meant. Why they're out to kill me.

"This hasn't been about you betraying the underworld," I say slowly as my gears turn. "They didn't want me to become queen. Whoever kidnapped me is pissed I'm still alive."

"I think so, yes. They're covering it up by labeling me the leader of a rebellion to unseat the queen Lucifer did marry. If he finds out people in his court conspired against him, it would mean true death for anyone involved." His eyes roam my face and his tone turns gravelly. "They were right to suspect I'd recognize you before long."

Relief spirals through me. The Devil hasn't spent three centuries looking for a lost queen he intends to wed. It doesn't matter if my true identity is Lilith, I don't want to be queen or marry anyone besides Alder, Matthias, and Valerian. I abandon my coffee on the railing to wrap my arms around his waist, breathing in the spicy sharpness in his smoky scent.

His fingers sink into my hair with a low growl. "They stole you away from me."

More images flash in my head—glimpses of how dedicated he was in protecting me, watching me wherever I went, the way we danced around each other but never acted on the spark between us. He shows me wielding my powers with deadly skill in some kind of tournament. Sneaking out of the castle to ride a beastly underworld creature and him tracking me down, but not forcing me back to a castle that makes me restless right away. Stolen moments of *what if* where our eyes would meet across the room.

Each memory he sends into my mind is tinged with the strength of his feelings for me, illicit yet inescapable. I can tell that much from the small flashes he allows me to see of our past. The depth of his love feels like it's spanned years, carried in his heart.

With a rough, broken noise, he pulls my head back by my hair and his mouth collides against mine. It's everything he's held back. The kiss is a passionate storm, all-consuming and wild. A claiming demand on my mouth, my heart, my very soul, telling me I'm his and will always be his. A cry escapes me and he drinks it in, his grip on me tightening as he devours my mouth.

Vale wrenches away, pressing his forehead to mine with a jagged breath that breaks my heart. "I failed you once before. The thought of ever losing you again terrifies me to the depths of my being."

He pulls back and a panicked noise leaves me at the thought of him retreating behind his brooding walls after that. I push on tiptoe and kiss him, unwilling to let him go. He clutches me to him as we kiss again, and again, and again until my heart feels ready to burst.

"I found you," he says against my mouth. "I won't let you go this time."

I shake my head, pressing so close I think I'm trying to climb inside him so we're never parted again.

Once my racing heart slows, I'm able to think more clearly. The others come outside, Alder sitting on the edge of the empty hot tub and Matthias hopping up to sit on the railing. Vale squeezes me like he doesn't want to share, but lets me slip out of his arms. I shyly fit myself between Matthias' knees to kiss his cocky smirk away, ending up smiling into our kiss. Then I go to Alder and give him a soft kiss, humming when he pets my hair.

He grazes my nose with his. "You're radiant."

My cheeks tingle and another smile breaks free. I return to Vale, leaning back against him. His tattooed arms move around me without the hesitation he's had with me before. At last my world's axis finds its alignment with all three of them.

"You said you had something important to discuss today," Alder says. "Are we ready to move?"

"Soon now that I'm healed. I know who Lily is." They both lean forward in anticipation. I trace his inked fingers interlocked around my waist, the abstract whorls shifting and curling around the places I touch. "Lilith."

"Lilith? *The* Lilith?" Alder's brows hike up.

"Shit," Matthias breathes.

"Shit indeed," Valerian mutters. "It brings the entire chain of command for the last few centuries into question. The council serves both as the overseers of the factions, and as royal council to Lucifer. We don't know which members are behind this other than speculating based on who benefited most in power."

The amount of time my demon has been missing stumps me. "If it was that long ago, how am I here now? I was found as a baby."

Alder crosses his arms, his muscles bulging. "Your bloodline is royalty amongst the demon fae. All demons descend from the primordial fae gods and the original Lilith is said to be one of those goddesses who reincarnated herself to become a demon because she fell in love. Every she-demon born to your bloodline inherits the original goddess' gifts. You are the daughter of a line that has never been broken, one of the strongest the underworld has. It's why you were destined for the throne."

Jesus. My gaze falls to my scarred hands. After everything I've been through, that's what awaited me in the place I truly come from? Respectfully, fuck that.

"That's some heavy shit," I mumble. "Still doesn't answer my question."

"Remember when I explained the laws surrounding reincarnation?" At my nod, he continues. "With your bloodline descending directly from our gods, it would take an immense amount of dark power to force you to reincarnate. It's likely they kept you on the brink of death for centuries wherever they had you hidden away before they were able to force you through it to bind you."

"Fuck," Matthias bites out fiercely.

Alder's expression hardens. "By weakening you enough to trap you in a changeling form, they probably thought their plan was complete since they never had anyone watching you. They kidnapped you. Tortured you. Then left you to die in the mortal realm by the humans' neglectful hands or by your own volatile untrained powers being too great for a human form to withstand."

Twenty Four
LILY

LEARNING THE TRUTH LEAVES ME TORN. I THOUGHT finding out the identity of the demon trapped inside me would make things clearer. It only leaves me conflicted.

Do I belong in the underworld realm I've forgotten, sitting on a throne I don't have any desire to take?

Am I Lilith? Or will she destroy me when we find a way to break the seal imprisoning her within me? I have her power, but a small corner of my mind still fears that who I am as Lily Sloane is only a stand-in shell born of her need to survive the mortal realm until her demon knight could rescue her. Someone who took the brunt of abuse while she remained hidden behind the magic seal trapping her inside me.

My throat tightens. Then why do I have a fated mate connection to all three of them? Is that hers, too? Would she have eventually found my warrior and trickster demons destined to love her?

No. The bond pulses in my chest in refusal. Fuck that. These demons are my home. My fate. No one will take them from me. They're the only good my rotten life has granted me.

They've given me so much already. I've experienced more life with them than I was ever allowed the privilege of before. I belong with them, allowed to take up space instead of being shunned and tossed aside.

I hold on to hope that we are one in the same, needing to believe I won't be separated from the three men who fill my heart.

"If this hadn't happened, would I have found you?" My throat constricts. "Vale knew me, but... How would I have found you guys if I was supposed to get married?"

"It's possible the reincarnation rewrote your magic. You're a rebirth of the Lilith I knew, and we never..." Valerian's forearms flex, his tattoos shifting restlessly with his thoughts. "The witch was right. You might not have most of your memories of your past life after going through hundreds of years of torture and surviving as a changeling that was likely meant to be your final death sentence."

"I've seen the underworld in my dreams." I slide my lips together, unsure why I'm trying to reassure him when I'm afraid he's only interested in *her* and not me. "Maybe it's not all gone. And…her memory lives on in you."

"What was between us was a possibility. This bond—" His palm splays over my heart and our bond swells to brush against his touch. His own heartbeat thumps against my back. "—is fated. You needed us and we needed you to bring us together. No one in the underworld would deny that as this incarnation Lilith, we are the mates fate chose for you."

Alder and Matthias come over and place their hands over Valerian's, the three of them circling me where they belong. The bond dances in my chest, the glow of warmth emanating through my skin. Fascinated, I turn my translucent, glowing hand back and forth.

"You're ours, Lily." Matthias takes my hand and brings my scarred knuckles to his lips.

"Fate brought us together. That's all that matters." Alder tucks my hair behind my ear. "Loving you is a gift bestowed upon us by the gods."

"Ours." Vale's embrace tightens with his rough echo.

"Yours," I murmur. "All of yours."

Three pleased rumbles sound around me. A happy, light laugh escapes me.

We stay like that for several moments until I think about everything standing between us and what I want—to be with them wherever our lives take us. We can't have that until we stop the corruption in the underworld that wants us all dead.

"So what will we do? As much as I'd love to ignore all of this, we can't stay here forever in our perfect bubble at the cabin."

Matthias jokes around with a scandalized gasp. "Don't let the Mothman shrine in the basement hear you talk about leaving him behind."

I give him a flat look. "No. You're not bringing that costume with us."

He grins. "I totally am, petal. I'll make Alder pin you down while I wear it and feed my cock to these gorgeous lips."

Maintaining my stern expression is hard when the mental image stirs a throb of desire in my core at the thought of Alder holding me down for Matthias to torment me with sinful pleasure. Damn him.

He laughs at my expression and leans in to kiss me. "Such a dirty girl. I love making you blush like that."

"She's right." Alder's gruff tone is thicker, his green eyes darkened with interest by Matthias' teasing. "We need to move and decide what to do."

I lift my head, my mouth set. "I don't want to keep running. I'm sick of it."

"We'll find out who did this to you, little flower," Vale promises. "And then we'll make them fucking pay."

The others echo his vengeful sentiment. It sends a shudder of adoration through me, leaving me weak in the knees.

"I'll call Rainer back before he gets far and meet up with him," he continues. "We'll strategize the best gate to use to sneak into the underworld. They blocked us from using ours and we wouldn't want to risk going through it if they've set up anyone there to capture us, but if we retrace our steps to an area they already tracked us it should provide enough cover to get to Hell."

"What about me?" A spike of anxiety hits me. "They've spent this long keeping me out of the underworld. We could go through the gate and it could destroy me."

Valerian crushes me against his chest and the others mutter unhappy sounds of refusal. "You are a powerful demon," Valerian says firmly. "Even though your kidnappers bound you, you chipped away at the seal, allowing your power to seep through. The portal's magic will recognize your place is in the underworld and grant you safe passage."

"Humans have come through the gates before," Alder reminds me. "As guards, we're meant to deal with them, but they have crossed over from the mortal realm. You'll also go through with us surrounding you as extra protection."

His reassurance that they won't make me go through this alone helps.

"Once we're in the underworld, I think we'll be able to break the seal by getting you back where you belong," Valerian says. "The energy of the realm will restore you to your full strength rather than keep you in this starved state. You'll have the power to break the seal on your own, shattering through the cracks to free yourself."

"I don't know. You really believe I can do that?" I push out of his arms to face the three of them, holding up my hands. "Guys, I've barely learned to control this in the last few weeks."

Alder steps forward to cradle my face. "You can do it. Trust in your own strength. And if you can't do that, then trust in us. When you falter, we're here to catch you. We believe in you even when you don't, mate."

My throat clogs and my eyes glisten as I stare back at him, then shift my attention to Matthias and Vale. Their solemn gazes choke me up even more. They believe I can do this. That for them, I'm enough.

Their support lends fortitude to my own tattered

belief in myself.

The ones who kidnapped me wanted to kill me and they almost succeeded. What they didn't know is that every time I've been knocked down, abused, rejected, tossed aside and forgotten, I've gotten the fuck back up and kept going. I survived and I'll keep fighting for my right to exist, to live on in spite of those who would rather see me dead.

Blinking away tears, I nod in determination. Alder kisses my forehead.

"I'll go find Rainer. Once I'm back, we'll leave and start our journey back up the coast," Valerian says.

Matthias gives me a crooked smile when Alder steps away and kisses me. Before I'm ready, I'm tugged away, Valerian's mouth claiming mine. He murmurs my true name against my lips like a prayer.

"I'm going to squeeze some practice in," I say.

"I'll be out shortly to join you," Alder says. "Don't overdo it."

"Yes, sir," I sass with a mock salute.

His scorching gaze sweeps over me and I smirk.

Matthias tugs on a lock of my short wavy hair as he passes, winking at me. "I'm going to pack up and see what I can scrounge up. If we're stocked longer, we'll only need to stop for gas."

"Don't even think about taking anything from that creepy ass shrine, Matthias," I warn.

The devious grin he flashes over his shoulder tells me he's absolutely going to do that. A soft, fond laugh leaves me.

Once I change into a pair of leggings and find a forgotten hair tie in the bathroom to secure my hair half up, I head out to my makeshift training course. Part of me is going to miss this cabin when we have to go. It's been our safe haven, and I'll always remember it as the place where my mates forged a deeper connection with me. Where I chased what I wanted and let them in.

Practice starts off rougher than I'd like as anxiety creeps back in. Even if we make it to the underworld without getting caught, what will it mean for me if I can break the seal?

I frown as the fire whip I visualize sputters out pitifully, nowhere near as badass as the whip Valerian wields. Switching to fire blasts, I start jogging, punching my shaky balls of flames through the air, imagining them hitting targets on the move.

My thoughts plague me while I continue to work. If I die, is that it, or will I reincarnate again? Or worse, when the seal breaks, will I return to my true form as Lilith and forget everything about myself as Lily? I don't want to give my fears life, but the second they flit into my head, they take flight, sweeping through me.

An unnatural explosive sound, followed by a

roar of pain, cuts through the woods and makes my heart stop. I swear that was Alder. It didn't come from the direction of the cabin. Forgetting about training, I cast a frantic gaze around to search for the source. Another yell that sounds like Matthias pierces my heart.

"Lily!" That angry, agonized bellow comes from Vale.

They're in trouble.

I take off, following the sounds of powers clashing as my pulse races. The steeper incline nearly trips me with uneven roots and the underbrush I crash through in my need to get to my mates. My heel slips on muddy leaves and I lose my balance. The wind knocks out of me when I land and slide down the hill for several feet, twigs and rocks jabbing my legs, my hair tie snagging and pulling free. Gritting my teeth, I push to my feet and keep going.

Three snarling howls echo around me, the familiar noises gutting me. I falter, my bond aching.

No, no, no. How did our enemies find us? This morning Valerian said there weren't any traces of demons in the area. Could they have masked their presence with magic and carefully planned an attack while we thought we were safe?

It doesn't matter. I have to get to them and help.

They are my everything. The matching shards

of my heart and soul that bind together to make us whole together. They're where I fit and I'm terrified of losing it and being isolated again without my fated mates.

I can't think straight. Can't breathe as terror settles like a leaden weight in the depths of my stomach.

Reaching the base of the hill, I burst out onto a backroad. An abandoned strip mall is across the street with the windows blacked out and half the buildings covered in graffiti. A crash inside an arcade at the end spurs me into action.

My ragged breaths scrape my throat and with a vicious slash of my hand, fire wraps around my fist. The locked handle melts beneath the searing heat covering my fingers and I shoulder my way inside.

"No!" I scream as I rush forward.

A frighteningly large demon with dark brown coiffed hair in a white suit oversees everything with a bored expression while several other thin, monstrous looking demons jump around the room chaotically, their features twisted in chilling fanged grins that stretch their skin. A woman in tight leather and a cloak shifts over to keep me at bay.

My worst fears play out before me.

Valerian, Alder, and Matthias fight the laughing demons that have them bound in chains. Valerian bares his fangs while Alder's claws spark against their bindings. Matthias' eyes glint with fury as he jerks against the restraints.

They won't break. They must be infused with magic to drain their strength because they're not using their flames.

Instinctively, my power takes over, fueled by my fury at seeing my mates hurt. Except when I push out to rain an attack on my enemies, the flames sputter out, stealing my breath as unbearable pain lances through my chest.

No. Not now. Don't fail me when I need to save them.

I try again. Again. *Again.*

Nothing. My powers won't obey while my mates are tortured before my eyes.

One of the demons stabs Matthias in the chest, right through his heart. Ice spreads through me, the stab echoing in my own chest as if those claws carved through my heart by stabbing my mate.

A wail wrenches from me as our eyes meet. He mouths my name before his eyes go dark. I freeze as his head slumps.

"Matthias!" The others fight harder at my shriek, calling for him to get up.

The demons make sure I'm watching as they position themselves behind Alder and Vale next. They struggle, but can't escape before the laughing demons rip their throats out with their teeth.

Raw power races through me as I fall apart with heavy sobs. It scalds me from the inside out, unable to unleash like I want it to. Like I need it to in a vengeful, raging torrent of hellfire for daring to hurt my mates. My power razes me instead of my enemies.

I keep trying until my arms sear with pain and I struggle to breathe, my skin cracking and burning like paper, embers eating away at my flesh. Ignoring the agonizing scorch of flames, I push myself harder because I can't lose them.

My failed attempts makes the demon near me peel back her blood red lips in a chilling, satisfied grin. "You should've died years ago," she hisses. "You're more trouble than you're worth. We won't have you wrecking our meticulous planning."

Two tall, thin demons flanking her release sinister, shrieking, high-pitched hysterical laughter. They dance around, relishing my increasing panic when nothing works. They remind me of Matthias—tricksters, but purely evil.

I can't break past an invisible barrier that kept me from running to them. Kicking dusty posters and a rotting piece of cardboard away from the floor, I gape at the eerie white glowing symbols circling around me. The bitchy demon and her minions laugh as I pound a fist weakly against the spell keeping me from getting to them.

I'm bound to a magic prison. They baited me. Lured me here after capturing my mates to force me to endure the agony of their deaths.

Twenty-Five
LILY

*L*ILY. VALERIAN'S VOICE IN MY HEAD CUTS THROUGH MY anguish. *Hold on, little flower. We're coming. I know it hurts. We sensed it. We're almost there.*

I stagger, clutching a pinball machine within the boundary trapping me. He's alive. They're all alive and they're coming for me. The cracked open cavern in my chest throbs, the cord connecting me to them pulled taut in the opposite direction.

The demons lured me with a trap, but it's not real. They've messed with my mind. Preyed on my worst fears with the cruel illusion of my mates in trouble.

With the last of my strength, I push a thought to him, hoping it reaches him. *I'm sorry.*

I believed I was coming to their rescue, but I

only fell for the trick. Now they could truly be in danger needing to rescue me. My vision is woozy from trying to use my power.

Hold on for me, Lily.

"What are you waiting for?" The demon in the suit unfolds his arms. "She stepped in the curse circle. Kill her now, Petra."

"Yes, sir." Petra approaches me with a gleam in her yellow eyes.

"Hell no, bitch," I wheeze. "I didn't survive sink or fucking swim just to die here."

Her brows furrow, not getting my meaning. It doesn't matter because the darkened windows shatter behind us and a strong gust of humid air knocks over the cluttered arcade games. My sweaty, blistered grip slips on the pinball machine as a relieved sigh escapes me at the sight of my guys charging through the broken window.

Alive.

I push through pain and exhaustion to drink in the sight of them, my faint heartbeat echoing as I bounce my gaze between them. Fresh tears well in my eyes, and I hate them for the few seconds they take away my ability to see my guys clearly.

"Petra?" Alder barks. "Cessair?"

"You understand duty best, warrior," the sinister demon in a white suit drawls. "If you stand down now, I'll show you mercy. My brothers and sisters on the council only demand Valerian's head for his betrayal to the demon court."

"No. The council is wrong. You will pay for attacking my mate!" Alder's bellow shakes the building.

"Then you die alongside the she-demon," Cessair says.

"You fucking bastard." Valerian's eyes flash a cold, deadly shade of blue, then he rushes Cessair.

Alder and Matthias flank him, their assault coordinated without speaking. Valerian clashes against a wall of flames Cessair erects while Matthias deals with the laughing demons, pinning one under his knee before he uses his claws to slice it from the corner of its jaw to its chest, black blood oozing out. Three of the demons vanish as if they never existed.

"I see through your shitty illusions, old man," Matthias grits out. "They're not as good as mine."

Alder has Petra by the throat after knocking her away from me with a fireball. His grip digs into her neck without mercy. My warrior is stronger than her and her eyes bulge as he squeezes with such force her throat collapses with a nauseating crunch. Not satisfied, he locks an arm around her body and twists her neck until her flesh tears, her head dangling from his white-knuckled grip.

"Cessair!" he shouts as he joins Valerian's fight.

The three of them trade fiery blows while

Matthias creates his own illusions to distract and give the others an advantage over Cessair. Several doubles of my guys materialize to join the fight.

Though I'm in excruciating discomfort, I see the difference. If he hadn't announced his were illusions, I'd believe these doubles of the three of them were real compared to the ones Cessair conjured to torture my mind with. Cessair's versions lacked the right details—the shades and length of hair off, their eyes not as bright—that Matthias perfectly nails in his. I only missed it because I was so fraught by the belief they were captured.

I try to keep my eyes open. My lids grow heavier with each labored, rattling breath I take. Darkness ebbs at the edge of my vision, the shadows encroaching until I'm unable to fight them off.

Someone yells my name as I collapse to the musty floor while the cacophony of fighting rages on.

"Is she alive?" Alder's gruff question sends a sharper needle of agony through me than the sweltering fire I wake to.

Did they burn the building down around us? My eyes refuse to crack open. It's so hot and my tongue sits heavy in my mouth.

346

Matthias lifts my upper body. I'm out of it, consumed by pain, but I recognize the comfort of his scent. It's sharper, tinged with anger.

He curses when he touches my scorched arms with shaking hands and draws a strangled noise from me. "Barely. She's all burned up and overheated. She needs to heal now."

I hold on to the fact I'm in his arms as he carries me. Then I'm passed off with a curt command, Valerian's bitter smoke scent twining around me.

"I've got you." His accented words are tight and cracking. He presses his lips to my temple. "My flower, my flower, my flower."

Each frayed whisper feels like he's pleading with me. Whatever he wants, I'll give it to him. He has me always and forever.

Everything aches with an acute, stinging throb. It's difficult to draw a full breath as if my lungs have seared away from the inside out.

"Fuck, that trickster demon's curse trapped her hellfire inside. It could've burned her internal organs without any outlet." Alder peels back my eyelids when Valerian sets me down.

It's soft, yet cold. Leaves? The treetops blur overhead. Still in the woods, then. Better than burning alive in the arcade, except I get no relief from the humidity compressing me in the open air.

"—re...safe?" My feeble voice cracks. "'m s'rry."

"Shh, petal." Matthias wedges in beside Alder, his expression fraught with worry. He tries to give me a smile and it crumbles. "You'll be okay. I promise."

I swallow thickly, hating the tremor in his voice. It's my fault it's there. If I hadn't been an idiot, if I hadn't fallen for the illusion that invaded my mind, he wouldn't be upset. Another fiery wave of pain passes through me and I grit my teeth to smother a scream.

"We don't have time," Valerian snaps.

Alder nods gravely and drags Matthias away. He fights, struggling to stay by my side.

"I want to stay with her, too," Alder barks. "But we have to keep her safe by guarding them while he saves her life."

Matthias wrestles away and lifts my hand to his face. A shuddering breath punches out of him. My tears spill over, stinging down my heated cheeks.

"Don't let our mate die, Vale," Matthias orders in a solemn, fractured tone.

"Never," Valerian snarls.

The only thing that soothes the misery of Alder dragging a reluctant Matthias away is Valerian's fierce kiss. I drown myself in it, focusing on him instead of everything else. Every glide of his lips and tongue against mine sends a spark along the invisible tether connecting us.

If this is the moment I die, then at least I'll go with the memory of his kiss on my lips.

He growls. "You're not fucking dying, Lily. I won't let you." He holds my jaw and deepens the kiss. "Keep surviving for me. For us."

I nod, clinging to him. I want that. I want to be with them always.

Valerian strips out of his clothes in record time and pulls me onto his lap. His fingers twist in my brittle hair and his jaw clenches.

The next kiss sweeps me away. Despite the blistering pain, I move against him, grinding against his hard length. My need comes on strong with a life of its own like the bond in my chest. A feral sound reverberates in his chest and my bond hums in response to my mate. I need him.

Let me in. Valerian's voice is warm and demanding in my head. *Give yourself to me, mate. I will make it all better.*

A piercing noise tears from me. *Yes. Please.*

That's it, little flower. He hears my unspoken plea.

Valerian growls, shredding what's left of my singed clothes with his claws to bear me for him. I grit my teeth. With a swift, brutal thrust, he enters me. My back bows and a cry lodges in my throat.

"Fuck," he rumbles. "Hold on. I know it hurts, but I swear to you it won't for much longer."

He sets a quick pace that steals my strained breath. The rough way he takes me reminds me I'm alive. The will to keep living for him, for Matthias and Alder, for *me* burns through me with flames that don't hurt.

Within moments, my heart beats stronger. He's right. The agony begins to subside.

The pleasure overtakes my pain, the heat between us erasing the discomfort, replacing it with a passionate hunger fueled by a wildfire. Our bond rewrites the hurts within me, the injuries covering my body, healing me with each kiss, each caress, each thrust that joins our bodies. The inferno moves from his body to mine and swirls around us, the flickering sparks creating rings of fire at the edges of my awareness.

As the building sensations crest, his tattooed fingers grasp my jaw. "You are mine. You hear me, Lily Sloane? *Mine*, and no one else will ever dare take you from me again. That includes you. Don't you dare retreat. You'll burn bright and vibrant, as the descendent of the fae goddess Lilith should. Promise me."

I nod frantically, my throat clogging. He sees me. He wants *me*. I am his Lilith.

The rings of fire race faster while we collide over and over like exploding stars, then burst in a rain of sparks that send up tendrils of smoke from the ground.

We moan in unison as his cock throbs inside me, the deep pulses triggering my orgasm. The bond goes crazy in my chest, heightening the intensity of everything—the sensation of fullness from his length buried in me, the heady mingling of our scents, both spicy and sweet, the thrumming in my chest that feels like I could reach out and touch the fated threads that tie our hearts together.

"My flower," he rasps. "My Lily flower."

There are no walls left between us. Though he held himself back from me the longest, my love for him overwhelms me.

My arms shake, no longer plagued by the searing, tight pain of my wounds. The burn marks fade as I lift them from his chest to wrap around his shoulders.

"It's not enough." He holds me against him, our hearts beating as one. "You need more."

It takes him several moments to pull out. When he does, he maps a path across my body with his mouth, guiding me to my back on the ground as he moves lower, settling between my legs. He leers up at me as he lowers his head, making sure I'm watching as his mouth covers my pussy.

I gasp as he devours me, his tongue stirring a new wave of arousal. He's relentless, his mouth moving on me mercilessly to bring me pleasure.

Before my thoughts fully form for what I need, he reads me through our bond and makes me come so hard my screams of ecstasy pierce the treetops above us and send birds flying through the air.

The fiery rings no longer surround us, yet the flow of energy along the tether connecting us continues as he worships my body. This is what he meant in the witch's cottage, the energy mates could share to replenish their strength, to heal each other.

An insistent throb pounds in my core. My fingers tug on his tousled black hair. I want him inside me again more than I desire my next breath.

"Vale. I need you. Please, I'm burning for you."

He understands, his piercing blue gaze smoldering as he gathers me in his lap again, our bodies moving together in anticipation before his hard cock sinks into me once more. A shivery moan slips out of me and my head tips back. This time the pace isn't as fast and urgent, the slower build even more intense, spreading tingling sparks through me.

He takes me by the throat with his inked fingers and squeezes slightly, dominating me with each hard thrust. "Ride my cock, mate. We're not stopping until you make a fucking mess on it."

My body bends to his will, the need in me growing more dizzying the more he takes control. I grab his wrist, holding his hand against my throat as my hips move, chasing the sweet oblivion building inside each time I slam down on his cock. When I come, I clench around him, greedy to feel this pleasure forever. He groans, fixing his mouth to my shoulder, sucking fiercely to leave proof I'm his on my skin. He releases my throat to grip me by the nape, hauling me closer.

Valerian teases my fevered skin with his fangs again as his knot swells within me. He buries a groan in the crook of my neck and I answer him as he fills me completely, our bodies locked together and our souls entwined.

The urge has come before and this time it's stronger than ever.

"Do it," I demand. "Mark me. Bite me. Make me yours."

My head tilts to give him better access and he releases a rough, primal sound at my neck on display, fingers digging into me. His cock pulses within me, stroking me so deep, the knot thickening even bigger. Groaning out a curse, he sinks his fangs into my skin.

We both tense at the breathtaking resonation in the bond between us. My fingers scrabble along his glistening muscles and he bands one arm around me, crushing me against his chest. His other hand drops to my ass and grabs it with bruising force.

Panting, he draws back, lapping at the bite with his forked tongue. Shudders rack my body, my sensitive nipples dragging against his firm chest. His luminous eyes collide with mine, full of enraptured possessiveness. His mouth curves into a feral grin, taking my hand and placing it over his drumming heartbeat.

"Mine," I whisper.

Twenty Six
LILY

It takes a few minutes for Valerian's knot to go down. This is the first time I've managed to remain awake through the experience, the sensation of his cock returning to normal as delicious as the stretch of the knot when it grows. When it's fully down, he pulls out, the flood of his come oozing out of me. He releases a filthy, satisfied sound and keeps me on his lap, his movements lethargic.

Exhaustion tugs at me, but I keep my eyes open, not willing to lose a second of basking in his arms wrapped around me. I have lost time to make up for and want every greedy moment with him I can get.

Even feeling his heartbeat against my breast, the unbearable sight of his throat being ripped out remains vivid in my mind. I shift as close as possible, needing to feel his skin on mine to reassure myself he's alive.

"I'm sorry," I whisper. "I didn't think—I couldn't. I thought you were in trouble and it killed me."

"It's not your fault. We should have protected you better. Shouldn't have left you alone." The scorn in his tone directed at himself makes my heart ache. He sighs harshly and strokes my back. "You're safe now. That's the only thing that matters."

His hands continue to wander my body and he kisses me endlessly. I like that he's so handsy with me. Affection glows in my chest for the side of himself my broody disgraced knight kept hidden behind his caustic barbs and abrasive attitude.

"We can't go again," I sass against his lips with a tired laugh.

He bucks against me, massaging my plump ass. "Even if I didn't have the strength to, I would, little flower. If you want my cock, then I'll give it to you until you can't take it anymore." He claims my mouth again with a rumble. "I need to make up for all the times I resisted the desire to do this. And this. This."

Valerian rains kisses on me, each one as devastating as the last, laying his claim to my heart and soul.

"How is she?" Matthias calls as he and Alder

356

return to check on us. My heart clenches at his voice. "We're clear, but if she's okay, we should move as soon as we can. I've got the car ready."

Alder kneels beside us, clasps my nape, and steals my breath with the force of his kiss. "We thought we'd lost you," he rasps.

He's no longer the stoic man of action, allowing his emotions to bleed through to engulf me. I swallow, pressing closer for another kiss to tell him how sorry I am to frighten him by putting myself in danger.

Matthias slots in behind me, ignoring the fact I'm still straddling my other mate's lap, completely nude in the woods. His heartbeat thumps against my back and his hands still tremble, moving over me gently. I lean against him, craving being near each of them to settle the echo of fearful despair in our bond.

He kisses every inch of skin he can reach, brushing his lips over the claiming bite Valerian marked me with. My breath catches. It's sensitive. I want the others to do the same with their own claiming bites to match it so I carry the marks of my mates.

"I shared enough energy with her through the bond to heal her internal wounds and external wounds to keep her from succumbing to the worst of it." Vale caresses my arms. "Let's go before we're found again. Lily, if you feel anything wrong, you tell us immediately, understand?"

I nod, still exhausted but feeling more of my strength return.

"If need be, we'll stop where we can and give her more of our life force," Alder says.

Inhaling sharply, I grab at him. "What?"

"I told you, little flower." Valerian rests his forehead against mine. "Demons can heal. I'll give you as much energy as you need."

I knew it was shared energy through the bond, but I didn't think it was his life force. Is that why he seems tired?

I shake my head. "What if it's enough to kill you?"

Alder hushes me, squeezing the back of my neck comfortingly. "It's not. The bond wouldn't allow you to kill your mate by absorbing their energy. Come on. I don't want to linger here any longer than necessary."

I'm in and out of consciousness on the drive, still recovering from the curse. At some point, I remember waking in Matthias', then Alder's arms, sprawled in the back seat wearing only the shirt Alder had on earlier. They each give me energy through the bond,

Matthias burying his head between my thighs, lapping at me gently for over an hour until I can't take another orgasm, then Alder fingering me with the same steadfast dedication for an endless stretch that leaves me floating in delirious bliss. Their touch restores my strength, soothing away my exhaustion and any lingering aches.

When I wake again with my head in Matthias' lap, the windows are down, fresh salty air whipping through the car. He has a hand out the window, surfing the wind while stroking my hair with the other.

"Feeling better?" he asks when I curl against the pillow of his leg.

"Yeah. A lot better." I sit up and lean into his side.

The lines etched around his tense mouth relax, his gaze softening as it roams my face. He drapes an arm over my shoulder and kisses the top of my head. "Good. I'll never accept seeing you hurt or losing you."

"Where are we?"

His warm chuckle trickles over me and a smile tugs at my lips. "We're almost there. The place you've wanted to see."

A seagull cries somewhere outside and I peer through the window curiously. My eyes light up at the sight of a bay when we drive across a bridge, the hazy coastline beyond it visible past the barrier islands separating the bay from the ocean. This water doesn't frighten me like the lakes, creeks, and ponds we've come across. The ocean smells fantastic.

"The beach?" A buzz sings through me at his broad smile. I'm not sure if it's my excitement feeding to him or his emanating from our bond. "I thought the plan was to retrace our steps to get to a gate?"

"We are," Alder assures me from the front, reaching back to touch my knee. I take his hand. "We were near here. This beach is closer to the gate we'll use."

"You said you wanted to go to the beach, pretty girl." Matthias kisses my temple. "And after this is over, we'll hit every beach topside and the shores of the underworld realms. You want beaches? We'll give you all of them."

A laugh bubbles out of me. "Thank you." *I love you. I love you all so much.*

They see me. Understand me. Care for me in ways I never dreamed to hope for. Happiness overflows in my chest, despite everything at stake, the hardships we've faced, and the attacks of our enemies. They still found a way to take me to the beach.

We roll the windows up and I take in the small beach town we drive through. It's quiet this late in the fall. The only stores open are a tiny supermarket and a flower shop with baskets of mums decorated with wooden turkeys and pumpkins. The car turns down a road one block from the ocean and I crane my neck to see past the dunes at every intersection.

"We'll go through the gate as soon as we're sure your strength is fully restored." Vale catches my eye in the rear view mirror, sending heat zipping down my spine at his leer. "Once we get to our destination, I'll contact Rainer and let him know to meet us when we're prepared. Cessair likely went back to the underworld after he retreated. I'll have Rainer track his movements to learn what we can before we face him in the underworld."

"That suit guy." I frown. "You all knew him. And the other demon with him."

"Petra," Alder growls. "Another warrior demon. She was a dedicated leader to her warrior clan and was always close with the council. Never a match against me, though."

"Is she, uh… Coming back from what you did? You said before the hellhounds could keep getting back up to track us."

"No, they're different. Arguably the hardest to put down. Cessair left Petra behind. Even immortal demons capable of reincarnation can be seriously wounded and killed in the mortal realm if they don't return to the underworld as quickly as possible.

Only the bond of a mate could have kept her alive long enough to heal from that. The assassins you killed when you were attacked at the witch's place, and the ones that attacked us at the motel outside of Brim Hills also met their ends."

Unlike Lane, I don't feel remorse that Petra died at Alder's hand. She's our enemy and he was protecting me. The three of them kill for me without mercy, even back when we hated each other, and I'd do the same for them.

"And Cessair is a trickster like me," Matthias says. "He's our boss and one of the oldest members on the council. Gate guards report directly to him."

"He's behind this." Vale's tattoos shift across his stiff knuckles. "Corruption is poisoning the council. If he's involved in it, then it might not have been a mere demotion when I was assigned my gate in Brim Hills."

Alder's grip clenches my hand. I soothe my thumb across his knuckles. "What makes you think that?"

Valerian works his jaw. "He was...aware of my interest in Lilith. That it went beyond what a demon knight should feel for the king's betrothed he's sworn to guard. I think he wanted to keep me distracted from looking for you and keep a close eye on me to ensure I never did." He releases a sharp laugh. "He underestimated you because you survived and found us instead."

"They're all like that," Matthias grumbles. "Old farts with superiority complexes the size of Texas."

I snort. "Do you know what you're saying?"

He shrugs, shooting me a lopsided grin that makes my heart flutter. "I've always wanted to use that one."

"He's not wrong," Alder says. "The demon council is made up of the oldest bloodlines. They're powerful and experienced."

The light mood in the car evaporates. They exchange glances, then Vale stares at me from his reflection.

"What?" I narrow my eyes. "New rule. No mind speak if you're going to exclude me. I hate being left out."

Valerian's lips twitch. "It's for your protection."

I hang my head, chewing on my lip. Honest vulnerability bleeds into my voice. "Don't keep me out of the loop. Please."

Alder twists to face me with a repentant expression. "They won't be easy to fight. Less so to kill."

"You'll need your full power for us to stand a chance against the council." The steering wheel creaks beneath Valerian's grip. "We're worried because Cessair alone almost killed you."

"The seal..." I trail off, pushing aside my

doubts about being able to break it myself. His gaze sharpens and I inject confidence into my tone to cover so he can't read my feelings so easily. "We just have to believe our plan will work. When we get to the underworld, I'll break it and bring the pain."

Matthias chuckles when I sit up and punch my fist against my palm, sending a gust of smoke and sparks into the air. "Our fierce little fighter."

"We're here," Valerian says.

A crumbling lighthouse stands at the end of the road. The car rolls to a stop at the gate with a dangling CONDEMNED sign. Alder gets out and wrenches the gate open with brute force, his muscles flexing. He trails after the car as we follow the sandy driveway to a small caretaker's house at the base.

"How did you know about this place?" I climb out and pause at the salty breeze shifting my hair and the distant sound of waves crashing beyond the lighthouse.

"The gate is inside the lighthouse," Alder says.

I smirk. "Oh, so when you said near our destination, you meant we're camping out right at the door to Hell."

"It's seldom used," Valerian says. "It's a one-way portal rather than one that grants access both ways, like in Brim Hills."

I follow them inside the tiny abandoned beach house, marveling at the glimpses of the shoreline through the windows. "Can I go down there?"

Alder catches me in his arms before I make it to the door. He cradles my face. "Do you still feel any pain?"

"No, I'm good as new. Look." I flash my hands back and forth. Only the scars of the fire from my childhood remain. "Please?"

"Someone go with her," Vale says. "She's not to be left alone for a second."

"I'll do the ward spells." Alder kisses my forehead and I hug him, enjoying his warm bare chest against my cheek. "Then I'll join you."

Matthias plops my beat up duffel on a rickety chair and coughs at the cloud of dust. "Do you want something warmer to wear before we go out, Lils?"

I pluck at Alder's shirt. "I'm good in this."

He flashes me a wink. "If you get cold, I'll be with you to warm you up, babe."

Valerian sighs behind me. He winds his arms around me and I spin to face him. The openness of his expression takes me by surprise. His mouth presses to mine in a fierce crush and he breathes me in like he's committing me to memory.

"I'll return to you," he promises.

"I'll be counting the seconds until you do," I murmur.

He steals another kiss before he leaves to meet Rainer. A piece of my heart goes with him, the hole left behind waiting for him to come back to me and make me complete again.

Matthias takes my hand. "Ready to see the beach? I wish we could take you to a nicer one as your first experience, but—"

"Yes." The corner of his mouth kicks up at the excitement brimming in my tone. "I don't care. I just want to see it."

"Let's go then, pretty girl." He kicks off his boots and leaves them behind.

We make our way through the back door that has a small deck and steps leading down to the sand. I freeze, staring past the break in the dunes protecting the old house from the tide.

"Wow," Matthias breathes.

"Yeah." I blink, realizing he's staring at me instead of the ocean. A blush colors my cheeks. "Come on."

The first touch of the chilly sand against my bare feet startles me. A delighted laugh slips out as I squish my toes in it. Matthias smiles at my joyful reactions. We move onto the beach and I pick up a shell. He holds out his hand and tucks it in his pocket for me.

It's beautiful. The beach is wild and unmaintained, but it's so perfect.

I watch the waves crash against the shore, the long drag as the saltwater rushes back out to sea, leaving its mark behind on the wet sand. Clumps of seaweed dot the sand and seagulls glide on the wind overhead.

This is amazing. I made it to the beach.

We stroll hand in hand along it. In the distance past an inlet that separates this part of the beach from the rest of the island, I spot a pier with a lone fisherman.

"Thank you," I murmur throatily. "This is the best gift."

"Anything for you." He grasps my chin and kisses my nose.

Beaming, I pull his face down for a kiss.

Twenty Seven
LILY

ALDER JOINS US ON OUR WALK BACK, HIS SMILE SOFT AND tender as I dip my toes in the water. Matthias splashes me first and I shriek at the frigid cold. He hides behind Alder and I scoop water into my hands and fling it at both of them to get him back. Alder glances between us with a lethal smirk and the two of us dash away as he chases us.

I laugh hard enough my belly cramps. His brawny arms catch me around my waist, lifting me. We're both soaked from the splash fight. I kick and scream as he wades deeper into the freezing waves, shirtless, strong, and unbelievably sexy.

"Truce?" I wriggle around to plant kisses all over his square jaw, licking away the salty droplets. He adjusts me in his arms, supporting me so my legs wrap around his waist. "It'll cost you a kiss, sweet blossom."

I grin. "I always want to kiss you."

His raspy laugh cuts off as I press my lips to his. A wave breaks against us, his rugged body not moving a muscle against it. I shiver, gliding my tongue against his.

"You're cold," he says.

"Not with you here to keep me warm." I glance back to the shore where Matthias picks out more shells. "Take me back to the beach?"

When we come out of the water, I hop down and race to Matthias, colliding with him with a happy yell. His arms circle me automatically and he laps at my damp skin with a playful growl.

"Did you like your swim?"

"It was short lived." I rub against him, my chilly damp shirt clinging to all my curves. "The water's cold as shit."

"Your nipples are like icicles." He touches my lips. "No more swimming, though. Even with you running a little warmer than a human should, I don't want you to catch a cold."

"Not without one of us taking you." Alder scrubs at his damp brown hair when he reaches us. "The current is strong."

"Here, I picked this one out for you." Matthias offers me a beautiful shell. The pearlescent shimmer has swirls of orange. "It reminded me of you."

I trace the wavy fan shape. "I love it."

Alder takes it and puts it in the pile we've collected, abandoning his soggy shoes. Matthias threads his fingers with mine and walks me back to the edge of the water. Our toes sink in the sand as the water rushes over our feet.

I wish Valerian was here with me, where he belongs. I want to enjoy our life together with only the four of us and no worries in the world.

He's coming back, I remind myself. He promised.

"Hey." Matthias holds my face, his golden eyes bounce between mine. "I love you more than anything. I just want you to know that."

My heart stutters recklessly. His soft smile grows, the tips of his fangs peeking out.

"I love you."

The words come out soft, stolen on the wind. I've never given them to anyone. Once they're out, I want to give them to Alder and Vale, too.

His thumbs sweep across my cheeks. "I know, baby. We all feel how big your love is. Here." He touches his chest. "Today, I was really scared of losing you."

"Me too."

He kisses me, the first gentle press of our lips quickly becoming more. Alder appears behind me while I make out with him.

Matthias burns me up with his kiss, warming me from the cold beach until I'm panting. He holds me close, mapping my curves with his clever sparking fingers. They tease higher, beneath the hem of my borrowed shirt. His tingling touch buzzes as he kneads my ass, then sinks between my cheeks.

I moan with wild abandon, hips bucking against the vibrations. Matthias swallows it as he teases me. Alder rumbles at my back, tracing my hips while he nibbles my shoulder. Being pinned between them is heaven.

Breaking away from Matthias, I face Alder and stare into the green depths of his handsome eyes. "I love you."

He presses his forehead to mine. "And my heart beats for you and you alone, mate."

I sense Vale's return before I see him. A hum lights up the bond and I gasp. Turning, I find him standing on the deck, his tousled dark hair whipping in the wind and his focus honed in on me. I need him. I need all of them.

"Come on." Alder scoops me up and carries me up the beach, back to my other mate.

Inside the house it's warmer, though it's not a natural warmth. It's coming from the four of us. From the desire growing from a flicker to a strong blaze now that we're here together. They take me upstairs. The bedroom is dusty, but I don't care. I don't need fine things and clean sheets—I only need my mates.

Alder sets me down and I immediately go to Valerian. I trace his sharp jaw. "You came back."

"Nothing will keep us apart again," he says roughly.

"Never," I echo with a swallow. "I love you."

He stills, his blue eyes flaring. "I've waited to hear those words from your lips for so long."

"I love you. I love you, I love you." The words won't stop coming, tinged with emotion after being locked up inside me, waiting and wishing to be let out for someone that loves me back.

I have the connection I've always longed for with my demons.

Valerian strokes my hair. "You are the only reason I exist, Lily. To love you for all eternity."

A whimper escapes me and I crash against him. He fists my hair and captures my mouth in a scorching kiss. *I love you*, he says reverently in my mind.

I grew up an orphan desperately aching to be loved. I never imagined I'd have three fated mates that match me so perfectly.

The room fills with my favorite scents. Woodsmoke and charcoal. Campfire roasted chestnut and maple. Rich, spiced hickory. And my own cinnamon scent dances with each of theirs. I want to be as connected to them as our scents are, the bond urging me on.

Alder strips out of his drenched sweatpants while Valerian stops kissing me long enough to divest his clothes, then tugs me back against him. Air rushes past my lips in anticipation. We don't need to say anything, not even through Valerian pushing thoughts into our heads. We all ride the tidal wave of desire crashing over us.

"We'll break the bed if we all climb on," Matthias says.

"Hold her up," Valerian suggests.

Alder peels my wet shirt off, baring me for them. Three leers drink me in. The wet shirt plops to the floor as Alder cups my breasts from behind me.

He bends and guides my arms around his neck. "Hold tight."

I do as he says and he stands tall, lifting me by my thighs. He opens my legs, and Valerian and Matthias freeze, their hot gazes dragging over me. Every time they look at me like that, I feel like the most gorgeous woman in existence.

"Fuck, I love the sight of you spread like that." Matthias discards his pants and fists his cock. "You're the most beautiful vision, petal."

"Agreed." Valerian strokes the insides of my thighs. "So soft and perfect."

"Fuck me," I beg. "Someone. Please."

They chuckle and Alder's grip flexes on my legs. Valerian nips at my lips and glides the tip of his cock through my slick folds. I strain my hips, but Alder won't let me have what I want.

"Please."

"You want my cock, little flower?" Vale rumbles.

My lashes flutter and I tip my head back on Alder's shoulder. "I need you inside me. I want all of you." A sharp cry escapes me when he stops teasing me and thrusts inside. "Yes. Please."

"We've got you," Matthias croons in my ear.

"You want all of us?" Alder murmurs.

I nod, gasping as Valerian pulls back and snaps his hips, filling me to the brim. My nipples tighten with a sweet ache. Matthias hums, playing with them.

"Give her to me," Vale orders. "Matthias, open her ass for Alder."

"With pleasure," Matthias says in a sinful tone.

A moan slips out of me as Alder guides my legs around Valerian's waist and lets him support me, his cock sinking deeper with every hard thrust. I cling to his shoulders, my nails digging into his inked skin. Matthias' touch skates down my spine, sending tingles straight to my core with the sparks buzzing in his fingers from his power. Just as he did earlier, he teases my ass, circling my hole. My pussy clenches on Valerian's cock and he groans, gathering me closer.

Matthias spreads my cheeks. "Spit, big guy. Let's get her nice and wet for you."

Alder kisses his way down my back as he bends and instead of spitting, his tongue drags across my tight hole. A throb pulses in my core and my breath hitches.

Valerian smirks and slams into me again. "She likes that. Her pussy is getting wetter."

"Next time," Alder promises. "I'll devote an entire day to feasting on every inch of you."

A thick glob of spit hits my asshole and I shiver as Matthias rubs his buzzing fingers through it. "Relax," he instructs. "It'll make it easier."

"I trust you." I mean it wholeheartedly.

It's not bad. The heat he warms his fingers with helps me ease open for him. Before I know it, my hips push back for more.

Alder shifts to watch as Valerian fucks me with slow, unrelenting precision and Matthias fingers me open to get me ready to take him. He jerks his massive cock, gathering the precome leaking from the tip. Stepping closer, he spreads my ass cheek more and adds his slickness to the spit Matthias uses to lubricate me.

I feel full already, the stimulation in my pussy and ass sending me right to the brink. My hazy gaze meets Valerian's and my lips part at the gleam in his eye.

"You're fucking beautiful like this," he rasps. "Getting fucked by your mates."

"Yes," I whimper.

"Are you ready for Alder to fuck you, petal?" Matthias kisses my shoulder. Cheeks hot, I nod fervently. "Good girl."

He moves out of the way, stroking his cock while he watches us. Valerian holds still, fluttering kisses up my neck as Alder spreads me to spit on my stretched hole again, then lines up. Even with Matthias' preparation, the first nudge of Alder's huge cock steals my breath.

"Open for us, my sweet blossom." Alder mouths at my neck. "I promise I won't hurt you."

"They'll feel so good filling you up, both of them at the same time." Matthias circles my nipples with his fingers, giving me electric jolts of ecstasy that throb in my clit. "And whoever finishes first, I'm taking their place to keep you so full you'll feel us everywhere for days. Because you're ours, mate. Ours to fuck. Ours to worship. Ours to pleasure. Every one of your sweet sounds when we make you come belongs to us."

"God, yes," I cry. "I belong to you. I'll always be yours."

I lose my breath again when Alder takes my

hips and sinks inside inch by inch, stretching my body further than I thought possible to fit his cock. Matthias fondles my breasts and draws my face to his for a kiss while Alder takes his time working his cock into my ass.

"Lean back against me." His arm wraps around my shoulders to guide me back against him. "Just feel."

He starts to move and my eyes roll back as he pulls out and pushes his cock back in. Then Valerian does the same. They work into a rhythm that leaves me lightheaded between their ridged lengths filling me at once.

It's overwhelming, but good. My senses are on overdrive, drunk on the blend of our arousal feeding through the bond between all four of us.

The connection between us sings in every inch of my being to the depths of my soul.

When my orgasm explodes from the slow build of taking them both, my body locks up and I scream. It's so intense, the erotic wave smashing through my core over and over. They support me while they fuck me, keeping me pinned between them. Alder holds me up, tethering me while my cresting pleasure threatens to sweep me away.

"Such a good girl, coming for us," Matthias praises. "So pretty when you fall apart."

I want him, too. My fingers reach for his cock and

he steps within reach. He slides his fingers between me and Vale, finding my clit. My chest heaves as he hits me with intermittent jolts of sparks to tease me over the edge again while the others fuck me. His cock leaks on my fingers continuously as I jerk it, his length growing slick with precome. I bring them to my mouth and taste him, wishing I could take him in my mouth.

"Let me taste you with me on your tongue." He tugs my hand back to his cock and leans in to kiss me with a groan.

I break away with a strangled cry as Valerian thrusts harder.

"Fuck." He tenses, burying his throbbing cock deep in my pussy as he comes.

Alder rumbles against my ear when my back arches and my muscles clamp on his length. "So tight."

Valerian trails biting kisses along my jaw. "Take good care of our girl."

The moment he pulls out, Matthias makes good on his promise to keep me full while Valerian steps back to watch. He sinks in with one smooth glide that sends a ripple of heat through me.

"So good," I whimper.

"Yeah, baby?" Matthias caresses my thigh wrapped around him and grinds deeper. "You love taking it."

"I do," I breathe. "Fuck me."

When they groan in unison as Matthias drives into me, my back arches. I never want this to end. It feels so right to have my mates inside me and I want more.

"Mark me. I want you both," I urge.

Alder releases a feral sound when I bare my neck. The scrape of his fangs on my skin is divine. His claiming bite makes my mouth part on a silent cry at the sensations racing through me from the bond. After he laps at it, he moves back and Mathias gives me a crooked grin. He kisses me, then trails his lips down my jaw, my neck, and sinks his fangs into me with his claiming bite, doubling the intense pulse from the bond.

The fated magic cord signs in harmony, connecting the four of us together. I shatter, falling into oblivion in my mates' arms. They have me. They'll never let me go.

This is how it's always meant to be. The three of them surrounding me, their bite marks left on my skin a permanent reminder that I'm irrevocably theirs.

Alder releases a deep groan and his cock pulses, filling my ass. It sets Matthias off and both of them dig their fingers into me while the three of us ride out our orgasms. We stay joined like that, panting and trembling.

Valerian tips my chin up for a soft kiss. "Are you okay?"

I nod, shivering with aftershocks. Alder pulls out first. I whimper at the loss and Matthias hushes me as he carefully does the same.

"You did so good, petal." He rests his forehead against mine.

"That was amazing." My smile is drowsy in a good, *no thoughts, only orgasm coma* way.

They've left my body singing, floating in a blissed out ebb and flow.

I can barely move after my last release. All I know is Matthias is holding me. Alder says something about a bath and a delirious laugh bubbles out of me. "This place is abandoned. I doubt there's a nice bathroom, let alone running water."

Yet it didn't occur to me that we're demons. He finds a basin and hauls it to the bedroom while Matthias massages my lower back with heat emanating from his hands. Valerian helps Alder fill it with seawater and in no time they have a steaming bath ready for me.

Valerian swirls his tattooed arm through the water. "What was that about doubting our ability to care for you, mate?"

"I'll never doubt you again." I stick my tongue out at him as Matthias helps lower me in, giggling when Valerian gives me a wry look and pinches my ass beneath the water.

The hot saltwater feels great against the ache between my legs and in my backside. I relax, closing my eyes as Valerian cards his fingers through my hair. Matthias perches on the other side of the basin and Alder kneels near my feet, reaching into the bath to massage my limbs.

They stay with me.

A smile tugs at my mouth. I have the missing pieces of my heart that have made me whole. Nothing will take this away from me.

Twenty Eight
LILY

A FTER TWO DAY'S REST AT OUR PRIVATE LITTLE STRIP of beach at the lighthouse, I grow antsy and announce I'm ready. Valerian doesn't want to hear it, but I argue with him that we're giving Cessair and the other dicks on the council more time to play kings with their home.

"Our home." Alder speaks firmly, getting between us before our fighting gets out of hand. "Yours and ours, Lily."

I rest a hand on his chest, over his heart. "My home is wherever I go with you three."

"You should rest more," Valerian grits out.

"No. You said it yourself. We're out of time." I sigh, moving around Alder to cup Valerian's jaw. He clasps my wrists. "We can't put this off. They've stolen enough from me."

A muscle in his cheek twitches and his grip digs into my wrists. "I know." He exhales jaggedly. "Forgive me for being selfish."

"I love that about you," I whisper, then press on tiptoe for a bittersweet kiss.

My fear of this slipping out of my grasp rears up. I shove it back down and bury it inside.

The flame burning inside me that kept me fighting to survive was almost snuffed out by the time fate guided me to cross paths with my mates. They stoked the flame back to life, feeding it to a roaring inferno.

They are my reason to fight. To survive. For them and for myself. For everything I've been denied being stuck on this earth destined to suffer until I found the ones who healed the jagged shards of my heart.

No more. I'm terrified of going through that portal, but I won't be less for anyone else ever again.

Vale's gaze bounces between mine. I feel echoes of his own fear of losing me again. I press closer to reassure both of us that it won't happen. Nothing will keep us apart.

"Lily," he says roughly.

"It's time," I say. "Those bastards thought they got away with this for the last three hundred years."

He grits his teeth. "Very well."

"Same plan?" Matthias leans against the wall. "We need to outsmart Cessair and whoever else is on Team Asshole. You know Cessair isn't calling the shots. Leadership isn't his style. He prefers to let someone else do the heavy lifting while he reaps the benefits."

"I know how he thinks. Sneaking back in under cover is out. All isn't lost, though." Valerian paces the small room, stroking his angular jawline. Alder's arms band around me and tug me against his broad chest. "This gate will put us close to a wellspring in the underworld."

My stomach turns. "A well?"

"Not necessarily a physical well," he answers. "Hell has many natural pockets of energy that provide the demon fae with their restorative power. It's how we can heal, even when we're in the mortal realm."

"River Styx?" Matthias' brows pinch. "Yeah. Cessair won't expect us to come through Hell where the human souls crossover."

"The waters will help undo the unnatural curse binding her," Alder says.

My nose wrinkles. "There will be souls in the water?"

"We're not making you eat souls, though it would help you regain your full power faster," Valerian says.

"Hard pass."

"The waters have absorbed the latent power of the souls that are ferried to their afterlife. We'll have to worry about any soul reaper demons and hellhounds in the area, but otherwise it's the nearest natural pocket of energy we can get you to. Once there, you'll be able to break the seal."

"And then we go for the council." The brittleness in Alder's tone is shocking. Compared to the demon I first got to know as someone who respects his orders and the chain of command, he sounds ready for bloodshed. "They'll pay for all they've made you endure. They're the ones who put you in the hands of the humans who harmed you."

I shiver at the vow of violent retribution bleeding into his words.

Valerian touches his wrist and murmurs, activating the glowing red symbol of his Demon's Pledge connecting him to Rainer. Concentration lines his sharp features to reach the demon knight across the realms, testing the limits of the spell. "The time has come, old friend."

Rainer's voice filters in Valerian's head, and he pushes it through to the rest of us with his telepathic gift. *I tracked Cessair as you asked. He returned to the council's wing of the castle. Most of the underworld is under their rule. They've been acting in place of the king and queen, not just on Lucifer's behalf, but with their own agenda in mind.*

"Do they believe they have the power to dispose of Lucifer to take the underworld for themselves?" Valerian frowns. "Their greedy hunger for power has gone to their heads."

Lucifer has yet to stop them. He's still nowhere to be found, Rainer answers. *I'll make my way to you.*

Valerian nods. "It's decided. We'll leave at dusk and set out to break Lily's seal."

That gives me a little over an hour to hide how much I'm freaking out. We have to do this. The council won't get away with what they've done to me and my mates. We're going to the underworld to kick ass so we can be left the hell alone.

"I'm going to change," I say.

And I need a minute alone to prepare for what awaits us.

"Not keen to rock up wearing nothing but your mate's stolen shirts, barefoot and commando beneath?" Matthias wriggles his fingers teasingly. "That's the way we like you. Easy access."

I level him with a sardonic expression. "Well, you dickheads kept shredding my clothes with those claws, so yeah, your shirts are offered up as acceptable sacrifices. I don't have much, but I fought with my elbows out to score my small collection of vintage pieces from secondhand shops."

He pops off the wall and threads his fingers in

my hair, tugging lightly. "I'll buy you new clothes, babe. You'll never want for anything ever again."

I nuzzle against his wrist with a soft sigh. I can't lose this.

"Okay. Be right back, I have to go get hot as shit for going to war." My clothes have always been my armor. My source of confidence.

"That's my girl." Matthias smacks my ass and makes me laugh on my way up the rickety, worn steps in the lighthouse caretaker's house we're squatting in.

I pick through my bag, smirking as I remember the first time Matthias saw me in my suspender skirt, how much Alder's found an appreciation for my crop tops, and how Vale's gaze flares when I'm in fishnets.

Cessair and his accomplices put me in this body, but it's mine. Every curve, every dimple, every roll. It's beautiful and fierce, and with this body they intended to be my downfall, I've survived.

I change into a tight red crop top, a leather jacket, and high waisted black distressed shorts. The fishnets aren't exactly practical for battle, yet they're a necessary part of the metaphoric armor I pull around myself. The difference between now and who I was when I stepped off the train into Brim Hills is that I'm no longer alone.

Leather boots finish off my outfit. I check the

cracked mirror and set my jaw at my reflection. How would the previous Lilith like this look? In my past life, I seemed so restless stuck in those gowns, but full of confident spirit. Drawing a breath, I search for that version of me in my mind.

The dreams I've had of another world are all that remains. Who knows what's locked beyond the magic seal?

Don't screw us, Lilith. I love our mates, and if you grant me your strength, I'll share them with you. Help me break this seal without destroying who I am now.

My amber eyes glisten in the reflection.

Rainer arrives by the time I return downstairs, looking every inch a roguish demon knight. He tips his head in greeting with a smirk. "Princess. I see you've sorted the balance between them since we last met."

"It's not princess anymore," I say. "Just Lily."

Matthias slips his hand into mine. His clever golden eyes see through the brave face I put on. "If you're not ready, we don't have to do this."

Damn it. I thought I was masking it. "I am. And we do."

Alder appears at my other side, squeezing the back of my neck. "We'll protect you no matter what."

"Let's go." Valerian meets my eye, trapping me in his astute gaze.

I keep hold of Matthias' hand and push past

him before he asks about why I'm barely keeping it together under the surface. It's all I can do to keep the worries plaguing me at bay, trying to stop my anxieties from feeding along the bond tethering me to my mates.

The climb up the rusted iron spiral steps in the lighthouse is only making it worse. To distract myself, I voice the first stray question that pops in my head.

"Does this Hell gate have an urban legend, too?" I crane my neck to look at the top of the lighthouse past the point the steps have deteriorated.

"Nailed it." Matthias brackets his hands on the railings on either side of me, climbing right behind me. "Locals claim it's haunted with steps that lead to nowhere and don't reach the top. The portal is past that point, but since it's a one-way trip it's less active."

The closer we get to the top, the more my breathing becomes strained. "And how do we activate it?"

"You'll feel it. This one doesn't have a ritual. It will recognize demons," Alder calls back from a few steps above us.

Rainer is ahead of him. Vale brings up the rear. Alder and Matthias are going to hold my hands, surrounding me as we go through together like they promised. It doesn't stop me from picturing being rejected by my true place.

"See you on the other side," Rainer says.

Shimmering static electricity like I saw in the Brim Hills graveyard crackles through the air above the broken steps. It looks like he needs to jump into it. My heartbeat drums erratically and my palms smoke as my emotions fray. He flashes a grin and steps on nothing—on air—and vaults himself through the portal that ripples around him with a flash of light.

Valerian pushes up to join me. He pins my hips against the cool brick wall. Alder plants himself at the top and Matthias blocks the path down. The three of them surround me, forcing me to face them.

"Don't lie to us, mate. We sense your fear. You can't hide it from the bond," Valerian rumbles. "Say the word and we call this off."

"We can't," I push out hoarsely.

"We'll do anything when it comes to you," Matthias says.

Alder cups my cheek and angles my face to his. He swipes the teardrops spilling over. "What are you afraid of?"

"Losing you." A shuddering breath hisses out of me. "Of being separated from you forever when I break the seal. I—I'm afraid that I don't exist. That the real Lilith is waiting to break free."

Valerian growls, getting in my face. "You

390

are Lilith, little flower. You. You're our mate. Our goddess incarnate."

The others make fierce noises of agreement. I swallow past the lump in my throat.

"We'll never be separated again. Right?" Vale gives me a hard, heart-stopping kiss.

"Never." I clutch his arms.

They study me for another beat. I nod, harnessing the flickering fire within me. This body is mine. This life is mine. Their love is mine. No one can take any of it from me—not even my past self locked behind the seal.

"Okay," I say.

"You can do this," Alder says. "You're a survivor."

"Our little fighter," Matthias adds fondly.

"And you're not alone." Valerian's knuckles graze my jaw. "With us, you'll never be alone."

Their belief in me twines around me, chasing away my doubts. When I falter, they're there to catch me. It's the reminder I need, the push that keeps me going.

We face the crackling air of the portal together. Anticipation of the unknown flutters through my stomach. Is this what the moment in isekai manga where the main character faces their new world feels like? Uncertainty, yet pulled in by the allure of the unknown? The thought stirs a rush in me. I always dreamed of that moment and this is my chance to live it as I step back into the place I truly belong.

"Ready?" Alder asks.

My chin dips in determination. "Let's do it."

Vale steps behind me and the others take my hands. We climb the last available steps. A faint wind blows through the portal that is much warmer than the damp, chilly air at the beach below. It feels nice.

Before I step through the gate, the hardest moments of my life flash through my mind. Mrs. Clark's wariness of how unnatural she claimed I was. The kids that bullied me because they were afraid of me. The times the world looked down on me and drilled it into my head I was not enough.

I am enough. I've always been enough.

Gritting my teeth, I jump into the shimmer in the air, Matthias and Alder squeezing my hands tight. My stomach plummets when it feels like we'll fall to our deaths before we're compressed on all sides and sucked through dark clouds of smoke. The sensation knocks the wind out of me. For a moment my panic spikes, remembering the black smoke portal in the castle.

The only thing keeping me upright when we hit hard ground is their grip on me.

"Sorry. We should've warned you the landing can be rough," Matthias says.

Valerian lands nearby in a swirl of smoke with

more skill than me. He comes to my side, grasping my chin to check me over.

"I'm fine."

Rainer, now sporting short horns, gets up from his perch on a rock and shakes his head with a smirk. "Thought you'd gotten lost. The area's clear. Hellhounds are up in the canyon's caverns, but I don't sense any soul reapers."

To underline his warning, a bone-rattling howl splits the balmy air.

Now that we're no longer in the mortal realm, my guys have dropped the small glamorous that masked their demon traits, their ears pointed and their eyes more luminous. Maybe it's the effect of being in the underworld, the natural power in tune with them.

My lips part as I take in our surroundings. We did it. We're in Hell. Some part of me recognizes it, unfurling inside me like a flower in bloom. It's strange to recognize a place I've only seen in my dreams and fragmented memories, to not feel the ever present ache of being out of place, yet have no idea what lies ahead.

At first glance, we could be at the base of any craggy ravine, but the sky above is a deep hue of red twilight with violet clouds that no sunset could create. Steps carved out of the dark colored stone rise in the distance, the top shrouded in fog. I wonder how far we are from the Devil's castle in the city reaching into the otherworldly sky.

"We should move before the hellhounds pick up our scent," Alder says.

Valerian gestures behind us to the mouth of a cave. Blue light like the kind put off by bioluminescent organisms casts a soft glow on the walls coming from a small stream weaving a meandering path through it white smoke bubbles from its surface.

"This way," he directs. "It's the fastest route to the river from here."

Twenty Nine
LILY

WE REMAIN ALERT ON OUR JOURNEY THROUGH THE cave. The deeper we go, the more faint whispers and the occasional eerie moan echoes off the cave walls.

"What is that?" I hiss when it sounds closer.

"Souls trapped in the waters. Well, what they've transformed into. A soul that cannot crossover because it follows the offshoots of the river becomes…lost." Alder crouches to pass a hand through it and shimmering apparitions race against the current for his hand with chilling screeches.

"Watch out!" I yank his arm. "What the hell, Alder?"

He chuckles and wipes his hand on his leg. "They won't hurt me. They're nothing more than mindless creatures that swarm when they sense stronger beings to leech from."

"Jesus," I mumble. "What a terrible fate. I thought demons eat souls for their power. Why let any get away?"

"We do," Matthias answers. "But fresh ones. We can't consume the ones in River Styx. It was one of the stipulations of the treaty the old humans made with the demon fae, granting safe passage to the afterlife as the gods always had."

"There's nothing to help the lost souls get back?" I frown at the bright blue water. For a long time, I was as lost as they are. "That's depressing."

"That's life," Vale says. "Keep moving. We don't have time to sightsee."

"But after." Matthias grins. "I'm starting a list. It will be an epic tour of beaches first, then the sights of the underworld realm I'm dying to show you. I can't wait to watch you experience it all."

He lightens the tense mood, helping me breathe easier. Despite the fact we're here to face our enemies, every moment I spend here lifts a weight off my shoulders. Little by little, Hell seems to seep into my bones, directly into my being through the soles of my feet from the damp stone.

Is this what Valerian meant by the natural restorative energy in the underworld? We haven't reached the wellspring yet, and I already feel—

something. Stronger. More in tune with the power thrumming inside me. I'm even able to sense the bond with my fated mates better, and beneath those threads connecting us, the hazy shape of the seal forms in my mind.

I halt, eyes unfocused. It's intricate, the symbols similar to the curse circle trap Cessair set in the arcade connected by the gnarled roots of a tree. They're a tangled mess, interwoven through the magic binding. An unwanted weed that took root and choked out everything else, growing a forest's worth of unruly vines.

"Lily?" Valerian rests a hand at the small of my back.

I wave him off. "I can...visualize the seal."

He inhales sharply, glancing at the others. "I was right. You're stronger here. Your scent is growing more potent." Grasping my jaw, he demands my attention. "Now you smell like a demon, little flower."

"Your eyes are glowing," Matthias says. "And you smell even more delicious, mate."

"Do you feel the source of your power?" Alder prompts.

I lift a palm and with much less effort than it takes me in the mortal realm, I create a dancing flame. Fascinated by how my power feels completely under my command, I add a ring of sparks to spiral around the flame, eyes widening when it works.

"Holy shit," I whisper. "I'm doing it."

"Good," Alder says. "This is a promising sign. Your power is coming through the cracks you've made in the seal with more ease because you're here where you've always belonged. The birthright of your goddess ancestor is flowing into you."

"They never could have kept you weak in the underworld. Not when twenty minutes has this effect on you after two decades away to emaciate your power," Vale says.

"The cave splits ahead. It's not far to the main river once we reach the other side," Rainer says.

I don't let my flame dissipate when we continue, marveling at its beautiful form. A thrill shoots down my spine. This is working. Our plan is going to work.

For the first time, relief creeps through, no longer shrouded by doubt about breaking the seal. Being in the underworld fills me with a breath of life that leaves me eager for more, to shed the cursed shackle binding me as a changeling and claim what's rightfully mine—my place here.

But not as Lucifer's bride. A smirk twitches my lips.

I could be useful in other ways. Carve my own path. In the memories Valerian shared with me, I seemed to have the same hunger for life. Possibility opens on the path of my future, waiting for me to chase it.

First I have to break this seal. I'm ready to see if I can form my own claws and use them to hack through the unwelcome roots keeping the seal magic in place.

The end of the cave lets out into a misty forest that thins as we make our way through the trees. The stream widens and flows down a waterfall into an underground pocket. More whispers follow us and I can't shake the sense we're being watched. I scan the trees, swearing small sets of glowing yellow eyes track us.

I catch up to Alder and lean into his side. "More lost souls?"

Valerian shakes his head. "The lesser beings of Hell. They're recognizing a superior power. Yours."

I slide my lips together. "Let's hope their gossip doesn't spread before I break the seal. We wouldn't want the council to find out we're sneaking in before we're ready to take them down."

"It's far too late for that, Lilith."

Fuck.

Our group tenses, whirling at Cessair's nasty voice. He appears through the trees, materializing out of thin air much like Rainer did the first time he found us when he drops the spell to hide his presence.

Cessair is joined by four others in matching

pompous white suits. One is stout with large horns curving back from his head, his sagging face in a permanent moe of sadness, and another with long, pointy gray horns has a venomous air about him, wrapped on his broad shoulders like a cloak. His thick lips curl back, baring his fangs at us.

"Shit," Rainer utters. "Brone and Samael."

Cessair defers to the tallest of the four, a man with pale skin stretched over unsettling angular features. His translucent skin is cracked with thin black lines that spread from his short, sharp red horns and around his fathomless dark eyes. His long white hair parts for pointed ears. The sight of him sends a chill down my spine.

"Alastor?" Matthias hisses. "You? But—you're Lucifer's closest friend! How could you betray him like this?"

Alastor's mouth forms a grim, hateful line. "It's simple, boy. I want what he has. Hell should be mine, not the arrogant, spoiled king's."

Valerian growls. "You aren't fit to rule the realms, you scheming bastard. None of you are."

"And yet we have the people's trust." Brone, the stout one, gives us a smile that's more of a grimace. "We have been at work putting the pieces into place. You won't stop what's in motion."

"We're primed to take our prize after centuries of planning," Samael says in a harsh, terrifying voice.

"Cessair." Alastor waves him forward with a clawed hand.

"You thought I let you win because you came to her rescue? We had spies watching you once I left the mortal realm."

Cessair holds out a hand and the whispers around us increase. The air crackles with static electricity and a small creature with delicate fairy wings materializes, landing in his palm. It's not cute or pretty like the fairies in my fantasy stories—its bared teeth are like needles and its fish-like eyes glow a sickly green.

"We've been waiting for you to arrive so we can end this as we should have long ago. It was clever of Valerian to think of the soul river. It probably would've worked. You've proven to be quite difficult to be rid of, Lilith. Even after we separated your body piece by piece until you were finally weak enough to bind, it seems you've still managed to fight your way past it instead of dying like a good little bitch."

My mates growl dangerously. Gritting my teeth, I surge forward, desperate to attack the bastards who did this to me. Alder's arm blocks me, tucking me behind him. They knew. They've been waiting, ready for us this whole time to stop us from reaching the river.

Keep them talking. Vale's voice echoes through the bond in my head. Matthias and Alder give barely perceptible nods, shifting in front of me while he moves behind me.

"You've broken sacred laws to satisfy your own ends," Alder says darkly.

Alastor laughs, the sound brittle and disconcerting. "Laws only stand in the way of those too weak to take the power they seek." He snatches a creature from a low hanging tree branch and crushes it in his fist without mercy. "We have no use for them. We've done whatever was necessary. Once we take Hell from its weak ruler, we'll restore the underworld as it should have always been. The treaty never should have existed."

"You can't mean destroying the barrier separating us from the mortals?" Matthias jerks his head in disgust. "That would be chaos."

"Precisely," Samael says.

"We won't allow you to continue," Alder counters.

Lily, get to the river. It's right past the trees. Valerian's urgent order enters my head while the others distract the council members. *We'll hold them off.*

"No," I hiss. "I'm not leaving you."

He fists my jacket and mutters against my ear. "Damn it, Lily—"

"I won't," I vow firmly. "I'll never leave you alone."

"Then you need to do it now without the river. Break the seal." His grip tightens and he hauls me closer. "You can do it. You have to."

"You won't be enough to stop us," Cessair boasts. "You've only escaped death thus far because we wanted to know why she survived."

"Yeah? Well we've killed everyone you've sent after us." I pull free of Valerian's grasp and push past Matthias. Alder grabs my jacket, freezing when I hold up a hand. "So far all I've heard is a bunch of douchebag men patting themselves on the back. I'm sick of it."

Alastor's mouth curls into a malevolent grin. "Just like your mother before you centuries ago. She met her end at my hand, and so shall you. The only mercy I'll grant is a swift end because you've already taken more than enough of my time."

My chest twinges and a sharp tingle spreads throughout my body. This demon has taken too much from me. I won't let him steal anything else— I'm done letting anyone decide my fate.

"No fucking way."

Flames spill down my arms into my hands. My nails lengthen into short red claws with the fierce anger coursing through my veins. My guys flank me, ready to go to war with me.

"This ends here," Valerian says.

The forest creatures hidden amongst the mist in the trees screech when I move for the first attack, creating a cacophony while the flames I push at our enemies clash against the twirling fire Brone wields to defend the group. Our hellfire illuminates the forest in violent bursts of light and oppressive heat.

Valerian and Alder charge Alastor while Matthias goes against Cessair. Rainer draws a sword and takes on Samael, and I fling another rush of flames at Brone.

This is nothing like the fights we've faced so far. It takes all my concentration to block Brone's rapid fireball attacks, my speed not as fast as his. Despite his stout stature, he's not slow. I barely have time to check on the others, too busy dodging like Alder taught me.

Rainer fights Samael, coating his blade in flames. They dance around each other in close combat, Rainer's sword and fist challenging Samael's powerful fiery hits matching him blow for blow. I think it's only Rainer's experience as a demon knight that keeps him on his feet as Samael gains ground, punching and slashing with burning fists to land vicious hits.

Matthias conjures fire and illusions to keep Cessair at bay, confusing him with doubles mimicking each move he makes so it's unclear where the true source is. His flames race to circle them, licking up the trees, and from those flames dog-like creatures made of molten stone and smoke burst free. Cessair smirks, unthreatened and counters with a fearsome flash that torches a path straight for Matthias, picking him out from the magic dopplegangers.

I yelp, moving mere seconds before Brone's spiraling fire molded like a spear catches me in the chest, knees skidding in the dirt. Heart pounding, I push to my feet and swing my arm to protect myself with a rush of hellfire. Though it's a strong burst, the flames sputter out before they reach him. He smirks, his sagging cheeks gruesomely folding over his mouth.

Don't panic. Break the seal, Valerian urges. In the corner of my eye, I watch in horror as Alastor rains endless hellfire on him and Alder. He splits his attention between the demon he fights and me, using his fire whip to force Alastor back several steps.

Don't let them win, Lily. Undo what they've done to you. We know you can do it.

My throat stings. We need to do something. My heartbeat stutters as I dodge another bout of blistering flames from Brone, flattening to the ground. How am I supposed to concentrate on breaking the seal by myself while fighting off the demons who did this to me?

They believe in me. It has to work.

Closing my eyes, I seek the seal in my mind, stomach plummeting at the thick roots and vines twisting through the ancient magic. I imagine claws to slice through the mess. Small pieces chip off, but I don't get far. The glowing symbols mock my inability to put a dent in my magic prison.

I gasp, eyes flying open at Alder's grunt of pain. Alastor has him by the throat, talons piercing his corded muscles. With a terrible bark of laughter, he throws my strong warrior aside against a thick tree trunk and turns his attention to Valerian.

"It's time for you to die," Alastor says.

"No!" I yell.

It's not enough. *I'm* not enough to save us—to save my mates. The harrowing truth I've always battled with shreds my heart.

We weren't ready. I can't break the seal and all the training they gave me isn't a match for the old, powerful demons corrupting Hell.

Dark smoke springs from Cessair's fingers like marionette strings, trapping Matthias in a magic swamp. He grunts, blocking the monstrous, skeletal creation Cessair pulls out of it, controlled by smoke, while trying to get his legs free. He's sinking and more illusions surface in the swamp, slashing at him, swarming him. They're too many for him to handle alone. He needs help.

"Matthias!" Alder calls hoarsely.

Valerian's flame whip catches Alastor's wrist and he wrenches. In the spare moment he gains the advantage in the fight, his gaze snaps to Matthias. Alastor knocks him back and pins him to the ground, claws slicing through his skin. Gritting his teeth, he struggles, raking his claws through the forest floor.

There's no curse circle trapping me this time. Before I make a move, Brone blocks my path to my mate, circling me with a ring of fire.

Cessair's grin is triumphant as Matthias chokes in pain when a creature sinks its teeth into his neck and pulls him deeper into the murky water. His golden eyes hold mine, their bright glow brimming with despair, with regret, with bittersweet love.

This isn't one of Cessair's cruel illusions. This time my worst nightmare is real.

"I'm sorry. Remember me, petal." Matthias' wry tone echoes with the melodic magic of his gift, trying to ease my mind, to convince me to believe this is okay, but it only carves deeper canyons in my aching heart when I don't allow his magic to sway my mind.

My mate's head disappears into the mucky swamp.

No. My heart stops. Frantic sounds escape me as I abandon my fight, leaping through the flames, ignoring the sear of pain, forcing my way to him. *No, no, no.* Please. I can't—I can't lose him. Not any of them.

Thirty
LILY

"Matthias! No!" My anguished, piercing screams send a pulsing wave of hot air out, knocking Brone away from me and blasting Cessair back from the magic swamp Matthias drowns in. "You promised! You promised not to leave me!"

A piece of my heart breaks off, threatening my ability to live whole ever again without him. He's my light. My reason to smile, the one who makes me laugh. I can't do this without him. Without Alder or Valerian. I need them all—without one of them, I'm lost.

"Matthias," I choke through a painful sob, clawing at the mud as the swamp recedes from my flaming hands burning out of my control, drying it

"Lily!" Valerian's yell is raw and broken.

"Lily, move!" Alder begs.

He staggers to his feet and dives to block Brone's fireball from hitting me. The force of it breaks over his body. He falls to the ground and doesn't get up. Again, my bond clamors in my chest as another piece of my heart fractures. Alastor growls and pins Valerian with enough force the crack of bones cuts through the air, the sound twisting my stomach. I scream through a wrecked sob.

It can't be like this. We didn't come this far for our enemies to win. I have to do something now to save us before we all die. I frantically turn my attention to the seal binding me from my true self.

These bastards barred me from the underworld and cast me into the mortal realm as a lost girl. Alastor, Cessair, Brone, and Samael will pay with their lives for their sins. I don't care how hard immortal demon fae are to kill. I will make them suffer.

The roots don't matter. They're a distraction. Another illusion to keep me out. To convince me I can't take what's always been mine.

The cursed seal they bound me with doesn't imprison a demon ready to erase me. I am Lilith. Not two separate parts—all of me. The truth sings clear in my veins now. It has from the moment I stepped foot in the underworld. The reject, troubled girl too afraid of myself with the royal blood of a fae goddess descendent within her.

I am Lily Sloane, the new incarnation of Lilith and *no one* will hurt me or my mates ever again.

I was terrified of losing myself to Lilith, but we're the same. They couldn't stamp me out, couldn't drown me, couldn't steal my power like they stole my life.

Sink or fucking swim.

Clenching my teeth, I drive my hands into the ground, chest collapsing when I feel Matthias buried under the earth. "I choose swim!"

My head flings back and I unleash a screech charged with a fury that awakens the slumbering power of a demon goddess in my blood. The heat of my rage scorches through me in a wild blaze, searing through my skin and exploding from my mouth, my chest, my hands. It's like the instinct that overcame me when we were attacked at the witch's cottage, but with the full strength within my grasp.

Driving my claws into the ground, I grasp what I want. I feel the seal shatter as I rise into the air, pulling Matthias free. My power flows through me, no longer locked away, giving me the strength needed to stop the corrupt demons.

A sharp breath catches in my throat. I remember. Not all of it—I remember being kidnapped from the castle halls through the black smoke portal. I remember the endless pain I endured, trapped by so many curses I couldn't escape.

"Lily." Matthias croaks. "Get that bastard, baby."

He coughs, spitting a mouthful of wet dirt. He's out of breath and caked in mud, but alive. *Alive.*

I smash my mouth to his, praying the hasty kiss triggers the bond to feed him my life force. He clutches the back of my head, breathing easier. When I pull back, his eyes gleam and he springs to his feet.

"Did you think that was enough to put me down, old man?" Matthias prowls toward Cessair, fiery fists poised to strike. "Putting me in the ground won't end me. Only slow me down."

Cessair narrows his eyes and looks past him dismissively to catch my eye. "We bound you once, Lilith. We will succeed again."

"Not before we kill you for doing it the first time," Matthias grits out.

Alder has recovered from taking Brone's attack to shield me, to my relief. Our eyes meet and I feel the echo of his pride in me emanating through the bond. He gets to his feet and uses his formidable brute strength to tackle Alastor, freeing Valerian to get to his feet. Vale abandons strategy and barrels into Alastor's other side, gripping him by the lapel and punching him with a flaming fist. Alastor growls and grabs his face, cutting open fresh wounds with his claws.

"Her power!" Brone squawks at the others. "She's freed her full power!"

"That's right, asshole. *My* power. The one you tried to take from me." My lip curls back from the fangs that lengthen in my mouth. "You failed."

His eyes go round, beady with apprehension. Without the seal, I realize how much my life was dulled down, tamped by magic. It wasn't me that made myself less—it was the curse. My senses sharpen, hearing what I couldn't before while the fighting rages around me, my eyesight keener to take in the nervous sweat beading Brone's saggy forehead.

I bolt to him through the charred trees with newfound speed, my hellfire springing forth before I visualize my attack. The ground turns molten wherever I step, the heat coming off me explosive from being bottled up, ready to let loose.

Brone collapses to his knees. "Mercy, Lilith. I beg of you."

"You're pathetic," I growl. "You fold at the first sign you won't win. Spoiler alert, shithead: you won't."

Grabbing him by one of his curved horns, I rake my claws across his greasy face. They're sharper and longer now that I've broken the curse, my demon traits no longer locked inside. He shrieks, wriggling

412

to escape.

"Samael! Cessair!"

"They won't help you," I hiss.

Kicking his chest, he flies back and crashes against a tree. I trace a circle in the air with my arms, calling on the natural power of the underworld feeding into the deep well of my power. It heeds my call, the ground splitting open with rattling fractures. A cloud of brimstone floods the misty air and fire rises from the depths of the underworld with molten earth to encase Brone against the tree.

His droopy features go slack. "That's not possible. No daughter of Lilith has power like this."

I clench a fist, then leap across the crevice separating us and drive it into his face. His head snaps to the side and I pull back again to throw another punch like Alder taught me. This one knocks him unconscious. And breaks his jaw, the bone crunching against my blazing knuckles.

I want to help Vale and Alder in their struggle against Alastor, but Rainer and Matthias are both fighting alone. Matthias is holding his own against Cessair, but Rainer has lost his sword to Samael.

When I join the fray, Samael's focus locks on me and he releases a hair-raising predatory sound. My heart pounds, recognizing it from the depths of my fragmented, lost memories. He was in charge of my torture, keeping me at the edge of death with curse upon curse.

Fucking bastard got off on every second of pain I endured.

My fire races to my fingertips, burning a bright, scorching blue. Panting, Rainer falls back a step from the sweltering heat coming off me. Blood trickles into his eye and his sleeve is torn.

"Go help the others," I say.

"And let you handle the fun on your own, princess?" He holds up his hands at the ferocious look I shoot him.

"I owe him a world of pain," I mutter.

Samael bares his teeth and sprints at me. I throw my hands up, dissipating the billow of flames he throws at me with my hotter ones, using them as my shield to get close enough to blast his head with an endless stream of blistering heat. He roars, skin burning. Jerking back, he swings a fist at me. The blow knocks me off balance. Alder's steady voice in my head reminds me to recenter myself to stay upright.

"You're twice as ugly now." I swipe the back of my hand across my mouth. "When Lucifer finds out what you've done, he'll charge you with treason and true death."

"He is a fool, hiding away in his castle. He practically handed the crown to us," Samael snarls.

"You're the idiots. You should've killed me

when you had the chance. Now I'm back and I'm pissed."

I launch myself at him, calling once more on the underworld to aid me. The ground melts at Samael's feet. His eyes widen and he sinks faster the more he thrashes to escape. I stop when he's up to his shoulders and wrench his head back by his hair.

"Hell and the underworld realms will never be yours," I spit before smashing his head down on my knee with ferocious strength repeatedly until he's unconscious.

Thirty One
LILY

Once I've dealt with Samael, I find Alder, Valerian, and Rainer handling Alastor with unrelenting attacks. Matthias is still on his own against Cessair.

I narrow my eyes. They've got this, and I want payback for the arcade and for trying to kill Matthias.

Cessair and Matthias trade blows with their blazing fists, both of them fighting off dueling illusions while brutally attacking each other. Serpents wrap around Cessair's leg, constricting tighter to knock him off balance, while Matthias deals with a horde of the nasty fairies Cessair had spying on us, their spindly teeth tearing into his arms and neck.

Closing the distance between us, I jump onto Cessair's back, winding one arm around his neck and clapping a hand over his eyes. Furious energy buzzes through me and I push a torrent of savage blue flames through my palm. His skin bubbles beneath my grip. I hope I'm melting his goddamn eyes.

"Augh! Fucking bitch!"

His arms pinwheel, claws biting into my skin, scrabbling over the short horns I've sprouted. The injuries he inflicts on me are nothing—they heal within moments as my power beats through me with the rhythm of my pulse. I won't let go, vicious in my attack to blind him.

"Get off, you little cunts." Matthias growls and twists in a spiral, blasting the horde of malicious fairies away from him with a burst of flame and humid wind. He plucks one from the air and pinches its head between his fingers, squashing it. Turning his attention back to us, his lips curl in satisfaction. "You picked the wrong fight, old man. Our girl is unstoppable."

Cessair reaches back and grabs me by the hair. I grit my teeth, digging into his face harder with a renewed shot of heat. He groans and collapses, taking me with him. I roll his body over and straddle his chest, squeezing his throat hard enough to pierce his skin with my sharp talons. His boiled skin and the charred remains of his eyes aren't enough.

He hurt Matthias. He hurt the others. He hurt

me. He doesn't deserve to live. None of them do.

A strangled sound leaves me as I claw at his filthy, tattered suit, the material shredding beneath my furious swipes. I slice through skin and bone, panting through my unshakeable anger. He slaps me and Matthias bolts over with a dangerous growl, pinning Cessair's arms in the smoking dirt.

"I'm going to rip your fucking hands off for that. Finger by finger," he promises. "And then I'll force feed them to you."

When I stop thrashing Cessair's chest, I'm panting and blood soaks my hands. Through his broken ribs and ravaged chest cavity, his exposed heart beats. I wrap my trembling fingers around it.

"Tell me why," I demand. "You're going to die anyway. You're done."

Cessair bucks, but between me and Matthias he's unable to gain leverage. He collapses with a squelched gargle when I squeeze his heart.

"Why?" It comes out low, rough, and shaky.

"Power," he grits out furiously. "You were too unpredictable. Not—susceptible to the influence I tried to plant in your mind."

I squeeze harder, ready to fucking burst his heart between my fingers and roast it in blue flames for retribution. His mouth falls open with a choked gasp when heat builds in my hands and the stench of smoking flesh and blood rises into the air.

"When we realized—you needed to go, we wanted to put our own queen on the throne to manipulate Lucifer." His breathing is labored. "But—But the pawn queen wouldn't be-behave. We knew we had to claim the throne for ourselves."

"Your greed is your downfall," I growl.

All the pain, heartache, fear, and uncertainty I've battled filters through me. The unbearable sight of Matthias disappearing beneath the surface of the swamp. Of Valerian when he was severely hurt guarding me from the demon assassins. Alder's fierce protectiveness against the demons that almost sliced him to ribbons in the motel. The looks on my mates' faces when I almost died trapped by Cessair's curse.

Tears sting my eyes and spill over as the riotous energy of my power culminates to a breaking point in my palms. Fire explodes through my hands, burning Cessair's rotten heart. His body jerks and Matthias holds him down while he babbles. A wet gasp leaves me as I squeeze harder until the seared muscle in my hands bubbles to a liquid state, oozing between my fingers.

Cessair twitches, then slumps. His sticky dark blood stains my hands.

"I killed him," I whisper.

Matthias covers my bloody hand with his, squeezing in support. "If you didn't, I was going to

419

do it. Or the others. Did you want to?"

I close my eyes. "Yes. Do you hate me for it?"

"No. Never." His tone is gentle. He leans in and kisses my temple. "Do you regret it?"

I shake my head. He fucking deserved it. He was going to kill me and my mates if I didn't end him.

"Let's see if the others need our help." He draws me to my feet. "I'm proud of you. We knew you could break the seal."

I don't spare Cessair's body another glance. He brought his fate on himself the moment he crossed me. My focus shifts to my other mates, to needing to help them end this.

Not far off, the others have Alastor on his knees. He's missing half an arm, the bloody limb on the ground, a scrap of Valerian's shirt clutched in the fist. My heart skips a beat and we rush to them.

"You have not won yet, Lilith," Alastor thunders. "You—"

I don't stop jogging, speeding up with a scowl. Alder yanks Valerian out of my path, pride glinting in his gaze as I coat my fist in ruthless blue flames and smash it into Alastor's face. His head snaps to the side from my punch and his chin slumps to his chest. The one hit knockout feels really damn good.

"Shut the fuck up," I grit out.

"Fiesty little princess." Rainer chuckles through

his exhaustion, slumping against a tree, using his sword to brace himself. "Consider our life debt repaid, old friend."

"Beautiful right hook," Alder praises warmly.

"Are you hurt?" Valerian grabs my wrist, examining my bloody hands.

I shake my head, leaning into his chest, covering his own torn up wounds. They mend beneath my touch. His arms close around me, speeding my own healing until I'm good as new. I bask in his embrace, breathing him in. He strokes my hair, holding me tight enough to let me know he's never letting me go.

When he lets me draw back, Alder takes me in his arms. I rub my cheek against his firm chest, passing my hands over him to check for wounds. He kisses the top of my head.

We did it. We're alive and we won.

I leave Alder's embrace to hug Matthias the hardest, still rattled from the threat of losing him. He lifts me and spins us around, face buried in my neck.

After he sets me down, the three of them close in around me, enveloping me in their smoky scents. Valerian catches my chin and draws it to him for a kiss while Alder's hug crushes me against his chest. I turn from Valerian to kiss Matthias. Alder's fingers move up my throat and he guides my head back to capture my lips for himself.

My heart flutters, brimming with love for my mates.

"If you four are going to fuck, can you give me a warning?" Rainer jokes. "The frenzy of battle does strange things to people. The comedown from all that adrenaline hits hard."

I laugh, pushing free of the circle. "Thank you for your help. You risked your life for us."

He smiles softly, patting my shoulder. "I would do it again. I owed Vale a debt, and more than that, he's my brother in arms."

"Will you be alright?" I eye Rainer's blood soaked sleeve, deep gashes from claws cover his skin.

"I'll heal soon." He smirks. "I don't have a mate bond to feed off of. Nifty trick."

I turn back to our defeated enemies with a frown. "What about any people that want them to rule? It can't be just them working alone for this long."

"I believe I'll take care of that," a new voice answers.

I whirl around, fire exploding around my fists, prepared to take on a new opponent.

"Your Highness." Rainer kneels, clasping a fist over his chest.

A moment later, Valerian and Alder do the same. Matthias remains on his feet, inclining his head with a murmur of respect for the demon.

That means—Lucifer.

Thirty Two
LILY

THE KING OF HELL IS TALL, WITH DARK DISHEVELED HAIR, pointed ears, and angelically handsome chiseled features. With one smirk, I know he's a dangerous, intelligent demon. Like the council, he wears a sharp suit, black with intricate details woven into the silk. A fur-edged cloak perches across his shoulders and rings decorate his fingers.

He surveys the destruction around the misty forest, lingering on each of the demon council that plotted to overthrow him. The corners of his mouth kick up in a smirk.

"Thanks for doing the heavy lifting." He strolls up to me and touches my face. "Welcome home, Lilith."

All of us tense at the honeyed tone and the

sweep of his eyes roving over me. The guys shift restlessly. This is their king, but I sense through the bond that they're ready to take him on to fight for me. In the corner of my eye, Rainer clasps Valerian's shoulder, holding him back, muttering in his ear.

Lucifer's brow lifts and he glides his fingertips down my neck.

"Hey!" My head jolts back as my three mates surge forward.

"My, my. You charge at your king like that?" Lucifer laughs, holding up a hand.

They freeze as a ring of brilliant blue fire traps them, blocking their path to me. Each of them set their jaws, prepared and willing to walk through fire for me. My heart pounds and panic floods me.

"W-wait. Please." Lucifer's attention returns to me. "What do you want? I promise to do anything if you'll spare them and let them go."

"What I want?" Lucifer's smile grows. "What would you like, Lilith? Shall I break the bonds you've formed with these demons so you can become the queen of Hell ruling at my side, as you were meant to?"

I shove away from him, fire erupting along my skin hot enough to rival the flames he trapped my guys with. If he won't allow my mates to fight for me, I'll fight for myself.

"No!" My fierce refusal is echoed by three

growled responses from Alder, Matthias, and Valerian. They grow more restless, trapped by Lucifer's hellfire. "I never wanted to be your queen. That much I remember. You won't take me from my mates."

Lucifer laughs, unbothered by my threatening stance. "Good."

I snuff out my flames, eyeing him warily. "Good? I don't get you, dude."

My suspicious distrust delights him. "I knew you were unhappy at the castle. You were much more yourself when you slipped past your guards and ventured out into the realm." He drops the blaze keeping my mates at bay. "I needed to be sure. Though my queen will not be happy with me for offering, even if I had no intention of taking you. She's quite the fiery spirit. You'd like her, I believe."

Keeping an eye on him, I back up, feeling the tethers connecting me to my demons as a guide. They close the distance between us in swift strides until I hit Valerian's chest. His arms lock around me, Alder and Matthias flanking us and taking my hands. Together we're a unified front, us against whatever threatens to tear us apart.

"I hope you can forgive me for testing you." Lucifer's smile falls into a chilling sneer as he takes in the incapacitated demons. He pauses on Alastor, his angelic features twisting, darkening. "I can't be too careful. Even those I trust enough to call a friend are quick to stab me in the back to sate their own greed."

Rainer hauls Alastor's unconscious body up and drags him, wrists bound with the glow of a spell. He moves to Samael and Brone, pausing to consider how to remove them from the ground I encased them in. "At your word, I'll alert the royal guard to prepare three cells, sir."

"Three?" Lucifer's gaze flicks between his council members, landing on Cessair's body. "Ah. I see."

I tense, remembering Alder's explanation of the sacred laws demons abide. I killed Cessair.

Sensing my stress, my guys press closer. They won't let any harm come to me.

"They planned to overthrow you, Your Highness," Valerian says gruffly. "The charge from the council that we betrayed you—that I was planning rebellion—was a lie to cover their schemes. They kidnapped Lily, tried to kill her, and sought to take the realm from you."

Lucifer chuckles dangerously, his crimson eyes flashing. "Oh, I'm not so easily manipulated. I'm the king of Hell and many have tried to fool me. I suspected something was at work when I heard of this."

Valerian's chin dips, grazing the top of my head.

"Sir."

"Truly, the first inclination something was wrong was when Lilith went missing. At first I thought you'd staged your own kidnapping as a way out of our betrothal. You always chased your wild ideas." Lucifer frowns. "But you never turned up. Then this treasonous claim and demons flocking through portals to the mortal realm didn't add up. I used you as bait to draw out those that sowed their corruption while I protected my queen."

"I hate being bait," I mutter.

Alder huffs in amusement, squeezing my hand. "What happens now?"

"Rainer," Lucifer says. "We'll need a prisoner transport."

Rainer bows, placing his fist over his heart before nodding to us. "Until next time, old friend."

"Uh, alright peace out, then." I elbow Valerian to get him to move.

"You're different, yet still much like yourself. Your true feelings shine through. It's good to see." Lucifer's grin shows a peek of fangs. "Where are you off to in such a hurry?"

I open and close my mouth. Right. He's the king of the underworld. We probably need his permission.

"Are we allowed to go? We collected your trash, so we're good, right?"

Matthias coughs to cover his laugh.

"Are you three not guardians of a gate?" Lucifer squints at my guys. "If that's where you wish to return, by all means. Unless you'd like to be reinstated to the knights, Valerian. Seeing as how the charge you guarded is now your mate."

Valerian is at a loss for words. I twist to see his wide-eyed gaze locked on the Devil, tremors of reprieve running along our bond. He's no longer disgraced now that Lucifer knows the truth about my disappearance.

"We'll go where you order us to, Your Highness," Alder says respectfully on Valerian's behalf.

Lucifer studies me for a moment. "I relieve you three from your duty as guards. For your loyalty and service to Hell, you're free to come and go as you please." At my quick inhale of excitement, he tilts his head. "On the condition you'll accept positions on my council, seeing as I have open positions to fill."

It's Alder's turn to be speechless. This must be a big deal.

"Council seats are inherited by descendants of a bloodline," Valerian murmurs in explanation.

"As long as we join the council, we can do whatever we want?" I bite my lip, waiting for another rug to be pulled out from under me—a habit I picked up growing up in the mortal realm.

Lucifer nods. "I wish you the grandest

adventure, Lilith."

"It's Lily now." I stick out my hand. "Nice to meet you."

A huff leaves him and he takes my hand to shake. "Lily. It suits you."

"It does." Warmth infuses Valerian's low rasp. "Perfectly."

"Then I leave you here." Lucifer gestures to Brone and Samael's forged prisons. "They're my— trash, as you put it, to deal with."

A weight lifts off my shoulders as my guys lead me away from our battleground. We make our way to the edge of the misty forest, the sprawling landscape of Hell opening up before us. The underworld flows through me, present in every breath I take. It's part of me, welcoming me back to the place I belong with open arms.

I stop to touch a tree in silent thanks for lending me extra strength to defeat our enemies. The guys give me soft smiles that touch the content bond wrapped around my heart.

"Where to first?" Matthias prompts.

The possibilities are endless. All that matters to me is that we're together. We will be, forever. Nothing will keep me and my mates apart.

A smile breaks free. "Let's go to the beach."

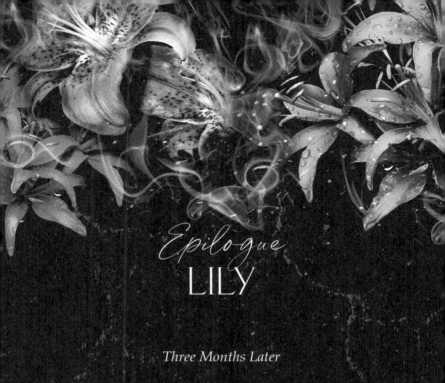

Epilogue
LILY

Three Months Later

"**Y**OU STILL NAPPING, PETAL? I FOUND YOU SOME more shells for our collect—oh." Matthias grins at the sight he walks in on in our tropical villa in Montego Bay, the third stop on our worldwide, multi-realm beach tour itinerary he planned.

Valerian has me on my hands and knees on the huge bed, taking me from behind. My sun hat is discarded by the door, my bathing suit bottoms hastily peeled down around my thighs, and my tits are spilling out of the flowy, off-shoulder sunflower print bikini.

Another strangled cry catches in my throat. I'm trying to be quiet, but Vale is making it his mission to make me scream after he challenged me to be quiet. My fists ball in the sheets as he drives into me harder with an audience.

His wicked chuckle lights me up, pushing me over the edge. "Shit!"

I press my face into the sheets to muffle a moan while I circle my hips, savoring the delicious glide of his cock filling me while my pussy flutters.

He fists my hair, drawing my head up. "No cheating. What's wrong, Lily? Can't you be a good girl and stay quiet?" He covers my back with his chest, bracing a tattooed hand on the bed. "Or does my cock make you scream?"

A breathy groan slips out of me. "You smug bastard."

"This is hot." Matthias grabs the instant camera he bought me when he announced the trip and snaps a photo. "Pull her hair again."

Vale complies, his hips snapping hard enough to make me see stars every time he slams into my pussy.

"Fuck," I breathe. "God, it's so good."

"I know, little flower."

"Hold that position. Yeah, like that. Mm, you're so sexy taking Vale's cock like that." He snaps another instant photo, the print fluttering to the floor for us to discover later. He tosses the camera to a bench and kneels on the huge bed, pushing his shorts down. "You look hungry, pretty girl."

Valerian lets go of my hair and grabs my hips for leverage. Matthias takes over, tugging a fistful hard enough my lashes flutter.

I lick my lips and open for him as he feeds me his cock. His head lolls back with a husky sigh and he pushes deeper into my mouth. I swirl my tongue, moaning around him when he thrusts, shallowly fucking my mouth.

Both of them fill me. I want to make them feel as good as they make me feel.

"Fuck, that's a sight, petal." Matthias cups my jaw. "Open wider. That's it. Shit, I'm not going to last. You're too fucking sexy like this."

He releases my hair and fists his dick, keeping just the tip resting on my tongue. His eyes gleam and his crooked smile shows a peek of his fangs before he grunts. His come shoots into my mouth. I swallow, some of it spilling down my chin. He catches it and pushes it back in alongside his dick. My tongue swirls around his finger and his cock, savoring the taste of him.

He pulls free, grasping my jaw to kiss me, swallowing every sound of pleasure I muffle into the kiss while Valerian picks up his pace and plays with my clit. I come with a gasp, burying my face in Matthias' neck, right where I've marked him with my own claiming bite. They each carry my possessive mark.

Valerian groans my name like a curse and a prayer rolled into one, slamming into me one last time as he comes. He presses a trail of kisses up my back, then pulls out. He spends a moment forcing his come back in me with his fingers before sprawling on the bed.

"You cheated again," he says in a rough, drowsy tone.

I flop onto my back beside him, chest heaving. "You never said I couldn't tag in outside help to stay quiet." My head turns on the pillow of Vale's arm to address Matthias when he stretches out on my other side. "Where's Alder?"

"Fascinated by swimming with sea turtles," Matthias answers. "He's going to be pissed when he figures out he's the odd man out."

A fond smile curves my mouth. "He's taking me stargazing on the beach tonight. I'm sucking his cock later. You two aren't invited."

Vale makes an unhappy sound, dragging me into his lap when he sits up. "We're invited if we want to be, mate. Maybe I'd like to watch these beautiful lips stretched for our brother."

"Agree to go parasailing with me," I barter. "I told you, I want it to be you. Then you can watch all night long."

His jaw clenches. "You drive a hard bargain."

I grin and kiss him. "Thank you. I'll hold your hand the whole time. We won't fall."

He grumbles until I kiss him again, then pats my thigh and gives me a wicked smirk. "I'm ordering Alder to fuck your throat raw tonight for this." My breath hitches and his luminous eyes glitter with satisfaction. "So perfect for us, mate."

Matthias takes my hand. "Come on. Let's head back to the beach. I want to make all the guys there jealous when I rub my gorgeous girl down with sunscreen. Then I want to show you the shells I scored for you."

Grinning, I slide my arms around his neck and kiss him.

Three Years Later

"Go, go, go!" I tap on Alder's shoulder to urge him on. The tattoos on my arm shift with my adrenaline, the lily flowers swirling into smoky shapes from my wrist to my elbow.

He cranes his neck, jogging down the narrow path we climbed to get here with me on his back. He's always been faster than me and grabbed me before I could move. "What made you think you could ride a wild isillion?"

"How was I supposed to know it would try to absorb me through its scales because that's where it keeps its extra teeth?" I shudder, reliving the moment my hand sank into a slimy mouth lined with sharp teeth. "I thought isillion were like dragons! I wanted to ride a dragon. Come on, that would've been badass if it worked."

Alder shakes his head and moves at an unmatched speed while the beast crashes out of its cave at the top of the mountain. "Next time you want to take some time off for an adventure, you're going to tell me exactly what your goals are so I don't have to relive watching you almost get eaten because you're obsessed with taming underworld beasts."

A laugh bubbles out of me and I hug him, kissing his cheek. "You love me."

"Old gods help me, I do, sweet blossom. With every fiber of my being. So much that I let my beautiful mate talk me into dangerous adventures for fun." There's a smile clear in his voice. He starts to laugh, deep and full of life. "The look on your face when you climbed on and it woke up."

My eyes widen as the huge creature takes flight, flapping leathery black wings beneath the blood moon rising in the sky. "I rode the smaller ones in Valerian's memories! I thought this would be the same."

"Those are the young!" He throws his head back and laughs harder. "We send warrior scouts into the mountains on missions to collect the eggs and raise them from hatchlings. They never open their scales and the teeth don't develop. You can't tame the fully grown wild ones at all, you crazy girl."

"Less talking, more running for our lives." I can't stop another giggle from escaping. "Vale's going to kill us."

"You're on your own there," he tosses over his shoulder as he twists to fling a fireball to deter the flying beast from snapping its deadly jaws at us.

"I thought you were my protector against all things?" I help him, conjuring a powerful whip made of flames to crack at the scaled isillion when it throws its antler-like horns at the cliff's edge.

"If he still lets me live after he finds out I let you come up here."

"I'll protect you, then." I crack my whip and tug on his shirt. "Stop for a second."

"Are you insane?" Alder slows, gesturing at the creature rearing back to attack us.

"Let me down."

"Lily—"

"For real, I've got this."

Reluctantly, he complies. I push up the sleeves of my sweater and adjust my tits. Alder rumbles at my side, prepared to jump in front of me. He

437

doesn't yet, trusting me to handle myself. I send him reassurance that I know what to do along our bond.

When the dragon-like creature with antlers charges the cliff, I fling my arms out, sending a strong gale of flames and hot air arcing out. It forces the isillion back and burns holes in its wings.

"Do you know who I am, beasty?" It screeches, circling around to try again and I grin. "I am Lily, bearer of the goddess Lilith's blood. Now sit the fuck down."

I build a fireball in my hand that grows larger as I spread my hands. The corner of my mouth kicks up as I send it flying with perfect accuracy. It hits the creature in the chest with enough force to make it fall several feet in the air until it recovers. It retreats, flapping its injured wings with an angry groan. It leaves us alone.

"See?" I turn to Alder with a triumphant smile. "Be the bigger baddie."

He shakes his head, clamping the back of my neck and hauling me close for a hard kiss. "I love you, you wild, fierce girl."

"I know." I hum and kiss him again. "Can I still get that piggyback ride?"

Nine Years Later

Valerian's fingertips lightly tracing the inside of my wrist, playing with my shifting tattoos that match the abstract ones covering his arms, distracts me from the demon council's discussion. He doesn't miss a beat, smirking at me before he interjects with his thoughts.

"We should think about the future. It's always best to consider all possible outcomes rather than wait for seeds of doubt to sow. Anticipating those outcomes helps us foster peace throughout the underworld."

Lucifer chuckles, chin propped against his fist in his throne, overseeing the meeting. "Sharp as ever, Valerian."

"Your Highness." Vale bows his head.

Whatever is said next goes over my head when he continues drawing lazy patterns on my sensitive skin. It takes me another moment to realize it's letters.

I love you. Over and over.

I peek at him through my lashes while Alder and another warrior demon on the council carry the discussion. His lips twitch.

Finally caught on, did you? He sends the words into my mind. I duck to hide my smile from the council. The last time I was caught flirting with my mates during a meeting, Vale made a bet with me that I couldn't sit through a whole meeting without getting distracted by them.

This so doesn't count because you're distracting me, not the other way around, I sass through our bond. *Also, I love you.*

His mouth curves and he traces the secret message into my skin again.

When the meeting ends, Valerian takes my hand and the four of us return to our home in Hell. It overlooks a pearlescent lavender lake with a balcony terrace where we've spent many nights enjoying each other and the view. I no longer fear water and my past can't hurt me anymore. I've overwritten all my bad memories with thousands of good ones with my mates by my side.

Between my many bookshelves packed with manga and a vast collection of books, we've covered the walls with photos of our travels, the little camera Matthias gifted me with working overtime to capture our memories—adventures exploring the underworld realm, traveling the mortal world three times over, and perfect little moments in between of our life together.

I stop in front of the portrait of all four of us that Matthias got enlarged. It's much like a dream I had once where they surrounded me on a throne. I've never wanted to be the queen of Hell, but Lucifer and his wife goaded me into sitting there during one of their opulent parties. My guys surrounded me as they did in that dream, taking their places at my side always, never leaving me alone. It's the only way it should ever be.

Matthias squeezes my shoulders. "Want to sit out on the balcony? The stars are sparkling off the lake and I got you something."

I smirk, catching the hint of mischief in his tone. "What are you up to?"

He tucks my hand in the crook of his elbow and escorts me outside. Grasping my waist, he boosts me onto the stone banister and fits himself between my legs, plucking at the suspenders of my corduroy skirt.

"I still remember when I first saw you wearing this," he rasps against my lips.

Pulling away from the kiss, he produces a small, plastic-wrapped treat. I turn it over and lift my brows.

"A Twinkie?"

"I didn't forget my promise." He winks. "We never made it back to any rest stops, so I wanted to bring it to you. I still want you to experience everything, Lils. We're not done by a long shot."

I wrap my arms around his shoulders to draw him closer. He settles his hands on my thighs and I smile.

"Thank you."

The way he always thinks of me with big and small gestures, and his boundless desire to see me live life with abandon makes my heart swell. Each of my mates takes care of me in their own way, and together as a group they fulfill me completely.

"There's my favorite sight," he murmurs. "Your smile is more beautiful than all the stars in every realm combined."

He takes the treat and feeds it to me while we watch the lake sparkle.

An Endless Lifetime Later

Time as an immortal fae being is fluid. Entire years can pass, yet it only seems like it's moments later.

With my fated mates, I've experienced everything I ever longed for in life. They sate my needs in every way, granting me a life full of exciting adventures fit for the stories I used to read to escape my pain. We've traveled far and wide, amongst the mortals and the fae.

There are so many that never wanted to see me live as I have. So many cruel people that stole my happiness. They don't matter now. They haven't for a long time.

The stars are beautiful tonight. We're in the abandoned Brim Hills cemetery on Halloween. We've come back to the place we started countless times over the years, but this is the first time we've spent Halloween here.

It's in a much worse state than all those years ago when I came to this town. Talbot House no longer stands beyond the woods and Brim Hills eventually died out as a town. Now it feels like it's our secret hideaway in the overgrown graveyard reclaimed by nature.

"Come here, petal." Matthias offers his hand. "Dance with me."

My fingers slip into his and I grant him a tender smile. He guides me into his arms and we twirl in a slow circle to the melody of our entwined heartbeats. He strokes my cheeks with a captivating smile.

"What?" I ask.

"Nothing. I was just thinking you're just as stunning as the night we first met."

"I don't look much different," I tease.

"It's your heart that's beautiful, mate," he murmurs before brushing his lips across mine.

Alder taps him on the shoulder. "I'd like to cut in."

"Happy birthday, Lils." Matthias grazes his nose against mine and hands me off to him.

"I still don't get why you all make a point of celebrating today," I say sardonically. "We know as demons we don't truly have birthdays to celebrate."

"We need little reason to show you we love you," Alder rumbles. "You are our treasure."

He spins me beneath his arm and pulls me back against his chest, kissing the top of my head. Valerian watches, leaning against the arch beneath the crumbled stairs of the chapel ruins. I don't need the ritual to activate the gate now. It recognizes the power in us and comes when we call it to return us to Hell.

On the next spin, Valerian and Alder switch seamlessly. He draws my hand to rest over his heart, caressing the swirling ink on my skin as he gazes at me, my magic tattoos as attuned to his touch as his are to mine.

"We celebrate your birthday because without your rebirth, we wouldn't have you," he says. "You're ours, Lily. Our goddess."

I sigh in contentment, resting my head against his chest. "And you're mine. My knight. My warrior. My trickster. I love you."

My mates make me happy. In them I have everything I've ever needed—beyond that. My protectors. My challengers. My perfect matches.

"Let's go home," Valerian says against my temple.

I smile as they circle me. "I've told you all hundreds of times. It doesn't matter where we go. In every realm, my home is with you, always."

Thank you so much for reading HELL GATE! Enjoy a special bonus by downloading three scenes from Alder, Matthias, and Valerian's points of view. Download the bonus scene at: **bit.ly/hellgatebonus**

Thank You
WHAT'S NEXT?

Thanks for reading Hell Gate! If you enjoyed it, please leave a review on your favorite retailer or book community! Your support means so much to me!

Need more Hell Gate right now? Have theories about which characters will feature next? Want exclusive previews of my next book? Join other readers in Veronica Eden's Reader Garden on Facebook!

Join: bit.ly/veronicafbgroup

Are you a newsletter subscriber?
By subscribing, you'll receive exclusive content

and news about upcoming releases, and be able to download a special deleted bonus scene from the Crowned Crows world.

Sign up to download it here:
veronicaedenauthor.com/bonus-content

Thank You
ACKNOWLEDGMENTS

Readers, I'm endlessly grateful for you! Thanks for reading this book. Lily's story was so fun and special for me to work on. I fell so in love with this world, with her, with her guys, and I hope you enjoyed the magical adventure! It means the world to me that you supported my work. I wouldn't be here at all without you! I love all of the comments and messages you send and live for your excitement for my characters!

Thanks to my husband for being you! He doesn't read these, but he's my biggest supporter. He keeps me fed and watered while I'm in the writer cave, and doesn't complain when I fling myself out of bed at odd hours with an idea to frantically scribble down

Thank you always to Dani, Becca, Ramzi, Sara, Kat, Jade, Sarah, Mia, Bre, Heather, Katie, and Erica for the supportive chats and keeping me arguably sane and on track until the end! And to my beta queens for reading my raw words and offering your time, attention to detail, and consideration of the characters and storyline in my books! With every book I write my little tribe grows and I'm so thankful to have each of you as friends to lean on and share my book creation process with!

To my lovely PA Heather, thank you for taking things off my plate and allowing me to disappear into the writing cave without having to worry. And for letting me infodump at you, because that's my love language hahaha! You rock and I'm so glad to have you on my team!

To my street team and reader group, y'all are the best babes around! Huge thanks to my street team for being the best hype girls! To see you guys get as excited as I do seriously makes my day. I'm endlessly grateful you love my characters and words! Thank you for your help in sharing my books and for your support of my work!

To Shauna and Wildfire Marketing Solutions, thank you so much for all your hard work and being so awesome! I appreciate everything that you do!

To Samantha & Brittni at Overbooked Author Services, thank you for your hard work and your booktok love!

To the bloggers and bookstagrammers, thank you for being the most wonderful community! Your creativity and beautiful edits, reviews, and videos are something I come back to visit again and again to brighten my day. Thank you for trying out my books. You guys are incredible and blow me away with your passion for romance!

About THE AUTHOR

Stay Up All Night Falling in Love

Veronica Eden is a USA Today & international bestselling author of addictive romances that keep you up all night falling in love with spitfire heroines, irresistible heroes, and edgy twists.

She loves exploring complicated feelings, magical worlds, epic adventures, and the bond of characters that embrace *us against the world*. She has always been drawn to gruff bad boys, clever villains, and the twisty-turns of a morally gray character. She is a sucker for a deliciously swoony hero with a devastating smirk. When not writing, she can be found soaking up sunshine at the beach, snuggling in a pile with her untamed pack of animals (her husband, dog and cats), and surrounding herself with as many plants as she can get her hands on.

CONTACT + FOLLOW
Email | Website | Facebook Group | Amazon

Other books
BY VERONICA

Dark Romance

Sinners and Saints Series
Wicked Saint
Tempting Devil
Ruthless Bishop
Savage Wilder
Sinners and Saints: The Complete Series

Crowned Crows Series
Crowned Crows of Thorne Point

Loyalty in the Shadows
A Fractured Reign

Standalone
Unmasked Heart
Devil on the Lake

Reverse Harem Romance
Standalone
Hell Gate
More Than Bargained

Contemporary Romance

Standalone
Jingle Wars
Haze

Printed in the USA
CPSIA information can be obtained
at www.ICGtesting.com
LVHW041147290724
786663LV00001B/25